Study Guide

Discovering Biological Psychology

SECOND EDITION

Laura A. Freberg

California Polytechnic State University, San Louis Obispo

Prepared by

Laura A. Freberg

California Polytechnic State University, San Louis Obispo

 WADSWORTH
CENGAGE Learning

Australia • Brazil • Japan • Korea • Mexico • Singapore • Spain • United Kingdom • United States

For product information and technology assistance, contact us at
Cengage Learning Customer & Sales Support,
1-800-354-9706

For permission to use material from this text or product, submit all requests online at **www.cengage.com/permissions**
Further permissions questions can be emailed to
permissionrequest@cengage.com

ISBN-13: 978-0-547-17785-4
ISBN-10: 0-547-17785-2

Wadsworth
10 Davis Drive
Belmont, CA 94002-3098
USA

Cengage Learning is a leading provider of customized learning solutions with office locations around the globe, including Singapore, the United Kingdom, Australia, Mexico, Brazil, and Japan. Locate your local office at: **international.cengage.com/region**

Cengage Learning products are represented in Canada by Nelson Education, Ltd.

For your course and learning solutions, visit **academic.cengage.com**

Purchase any of our products at your local college store or at our preferred online store **www.ichapters.com**

Printed in the United States of America
1 2 3 4 5 6 7 12 11 10 09

Contents

Preface

The purpose of this study guide is to help you master as quickly and as easily as possible the material in the textbook, ***Discovering Biological Psychology, Second Edition***. This is not an easy course, but the study guide will help you focus and evaluate your work as you go forward, resulting in your getting the best grade possible.

This preface begins with a section titled, Getting the Most from Your Textbook. Even though you've been reading textbooks for years, you will probably learn some new tips and tricks by going through this section. The next section of the preface is Getting the Most from Your Study Guide. There you will find instructions for completing the three types of exercises you will find within the chapters: Indentifying Key Terms and Their Definitions, Learning by Coloring, and Practice Quiz. In the last section of this preface I'll tell you about the useful information in the appendix that will help you master the Latin terminology in the biological psychology course.

GETTING THE MOST FROM YOUR TEXTBOOK

We all know how to read. However, reading a textbook is different from any other kind of reading because you need to remember far more than just the plot line of a novel or the gist of a news article. If you are like most college students, you do not have unlimited time for studying. So your goal must be to move information from your textbook into your long-term memory as quickly and efficiently as possible. Although some of the strategies discussed below look like more work than you're used to doing, you will be surprised at how quickly you can master material when you study this way.

You have probably been told many times that cramming is a bad thing. Let's look at this a different way. Do you think NBA stars lie around doing nothing for days or weeks and then pull an all-nighter to practice for a big game? The brain doesn't treat learning about basketball any different from other types of learning. If cramming doesn't work for athletes and musicians, it's not going to work for students. Break the cramming habit now. A little work done every day pays off at exam time.

Approaching your textbook involves planning, reading, reviewing, and maintaining your concentration as you work.

Planning
- Establish a good physical environment. Some students can read with the TV on, others cannot. Evaluate your own needs and set up your ideal situation for good concentration.
- Relax and think positively. Remind yourself of your goals to succeed in this course, in your academic career, and after college.
- Review your syllabus and any other relevant instructions from your professor. For example, a professor might tell you to read only certain pages from a chapter.
- Review your lecture notes. Ideally, you should at least scan a chapter before the relevant lecture, because this increases your understanding of the lecture. However, once a topic has been covered in lecture, your notes will show you the topics where your understanding is missing or incomplete. Don't depend on the professor to talk about all the topics you're expected to know. Mark the topics in your text that will need extra attention from you.
- Think about what you already know about the topic. How do the topics help you understand your own experience? Why are experts interested in these topics? How can we apply our understanding of this topic in everyday life?
- Preview the assignment. Don't just start reading right away, or you will have a hard time figuring out how the information fits into the whole.
  - Read through the Learning Objectives and Chapter Outline.
  - Scan the headings in the chapter.

- o   In each major section, read the introductory and concluding paragraphs.
- o   Read any term that is in bold font, and read the margin definitions of terms that are unfamiliar to you.
- o   Look at the photos and other illustrations and read the captions.
- o   Read the interim and chapter summaries.

Reading

- Think like a professor.
  - o   Turn the material you read into questions. How would a professor ask a question about what you just read?
  - o   Most of the important content of a textbook answers questions of "what," "why," and "how."
- At the end of sentences or paragraphs, restate the ideas in your own words. Imagine that you are explaining the concepts to a parent or friend. If you can't do this, you probably need to go over the material again.
- Reread the Learning Objectives, Chapter Outline, headlings, and captions for each section before beginning the section (refreshing your preview).
- Mark your book! Use highlighters, pens, pencils, or post-its. There are good ways and bad ways to do this. Simply using a highlighter at random is not going to help you much.
  - o   **NEVER** mark your book the first time you read a section. Usually, we need to see where information fits in the larger picture before we can make useful decisions about key concepts.
  - o   During your **SECOND** reading, mark concepts, definitions, examples, and details that appear interesting or important.
  - o   Use the margins!
    - ▪   Place a "?" by sections you do not understand, and raise the question with your professor in class or office hour. Circle terms that you need to look up in margin definitions or a dictionary. You can't remember material you do not understand.
    - ▪   Mark sources of answers to potential exam questions, perhaps by labeling a sentence, illustration, or definition with an EQ.
    - ▪   Summarize sections briefly in your own words. Add your own examples, and note comparisons, contrasts, and causal relationships that you read.
    - ▪   Note your personal reactions to the material. Does it make you feel positive? Negative? Do you agree or disagree?
- Make 3x5 flashcards of vocabulary terms as you go.
- Visualization often helps people comprehend what they read better. Close your eyes and try to visualize a process. Take advantage of the animations available on the student website for this textbook and do the labeling and coloring exercises in this study guide.

Reviewing

Reviewing can be broken up into *immediate reviewing,* following a study session, and *periodic reviewing,* which is needed to prepare for exams. A good deal of un-reviewed textbook material can be forgotten in a single day and 80 percent of un-reviewed textbook material is lost in two weeks.

- Immediate reviewing should take place right after you finish a reading session (I recommend between 30-40 minutes of concentrated work), do the following steps:
  - o   Review the questions you posed during the planning stage. If you can't answer one, reread the markings you made in that section.

- o Check any questions posed in the Interim Summaries and Chapter Summaries. If you can't answer these, return to the section and review your notes.
- Periodic reviewing should be calendared at regular intervals throughout the term.
  - o Try to consolidate the material you've read with other sources of information on the same topics, such as your lecture notes.
  - o Test yourself. Use the practice quizzes in this study guide and make your own. Write questions and answers on either side of 3x5 flashcards and use spare time between classes to review them.
  - o Use a study group, but make sure the group doesn't meet until everyone is familiar with the material. Talk about the material you have read in your own words and quiz each other using your study questions.
  - o Unfortunately, the stress of an exam can interfere with our retrieval of information. Most of us would struggle to retrieve our own names as a contestant on a game show where millions are at stake. To avoid blanking out in panic when you sit for an exam, review the material one more time after you get the "I know this" message. It's boring, but it will really help to avoid test anxiety.
  - o Just before your exam, quickly scan through the main headings of your text and notes to refresh your memory.

Maintaining Concentration

I have worked very hard to make *Discovering Biological Psychology* as accessible as it can be for students. But let's face facts—it is still more challenging to read than *Harry Potter.* So you need to adjust your habits accordingly. Watch your behavior and try to identify times of day, length of reading sessions, and other habits that contribute to your best concentration.

- Engineer your environment. Stay away from temptations, like outdoor views, television, your cell phone or computer, or interruptions from friends and relatives. Sit comfortably but not so comfortably that it makes you drowsy. Avoid lying on a sofa or slouching in a cushy armchair when you study.
- If you find your mind wandering, find something that will help you wake up. Do a couple of pushups, jumping jacks, or crunches. Get a drink of water or do deep breathing for a couple of minutes.
- Make your study environment pleasant. Surround yourself with pleasant colors. Sip a cup of tea. Play relaxing background music.
- Reward yourself. After you complete a reading assignment, check your text messages, get a snack, do something fun.

GETTING THE MOST FROM THIS STUDY GUIDE

Textbooks are for learning and study guides are for remembering. The purpose of this study guide is to reinforce your memory of the material in the textbook. The exercises in every chapter provide different modes of practicing. In the first exercise in every chapter, you will reinforce your memory of the material by matching terms with their definitions. In a second exercise (in every chapter except the first and the last two) you will reinforce your memory of the material through use of your visual skills to color and label figures based on the figures in the textbook. And finally, you will take a practice quiz, score it, and evaluate your needs for further study. Because I wrote the questions both for this study guide and the test bank from which many instructors take test items to make up their exams, these quizzes should give you a very good idea of whether or not you are prepared for your class exams.

Identifying Key Terms and Their Definitions

In the spaces provided, write the terms that match the definitions. Try to complete as many as you can on your own—it's the best way to learn—referring to the bulleted list of terms below the table only when you need help. Note that the terms in the bulleted lists have been scrambled; so simply placing them in the same order in the numbered boxes won't work.☺ Check your work when you are done against the answers at the end of the exercise.

Learning by Coloring
In all but the first and last two chapters, you will find a fun coloring book feature that will help you learn the location of important structures in the nervous system. The instructions for each one is on the same page. You don't have to be a terrific artist to enjoy these activities.

Practice Quiz
Finally, you can complete your review of each chapter by taking a practice quiz containing true-false items, multiple choice items, fill-in items, and for some chapters, a labeling exercise. Take each quiz as though you are actually taking it in class, that is, set aside enough time to complete it all at one sitting and give yourself only the amount of time allotted (the allotted time is listed at the beginning of each quiz.)

When you are done taking a quiz, take advantage of the table provided at the end of the quiz to check your answers, add up your score, analyze which sections of the text chapter you need to review, and write up a plan to reread the relevant text pages. For each item answered correctly, give yourself the indicated number of points. For each item answered incorrectly, give yourself zero points. (For fill-in and short answer/labeling questions you may give yourself a partial score if you answered part of the question correctly.) After adding up your score, circle or highlight the items you missed on the Analyze Your Performance side of the scoring table, which is organized by learning objective and text page. Next to each incorrect item make a brief note of your plan for further review.

Appendix: Latin Pronunciation Guide
Finally, in the Appendix of this Study Guide, I've added a unique section to help you tackle the many Latin terms that appear in the anatomical lexicon. Even if you don't pronounce the words perfectly, it's important to try. Your instructor (not to mention your classmates) will be impressed by your correct, or close-to-correct, pronunciation of Latin-derived terms when you ask a question or are called on to answer a question in class. Most importantly, speaking these terms out loud in your study group—or to yourself as you read the textbook and do the exercises in this guide—will help you remember them later on.

Good luck on your adventure into the fascinating world of biological psychology! If you have any suggestions or comments about this study guide, I would love to hear from you. Join me on my Facebook page, Discovering Biological Psychology, or contact me via email or twitter:

> lfreberg@calpoly.edu
> http://www.laurafreberg.com/blog
> http://www.twitter.com/lfreberg

Laura Freberg
California Polytechnic State University, San Luis Obispo

Chapter 1. Introducing Biological Psychology

EXERCISE 1.1 IDENTIFYING KEY TERMS AND THEIR DEFINITIONS

A. Historical Terms

1.	A philosophical perspective put forward by René Descartes in which the body is mechanistic, whereas the mind is separate and nonphysical.
2.	The branch of psychology in which the biological foundations of behavior, emotions, and mental processes are studied.
3.	A philosophical perspective characteristic of the neurosciences in which the mind is viewed as the product of activity in the brain and nervous system.

- biological psychology
- monism
- mind-body dualism

B. Imaging and Recording Technologies

1.	An imaging technology in which computers are used to enhance X-ray images.
2.	An imaging technique that provides very high-resolution structural images.
3.	A technique for stimulating the cortex at regular intervals by applying a magnetic pulse through a wire coil encased in plastic and placed on the scalp.
4.	A technology for studying the activity of the brain through recordings from electrodes placed on the scalp.
5.	A technology for recording the magnetic output of the brain.
6.	A technology using a series of MRI images taken one to four seconds apart in order to assess the activity of the brain.
7.	An alteration in the EEG recording produced in response to the application of a particular stimulus.
8.	An imaging technique that provides information regarding the localization of brain activity.

- magnetic resonance imaging (MRI)
- functional magnetic resonance imaging (fMRI)
- evoked potential
- computerized tomography (CT)
- repeated transcranial magnetic stimulation (rTMS)
- electroencephalogram (EEG)
- magnetoencephalography (MEG)
- positron emission tomography (PET)

C. Terms in Stimulation, Biochemical, and Genetic Research

1.	The amount of variability of a trait in a population that is due to genetics.
2.	A technique for assessing the chemical composition of a very small area of the brain.
3.	Genes that take the place of normal genes but that fail to produce the specific protein produced by the normal genes.

4.	Pathological or traumatic damage to tissue.
5.	The surgical removal of tissue.
6.	The examination of body tissues following death.
7.	An undifferentiated cell that can divide and differentiate into other types of cells.
8.	The study of cells and tissues on the microscopic level.

- ablation
- microdialysis
- knockout genes
- histology

- heritability
- autopsy
- lesion
- stem cell

EXERCISE 1.1 ANSWER KEY

A. Historical Terms
1. mind-body dualism (p. 4)
2. biological psychology (p. 3)
3. monism (p. 4)

B. Imaging and Recording Technologies
1. computerized tomography (CT) (p. 10)
2. magnetic resonance imaging (MRI) (p. 10)
3. repeated transcranial magnetic stimulation (rTMS) (p. 16)
4. electroencephalogram (EEG) (p. 12)
5. magnetoencephalography (MEG) (p. 13)
6. functional magnetic resonance imaging (fMRI) (p. 10)
7. evoked potential (p. 13)
8. positron emission tomography (PET) (p. 10)

C. Terms Used in Stimulation, Biochemical, and Genetic Research
1. heritability (p. 19)
2. microdialysis (p. 18)
3. knockout genes (p. 19)
4. lesion (p. 16)
5. ablation (p. 17)
6. autopsy (p. 9)
7. stem cell (p. 19)
8. histology (p. 8)

EXERCISE 1.2 PRACTICE QUIZ

Time: 45 minutes

True–False

1. Herophilus, Galen, and Descartes shared the mistaken notion that fluids played a very important role in the transmission of messages by the nervous system.

      T   F

2. More information about the localization of brain activity is provided by electroencephalography (EEG) than by magnetoencephalography (MEG).

      T   F

3. Even though a university is receiving federal funding in the form of student grants and loans, researchers at that university are only subject to federal ethical guidelines if their research is funded by the federal government.

      T   F

Multiple Choice

4. Biological psychology is defined as the
   A) study of brain physiology.
   B) study of the neurosciences.
   C) study of behavior and mental processes.
   D) branch of psychology that studies the biological foundations of behavior, emotions, and mental processes.

5. If you were examined by a phrenologist, you would
   A) have the bumps on your skull evaluated for personality traits.
   B) be administered a radioactive tracer.
   C) have your DNA evaluated for vulnerabilities for disease.
   D) have the electrical activity of your brain recorded through electrodes on your scalp.

6. If you want to compare the distribution of cell bodies in the hippocampus of patients with schizophrenia to healthy controls, you would probably use
   A) a Golgi stain.
   B) horseradish peroxidase.
   C) a Nissl stain.
   D) monoclonal antibodies.

7. Strong magnets are used in which of the following imaging technologies?
   A) CT
   B) MRI
   C) PET
   D) MEG

8. Which of the following technologies uses sensors known as SQUIDs?
   A) MRI
   B) fMRI
   C) EEG
   D) MEG

9.   The function of a particular part of the brain can be studied by using
      A) lesions, but not electrical stimulation.
      B) electrical stimulation, but not lesions.
      C) both lesions and electrical stimulation.
      D) neither lesions nor electrical stimulation.

10.   Which of the following techniques allows researchers to assess the chemicals present
      in a small part of the brain?
      A) lesion
      B) microdialysis
      C) electrical stimulation
      D) single cell recording

11.   Fraternal twins have
      A) fewer genes in common than identical twins, but have more genes in common than
          non-twin siblings.
      B) about the same number of genes in common as identical twins.
      C) about the same number of genes in common as non-twin siblings.
      D) fewer genes in common than non-twin siblings.

12.   Embryonic stem cells are derived from
      A) embryos at the blastocyst stage.
      B) umbilical cord blood.
      C) non-fertilized eggs.
      D) embryos at about 3 weeks post-conception.

13.   Informed consent refers to the
      A) information provided by a researcher to his or her campus review board.
      B) debriefing given to research participants after the experiment is complete.
      C) information about research funding provided to the journal in which the results are
          published.
      D) information provided to a prospective volunteer for a research study.

Fill In

14.   Descartes supported the idea of mind-body _____, in which the body is

      viewed as mechanical and the mind as non-physical; whereas contemporary

      neuroscientists support _____, the perspective that sees the "mind" as the

      result of the activity of neurons.

15.   Three major types of imaging technologies include _____,

      _____, and _____.

16.   _____ are special types of EEG recordings that allow researchers to

      study the brain's response to environmental stimuli.

17. Naturally occurring or deliberately produced brain damage, or _____, can help neuroscientists identify the functions of specific areas of the brain.

18. We can use _____ rates in twins to evaluate the genetic contributions to a particular psychological disorder.

19. _____ cells can differentiate into all types of tissue.

Short Answer/Labeling

20. Why must we be cautious in our interpretations of stimulation and lesion results?

_____

_____

_____

_____

_____

_____

21. Why is the process of informed consent so important in protecting human research participants?

_____

_____

_____

_____

_____

_____

EXERCISE 1.2 ANSWER KEY

True-False: 1. T; 2. F; 3. F. **Multiple Choice:** 4. D) 5. A) 6. C) 7. B) 8. D) 9. C) 10. B) 11. C) 12. A) 13. D). **Fill-In:** 14. dualism; monism. 15. CT; PET; MRI. 16. Evoked potentials. 17. lesions. 18. concordance. 19. Pluripotent. **Short Answer/Labeling:** 20. Brain structures are richly connected. Behaviors resulting from stimulation or lesion might be caused directly by the stimulated or lesioned structure or indirectly by other structures connected to the stimulated or lesioned structure. 21. We do not believe that people should be coerced in any way to participate in research. To ensure that people are volunteering freely, an informed consent form should outline any possible risks that might occur as a result of participating.

Tally Your Score			Analyze Your Performance/Plan Your Review			
Test Item	Point Value	Your Score	LO	Test Item	Text Page	Your Review Plan
1.	2		1.1	4	3	
2.	2		1.2	1	4	
3.	2			14	4	
4.	4			5	6	
5.	4		1.3	6	8	
6.	4		1.4	15	9	
7.	4			7	10	
8.	4		1.5	2	13	
9.	4			16	13	
10.	4			8	14	
11.	4		1.6	20	15	
12.	4			9	16	
13.	4			17	16	
14.	6		1.7	10	18	
15.	6		1.8	11	18	
16.	6			18	18	
17.	6		1.9	12	19	
18.	6			19	19	
19.	6		1.10	3	21	
20.	9			13	23	
21.	9			21	23	
TOTAL	100					

Chapter 2. The Anatomy and Evolution of the Nervous System

EXERCISE 2.1 IDENTIFYING KEY TERMS AND THEIR DEFINITIONS

A. Terms of Anatomical Direction

1.	An anatomical section that is parallel to the midline.
2.	A directional term meaning toward the tail of a four-legged animal.
3.	An imaginary line dividing the body into two equal halves.
4.	A directional term meaning toward the back of a four legged animal.
5.	A directional term referring to structures on opposite sides of the midline.
6.	A directional term meaning farther away from another structure, usually in reference to limbs.
7.	A directional term meaning toward the head of a four-legged animal.
8.	A directional term referring to structures on the same side of the midline.
9.	A directional term meaning toward the midline.
10.	A directional term meaning away from the midline.
11.	A directional term that means closer to center; usually applied to limbs; opposite of distal.
12.	A directional term meaning toward the belly of a four-legged animal.
13.	An anatomical section dividing the brain front to back, parallel to the face. Also known as a frontal section.
14.	An anatomical section that divides the brain from top to bottom.
15.	An imaginary line that runs the length of the spinal cord to the front of the brain.

- rostral / anterior
- inferior / ventral
- neuraxis
- caudal / posterior
- superior / dorsal
- contralateral
- coronal section
- distal
- ipsilateral
- lateral
- medial
- midline
- proximal
- sagittal section
- horizontal / axial section

B. Terms Related to Nervous System Protection and Blood Supply

1.	The small midline channel in the spinal cord that contains cerebrospinal fluid.
2.	The middle layer of the meninges covering the central nervous system.
3.	The innermost of the layers of meninges, found in both the central and peripheral nervous systems.
4.	A space filled with cerebrospinal fluid that lies between the arachnoid and pia mater layers of the meninges in the central nervous system.

5.	The special plasmalike fluid circulating within the ventricles of the brain, the central canal of the spinal cord, and the subarachnoid space.
6.	One of four hollow spaces within the brain that contain cerebrospinal fluid.
7.	The layers of membranes that cover the central nervous system and the peripheral nerves.
8.	The outermost of the three layers of meninges, found in both the central and peripheral nervous systems.

- dura mater
- meninges
- arachnoid layer
- central canal
- cerebrospinal fluid (CSF)
- pia mater
- subarachnoid space
- ventricle

C. General Nervous System Terms

1.	An area of neural tissue primarily made up of myelinated axons.
2.	An area of neural tissue primarily made up of cell bodies.
3.	The nerves exiting the brain and spinal cord that serve sensory and motor functions for the rest of the body.
4.	A long cylinder of nervous tissue extending from the medulla to the first lumbar vertebra.
5.	Gray matter in the spinal cord that contains sensory neurons.
6.	The brain and spinal cord.
7.	An involuntary action or response.
8.	The most caudal division of the brain, including the medulla, pons, and cerebellum.
9.	The division of the brain lying between the hindbrain and forebrain.
10.	The division of the brain containing the diencephalon and the telencephalon.
11.	The lower two thirds of the brain, including the hindbrain and midbrain.

- central nervous system (CNS)
- peripheral nervous system (PNS)
- spinal cord
- dorsal horns
- gray matter
- reflex
- white matter
- midbrain / mesencephalon
- hindbrain
- forebrain
- brainstem

D. Terminology of the Hindbrain and Midbrain

1.	The division of the hindbrain containing the pons and cerebellum.
2.	Midbrain nuclei that communicate with the basal ganglia of the forebrain.
3.	A collection of brainstem nuclei, located near the midline from the rostral medulla up into the midbrain, that regulate sleep and arousal.
4.	The small channel running along the midline of the midbrain that connects the third and fourth ventricles.
5.	A structure located in the metencephalon that participates in balance, muscle tone, muscle coordination, some types of learning, and possibly higher cognitive functions in humans.
6.	Nuclei located in the pons that participate in the regulation of sleep and arousal.
7.	A structure in the pons that participates in arousal.
8.	The most caudal part of the hindbrain.
9.	A structure located in the metencephalon between the medulla and midbrain; part of the brainstem located in the hindbrain.

- cerebellum
- metencephalon
- myelencephalon / medulla
- pons
- reticular formation
- locus coeruleus
- raphe nuclei
- cerebral aqueduct
- substantia nigra

E. Terms for the Forebrain

1.	An almond-shaped structure in the rostral temporal lobes that is part of the limbic system.
2.	A division of the forebrain made up of the hypothalamus and the thalamus.
3.	One of the two large, globular structures that make up the telencephalon of the forebrain.
4.	A structure in the diencephalon that processes sensory information, contributes to states of arousal, and participates in learning and memory.
5.	A segment of older cortex just dorsal to the corpus callosum that is part of the limbic system.
6.	A collection of nuclei within the cerebral hemispheres that participate in the control of movement.
7.	A collection of forebrain structures that participate in emotional behavior and learning.
8.	A structure deep within the cerebral hemispheres that is involved with the formation of long-term declarative memories; part of the limbic system.
9.	A structure found in the diencephalon that participates in the regulation of hunger, thirst, sexual behavior, and aggression; part of the limbic system.
10.	The division of the brain comprising the cerebral hemispheres.

- cerebral hemisphere
- diencephalon
- telencephalon
- thalamus
- basal ganglia

- hypothalamus
- limbic system
- amygdala
- hippocampus
- cingulate cortex

F. Terms for the Cortex

1.	An area located at the top and sides of the frontal lobe that participates in executive functions such as attention and the planning of behavior.
2.	One of the "hills" on the convoluted surface of the cerebral cortex.
3.	A wide band of axons connecting the right and left cerebral hemispheres.
4.	Areas of the cortex that link and integrate sensory and motor information.
5.	The fissure separating the frontal and parietal lobes of the cerebral cortex.
6.	One of the four lobes of the cerebral cortex; located between the frontal and occipital lobes.
7.	The lobe of the cerebral cortex lying ventral and lateral to the frontal and parietal lobes and rostral to the occipital lobe.
8.	The fold of parietal lobe tissue just caudal to the central sulcus; the location of the primary somatosensory cortex.
9.	The most caudal lobe of the cortex; location of primary visual cortex.
10.	The most rostral lobe of the cerebral cortex, separated from the parietal lobe by the central sulcus and from the temporal lobe by the lateral sulcus.
11.	A small bundle of axons that connects structures in the right and left cerebral hemispheres.
12.	A "valley" in the convoluted surface of the cerebral cortex.

- gyrus/gyri
- sulci/sulcus
- central sulcus
- frontal lobe
- temporal lobe

- anterior commissure
- association cortex
- parietal lobe
- occipital lobe
- corpus callosum

- postcentral gyrus
- dorsolateral prefrontal cortex

G. Terms for the Peripheral Nervous System

1.	A string of cell bodies outside the spinal cord that receive input from sympathetic neurons in the central nervous system and that communicate with target organs.
2.	A cranial nerve that controls muscles of the eye.
3.	The division of the autonomic nervous system responsible for rest and energy storage.
4.	Twelve pairs of nerves that exit the brain as part of the peripheral nervous system.
5.	The division of the peripheral nervous system that directs the activity of the glands, organs, and smooth muscles of the body.

- autonomic nervous system
- cranial nerves
- oculomotor nerve

- sympathetic chain
- parasympathetic nervous system

H. Evolutionary Terms

1.	The species of modern humans.
2.	The phylum of animals that possess true brains and spinal cords. Also known as vertebrates.
3.	A primate in the family Hominidae, of which *Homo sapiens* is the only surviving member.

- chordates
- hominids
- *Homo sapiens*

EXERCISE 2.1 ANSWER KEY

A. Terms of Anatomical Direction
1. sagittal section (p. 28)
2. caudal / posterior (p. 27)
3. midline (p. 28)
4. superior / dorsal (p. 27)
5. contralateral (p. 28)
6. distal (p. 28)
7. rostral / anterior (p. 27)
8. ipsilateral (p. 28)
9. medial (p. 28)
10. lateral (p. 28)
11. proximal (p. 28)
12. inferior / ventral (p. 27)
13. coronal section (p. 28)
14. horizontal / axial section (p. 28)
15. neuraxis (p. 27)

B. Terms Related to Nervous System Protection and Blood Supply
1. central canal (p. 30)
2. arachnoid layer (p. 30)
3. pia mater (p. 30)
4. subarachnoid space (p. 30)
5. cerebrospinal fluid (CSF) (p. 30)
6. ventricle (p. 30)
7. meninges (p. 29)
8. dura mater (p.29)

C. General Nervous System Terms
1. white matter (p. 34)
2. gray matter (p. 34)
3. peripheral nervous system (PNS)
4. spinal cord (p. 33)
5. dorsal horns (p. 33)
6. central nervous system (CNS) (p. 33)
7. reflex (p. 34)
8. hindbrain (p. 35)
9. midbrain / mesencephalon (p. 35)
10. forebrain (p. 35)
11. brainstem (p. 35)

D. Terminology of the Hindbrain and Midbrain
1. metencephalon (p. 35)
2. substantia nigra (p. 37)
3. reticular formation (p. 37)
4. cerebral aqueduct (p. 37)
5. cerebellum (p. 35)
6. raphe nuclei (p. 36)
7. locus coeruleus (p. 36)
8. myelencephalon / medulla (p. 35)
9. pons (p. 35)

E. Terms for the Forebrain
1. amygdala (p. 40)
2. diencephalon (p. 38)
3. cerebral hemisphere (p. 38)
4. thalamus (p. 38)
5. cingulate cortex (p. 41)
6. basal ganglia (p. 39)
7. limbic system (p. 40)
8. hippocampus (p. 40)
9. hypothalamus (p. 39)
10. telencephalon (p. 38)

F. Terms for the Cortex
1. dorsolateral prefrontal cortex.
2. gyrus/gyri (p. 42)
3. corpus callosum (p. 44)
4. association cortex (p. 44)
5. central sulcus (p. 43)
6. parietal lobe (p. 43)
7. temporal lobe (p. 43)
8. postcentral gyrus (p. 44)
9. occipital lobe (p. 43)
10. frontal lobe (p. 43)
11. anterior commissure (p. 44)
12. sulcus/sulci (p. 42)

G. Terms for the Peripheral Nervous System
1. sympathetic chain (p. 50)
2. oculomotor nerve (p. 47)
3. parasympathetic nervous system (p. 50)
4. cranial nerves (p. 47)
5. autonomic nervous system (p. 47)

H. Evolutionary Terms
1. *Homo sapiens* (p. 55)
2. chordates (p. 54)
3. hominid (p. 55)

EXERCISE 2.2 LEARNING BY COLORING

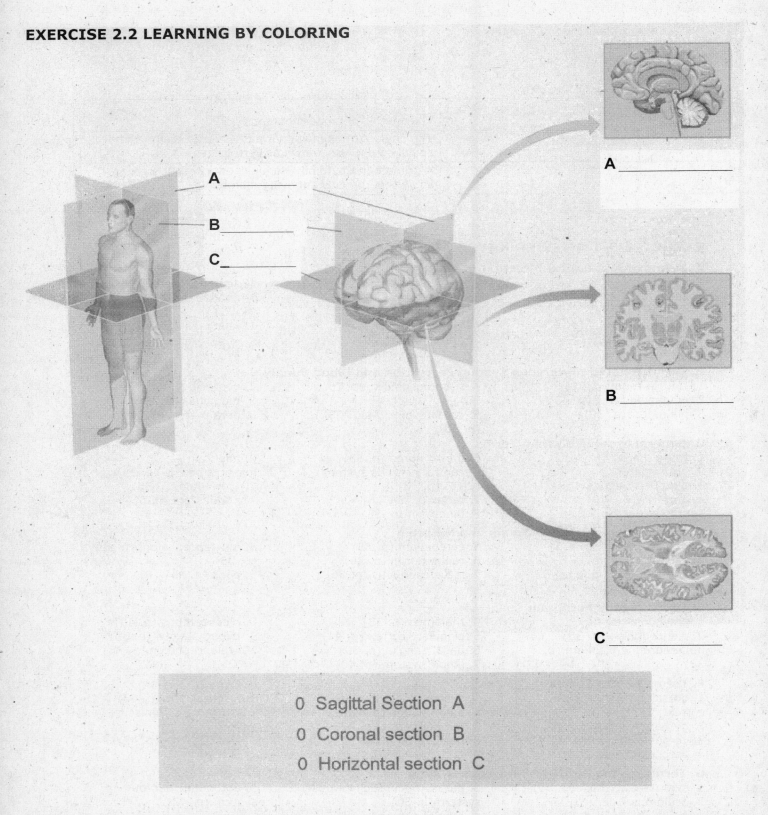

A _____

B _____

C _____

0 Sagittal Section A

0 Coronal section B

0 Horizontal section C

Figure 2.2   Anatomists use planes of section to view the three-dimensional structures of the brain in two-dimensional images.

Color each plane the same color in the man, brain, and section images. Fill in the boxes and lines with the appropriate labels.

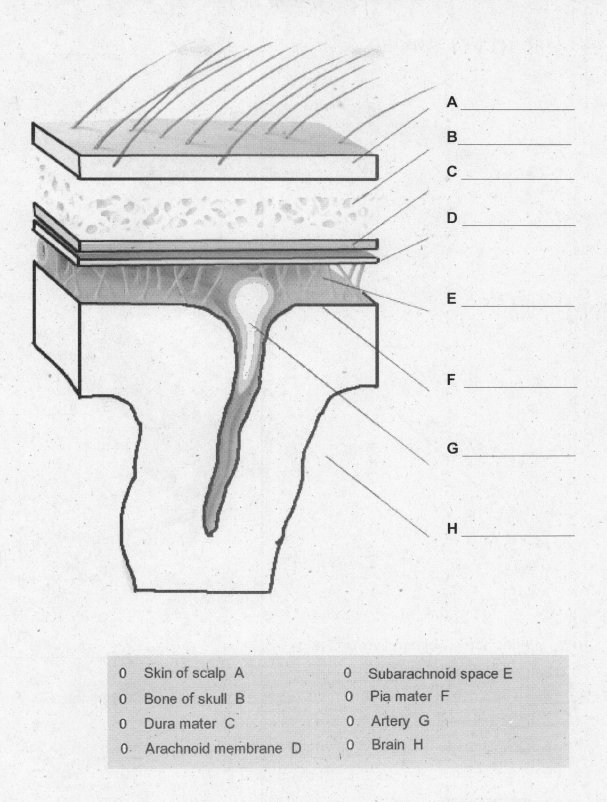

A _____

B _____

C _____

D _____

E _____

F _____

G _____

H _____

0   Skin of scalp A   0   Subarachnoid space E

0   Bone of skull B   0   Pia mater F

0   Dura mater C   0   Artery G

0   Arachnoid membrane D   0   Brain H

Figure 2.3 The skull bones and three layers of meninges protect the brain.

**Color the scalp a skin-tone color, and the bone a light yellow. Choose four
different colors for the three layers of meninges and the subarachnoid space.
Color the artery red. Color the gray matter of the brain a darker gray, and leave
the white matter (outside the black line) as white.**

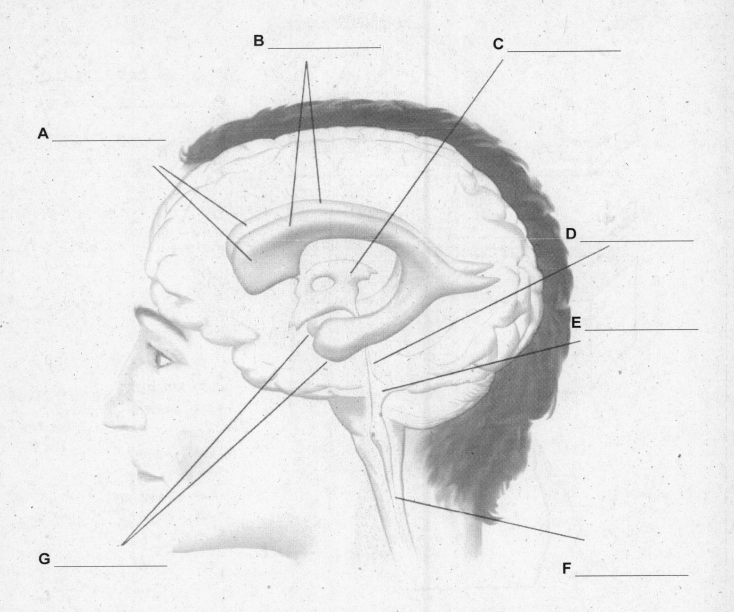

B _____

C _____

A _____

D _____

E _____

G _____

F _____

0   Anterior horns of lateral ventricles A

0   Lateral ventricles B   0   Central canal F

0   Third ventricle C   0   Inferior horns of lateral ventricles G

0   Cerebral aqueduct D

0   Fourth ventricle E

Figure 2.5a The Ventricles

Select a color for each type of ventricle, the cerebral aqueduct, and the central canal. Use different shades of the color selected for the lateral ventricles to color the anterior and inverior horns.

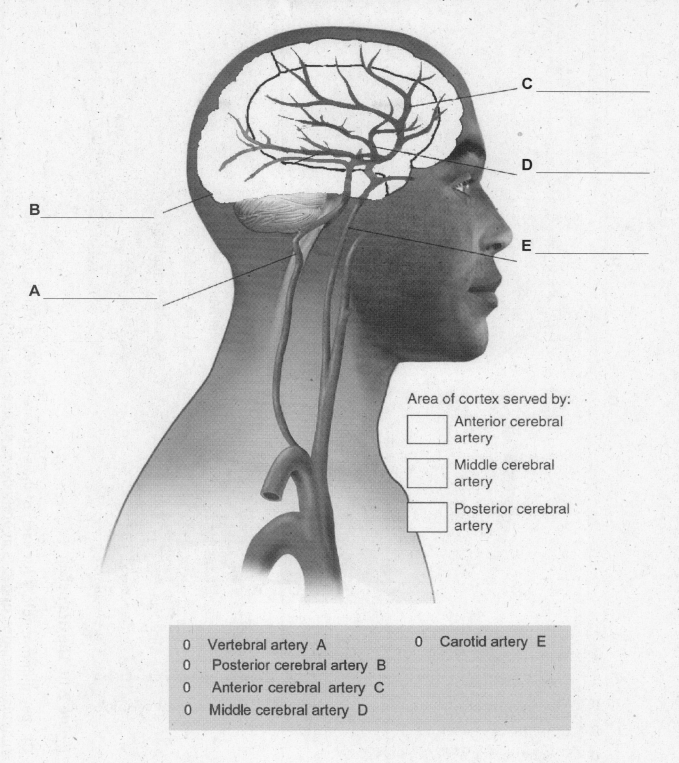

C _____

D _____

B _____

E _____

A _____

Area of cortex served by:

☐ Anterior cerebral artery

☐ Middle cerebral artery

☐ Posterior cerebral artery

0	Vertebral artery A	0	Carotid artery E
0	Posterior cerebral artery B		
0	Anterior cerebral artery C		
0	Middle cerebral artery D		

Figure 2.7 The brain's blood supply

Color the vertebral and carotid arteries two different shades of red.

Color the areas of the brain served by the anterior, middle, and posterior cerebral arteries three different colors. Use the appropriate colors for the key.

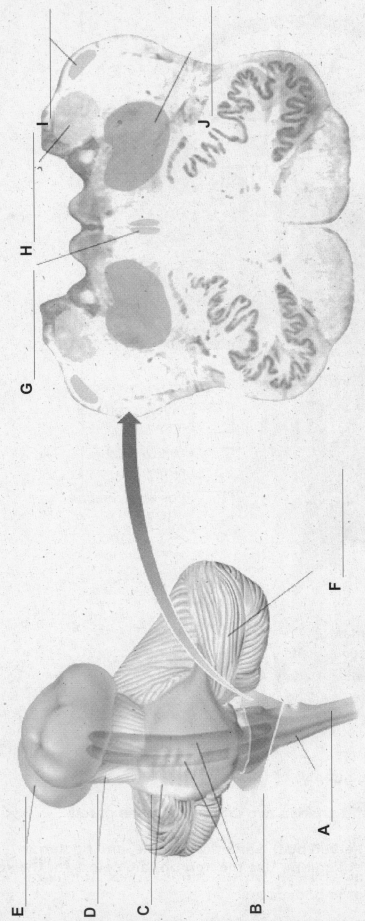

Figure 2.10 The Brainstem

0 Medulla A	0 Raphe nucleus G
0 Reticular formation B	0 Vestibular nucleus H
0 Pons C	0 Cochlear nucleus I
0 Midbrain D	0 Reticular formation J
0 Thalamus E	
0 Cerebellum F	

Choose different colors for each of the structures listed in this figure. The reticular formation appears in both views, so use the same color in both cases.

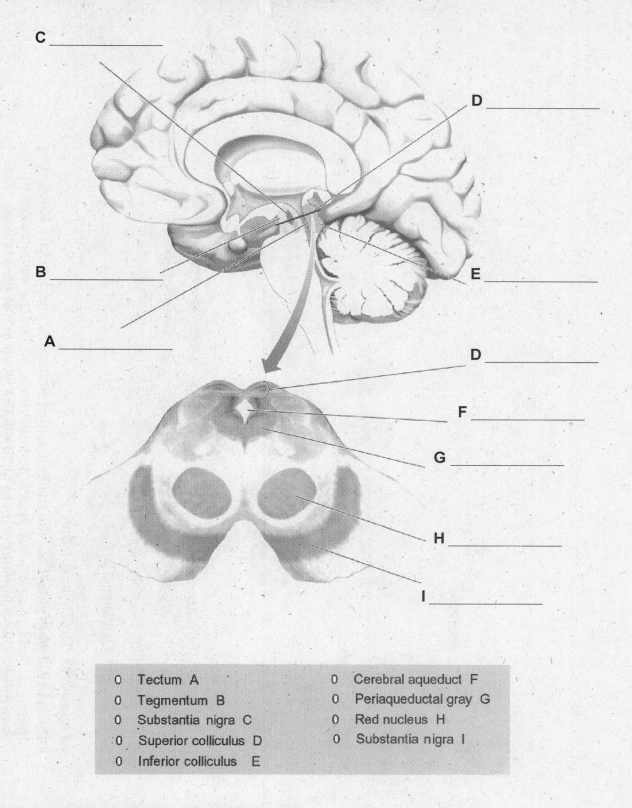

C _____

D _____

B _____

A _____

D _____

E _____

F _____

G _____

H _____

I _____

0 Tectum A	0 Cerebral aqueduct F
0 Tegmentum B	0 Periaqueductal gray G
0 Substantia nigra C	0 Red nucleus H
0 Superior colliculus D	0 Substantia nigra I
0 Inferior colliculus E	

Figure 2.11 Structures of the Midbrain

Select a different color for each of the structures found in this figure. The superior and inferior colliculi are both part of the tectum, so use darker shades of the color you select for the tectum for these two structures. Substantia nigra appears twice, so use the same color in both cases.

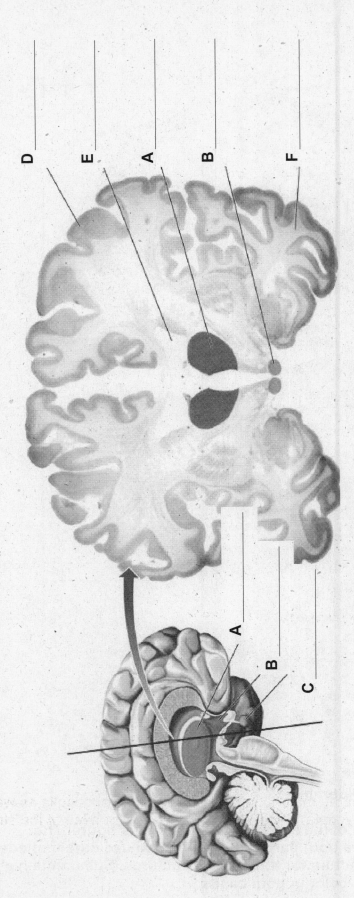

D

E

A

B

F

A

B

C

0   Thalamus   A

0   Hypothalamus   B

0   Pituitary gland   C

0   Parietal lobe   D

0   Lateral ventricle   E

0   Temporal lobe   F

Figure 2.12 The Diencephalon

Choose different colors for the thalamus, hypothalamus, and pituitary gland. The thalamus and hypothalamus appear in both views, so use the same colors in both cases. Use different colors to fill in the lateral ventricle, parietal lobe, and temporal lobe in the image on the right.

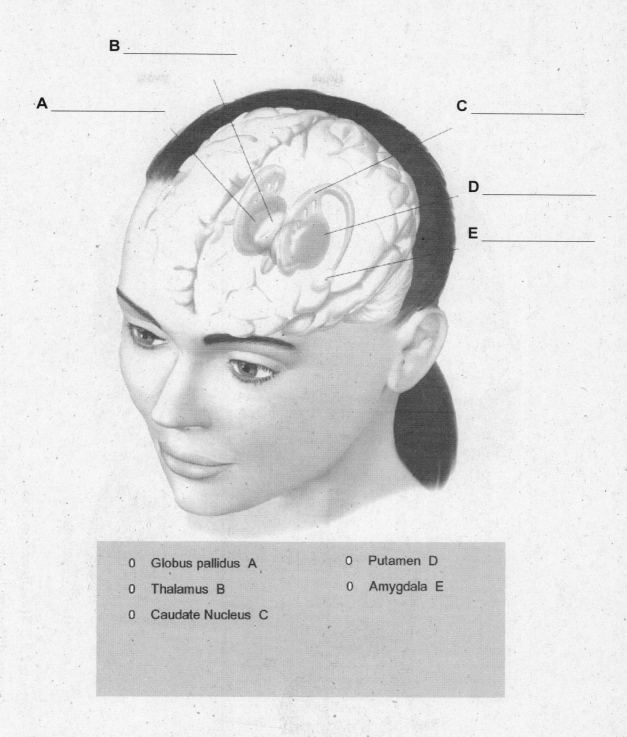

B _____

A _____

C _____

D _____

E _____

O	Globus pallidus A	O	Putamen D
O	Thalamus B	O	Amygdala E
O	Caudate Nucleus C		

Figure 2.13 The Basal Ganglia

This image illustrates three of the major components of the basal ganglia as well as the nearby thalamus and amygdala. Choose a different color for each of the structures shown.

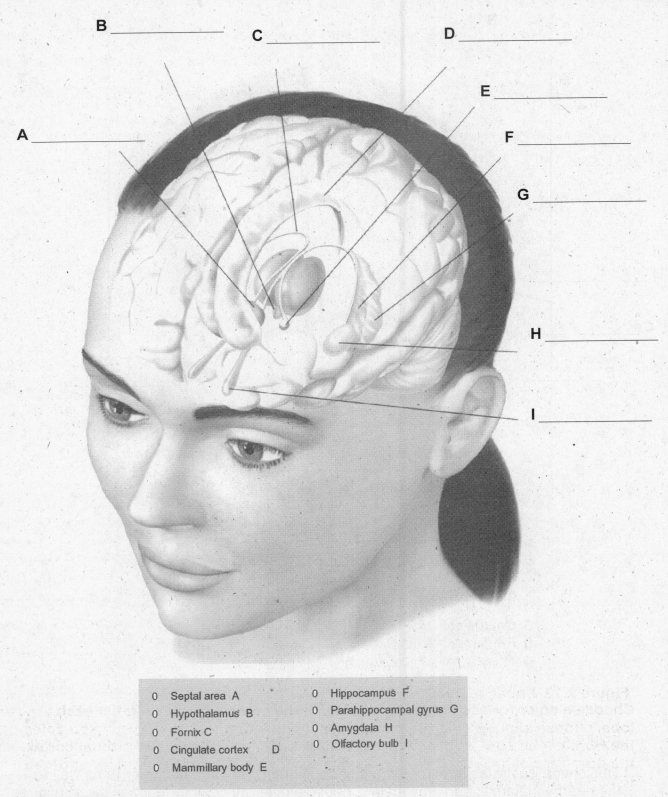

B_____   C_____   D_____

E_____

A_____   F_____

G_____

H_____

I_____

0	Septal area A	0	Hippocampus F
0	Hypothalamus B	0	Parahippocampal gyrus G
0	Fornix C	0	Amygdala H
0	Cingulate cortex D	0	Olfactory bulb I
0	Mammillary body E		

Figure 2.14 The Limbic System

Choose a different color for each of these structures.

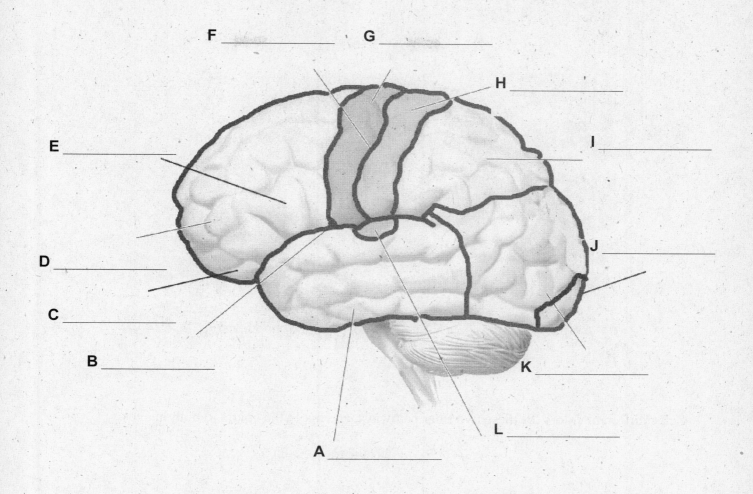

F _____   G _____

H _____

E _____

I _____

D _____

J _____

C _____

B _____

K _____

L _____

A _____

0 Temporal lobe A   0 Parietal lobe I
0 Lateral sulcus B   0 Primary visual cortex J
0 Orbitofrontal cortex C   0 Occipital lobe K
0 Frontal lobe D   0 Primary auditory cortex
0 Dorsolateral prefrontal cortex E   L
0 Central sulcus F
0 Precentral gyrus G
0 Postcentral gryus H

Figure 2.19 Lobes of the Cortex
Choose a color for each of the four lobes of the cerebral cortex. Within each lobe, choose slightly different shades for each feature. For example, if you color the frontal lobe blue, choose different shades of blue for the orbitofrontal cortex, the dorsolateral prefrontal cortex, the precentral gyrus, and the remainder of the lobe. The lateral and central sulci are already black, but you can shade over them with additional color☐☐

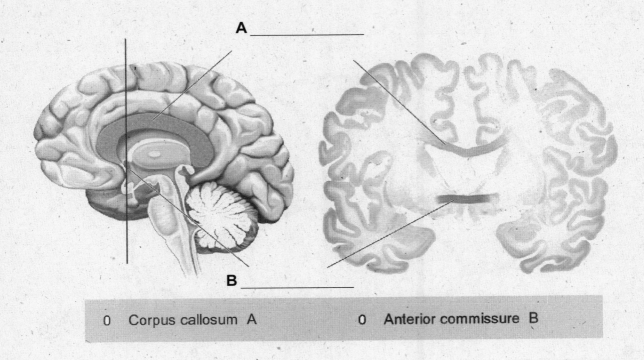

A _____

B _____

| 0   Corpus callosum A | 0   Anterior commissure B |

Select different colors for these two fiber pathways, and apply the colors to both images.

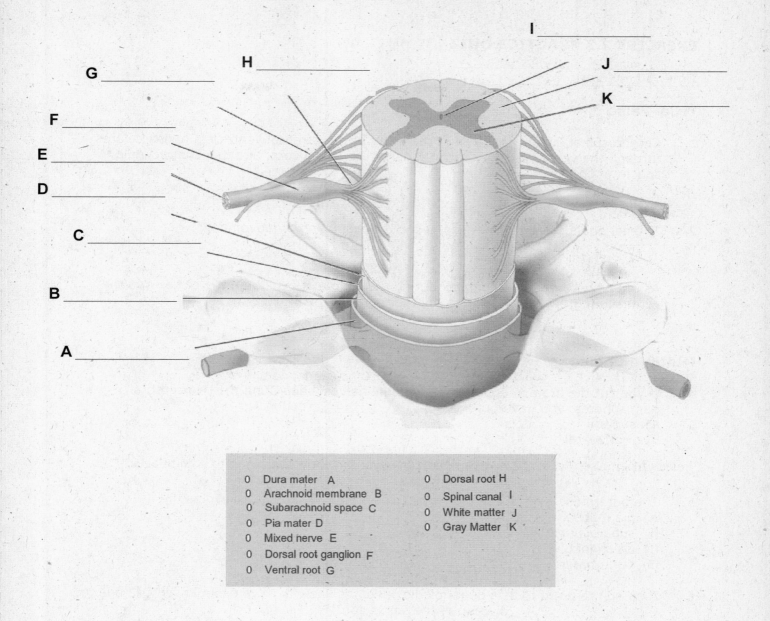

G _____

F _____

E _____

D _____

C _____

B _____

A _____

H _____

I _____

J _____

K _____

0	Dura mater A	0	Dorsal root H
0	Arachnoid membrane B	0	Spinal canal I
0	Subarachnoid space C	0	White matter J
0	Pia mater D	0	Gray Matter K
0	Mixed nerve E		
0	Dorsal root ganglion F		
0	Ventral root G		

Figure 2.23 Structure of the Spinal Cord

Select different colors for dorsal and ventral, and apply these to the appropriate arrows, roots, and ganglia. Select other colors for the remaining features in this image.

EXERCISE 2.3 PRACTICE QUIZ

Time: 50 minutes

True–False

1. Cerebrospinal fluid is produced in the lining of the cerebral ventricles, and circulates through the ventricles, the central canal of the spinal cord, and the subarachnoid space.

    T   F

2. The periaqueductal gray participates in the regulation of movement.

    T   F

3. As brains became more complex during the course of evolution, the cortex and the cerebellum grew in size relative to other parts of the brain.

    T   F

Multiple Choice

4. If you cut the brain in approximately equal halves, separating the two cerebral hemispheres, you have produced a _____ section.
    A) sagittal
    B) horizontal
    C) frontal
    D) coronal

5. The outermost layer of the meninges, closest to the skull, is known as the
    A) pia mater.
    B) subarachnoid.
    C) arachnoid.
    D) dura mater.

6. A person referred to as a quadriplegic patient is likely to have experienced damage to the _____ division of the spinal cord.
    A) thoracic
    B) lumbar
    C) cervical
    D) sacral

7. Another name for the myelencephalon is the
    A) cerebellum.
    B) medulla.
    C) midbrain.
    D) pons.

8. Hunger, thirst, and body temperature are regulated by the
    A) amygdala.
    B) hippocampus.
    C) thalamus.
    D) hypothalamus.

9. The frontal and parietal lobes are separated by the
    A) longitudinal fissure
    B) lateral sulcus
    C) central sulcus
    D) corpus callosum

10. The precentral gyrus consists of _____ cortex.
    A) motor
    B) sensory
    C) association
    D) undifferentiated

11. Information traveling to muscles exits the spinal cord via the
    A) dorsal roots.
    B) ventral roots.
    C) both the dorsal and ventral roots.
    D) central canal.

12. When your sympathetic nervous system is active
    A) your heart rate slows down.
    B) salivation is stimulated.
    C) the pupils of your eyes are dilated.
    D) your bladder is stimulated.

13. Brain size in *Homo sapiens*
    A) increased at a steady pace.
    B) increased rapidly and then leveled off.
    C) increased rapidly since the advent of agriculture.
    D) has not changed much since the species first appeared.

Fill In

14. Structures located towards the nose of an animal are _____ or _____, whereas structures towards the tail of an animal are _____ or _____.

15. The forebrain can be divided into the _____, which contains the thalamus and hypothalamus, and the _____, which contains the remainder of the cerebral hemispheres.

16. The basal ganglia include the _____, _____, _____, and _____.

17. The four lobes of the cerebral cortex are the _____ lobe, the _____ lobe, the _____ lobe, and the _____ lobe.

18. The two hemispheres are connected by the _____ and the
    _____.

19. Twelve pairs of _____ nerves exit the brain, and 31 pairs of _____
    nerves exit between the vertebrae in five divisions: _____,
    _____, _____, _____, and _____.

Short Answer/Labeling

20. Describe the major functions of the cerebellum.

    _____

    _____

    _____

    _____

    _____

    _____

21. What are the roles of the dorsolateral prefrontal cortex and the orbitofrontal cortex?

    _____

    _____

    _____

    _____

    _____

    _____

22. Complete the labels in the figure that follows.

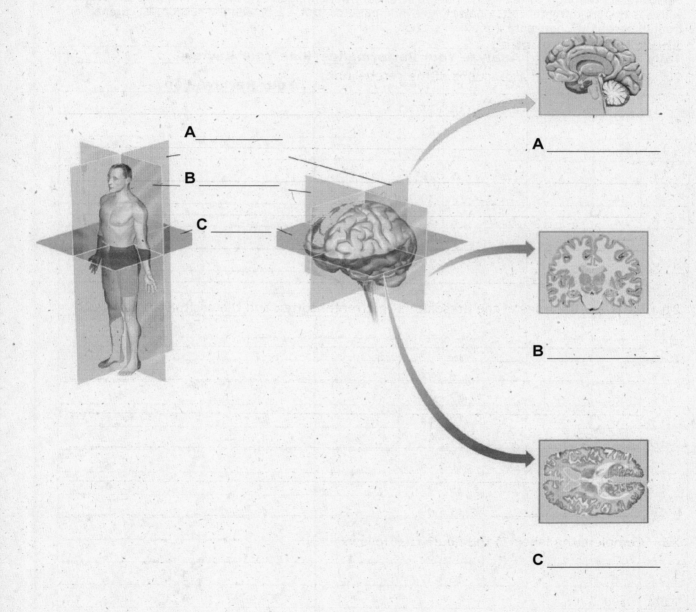

A_____

B_____

C_____

A_____

B_____

C_____

Exercise 2.3 ANSWER KEY

True-False: 1. T; 2. F; 3. T. **Multiple Choice:** 4. A) 5. D) 6. C) 7. B) 8. D) 9. C) 10. A) 11. B) 12. C) 13. D). **Fill In:** 14. rostral; anterior; caudal; posterior. 15. diencephalon; telencephalon. 16. caudate nucleus; putamen; globus pallidus; subthalamic nuclei. 17. frontal; parietal; temporal; occipital. 18. corpus callosum; anterior commissure. 19. cranial; spinal; cervical; thoracic; lumbar; sacral; coccygeal. **Short Answer/Labeling:** 20. The cerebellum participates in balance and motor coordination, as well as higher cognitive functions including learning and language. 21. The dorsolateral prefrontal cortex contributes to attention, working memory, and the planning of behavior, whereas the orbitofrontal cortex participates in impulse control. 22. A. sagittal section; B. coronal (or frontal) section; C. horizontal (or axial) section.

Tally Your Score

Test Item	Point Value	Your Score
1.	2	
2.	2	
3.	2	
4.	4	
5.	4	
6.	4	
7.	4	
8.	4	
9.	4	
10.	4	
11.	4	
12.	4	
13.	4	
14.	6	
15.	6	
16.	6	
17.	6	
18.	6	
19.	6	
20.	6	
21.	6	
22.	6	
TOTAL	100	

Analyze Your Performance/Plan Your Review

LO	Test Item	Text Page	Your Review Plan
2.1	14	27	
	4	28	
	22	29	
2.2	5	29	
	1	30	
2.3	6	35	
2.4	7	35	
	2	37	
	20	37	
	15	38	
	8	39	
	16	39	
2.5	9	44	
	17	44	
	18	44	
	21	45	
2.6	10	44	
2.7	19	47	
	11	49	
2.8	12	51	
2.9	3	55	
	13	57	

Chapter 3. Cells of the Nervous System

EXERCISE 3.1 IDENTIFYING KEY TERMS AND THEIR DEFINITIONS

A. Terms for Structures of Neural Communication

1.	A cell of the nervous system that is specialized for information processing and communication.
2.	Cells in the nervous system that support the activities of neurons.
3.	The main mass of a neuron, containing the nucleus and many organelles.
4.	The branch of a neuron that generally receives information from other neurons.
5.	The branch of a neuron usually responsible for carrying signals to other neurons.
6.	The junction between two neurons at which information is transferred from one to another.

- axon
- cell body / soma
- dendrite
- glia
- neuron
- synapse

B. Terms Related to Neuron Membranes

1.	An ion channel that opens or closes in response to the local electrical environment.
2.	An ion pump that uses energy to transfer three sodium ions to the extracellular fluid for every two potassium ions retrieved from the extracellular fluid.
3.	The fluid inside a cell.
4.	The fluid surrounding a cell.
5.	An electrically charged particle in solution.
6.	A chemical messenger that transfers information across a synapse.
7.	An ion channel in the neural membrane that responds to chemical messengers.

- extracellular fluid
- intracellular fluid
- ion
- voltage-dependent channel
- ligand-gated channel
- sodium-potassium pump
- neurotransmitter

C. Neuron Structural Support Terms

1.	The smallest fiber found in the cell cytoskeleton that may participate in the changing of the length and shape of axons and dendrites.
2.	A knob on the dendrite that provides additional membrane area for the formation of synapses with other neurons.

3.	A network of filaments that provides the internal structure of a neuron.
4.	A neural fiber found in the cell cytoskeleton that is responsible for structural support.
5.	The largest fiber in the cell cytoskeleton, responsible for the transport of neurotransmitters and other products to and from the cell body.

- cytoskeleton
- microtubule
- dendritic spine

- microfilament
- neurofilament

D. Terms for Key Neuron Components

1.	The fatty insulating material covering some axons that boosts the speed and efficiency of electrical signaling.
2.	The uncovered section of axon membrane between two adjacent segments of myelin.
3.	The cone-shaped segment of axon located at the junction of the axon and cell body that is specialized for the generation of action potentials.
4.	A small structure in the axon terminal that contains neurotransmitters.
5.	The tiny fluidfilled space between neurons forming a synapse.
6.	The swelling at the tip of an axon collateral specialized for the release of neurotransmitter substances.

- synaptic gap
- axon hillock
- axon terminal

- myelin
- node of Ranvier
- synaptic vesicle

E. Terms Related to Glia

1.	A neuron with one branch that extends a short distance from the cell body then splits into two branches.
2.	A neuron with two branches: one axon and one dendrite.
3.	A neuron that has multiple branches, usually one axon and numerous dendrites.
4.	A specialized neuron that communicates with muscles and glands.
5.	A specialized neuron that translates incoming sensory information into electrical signals.
6.	A glial cell that forms the myelin on central nervous system axons.
7.	A large, star shaped glial cell of the central nervous system, responsible for structural support, isolation of the synapse, control of the extracellular chemical environment at the synapse, and communication.
8.	Tiny, mobile glial cells that migrate to areas of damage and digest debris.
9.	Large glial cells, including astrocytes, oligodendrocytes, and Schwann cells.
10.	A glial cell that forms the myelin on axons in the peripheral nervous system.

- astrocyte
- bipolar neuron
- macroglia
- microglia
- motor neuron
- multipolar neuron
- oligodendrocyte
- Schwann cell
- sensory neuron
- unipolar neuron

F. Terms Involved with Neural Signaling

1.	The movement of an action potential down the length of an unmyelinated axon.
2.	The measurement of the electrical charge across the neural membrane when the cell is not processing information.
3.	The nerve impulse arising in an axon.
4.	The period following an action potential in which larger than normal input will produce a second action potential but in which normal input will be insufficient.
5.	The movement of an action potential from node of Ranvier to node of Ranvier, down the length of a myelinated axon.
6.	The movement of an electrical charge within a cell in a more positive direction.
7.	The period in which an action potential will not occur in a particular location of an axon regardless of input.
8.	The level of depolarization at which an action potential is initiated.

- action potential
- resting potential
- depolarization
- threshold
- absolute refractory period
- relative refractory period
- passive conduction
- saltatory conduction

G. Terms Involved with Neuron Signal Reception

1.	A process for ending the action of neurotransmitters in the synaptic gap in which the presynaptic membrane recaptures the transmitter molecules.
2.	A small hyperpolarization produced in the postsynaptic cell as a result of input from the presynaptic cell.
3.	A small depolarization produced in the postsynaptic cell as a result of input from the presynaptic cell.
4.	Neural integration in which the combined inputs from many synapses converge on the axon hillock, where an action potential will result if threshold is reached.
5.	Receptor site located on the presynaptic neuron that provides information about the cell's own activity levels.
6.	At a synapse between two axons, the increase of neurotransmitter release by the postsynaptic axon as a result of input from the presynaptic axon.
7.	Neural integration in which excitation from one active synapse is sufficient to initiate the formation of an action potential.
8.	The process in which vesicles fuse with the membrane of the axon terminal and release neurotransmitter molecules into the synaptic gap.

9.	At a synapse between two axons, the decrease of neurotransmitter release by the postsynaptic axon as a result of input from the presynaptic axon.
10.	A protein structure embedded in the postsynaptic membrane containing a recognition site and a G protein. Neurotransmitters binding to these receptors do not directly open ion channels.
11.	A receptor protein in the postsynaptic membrane in which the recognition site is located in the same structure as the ion channel.

- autoreceptor
- exocytosis
- ionotropic receptor
- metabotropic receptor
- reuptake
- presynaptic facilitation

- excitatory postsynaptic potential (EPSP)
- inhibitory postsynaptic potential (IPSP)
- presynaptic inhibition
- spatial summation
- temporal summation

EXERCISE 3.1 ANSWER KEY

A. Terms for Structures of Neural Communication
1. neuron (p. 61)
2. glia (p. 61)
3. cell body / soma (p. 61)
4. dendrite (p. 61)
5. axon (p. 61)
6. synapse (p. 63)

B. Terms Related to Neuron Membranes
1. voltage-dependent channel (p. 62)
2. sodium-potassium pump (p. 63)
3. intracellular fluid (p. 62)
4. extracellular fluid (p. 62)
5. ion (p. 62)
6. neurotransmitter (p. 63)
7. ligand-gated channel (p. 63)

C. Neuron Structural Support Terms
1. microfilament (p. 65)
2. dendritic spine (p. 65)
3. cytoskeleton (p. 63)
4. neurofilament (p. 65)
5. microtubule (p. 63)

D. Terms for Key Neuron Components
1. myelin (p. 67)
2. node of Ranvier (p. 67)
3. axon hillock (p. 67)
4. synaptic vesicle (p. 67)
5. synaptic gap (p. 65)
6. axon terminal (p. 67)

E. Terms Related to Glia
1. unipolar neuron (p. 68)
2. bipolar neuron (p. 68)
3. multipolar neuron (p. 68)
4. motor neuron (p. 68)
5. sensory neuron (p. 68)
6. oligodendrocyte (p. 68
7. astrocyte (p. 68)
8. microglia (p. 68)
9. macroglia (p. 68)
10. Schwann cell (p. 68)

F. Terms Involved with Neural Signaling
1. passive conduction (p. 80)
2. resting potential (p. 74)
3. action potential (p. 61)
4. relative refractory period (p. 79)
5. saltatory conduction (p. 81)
6. depolarization (p. 77)
7. absolute refractory period (p. 78)
8. threshold (p. 77)

G. Terms Involved with Neuron Signal Reception
1. reuptake (p. 87
2. inhibitory postsynaptic potential (IPSP) (p. 88)
3. excitatory postsynaptic potential (EPSP) (p. 88)
4. spatial summation (p. 91)
5. autoreceptor (p. 85)
6. presynaptic facilitation (p. 91
7. temporal summation (p. 91
8. exocytosis (p. 85)
9. presynaptic inhibition (p. 91)
10. metabotropic receptor (p. 86)
11. ionotropic receptor (p. 86)

EXERCISE 3.2 LEARNING BY COLORING

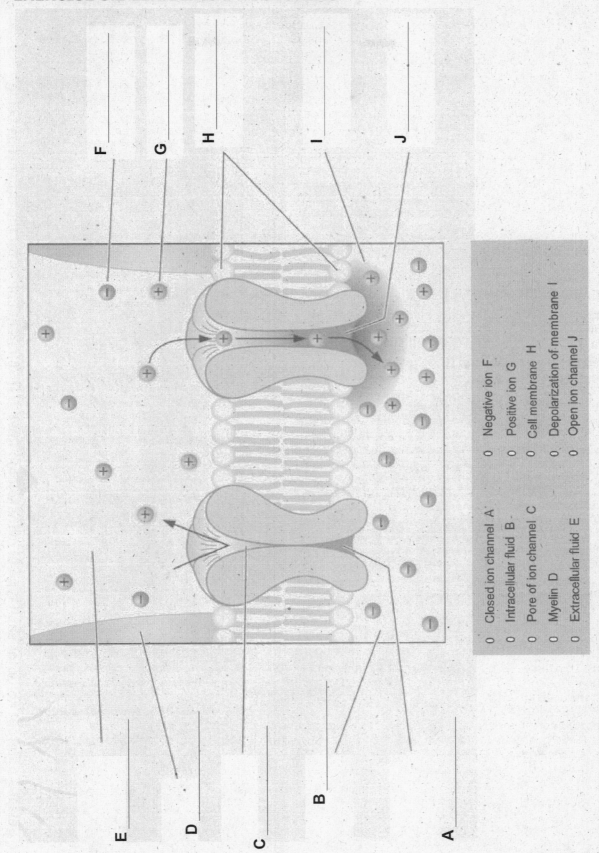

Figure 3.2 The Neural Membrane

Select a different color for each of the features in this image. Use one color for all positively charged ions and another color for all negatively charged ions.

- 0 Closed ion channel A
- 0 Intracellular fluid B
- 0 Pore of ion channel C
- 0 Myelin D
- 0 Extracellular fluid E
- 0 Negative ion F
- 0 Positive ion G
- 0 Cell membrane H
- 0 Depolarization of membrane I
- 0 Open ion channel J

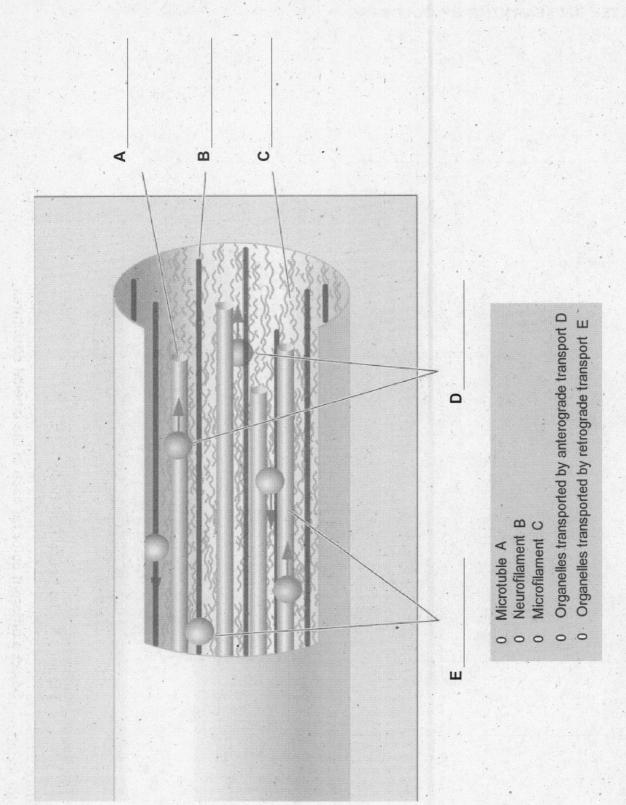

A

B

C

D

E

Figure 3.3 The Neural Cytoskeleton

Select a different color for each type of cytoskeleton fiber. Use different colors for the organelles being transported by anterograde and retrograde transport.

0 Microtuble A
0 Neurofilament B
0 Microfilament C
0 Organelles transported by anterograde transport D
0 Organelles transported by retrograde transport E

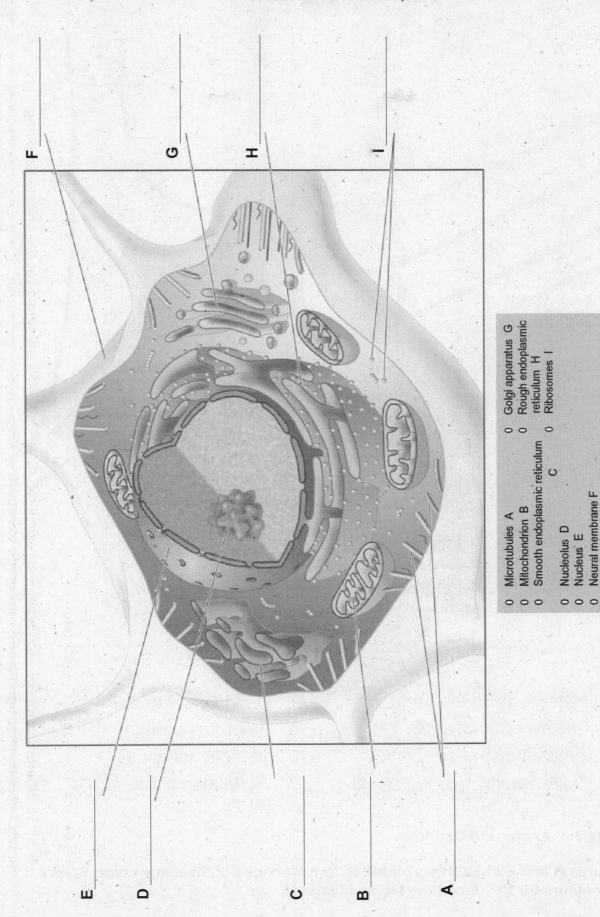

Figure 3.5 The Neural Cell Body

Select a different color for each of the labeled structures.

0 Microtubules A
0 Mitochondrion B
0 Smooth endoplasmic reticulum C

0 Nucleolus D
0 Nucleus E
0 Neural membrane F

0 Golgi apparatus G
0 Rough endoplasmic
    reticulum H
0 Ribosomes I

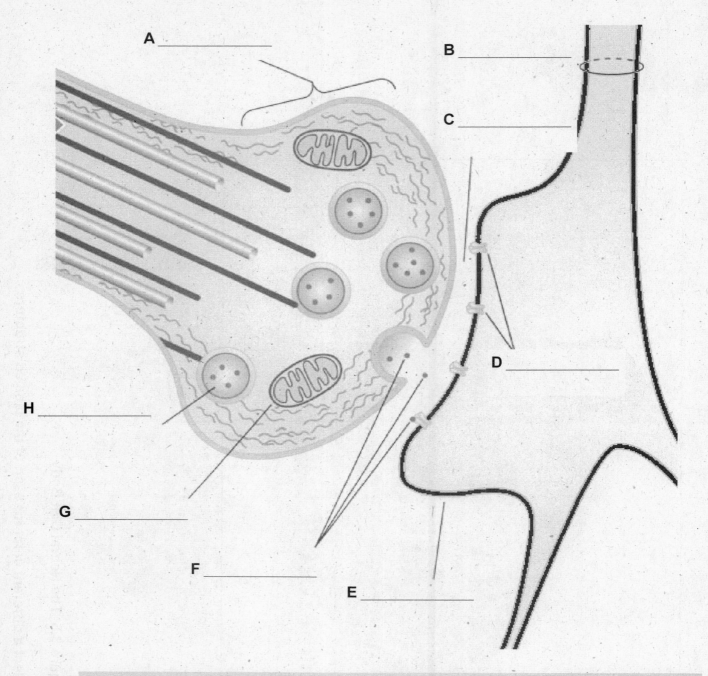

A _____

B _____

C _____

D _____

E _____

F _____

G _____

H _____

0	Presynaptic axon terminal A	0	Dendrite spine E
0	Postsynaptic dendrite B	0	Neurotransmitter F
0	Synaptic gap C	0	Mitochondrion G
0	Postsynaptic receptors D	0	Synaptic vesicle H

Figure 3.6 Axons and Dendrites

Features B and E should be colored different shades of the same color. Select other colors for the remaining labeled features.

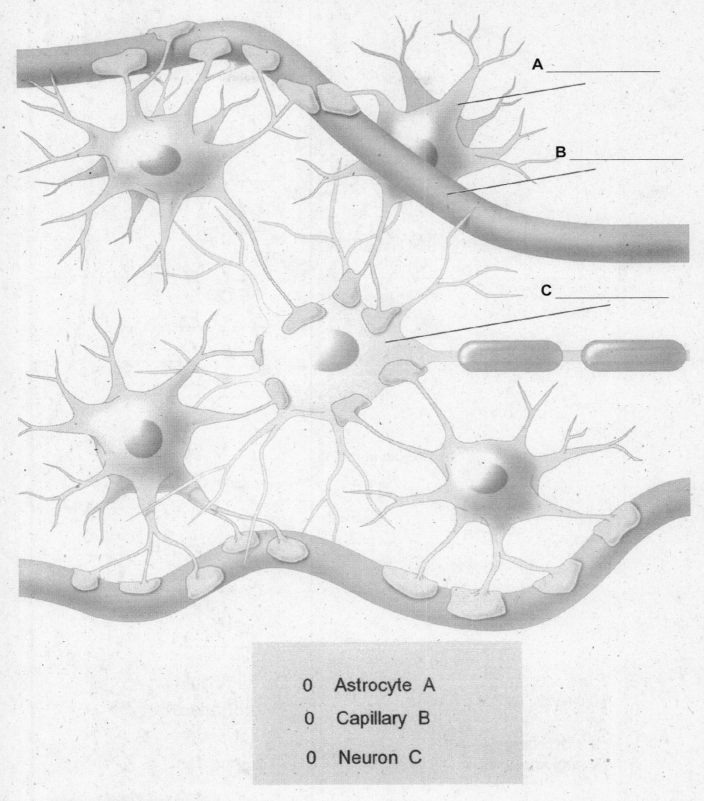

A_____

B_____

C_____

0   Astrocyte A

0   Capillary B

0   Neuron C

Figure 3.9 Astrocytes

Select a different color for each of the labeled features in this image. There is one neuron, but multiple astrocytes.

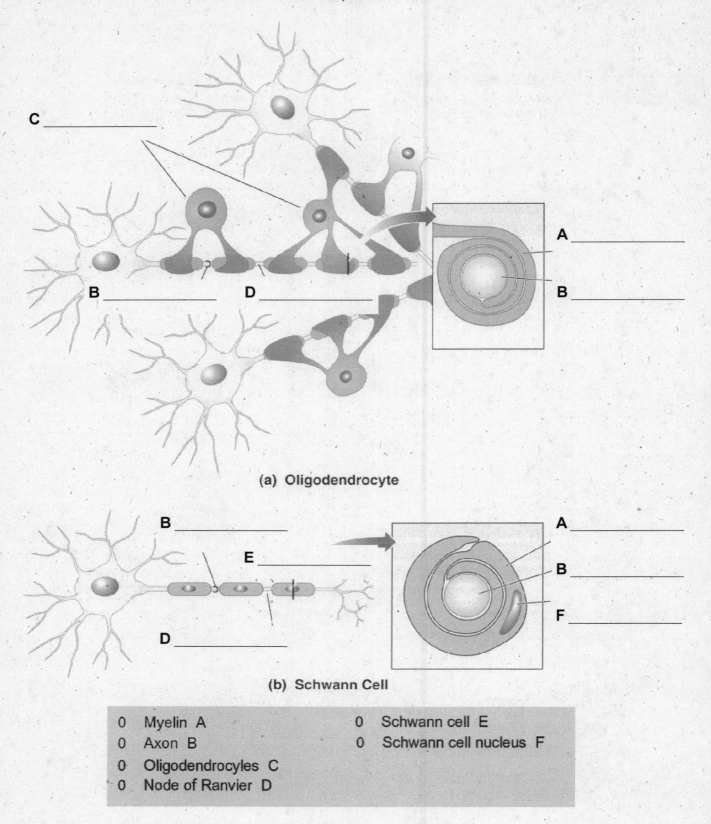

(a) Oligodendrocyte

(b) Schwann Cell

0	Myelin A		0	Schwann cell E
0	Axon B		0	Schwann cell nucleus F
0	Oligodendrocyles C			
0	Node of Ranvier D			

Figure 3.10 Oligodendrocytes and Schwann Cells

Select a color for each labeled feature. Note that the same feature appears multiple times in the image.

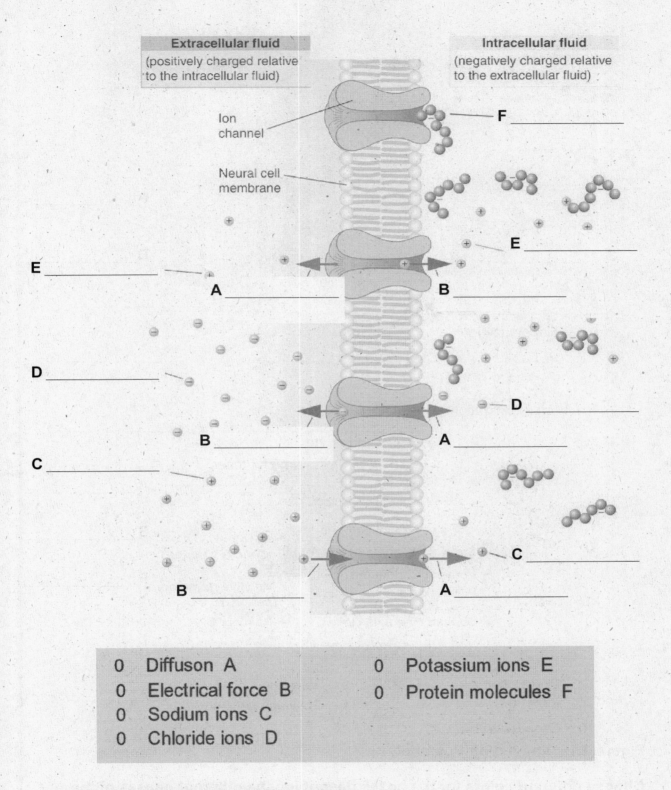

Extracellular fluid
(positively charged relative to the intracellular fluid)

Intracellular fluid
(negatively charged relative to the extracellular fluid)

Ion channel

Neural cell membrane

F _____

E _____

E _____

A _____   B _____

D _____

D _____

B _____   A _____

C _____

C _____

B _____   A _____

0   Diffuson A   0   Potassium ions E
0   Electrical force B   0   Protein molecules F
0   Sodium ions C
0   Chloride ions D

Figure 3.14 Diffusion and Electrical Force

Choose one color for all of the diffusion arrows and another for all the electrical force arrows. Select different colors for the four types of molecules and color all instances of each type.

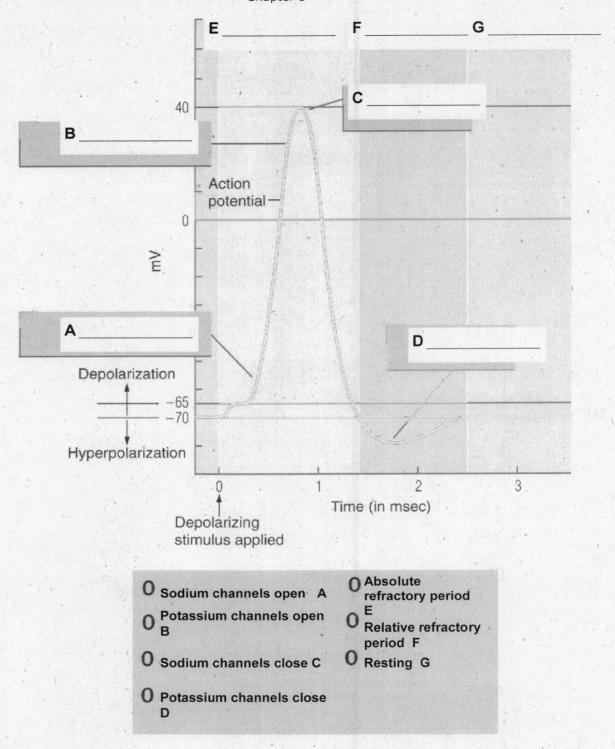

Figure 3.15 The Action Potential

Choose different colors for the boxes describing the different phases of the action potential, and match those colors to the appropriate line segments. Lightly shade the resting and refractory periods in the background of the image.

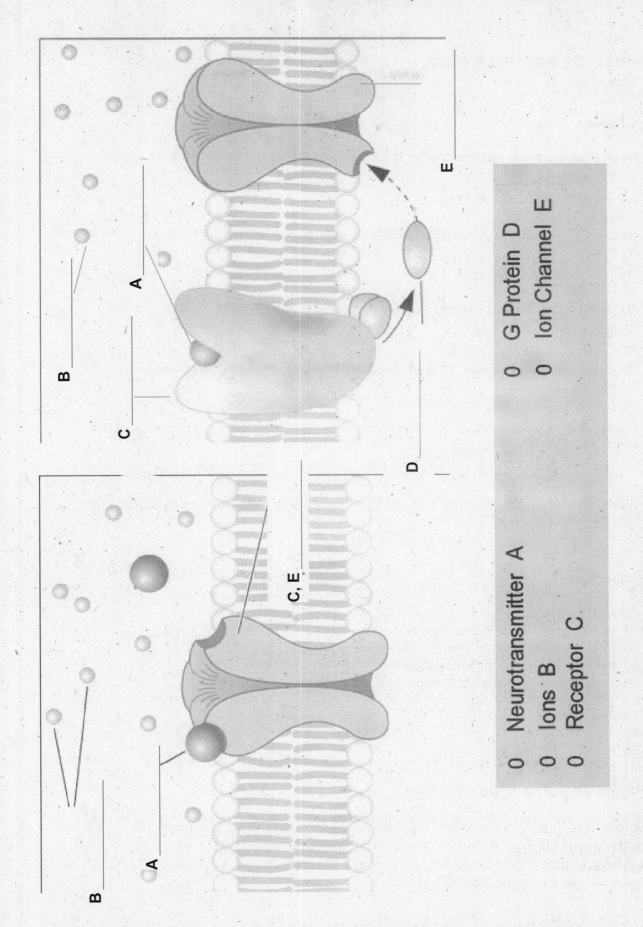

Figure 3.20 Ionotropic and Metabotropic Receptors

Select a single color for each of the labeled features, and apply the color in both illustrations.

0   Neurotransmitter   A
0   Ions   B
0   Receptor   C
0   G Protein   D
0   Ion Channel   E

EXERCISE 3.3 PRACTICE QUIZ

Time: 55 minutes

True–False

1. Neurofilaments are responsible for retrograde and anterograde transport within neurons.

    T   F

2. The areas of axon membrane between two segments of myelin are known as nodes of Ranvier.

    T   F

3. The majority of neurons in the human nervous system are bipolar.

    T   F

4. Microglia are able to move to areas where the nervous system is damaged.

    T   F

5. During an action potential, sodium channels remain open longer than potassium channels.

    T   F

6. IPSPs can result from the opening of either chloride or potassium channels on the postsynaptic membrane.

    T   F

Multiple Choice

7. Glia are found
    A) in the central nervous system only.
    B) in the peripheral nervous system only.
    C) in both the central and peripheral nervous systems.
    D) circulating in the cerebrospinal fluid.

8. Tau proteins hold _____ in place.
    A) microtubules
    B) neurofilaments
    C) microfilaments
    D) synaptic vesicles

9. An organelle responsible for packaging proteins for transport within the cell is the
    A) mitochondria.
    B) Golgi apparatus.
    C) nucleolus.
    D) smooth endoplasmic reticulum.

10. Electrical signals move from the axon _____ to the axon _____.
    A) terminal; hillock
    B) hillock; terminal
    C) collateral; hillock
    D) terminal; collateral

11. Cells that have one branch that leaves the cell body are known as
    A) multipolar cells.
    B) bipolar cells.
    C) unipolar cells.
    D) von Economo neurons.

12. Which type of glia participate in the blood-brain barrier?
    A) Microglia
    B) Oligodendrocytes
    C) Schwann cells
    D) Astrocytes

13. Immediately following an action potential, the axon membrane
    A) returns to the resting potential.
    B) remains slightly depolarized.
    C) remains slightly hyperpolarized.
    D) returns to threshold.

14. The amount of neurotransmitter released during exocytosis is a function of the
    A) amount of calcium entering the axon terminal.
    B) size of the action potential.
    C) length of the axon.
    D) number of mitochondria in the axon terminal.

15. Opening postsynaptic potassium channels will result in the production of
    A) an EPSP.
    B) an IPSP.
    C) an action potential.
    D) exocytosis.

16. Presynaptic facilitation involves a synapse between
    A) an axon and a dendrite.
    B) an axon and a cell body.
    C) two axons.
    D) two dendrites.

Fill In

17. _____ channels in the neural membrane open in response to
    contact with specific chemicals, and _____ channels open in response
    to the electrical status of adjacent areas of membrane.

18. _____ form myelin in the central nervous system, whereas
    _____ form myelin in the peripheral nervous system.

19. Extracellular fluid is rich in _____ and _____,
    but contains little _____ compared to the intracellular fluid.

20. In the resting neuron, potassium moves into the cell due to _____ and
    out of the cell due to _____.

21. _____ conduction occurs in myelinated axons, and
    _____ conduction occurs in unmyelinated axons.

22. _____ receptors feature recognition sites located on an ion channel,
    and _____ receptors release G proteins internally.

Short Answer/Labeling

23. Describe the sequence of events that occur during an action potential.

    _____

    _____

    _____

    _____

    _____

    _____

24. Describe the process of exocytosis.

    _____

    _____

    _____

    _____

    _____

    _____

25. Complete the labels in the figure that follows.

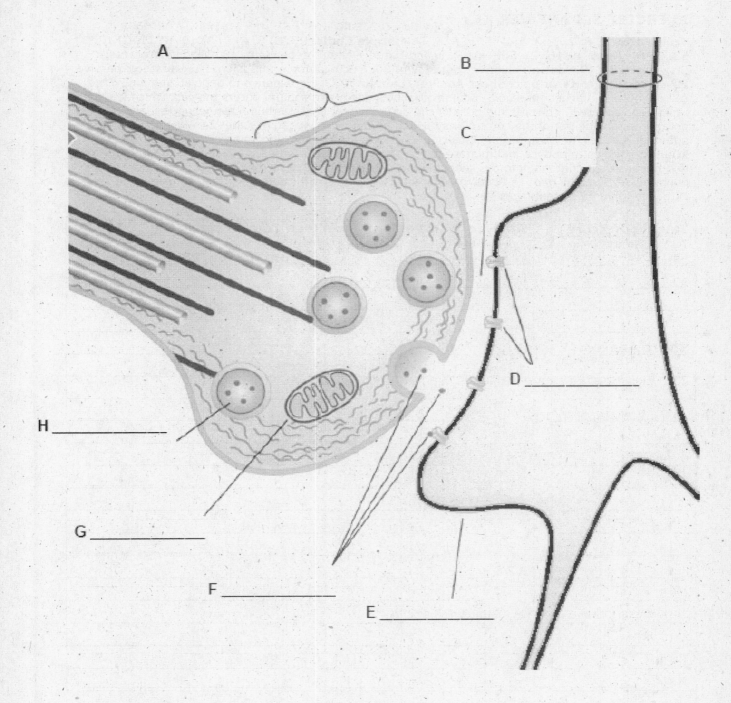

A_____

B_____

C_____

D_____

E_____

F_____

G_____

H_____

EXERCISE 3.3 ANSWER KEY

True-False: 1. F; 2. T; 3. F; 4. T; 5. F; 6. T. **Multiple Choice:** 7. C) 8. A) 9. B) 10. B) 11. C) 12. D) 13. C) 14. A) 15. B) 16. C). **Fill In:** 17. ligand-gated; voltage-dependent. 18. Oligodendrocytes; Schwann cells. 19. sodium; chloride; potassium. 20. electrical force; diffusion. 21. Saltatory; passive. 22. Ionotropic; metabotropic. **Short Answer/Labeling:** 23. In response to depolarizing input, the cell membrane reaches threshold. Sodium channels open, and sodium enters the cell, which leads to a rapid depolarization. Towards the peak of the action potential, potassium channels open, and potassium moving out of the cell returns the cell to its former negative state. 24. When an action potential reaches the axon terminal, calcium channels are opened. Incoming calcium ions signal synaptic vesicles to undock and migrate to the cell membrane, where they fuse with the membrane and release their contents into the synaptic gap. 25. A. Presynaptic axon terminal; B. Postsynaptic dendrite; C. Synaptic gap; D. Postsynaptic receptors; E. Dendritic spine; F. Neurotransmitters; G. Mitochondrion; H. Synaptic vesicle.

Tally Your Score

Test Item	Point Value	Your Score
1.	1	
2.	1	
3.	1	
4.	1	
5.	1	
6.	1	
7.	4	
8.	4	
9.	4	
10.	4	
11.	4	
12.	4	
13.	4	
14.	4	
15.	4	
16.	4	
17.	6	
18.	6	
19.	6	
20.	6	
21.	6	
22.	6	
23.	6	
24.	6	
25.	6	
TOTAL	100	

Analyze Your Performance/Plan Your Review

LO	Test Item	Text Page	Your Review Plan
3.1	7	61	
3.2	17	62	
	1	63	
	8	64	
3.3	9	65	
3.4	25	66	
	2	67	
	10	67	
3.5	3	68	
	11	68	
3.6	12	70	
	18	71	
	4	72	
3.7	19	73	
	20	75	
	23	77	
	5	78	
	13	78	
	21	80	
3.8	14	85	
	24	85	
	22	87	
3.9	6	88	
	15	88	
3.10	16	91	

Chapter 4. Psychopharmacology

EXERCISE 4.1 IDENTIFYING KEY TERMS AND THEIR DEFINITIONS

A. General Terms for Chemical Messengers

1.	A chemical messenger that communicates with target cells more distant than the synapse by diffusing away from the point of release.
2.	A chemical messenger that communicates with target cells at great distance, often by traveling through the circulation.
3.	A chemical messenger that communicates across a synapse.

- neurotransmitter
- neuromodulator
- neurohormone

B. Terms for the Neurotransmitters of Cholinergic Neurons

1.	A postsynaptic receptor that responds to both ACh and muscarine.
2.	A postsynaptic receptor that responds to nicotine and ACh.
3.	An enzyme that breaks down the neurotransmitter acetylcholine.
4.	A major small-molecule neurotransmitter used at the neuromuscular junction, in the autonomic nervous system, and in the central nervous system.

- acetylcholine (ACh)
- acetylcholinesterase (AChE)

- muscarinic receptor
- nicotinic receptor

C. Terms for the Monoamines

1.	One of a subgroup of monoamines, including serotonin and melatonin.
2.	One of a major group of biogenic amine neurotransmitters, including dopamine, norepinephrine, epinephrine, and serotonin.
3.	A member of a group of related biogenic amines that includes dopamine, epinephrine, and norepinephrine.
4.	One of the monoamine/ catecholamine neurotransmitters; also known as adrenaline.
5.	An enzyme that breaks down monoamines.
6.	A major monoamine and catecholamine neurotransmitter.
7.	A major monoamine and catecholamine neurotransmitter implicated in motor control, reward, and psychosis.

- dopamine
- epinephrine
- indoleamine
- monoamine

- monoamine oxidase (MAO)
- norepinephrine
- catecholamine

D. Amino Acid and Gaseous Neurotransmitter Terms

1.	A gas that performs a type of signaling between neurons.
2.	A major monoamine and indoleamine neurotransmitter believed to participate in the regulation of mood, sleep, and appetite.
3.	A major inhibitory amino acid neurotransmitter.
4.	A byproduct of adenosine triphosphate (ATP) that functions as a neurotransmitter.
5.	A major excitatory amino acid neurotransmitter.

- gamma-aminobutyric acid (GABA)
- glutamate
- serotonin
- adenosine
- nitric oxide (NO)

E. Terms Related to Drug Actions and Effects

1.	Perceived benefit from inactive substances or procedures.
2.	A brainstem area, in which the blood–brain barrier is more permeable, that triggers vomiting in response to the detection of circulating toxins.
3.	A dopaminergic structure believed to participate in reward and addiction.
4.	A compulsive craving for drug effects or other experience.
5.	The symptoms that occur when certain addictive drugs are no longer administered or are administered in smaller quantities.
6.	The process in which more of a drug is needed to produce the same effect.
7.	Substance that promotes the activity of a neurotransmitter.
8.	Substance that reduces the action of a neurotransmitter.

- agonist
- antagonist
- area postrema
- placebo effect
- tolerance
- withdrawal
- nucleus accumbens
- addiction

F. Terms Related to Psychoactive Drugs

1.	A stimulant drug that is the major active component found in tobacco.
2.	An illegal liquid sedative that appears to affect the thresholds of response for a number of neurotransmitters.
3.	The major ingredient of cannabis.
4.	A hallucinogenic drug that resembles serotonin.
5.	An herb that is frequently used to selftreat mild depression
6.	A hallucinogen that acts as an antagonist at the NMDA glutamate receptor
7.	The active hallucinogenic ingredient found in the peyote cactus.

8.	A stimulant drug found in coffee, tea, cola, and chocolate that acts as an antagonist to adenosine.
9.	A drug that produces changes in mental processes.
10.	A close relative of amphetamine that produces its behavioral effects by stimulating the release of serotonin.
11.	A naturally occurring neuropeptide that is very closely related to opioids.
12.	A highly addictive drug that acts as a potent dopamine agonist.
13.	An active substance derived from the opium poppy.
14.	A variation of amphetamine that is cheaply produced and widely abused in the United States.
15.	A powerful, addictive dopamine agonist derived from the leaves of the coca plant of South America.

- caffeine
- psychoactive drug
- nicotine
- amphetamine
- cocaine
- ecstasy (MDMA)

- methamphetamine
- opiate
- endorphin
- tetrahydrocannabinol (THC)
- St. John's wort

- lysergic acid diethylamide (LSD)
- mescaline
- phencyclidine (PCP)
- gamma-hydroxybutyrate (GHB)

EXERCISE 4.1 ANSWER KEY

A. General Terms for Chemical Messengers
1. neuromodulator (p. 95
2. neurohormone (p. 95)
3. neurotransmitter (p. 95)

B. Terms for the Nuerotransmitters of Cholinergic Neurons
1. muscarinic receptor (p. 97)
2. nicotinic receptor (p. 97)
3. acetylcholinesterase (AChE) (p. 97
4. acetylcholine (ACh) (p. 97)

C. Terms for the Monoamines
1. indoleamine (p. 98)
2. monoamine (p. 98)
3. catecholamine (p. 99)
4. epinephrine (p. 98)
5. monoamine oxidase (MAO) (p. 98)
6. norepinephrine (p. 98)
7. dopamine (p. 98)

D. Amino Acid and Gaseous Neurotransmitter Terms
1. nitric oxide (NO) (p. 102
2. serotonin (p. 100
3. gamma-aminobutyric acid (GABA)(p. 100)
4. adenosine (p. 102
5. glutamate (p. 100)

E. Terms Related to Drug Actions and Effects
1. placebo effect (p. 109)
2. area postrema (p. 108)
3. nucleus accumbens (p. 111)
4. addiction (p. 111)
5. withdrawal (p. 111)
6. tolerance (p. 111)
7. agonist (p. 105)
8. antagonist (p. 105)

F. Terms Related to Psychoactive Drugs
1. nicotine (p. 114)
2. gamma-hydroxybutyrate (GHB)(p. 116)
3. tetrahydrocannabinol (THC) (p. 118)
4. lysergic acid diethylamide (LSD)(p. 120)
5. St. John's wort (p. 121)
6. phencyclidine (PCP) (p. 120)
7. mescaline (p. 120)
8. caffeine (p. 113)
9. psychoactive drug (p. 113)
10. ecstasy (MDMA) (p. 115)
11. endorphin (p. 117)
12. amphetamine (p. 115)
13. opiate (p. 116)
14. methamphetamine (p. 115)
15. cocaine (p. 115)

EXERCISE 4.2 LEARNING BY COLORING

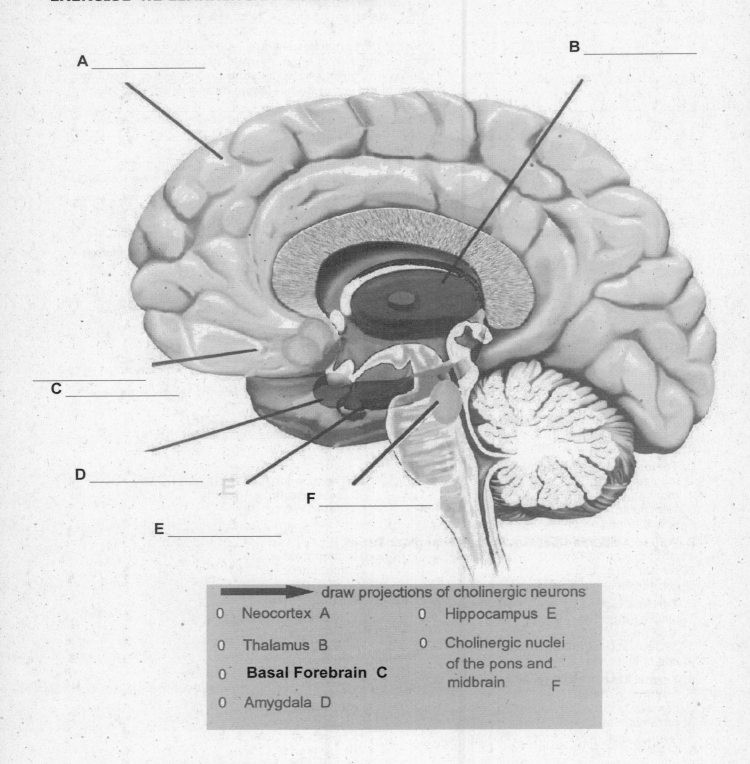

A_____

B_____

C_____

D_____

E_____

F_____

draw projections of cholinergic neurons

0	Neocortex A	0	Hippocampus E
0	Thalamus B	0	Cholinergic nuclei of the pons and midbrain F
0	**Basal Forebrain C**		
0	Amygdala D		

Figure 4.3 Cholinergic Pathways

Use a different color for each of the labeled structures. Choose one additional color and draw arrows to indicate the major cholinergic pathways in the brain.

A _____

B

D _____

E _____

F _____

G _____

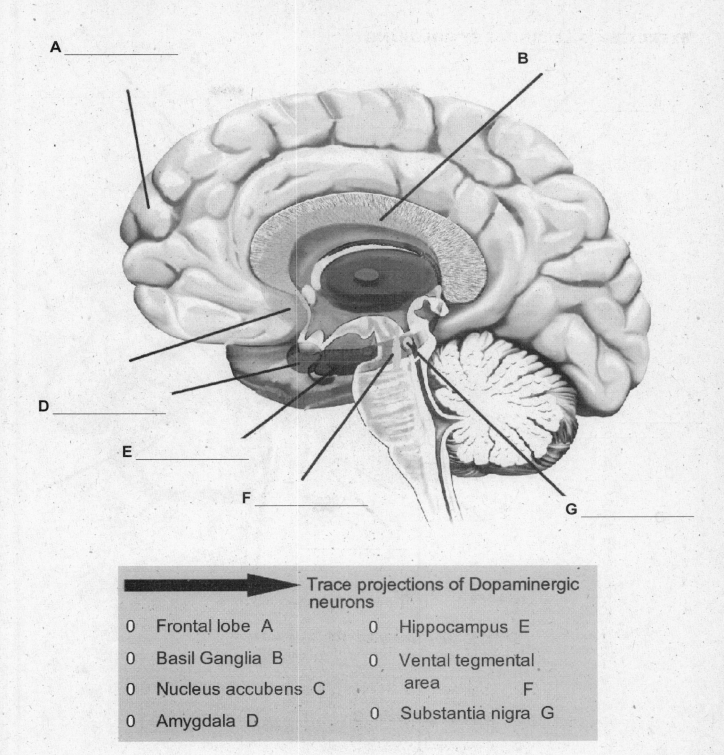

Trace projections of Dopaminergic neurons

0	Frontal lobe A	0	Hippocampus E
0	Basil Ganglia B	0	Vental tegmental area F
0	Nucleus accubens C		
0	Amygdala D	0	Substantia nigra G

Figure 4.5 Dopaminergic Pathways

Select different colors for each of the labeled structures. Choose a new color to draw arrows indicating the major dopaminergic pathways in the brain.

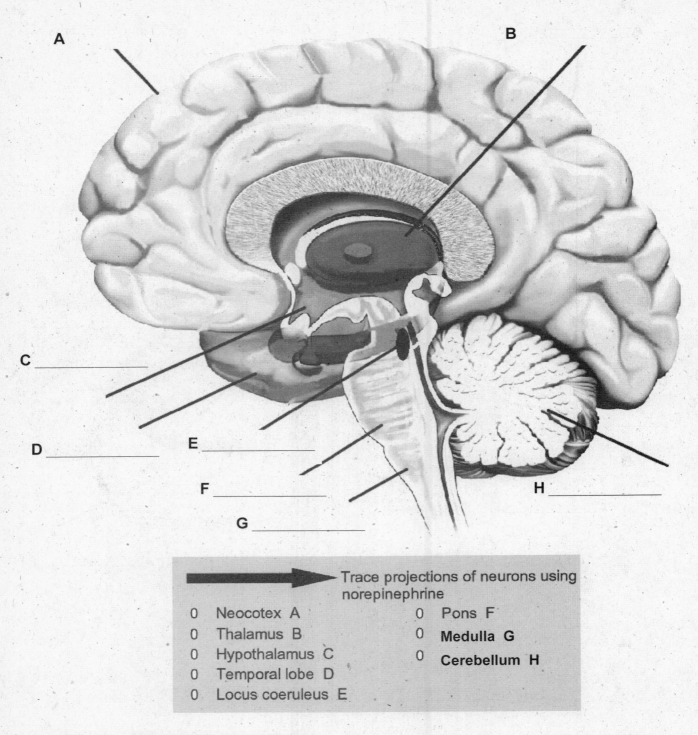

A

B

C _____

D _____

E _____

F _____

G _____

H _____

Trace projections of neurons using
norepinephrine

0   Neocotex A   0   Pons F
0   Thalamus B   0   **Medulla G**
0   Hypothalamus C   0   **Cerebellum H**
0   Temporal lobe D
0   Locus coeruleus E

Figure 4.6 Norepinephrine Pathways

Select a different color for each of the labeled structures. Choose one additional color,
and use it to draw arrows indicating the projections of neurons using norepinephrine as
their major neurotransmitter.

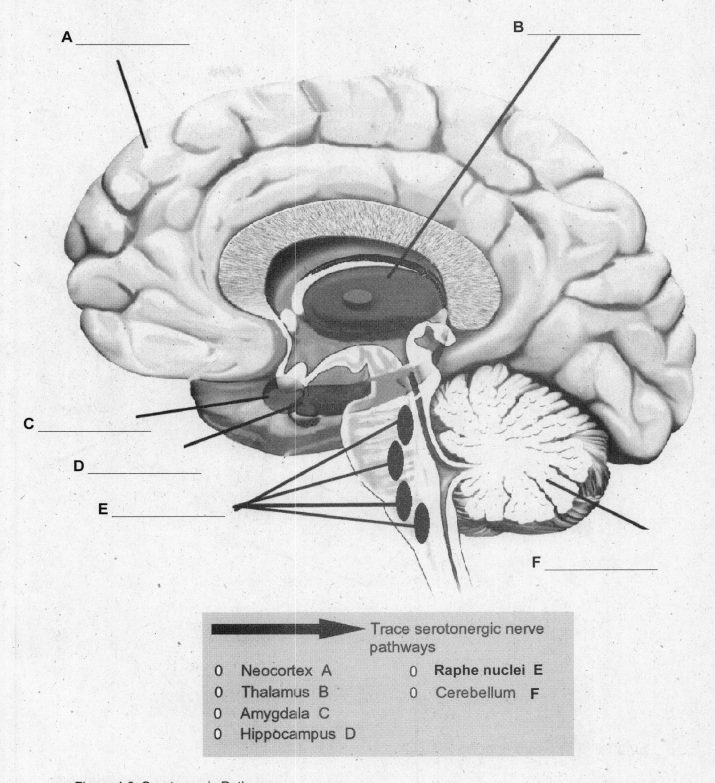

A _____

B _____

C _____

D _____

E _____

F _____

Trace serotonergic nerve pathways

0	Neocortex A	0	**Raphe nuclei** **E**
0	Thalamus B	0	Cerebellum **F**
0	Amygdala C		
0	Hippocampus D		

Figure 4.8 Serotonergic Pathways

Select different colors for each of the labeled structures. Choose a new color to draw arrows indicating the major serotonergic pathways in the brain.

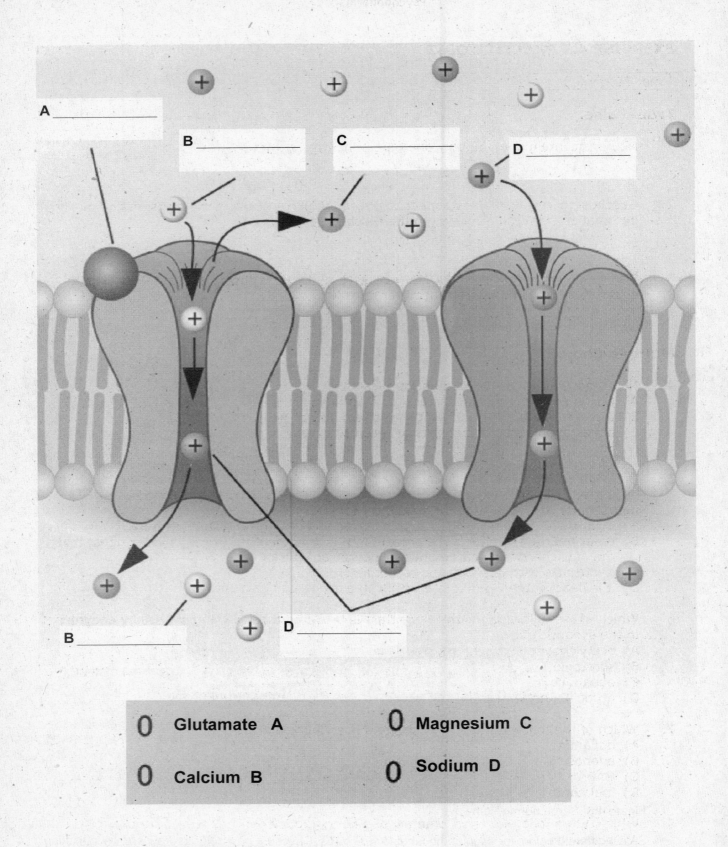

A _____

B _____   C _____   D _____

B _____   D _____

| 0 | Glutamate A | 0 | Magnesium C |
| 0 | Calcium B | 0 | Sodium D |

Figure 4.9 The NMDA Glutamate receptor

Choose colors for each of the four types of molecules, and color all instances of each type.

EXERCISE 4.3 PRACTICE QUIZ

Time: 50 minutes

True–False

1. Neurons contain one and only one type of neurotransmitter.

    T   F

2. Gaseous neurotransmitters appear to play an important role in the transmission of information from the thalamus to the cerebral cortex.

    T   F

3. Black widow spider venom, MDMA (ecstasy), and amphetamine exert their agonistic effects by increasing neurotransmitter release.

    T   F

Multiple Choice

4. Neuromodulators are defined as chemicals that
    A) act on adjacent neurons across a synaptic gap.
    B) travel through the blood supply to affect distant neurons.
    C) act as agonists or antagonists at receptor sites.
    D) diffuse away from the synapse to influence more distant neurons.

5. Dr. Williams discovers a new chemical that is synthesized in neurons and appears to be released in response to action potentials. To be certain that the new chemical is a neurotransmitter, Dr. Williams should try to determine whether
    A) it travels through the blood supply before interacting with other neurons.
    B) other neurotransmitters are present in the same neuron, which would suggest that the new chemical can't be another neurotransmitter.
    C) it interacts with postsynaptic receptors.
    D) it is deactivated when it interacts with extracellular calcium.

6. Which of the following neurotransmitters is broken down following release by enzymes in the synaptic gap?
    A) acetylcholine
    B) serotonin
    C) dopamine
    D) norepinephrine

7. Which of the following neurotransmitters is an indoleamine?
    A) dopamine
    B) adenosine
    C) GABA
    D) melatonin

8. Which of the following is an example of a neuropeptide?
    A) serotonin
    B) oxytocin
    C) melatonin
    D) acetylcholine

9.   Which of the following is an example of an antagonist?
      A) Prozac, because it interferes with the reuptake of serotonin
      B) black widow spider venom, because it enhances the release of acetylcholine
      C) caffeine, because it blocks adenosine receptors
      D) heroin, because it activates endorphin receptors

10.   Which of the following drugs interferes with the storage of monoamines within synaptic vesicles?
      A) reserpine
      B) botulin toxin
      C) curare
      D) cobra venom

11.   When a person becomes tolerant of a drug, it means that he or she
      A) is addicted to the drug.
      B) needs more of the drug to obtain the same effects.
      C) is experiencing symptoms due to the removal of the drug.
      D) has a genetic predisposition that prevents much reaction to the drug.

12.   Which of the following drugs leads to enhanced release of serotonin?
      A) GHB
      B) PCP
      C) MDMA (ecstasy)
      D) LSD

13.   Anandamide is suspected of being an endogenous version of which of the following drugs?
      A) LSD
      B) opiates
      C) caffeine
      D) marijuana

Fill In

14.   The catecholamines include _____, _____, and
      _____, and the indoleamines include _____ and
      _____.

15.   _____ is a neuropeptide that might participate in feelings of
      pain.

16.   _____ is an inhibitory amino acid neurotransmitter, and
      _____ is an excitatory amino acid neurotransmitter.

17.   Dopamine reuptake is inhibited by _____,
      _____, and _____.

18. _____ occurs when more of a drug is needed to obtain the same effects, and _____ occurs when symptoms result when use of a drug is discontinued.

19. _____ is a relatively untested herbal remedy often taken in response to depression.

Short Answer/Labeling

20. Describe the major systems that use the neurotransmitter acetylcholine.

_____

_____

_____

_____

_____

_____

21. Define the term *placebo* and describe research methods designed to control for placebo effects.

_____

_____

_____

_____

_____

22. How does caffeine achieve its behavioral effects?

_____

_____

_____

_____

_____

23. Complete the labels in the figure that follows.

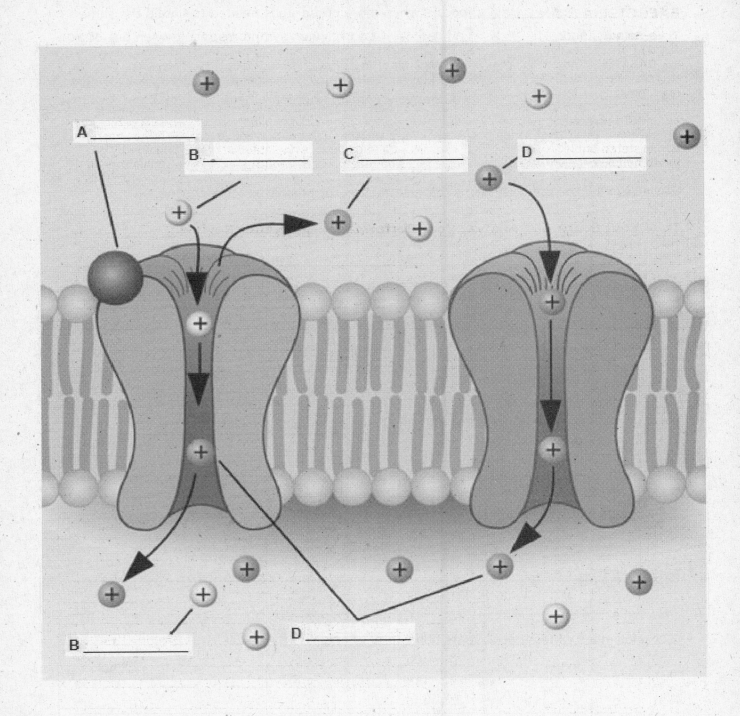

A _____

B _____

C _____

D _____

B _____

D _____

EXERCISE 4.3 ANSWER KEY

True-False: 1. F; 2. T; 3. T. **Multiple Choice:** 4. D) 5. C) 6. A) 7. D) 8. B) 9. C) 10. A) 11. B) 12. C) 13. D) **Fill In:** 14. dopamine; norepinephrine; epinephrine; serotonin; melatonin. 15. Substance P. 16. GABA; glutamate. 17. cocaine, amphetamine; methylphenidate (Ritalin). 18. Tolerance; withdrawal. 19. St. John's Wort. **Short Answer/Labeling:** 20. Cholinergic neurons are found in the autonomic nervous system, the neuromuscular junction, and in parts of the brain involved with arousal, learning, and memory. 21. A placebo is an inactive ingredient that provides a perceived benefit. To control for placebo effects, researchers use the "double blind" procedure, in which neither the research participant nor the observer knows whether a placebo or active ingredient has been administered until the experiment is over. 22. Caffeine acts as an antagonist for the inhibitory neuromodulator adenosine by blocking adenosine receptors. By reducing adenosine's inhibitory effects, caffeine leads to alertness. 23. A. Glutamate; B. Calcium (Ca^{2+}); C. Magnesium (Mg^{2+}); D. Sodium (Na^+).

Tally Your Score

Test Item	Point Value	Your Score
1.	1	
2.	1	
3.	1	
4.	4	
5.	4	
6.	4	
7.	4	
8.	4	
9.	4	
10.	4	
11.	4	
12.	4	
13.	4	
14.	5	
15.	5	
16.	5	
17.	5	
18.	5	
19.	5	
20.	6	
21.	6	
22.	6	
23.	9	
TOTAL	100	

Analyze Your Performance/Plan Your Review

LO	Test Item	Text Page	Your Review Plan
4.1	4	95	
4.2	5	95	
	1	96	
4.3	6	97	
	20	97	
	16	100	
	23	101	
4.4	14	98	
	7	100	
	2	102	
4.5	8	102	
	15	102	
4.6	9	105	
4.7	10	105	
	17	107	
4.8	21	109	
	11	110	
	18	110	
4.9	3	106	
	22	114	
	12	116	
	13	118	
	19	121	

Chapter 5. Genetics and the Development of the Human Brain

EXERCISE 5.1 IDENTIFYING KEY TERMS AND THEIR DEFINITIONS

A. Terms Related to Genetics and Behavior

1.	Molecules that compose chromosomes.
2.	A strand of DNA found within the nucleus of a cell.
3.	The observable appearance of an organism.
4.	The genetic composition of an organism.
5.	Alternative version of a particular gene.
6.	The translation of the genotype into the phenotype of an organism.
7.	A functional hereditary unit made up of DNA that occupies a fixed location on a chromosome.

- allele
- chromosome
- gene
- gene expression

- genotype
- phenotype
- deoxyribonucleic acid (DNA)

B. Terms Related to Genetic Diversity

1.	Having two different alleles for a given gene.
2.	Having two identical alleles for a given gene.
3.	A gene that produces its phenotype regardless of whether its paired allele is heterozygous or homozygous.
4.	A molecule that is similar to DNA that participates in the translation of genetic sequences into proteins.
5.	A gene of which only the mother's or the father's copy is expressed, but not both in the normal Mendelian sense.
6.	A degenerative, ultimately fatal condition marked initially by memory loss.
7.	A heritable alteration of genes.
8.	A gene that will produce its characteristic phenotype only when it occurs in a homozygous pair
9.	Cell division in sexually reproducing organisms that reduces the number of chromosomes in half in the reproductive cells, such as sperm, eggs, and spores.
10.	The characteristic of genes located adjacent to one another to be passed along as a group.
11.	A process occurring during meiosis in which chromosomes exchange equivalent segments of DNA material.

- crossing over
- dominant allele
- heterozygous
- homozygous
- imprinted gene
- linkage
- meiosis
- recessive allele
- ribonucleic acid (RNA)
- mutation
- Alzheimer's disease

C. Terms Related to Neuronal Development

1.	Special glia that radiate from the ventricular layer to the outer edge of the cerebral cortex, serving as a pathway for migrating neurons.
2.	One of the initial three germ layers of the embryo, the source of many internal organs.
3.	One of the initial three germ layers of the embryo, the source of skin and neural tissue.
4.	The unborn offspring; used to refer in humans to the developing individual following the embryonic stage until birth.
5.	One of the initial three germ layers of the embryo that will form connective tissue such as ligaments, muscles, blood vessels, and the urogenital systems.
6.	An organism in its early stage of development; in humans, the developing individual is referred to as an embryo between two and eight weeks following conception.
7.	A structure formed by the developing embryonic neural plate that will eventually form the brain and spinal cord, with the interior of the tube forming the ventricle system of the adult brain.
8.	The cell formed by the two merged reproductive cells.
9.	Substance released by target cells that contributes to the survival of presynaptic neurons
10.	Programmed cell death.
11.	The process in which functional synapses are maintained and nonfunctional synapses are lost.
12.	The swelling at the tip of a growing axon or dendrite that helps the branch reach its synaptic target.
13.	The process of cell division that produces two identical daughter cells.

- embryo
- endoderm
- fetus
- mesoderm
- mitosis
- neural tube
- radial glia
- growth cone
- apoptosis
- neurotrophin
- synaptic pruning
- zygote
- ectoderm

D. Terms Related to Neuronal Degeneration

1.	The deterioration of the cell body and remaining axon stub produced by damage to an axon.
2.	An intracellular protein responsible for maintaining the structure of microtubules; broken down in conditions such as Alzheimer's disease.

3.	The birth of new neural cells.
4.	A protein associated with the degeneration of tissue, such as in patients with Alzheimer's disease and other types of dementia.
5.	An abnormal internal structure of neurons found in cases of Alzheimer's disease.
6.	The deterioration of postsynaptic cells in response to loss of input from damaged presynaptic neurons.
7.	The deterioration of the axon segment separated from the cell body by damage to the axon.

- anterograde degeneration
- retrograde degeneration
- transneuronal degeneration
- neurofibrillary tangles

- neurogenesis
- tau
- amyloid

EXERCISE 5.1 ANSWER KEY

A. Terms Related to Genetics and Behavior
1. deoxyribonucleic acid (DNA) (p. 125)
2. chromosome (p. 125)
3. phenotype (p. 125)
4. genotype (p. 125)
5. allele (p. 125)
6. gene expression (p. 125)
7. gene (p. 125)

B. Terms Related to Genetic Diversity
1. heterozygous (p. 126)
2. homozygous (p. 126)
3. dominant allele (p. 126
4. ribonucleic acid (RNA) (p. 126)
5. imprinted gene (p. 126)
6. Alzheimer's disease (p. 130)
7. mutation (p. 128)
8. recessive allele (p. 126)
9. meiosis (p. 126)
10. linkage (p. 126)
11. crossing over (p. 126)

C. Terms Related to Neuronal Development
1. radial glia (p. 135)
2. endoderm (p. 133)
3. ectoderm (p. 133)
4. fetus (p. 133)
5. mesoderm (p. 133)
6. embryo (p. 133)
7. neural tube (p. 134)
8. zygote (p. 133)
9. neurotrophin (p. 139)
10. apoptosis (p. 139)
11. synaptic pruning (p. 140)
12. growth cone (p. 137)
13. mitosis (p. 134)

D. Terms Related to Neuronal Degeneration
1. retrograde degeneration (p. 147)
2. tau (p. 149)
3. neurogenesis (p. 149)
4. amyloid (p. 150)
5. neurofibrillary tangles (p. 149)
6. transneuronal degeneration (p. 147)
7. anterograde degeneration (p. 147)

EXERCISE 5.2 LEARNING BY COLORING

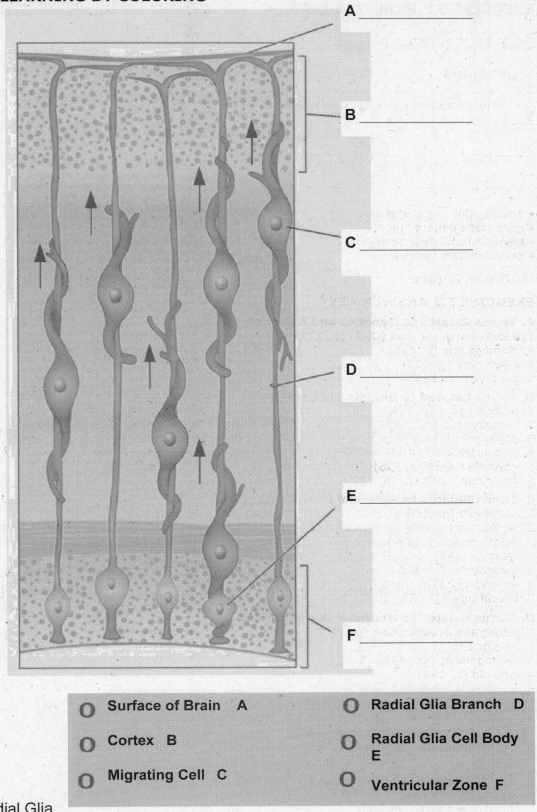

A _____

B _____

C _____

D _____

E _____

F _____

O Surface of Brain A	O Radial Glia Branch D
O Cortex B	O Radial Glia Cell Body E
O Migrating Cell C	O Ventricular Zone F

Figure 5.16 Radial Glia

Select different colors for structures A, B, C, and F. Use different shades of the same color for D and E.

EXERCISE 5.3 PRACTICE QUIZ

Time: 50 minutes

True–False

1. The majority of mutations influence phenotypical traits.

    T   F

2. Neurons will develop from cells located in the ectoderm layer of the embryo.

    T   F

3. Fragile X syndrome accounts for the majority of cases of autism.

    T   F

Multiple Choice

4. A person's phenotype consists of his or her
    A) observable characteristics, such as hair color.
    B) set of genetic instructions.
    C) characteristics that result from environment and experience.
    D) mitochondrial DNA.

5. Linkage refers to the
    A) process in which genes exchange equivalent sections of genetic material.
    B) passing along of genes that are close together on the same chromosome.
    C) division of cells into eggs or sperm.
    D) inheritance of recessive traits over several generations.

6. Heritability is defined as the
    A) amount of genetic influence on a trait observed in an individual.
    B) proportion of genes that a person has in common with his or her parents.
    C) amount of variability between two populations that is the result of genetics.
    D) likelihood that a person's offspring will inherit a particular trait.

7. The neural tube begins to close during the _____ month following conception.
    A) first
    B) third
    C) fifth
    D) seventh

8. Apoptosis refers to the
    A) formation of new synapses.
    B) birth of new daughter cells in the ventricular layer.
    C) movement of neurons along radial glia.
    D) programmed death of some neurons.

9. Where would you look to find filopodia?
    A) on growth cones
    B) on guidepost cells
    C) in molecules of DNA
    D) on radial glia

10. Which of the following practices remains "plastic" throughout life?
    A) vision
    B) language
    C) mathematical skills
    D) imprinting

11. Multiple repeats of codons on the *FMR-1* gene are responsible for
    A) Down syndrome
    B) phenylketonuria
    C) Huntington's disease
    D) fragile X syndrome

12. In anterograde degeneration,
    A) the segment of axon between a point of damage and the terminal will degenerate.
    B) the segment of axon between a point of damage and the cell body will degenerate.
    C) cells that receive input from a cell will degenerate when that cell is damaged.
    D) cells that communicate with a cell will degenerate when that cell is damaged.

13. Amyloid plaques appear in the brains of people with
    A) fragile X syndrome
    B) fetal alcohol syndrome
    C) Alzheimer's disease
    D) phenylketonuria

Fill In

14. When two different alleles differ at only one location, we refer to this location as a

    _____.

15. The three embryonic germ layers are the _____,

    _____, and _____.

16. The inducing factor _____ is responsible for organizing the ventral neural

    tube for _____ systems, and the inducing factor _____ is

    responsible for organizing the dorsal neural tube for _____ systems.

17. Failure of the caudal neural tube to close produces _____, and

    failure of the rostral neural tube to close produces _____.

18. When an axon is damaged, _____ occurs between the site

    of damage and the axon terminal, _____ occurs between the site

    of damage and the cell body, and _____ occurs in cells

    that normally receive input from the damaged cell.

19. At the microscopic level, Alzheimer's disease is characterized by structural deformities

    known as _____ and _____.

Short Answer/Labeling

20. What is a sex-linked characteristic?

_____

_____

_____

_____

_____

21. Describe the process of cell migration from the ventricular layer to the cerebral cortex.

_____

_____

_____

_____

_____

_____

22. Describe the brain development that occurs in adolescence.

_____

_____

_____

_____

_____

23. Complete the labels in the figure that follows.

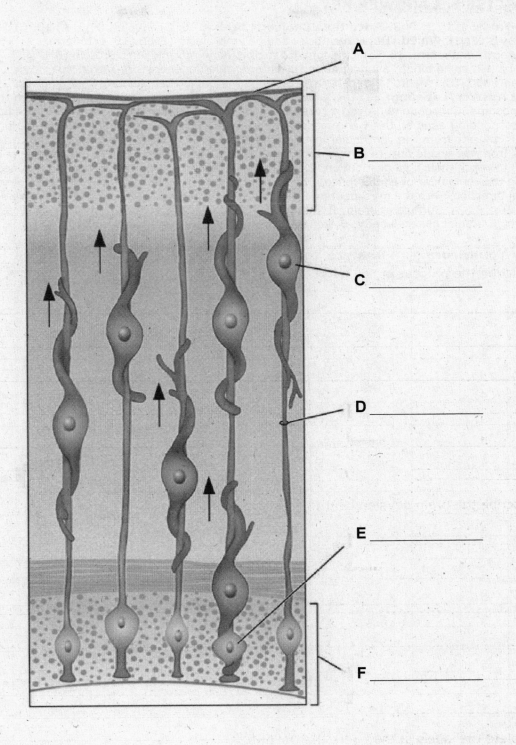

A _____

B _____

C _____

D _____

E _____

F _____

EXERCISE 5.3 ANSWER KEY

True-False: 1. F; 2. T; 3. F. **Multiple Choice:** 4. A) 5. B) 6. C) 7. A) 8. D) 9. A) 10. C) 11. D) 12. A) 13. C). **Fill In:** 14. single nucleotide polymorphism (SNP). 15. ectoderm; mesoderm; endoderm. 16. sonic hedgehog; motor; bone morphogenic protein (BMP); sensory. 17. spina bifida; anencephaly. 18. anterograde degeneration; retrograde degeneration; transneuronal degeneration. 19. neurofibrillary tangles; amyloid plaques.

Short Answer/Labeling: 20. The X chromosome contains genes that are not found on the Y chromosome. Consequently, even a recessive gene on the X chromosome that does not have a corresponding gene on the Y chromosome will produce a phenotypic trait. 21. The majority of cells migrate from the ventricular layer to the cerebral cortex along radial glia. The cortex grows from the inside out. In other words, later arriving neurons must pass through existing layers to reach their final destination. 22. At puberty, a second wave of cortical growth occurs. During the remainder of adolescence, thinning of the cortex occurs. Myelination continues in a rostral direction, with the myelination of the frontal lobes finally being completed in a person's early 20s. 23. A. Surface of brain; B. Primitive cortex; C. Migrating cells; D. Radial glial cell branch; E. Radial glial cell body; F. Ventricular zone.

Tally Your Score		
Test Item	Point Value	Your Score
1.	1	
2.	1	
3.	1	
4.	4	
5.	4	
6.	4	
7.	4	
8.	4	
9.	4	
10.	4	
11.	4	
12.	4	
13.	4	
14.	5	
15.	5	
16.	5	
17.	5	
18.	5	
19.	5	
20.	6	
21.	6	
22.	6	
23.	9	
TOTAL	100	

Analyze Your Performance/Plan Your Review			
LO	Test Item	Text Page	Your Review Plan
5.1	4	125	
5.2	5	126	
	1	128	
	20	128	
	14	129	
5.3	6	130	
5.4	2	133	
	15	133	
	7	135	
5.5	16	136	
	21	136	
	23	136	
	9	137	
	8	139	
5.6	10	141	
5.7	11	145	
	17	145	
	3	146	
5.8	12	147	
	18	147	
5.9	22	141	
	19	149	
	13	150	

Chapter 6. Vision

EXERCISE 6.1 IDENTIFYING KEY TERMS AND THEIR DEFINITIONS

A. Terms for Eye Anatomy

1.	The opening in the front of the eye controlled by the iris.
2.	The clear structure behind the pupil and iris that focuses light on the retina.
3.	The elaborate network of photoreceptors and interneurons at the back of the eye that is responsible for sensing light.
4.	A small pit in the macula specialized for detailed vision.
5.	The fiber pathway formed by the axons of the ganglion cells as they leave the eye.
6.	The transparent outer layer of the eye.
7.	The circular muscle in the front of the eye that controls the opening of the pupil.
8.	The white outer covering of the eye.

- cornea
- iris
- pupil
- sclera
- lens
- optic nerve
- retina
- fovea

B. The Terminology of Photoreception

1.	Specialized sensory cell in the retina that responds to light.
2.	A retinal interneuron located in the inner nuclear layer that integrates signals from across the surface of the retina.
3.	A photoreceptor that operates in bright conditions and responds differentially to color.
4.	A photoreceptor that responds to low levels of light but not to color.
5.	The ability to perceive visual stimuli under bright light conditions due to the activity of cones.
6.	A pigment contained in the photoreceptors of the eye that absorbs light.
7.	The process of translating a physical stimulus into neural signals.
8.	The ability to perceive visual stimuli in near darkness due to the activity of rods.
9.	A cell in the inner nuclear layer of the retina that forms part of the straight pathway between the photoreceptors and the ganglion cells.
10.	The process in which active cells limit the activity of neighboring, less active cells.
11.	A location on the retina at which light affects the activity of a particular visual interneuron.

12.	The steady depolarization maintained by photoreceptors when no light is present.
13.	A retinal interneuron in the inner nuclear layer that integrates signals across adjacent segments of the retina.
14.	The ability to perceive visual stimuli focused on the macula of the retina.
15.	The ability to perceive visual stimuli that are off to the side while looking straight ahead.

- photoreceptor
- amacrine cell
- bipolar cell
- central vision
- peripheral vision

- horizontal cell
- cone
- photopic vision
- photopigment
- rod

- scotopic vision
- transduction
- dark current
- receptive field
- lateral inhibition

C. Terms for Processing Visual Input

1.	A cortical interneuron that shows a preferred stimulus size and orientation but not location within the visual field. oxidase that responds to color.
2.	The fiber pathways between the optic chiasm and destinations in the forebrain and brainstem.
3.	A column of primary visual cortex that responds to lines of a single angle.
4.	An area of primary visual cortex rich in the enzyme cytochrome
5.	A column of cortex perpendicular to the cortical surface that responds to input from either the right or left eye, but not to both.
6.	A structure in the tectum of the midbrain that guides movements of the eyes and head toward newly detected objects in the visual field.
7.	The area at the base of the brain where the optic nerves cross to form the optic tracts; the location of a partial decussation of the optic nerves in humans.
8.	A cell that responds to stimuli in the shape of a bar or edge with a particular slant or orientation in a particular location on the retina.
9.	A pathway of information from the primary visual cortex to the inferior temporal lobe that is believed to process object recognition.
10.	A complete set of orientation columns.
11.	The location in the occipital lobe for the initial cortical analysis of visual input. Also known as striate cortex.
12.	A unit of primary visual cortex containing two sets of ocular dominance columns, 16 blobs, and two hypercolumns.
13.	A pathway leading from the primary visual cortex in a dorsal direction thought to participate in the perception of movement.
14.	The nucleus within the thalamus that receives input from the optic tracts.

- lateral geniculate nucleus (LGN)
- optic chiasm
- optic tracts
- superior colliculus

- primary visual cortex
- simple cortical cell
- complex cortical cell
- cortical module
- cytochrome oxidase blobs

- hypercolumn
- ocular dominance column
- orientation column
- dorsal stream
- ventral stream

D. Terms Related to Visual Perception

1.	The theory that suggests human color vision is based on our possessing three different color photopigments.
2.	The fact that colors can look different depending on the surrounding colors.
3.	The concept that an object's color looks the same regardless of the type of light falling on the object.
4.	The process of obtaining information about the environment and transmitting it to the brain for processing.
5.	A theory of human color vision based on three antagonistic color channels: red-green, blue-yellow, and black-white.
6.	The process of interpreting sensory signals sent to the brain.

- perception
- sensation
- opponent process theory

- trichromacy theory
- color constancy
- color contrast

EXERCISE 6.1 ANSWER KEY

A. Terms for Eye Anatomy
1. pupil (p. 159)
2. lens (p. 160)
3. retina (p. 160)

4. fovea (p. 161)
5. optic nerve (p. 160)
6. cornea (p. 159)

7. iris (p. 159)
8. sclera (p. 159)

B. The Terminology of Photoreception
1. photoreceptor (p. 160)
2. horizontal cell (p. 162)
3. cone (p. 162)
4. rod (p. 162)
5. photopic vision (p. 162)
6. photopigment (p. 162)
7. transduction (p. 162)
8. scotopic vision (p. 162)

9. bipolar cell (p. 161)
10. lateral inhibition (p. 168)
11. receptive field (p. 165)
12. dark current (p. 163)
13. amacrine cell (p. 161)
14. central vision (p. 161)
15. peripheral vision (p. 161)

C. Terms for Processing Visual Input
1. complex cortical cell (p. 172)
2. optic tracts (p. 169)
3. orientation column (p. 172)
4. cytochrome oxidase blobs (p. 172)
5. ocular dominance column (p. 172)
6. superior colliculus (p. 169)
7. optic chiasm (p. 169)

8. simple cortical cell (p. 171)
9. ventral stream (p. 174)
10. hypercolumn (p. 172)
11. primary visual cortex (p. 171)
12. cortical module (p. 172)
13. dorsal stream (p. 174)
14. lateral geniculate nucleus (LGN)(p. 169)

D. Terms Related to Visual Perception
1. trichromacy theory (p. 179)
2. color contrast (p. 181)

3. color constancy (p. 180)
4. sensation (p. 176)

5. opponent process theory (p. 179)
6. perception (p. 176)

EXERCISE 6.2 LEARNING BY COLORING

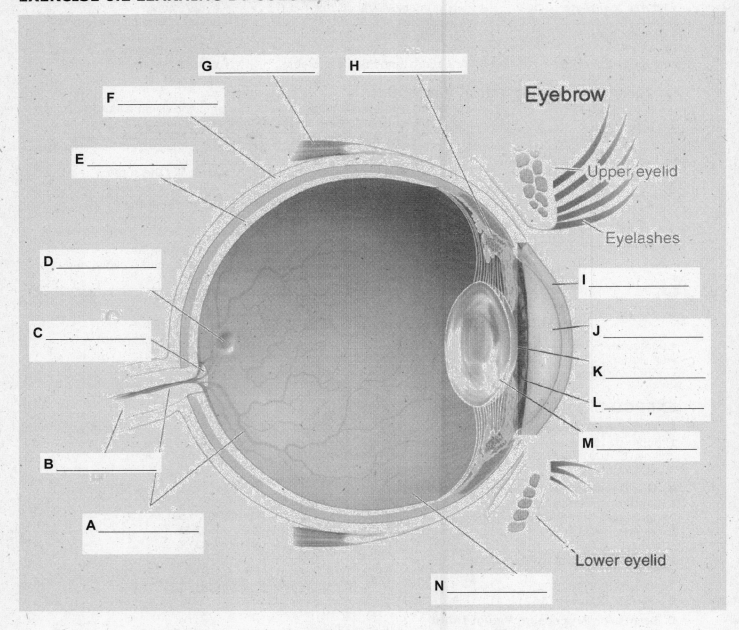

Figure 6.6 The Eye

Use different colors for each of the labeled structures.

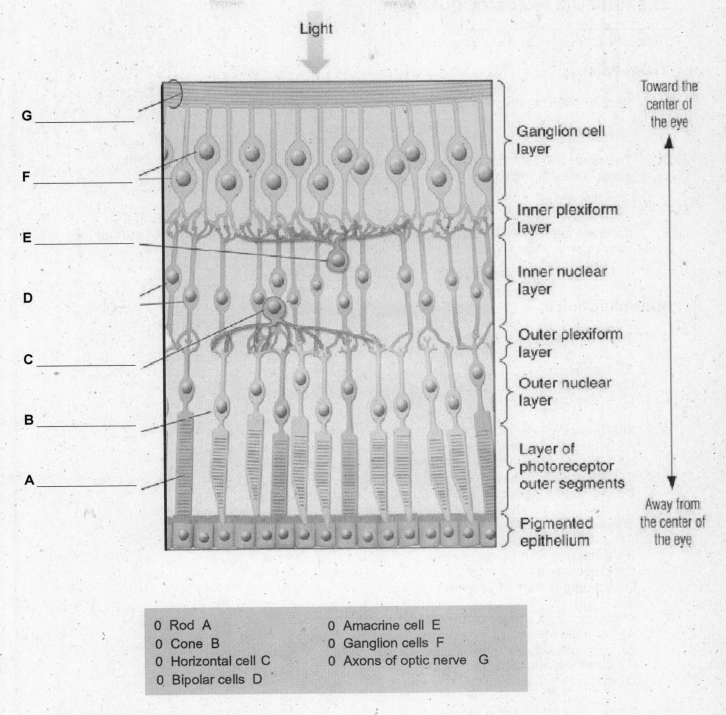

Figure 6.9 The Layers of the Retina

Select a color for each different type of cell found in the retina, and color all examples of each type.

EXERCISE 6.3 PRACTICE QUIZ

Time: 50 minutes.

True–False

1.   Neither the cornea nor the lens contains any blood vessels.

             T   F

2.   The dorsal stream participates in object recognition, and the ventral stream participates in motion detection.

             T   F

3.   Contrast sensitivity functions allow us to assess the visual capabilities of human infants and other species.

             T   F

Multiple Choice

4.   The brightness of a light wave corresponds to its
     A) amplitude.
     B) frequency.
     C) complexity.
     D) saturation.

5.   The optic disk is
     A) a clear structure that bends light towards the retina.
     B) a round area in the retina that is not covered by blood vessels.
     C) the area in the retina where blood vessels and the optic nerve leave the eye.
     D) the pigmented cells that support the photoreceptors.

6.   The outer nuclear layer of the retina contains
     A) ganglion cells.
     B) amacrine and bipolar cells.
     C) bipolar and horizontal cells.
     D) the cell bodies of photoreceptors.

7.   Rhodopsin is a photopigment found in
     A) long wavelength (red) cones.
     B) medium wavelength (green) cones.
     C) short wavelength (blue) cones.
     D) rods.

8.   Action potentials are produced by
     A) all neurons in the retina.
     B) amacrine and horizontal cells.
     C) ganglion cells.
     D) bipolar cells and photoreceptors.

9.   Visual input to the thalamus is sent to the
     A) medial geniculate nucleus.
     B) lateral geniculate nucleus.

C) ventral posterior nucleus.
D) intralaminar nuclei.

10. A cell that responds to bars of light with a particular orientation falling on a particular location in the retina is a _____ cell.
   A) simple cortical
   B) complex cortical
   C) koniocellular
   D) ganglion

   Ans: ____

11. Retinal disparity provides information about
   A) color contrast.
   B) frequency.
   C) depth.
   D) color constancy.

12. Tetrachromats possess
   A) one photopigment.
   B) two photopigments.
   C) three photopigments.
   D) four photopigments.

13. Presbyopia refers to a condition in which
   A) the eyes do not focus together.
   B) accommodation to changes in focal distance is reduced.
   C) the cornea is misshapen, producing a blurry image on the retina.
   D) people cannot recognize the faces of familiar people.

Fill In

14. When light is retained by an object, it is _____; when it is bent back from an object, it is _____; and when it changes at a boundary between air and water, it is _____.

15. Light is focused on the retina by the _____ and the _____.

16. Rods are responsible for _____ vision, and cones are responsible for _____ vision.

17. Information from the retina travels to the _____ of the hypothalamus, to the _____ of the midbrain, and to the _____ of the thalamus.

18. The three types of layers in the lateral geniculate nucleus are the

_____ layers, the _____ layers, and the

_____ layers.

19. An elongated eyeball results in _____, a shortened eyeball results in

_____, and a misshapen cornea results in _____.

Short Answer/Labeling

20. What is the dark current?

_____

_____

_____

_____

_____

21. What is a feature detector?

_____

_____

_____

_____

_____

22. What are the major types of colorblindness?

_____

_____

_____

_____

_____

_____

23. Complete the labels in the figure that follows.

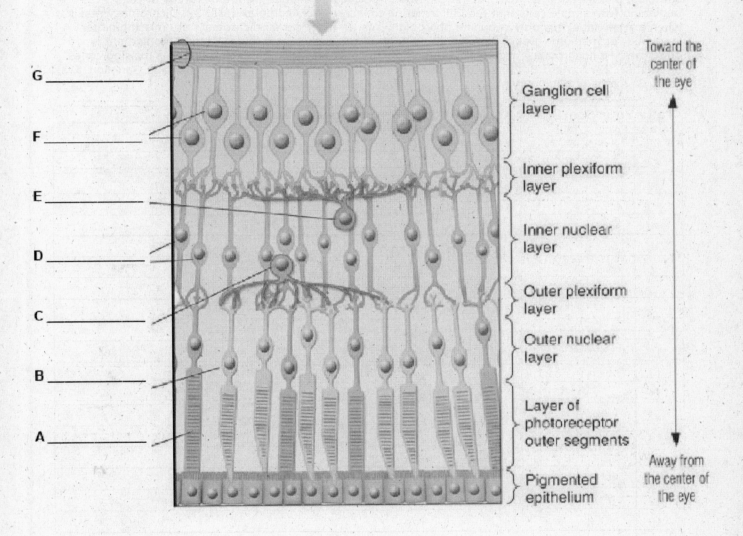

Light

G _____

F _____

E _____

D _____

C _____

B _____

A _____

Ganglion cell layer

Inner plexiform layer

Inner nuclear layer

Outer plexiform layer

Outer nuclear layer

Layer of photoreceptor outer segments

Pigmented epithelium

Toward the center of the eye

Away from the center of the eye

EXERCISE 6.3 ANSWER KEY

True-False: 1. T; 2. F; 3. T. **Multiple Choice:** 4. A) 5. C) 6. D) 7. D) 8. C) 9. B) 10. A) 11. C) 12. D) 13. B). **Fill In:** 14. absorbed; reflected; refracted. 15. cornea; lens. 16. scotopic; photopic. 17. suprachiasmatic nucleus; superior colliculi; lateral geniculate nucleus. 18. parvocellular; magnocellular; koniocellular. 19. myopia; hyperopia; astigmatism. **Short Answer/Labeling:** 20. When a photoreceptor is in the dark, it is slightly depolarized to about -30 mV by the inward movement of sodium ions through the outer-segment membrane. Sodium channels are kept open by cGMP. 21. A feature detector is a hypothetical cell that is capable of responding to a single complex stimulus, and no other stimuli. Such a cell would receive information from a hierarchy of cells beginning with simple cells that feed information to increasingly complex cells. 22. Dichromacy results when an individual has only two cone photopigments. In most cases, dichromats are missing either long (red) or medium (green) cone photopigments. Lack of the short (blue) cone photopigment is quite rare. Monochromacy occurs when a person has only one cone photopigment or is missing cones altogether. 23. A. Rod; B. Cone; C. Horizontal cell; D. Bipolar cells; E. Amacrine cells; F. Ganglion cells; G. Axons of optic nerve.

Tally Your Score

Test Item	Point Value	Your Score
1.	1	
2.	1	
3.	1	
4.	4	
5.	4	
6.	4	
7.	4	
8.	4	
9.	4	
10.	4	
11.	4	
12.	4	
13.	4	
14.	5	
15.	5	
16.	5	
17.	5	
18.	5	
19.	5	
20.	6	
21.	6	
22.	6	
23.	9	
TOTAL	100	

Analyze Your Performance/Plan Your Review

LO	Test Item	Text Page	Your Review Plan
6.1	4	155	
	14	156	
6.2	1	159	
	15	159	
	5	160	
	6	162	
6.3	7	162	
	16	162	
	20	163	
6.4	23	161	
	8	168	
	9	169	
	17	169	
	18	170	
	2	174	
6.5	10	171	
6.6	21	177	
	3	178	
	11	179	
	22	180	
	12	181	
6.7	13	182	
	19	184	

Chapter 7. Nonvisual Sensation and Perception

EXERCISE 7.1 IDENTIFYING KEY TERMS AND THEIR DEFINITIONS

A. Terms for Sound

1.	A unit used to express a difference in intensity between two sounds, equal to 20 times the common logarithm of the ratio of the two levels.
2.	The sense of hearing.
3.	A unit of sound frequency equal to one cycle per second.
4.	The height of a periodic curve measured on its vertical axis.
5.	The number of cycles of a periodic wave per unit of time.

- audition
- amplitude
- decibel (dB)

- frequency
- hertz (Hz)

B. Terms for Hearing

1.	The fluid-filled structure of the inner ear containing auditory receptors.
2.	Areas surrounding Heschl's gyrus in the temporal lobe that process more complex types of stimuli.
3.	A structure in the cochlea that separates the tympanic canal and the cochlear duct.
4.	Cortex located just below the lateral fissure in the temporal lobe that provides the initial cortical processing of auditory information.
5.	The part of the human secondary auditory cortex that specifically decodes speech.
6.	The nerve that makes contact with the hair cells of the cochlea; cranial nerve VIII.
7.	The membrane separating the outer and middle ears.
8.	The visible part of the outer ear.
9.	The bones of the middle ear.
10.	Nucleus of the thalamus that receives auditory input.

- ossicles
- pinna
- tympanic membrane
- basilar membrane

- cochlea
- medial geniculate nucleus
- primary auditory cortex
- secondary auditory cortex

- Wernicke's area
- auditory nerve (cranial nerve VIII)

C. Terms Involved in Sensing Position and Movement

1.	The system that provides information about the body senses, including touch, movement, pain, and temperature.

2.	Cortex located in the postcentral gyrus of the parietal lobe that is responsible for the initial cortical processing of somatosensory input.
3.	A structure in the inner ear vestibular system that provides information about the angle of the head relative to the ground and about linear acceleration.
4.	The sensory system that provides information about the position and movement of the head.
5.	The nucleus of the thalamus that receives information regarding pain, touch, and the position and movement of the head.
6.	One of three looping chambers found in the inner ear that provide information regarding the rotation of the head.

- otolith organ
- semicircular canal
- somatosensory system

- vestibular system
- primary somatosensory cortex
- ventral posterior (VP) nucleus

D. Terms for Touch

1.	The area of the skin surface served by the dorsal roots of one spinal segment.
2.	A nerve ending that responds to painful stimuli.
3.	A small, unmyelinated fiber that carries information about temperature, itch, and dull, aching pain to the central nervous system.
4.	An encapsulated, fast-adapting mechanoreceptor with small receptive field that responds primarily to pressure.
5.	Areas in the parietal lobe adjacent to primary somatosensory cortex that process a wide variety of complex somatosensory inputs.
6.	An encapsulated, rapidly adapting mechanoreceptor with large receptive field that provides information about pressure and vibration.
7.	A nonencapsulated, slow-adapting mechanoreceptor with small receptive field that provides information primarily about pressure.
8.	A nerve ending in the skin that responds to surface temperature.
9.	A skin receptor that senses touch, pressure, or vibration.
10. Ruffini's ending (p. 205)	A nonencapsulated, slow-adapting mechanoreceptor with large receptive field that provides information regarding stretch.

- mechanoreceptors
- Meissner's corpuscle
- Merkel's disk
- Pacinian corpuscles
- Ruffini's ending

- C fiber
- dermatome
- secondary somatosensory cortex
- thermoreceptor
- nociceptor

E. Terms for the Chemical Senses

1.	The sense of smell.
2.	Cortex in the frontal lobe that responds to the sense of smell.
3.	The nucleus of the thalamus that receives information regarding taste.
4.	Structures found within the olfactory bulbs.
5.	A fiber pathway connecting the olfactory bulbs to the olfactory cortex.

- olfaction
- glomerulus/glomeruli
- olfactory cortex

- olfactory tract
- ventral posterior medial (VPM) nucleus

EXERCISE 7.1 ANSWER KEY

A. Terms for Sound
1. decibel (dB) (p. 190)
2. audition (p. 189)
3. hertz (Hz) (p. 192)
4. amplitude (p. 190)
5. frequency (p. 190)

B. Terms for Hearing
1. cochlea (p. 193)
2. secondary auditory cortex (p. 198)
3. basilar membrane (p. 193)
4. primary auditory cortex (p. 198)
5. Wernicke's area (p. 198)
6. auditory nerve (cranial nerve VIII) (p. 195)
7. tympanic membrane (p. 192)
8. pinna (p. 192)
9. ossicles (p. 192)
10. medial geniculate nucleus (p. 198)

C. Terms Involved in Sensing Position and Movement
1. somatosensory system (p. 202)
2. primary somatosensory cortex (p. 204)
3. otolith organ (p. 202)
4. vestibular system (p. 202)
5. ventral posterior (VP) nucleus (p. 204)
6. semicircular canal (p. 202)

D. Terms for Touch
1. dermatome (p. 206)
2. nociceptor (p. 212)
3. C fiber (p. 206)
4. Meissner's corpuscle (p. 205)
5. secondary somatosensory cortex (p. 209)
6. Pacinian corpuscles (p. 205)
7. Merkel's disk (p. 205)
8. thermoreceptor (p. 211)
9. mechanoreceptors (p. 205)
10. Ruffini's ending (p. 205)

E. Terms for the Chemical Senses
1. olfaction (p. 216)
2. olfactory cortex (p. 219)
3. ventral posterior medial (VPM) nucleus (p. 221)
4. glomerulus/glomeruli (p. 218)
5. olfactory tracts (p. 219)

EXERCISE 7.2 LEARNING BY COLORING

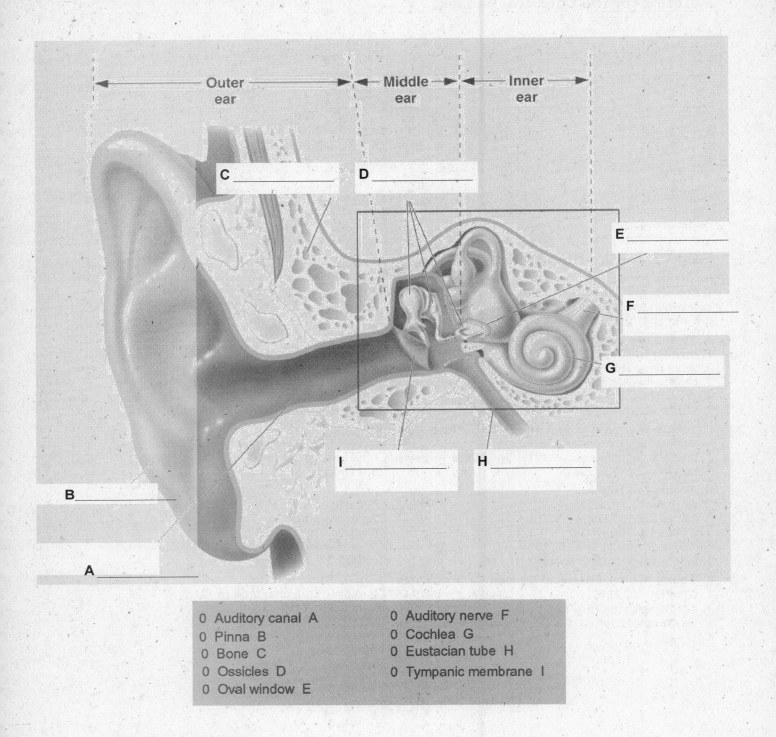

Outer ear   Middle ear   Inner ear

C _____   D _____

E _____

F _____

G _____

B _____

A _____

I _____   H _____

0 Auditory canal A   0 Auditory nerve F
0 Pinna B   0 Cochlea G
0 Bone C   0 Eustacian tube H
0 Ossicles D   0 Tympanic membrane I
0 Oval window E

Figure 7.4 The Ear

Select a different color for each of the labeled structures.

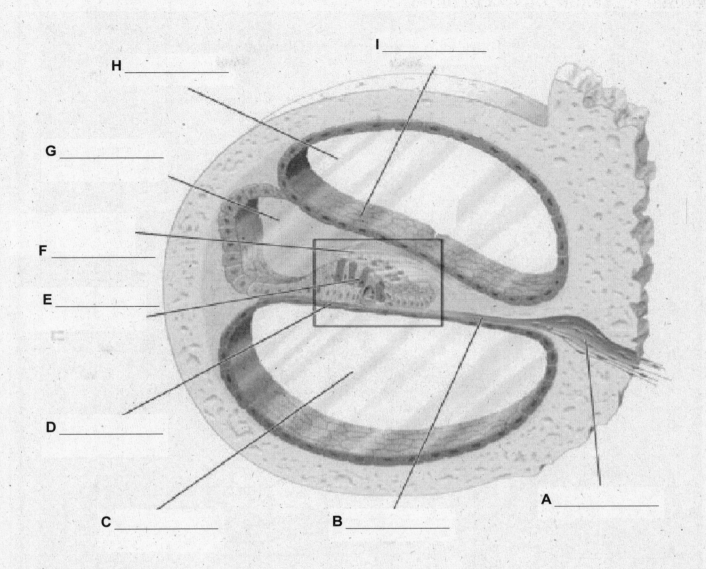

Figure 7.5 The Cochlea

Select a different color for each of the labeled structures.

0 Spiral ganglion A
0 Spiral ganglion cell fibers B
0 Tympanic canal (contains perilymph) C
0 Basilar membrane D
0 Organ of Corti E
0 Tectorial membrane F
0 Cochlear duct (contains endolymph) G
0 Vestibular canal (contains perilymph) H
0 Reissner's membrane I

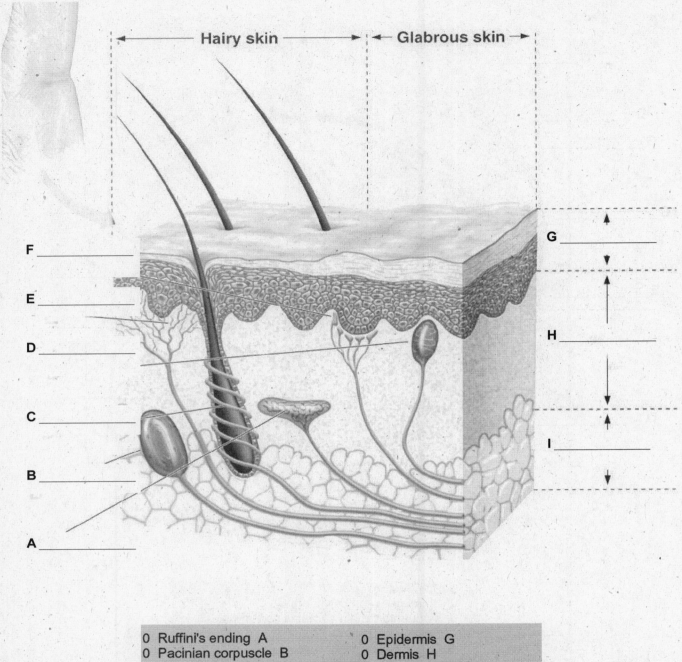

Figure 7.14 The Mechanoreceptors

Choose a different color for each of the labeled structures.

The labeled structures:

0 Ruffini's ending A
0 Pacinian corpuscle B
0 Hair follicle receptor C
0 Meissner's corpuscle D
0 Free nerve ending E
0 Merkel's disk F

0 Epidermis G
0 Dermis H
0 Subcutaneous tissue   I

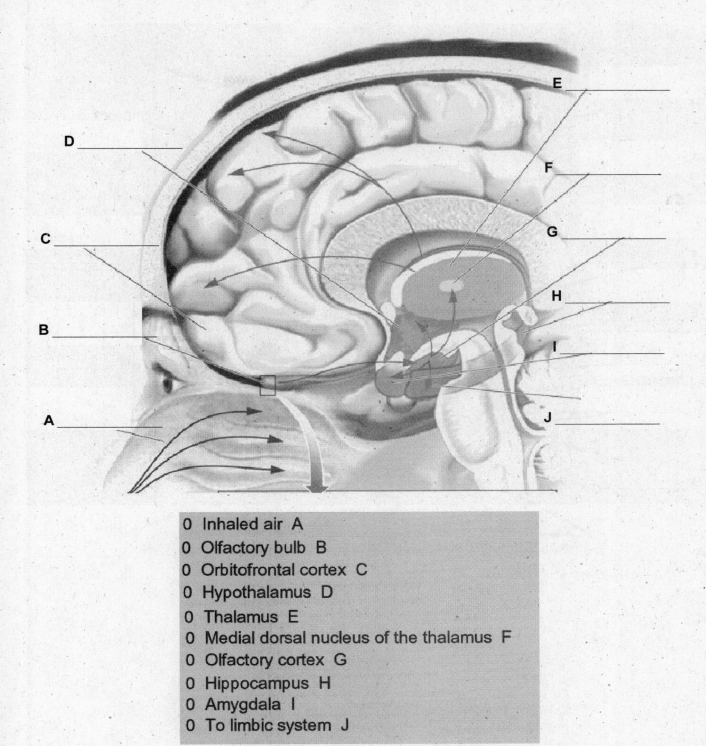

Figure 7.26a Central Olfactory Pathways

Select a different color for each of the labeled structures.

0 Inhaled air A
0 Olfactory bulb B
0 Orbitofrontal cortex C
0 Hypothalamus D
0 Thalamus E
0 Medial dorsal nucleus of the thalamus F
0 Olfactory cortex G
0 Hippocampus H
0 Amygdala I
0 To limbic system J

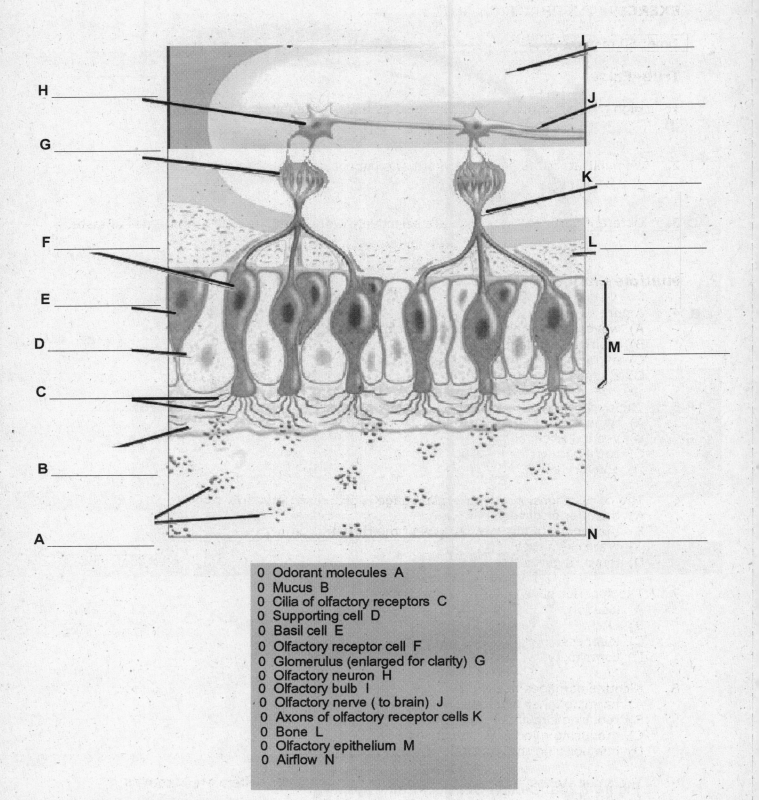

H _____

G _____

F _____

E _____

D _____

C _____

B _____

A _____

L _____

J _____

K _____

L _____

M _____

N _____

0 Odorant molecules A
0 Mucus B
0 Cilia of olfactory receptors C
0 Supporting cell D
0 Basil cell E
0 Olfactory receptor cell F
0 Glomerulus (enlarged for clarity) G
0 Olfactory neuron H
0 Olfactory bulb I
0 Olfactory nerve (to brain) J
0 Axons of olfactory receptor cells K
0 Bone L
0 Olfactory epithelium M
0 Airflow N

Figure 7.26b Olfactory Receptors

Select a different color for each of the labeled structures.

EXERCISE 7.3 PRACTICE QUIZ

Time: 50 minutes

True–False

1. High frequency sounds are perceived as having high pitch.

    T   F

2. Unmyelinated C fibers carry information about both pain and itch.

    T   F

3. Different parts of the tongue are selectively more sensitive to different types of taste.

    T   F

Multiple Choice

4. A pure tone has
    A) waves that do not have a regular pattern.
    B) multiple frequencies.
    C) multiple harmonics.
    D) a single frequency.

5. The oval window covers the
    A) tympanic canal.
    B) vestibular canal.
    C) cochlear duct.
    D) auditory canal.

6. The comprehension of spoken language is processed primarily by
    A) the inferior olive.
    B) the medial geniculate nucleus of the thalamus.
    C) Wernicke's area.
    D) Heschl's gyrus.

7. The superior olive is essential for determining a sound's
    A) location.
    B) pitch.
    C) loudness.
    D) complexity.

8. Nicotine damages hearing by
    A) harming inner hair cells.
    B) reducing circulation to the ear.
    C) producing middle ear infections.
    D) immobilizing the ossicles.

9. The small stones attached to hair cells in the vestibular system are known as
    A) saccules.
    B) utricles.
    C) ossicles.
    D) otoliths.

10. Ruffini's endings are particularly good at sensing
    A) pressure.
    B) pain.
    C) stretch.
    D) vibration.

11. Alpha-beta fibers carry information about
    A) pain.
    B) cold temperatures.
    C) warm temperatures.
    D) touch.

12. The olfactory cortex is located in the _____ lobe.
    A) frontal
    B) parietal
    C) temporal
    D) occipital

13. Umami refers to
    A) the taste of hot peppers.
    B) a meaty or savory flavor.
    C) the neurotransmitter used by taste fibers.
    D) the bumps on the tongue that contain taste buds.

Fill In

14. The three bones of the ossicles are the _____,
    _____, and _____.

15. The three membranes found in the cochlea are the _____, the
    _____, and the _____.

16. The otolith organs include the _____ and _____.

17. Information from nociceptors travels to the _____, the
    _____ nucleus and the _____ nuclei of the
    thalamus, and the _____ and _____ lobe.

18. Olfactory receptor fibers synapse on structures known as _____,
    which are located in the _____.

19. Taste information travels from the taste receptors to the _____
    nucleus in the medulla, which makes contact with the _____
    nucleus in the thalamus, which sends information to the gustatory cortex in the
    _____ lobe.

Short Answer/Labeling

20. How does the basilar membrane encode different frequencies of sound?

    _____

    _____

    _____

    _____

    _____

    _____

21. What do we mean by "plasticity" of touch?

    _____

    _____

    _____

    _____

    _____

    _____

22. Describe the role of descending pathways from the brain on our perception of pain.

    _____

    _____

    _____

    _____

    _____

    _____

23. Complete the labels in the figure that follows.

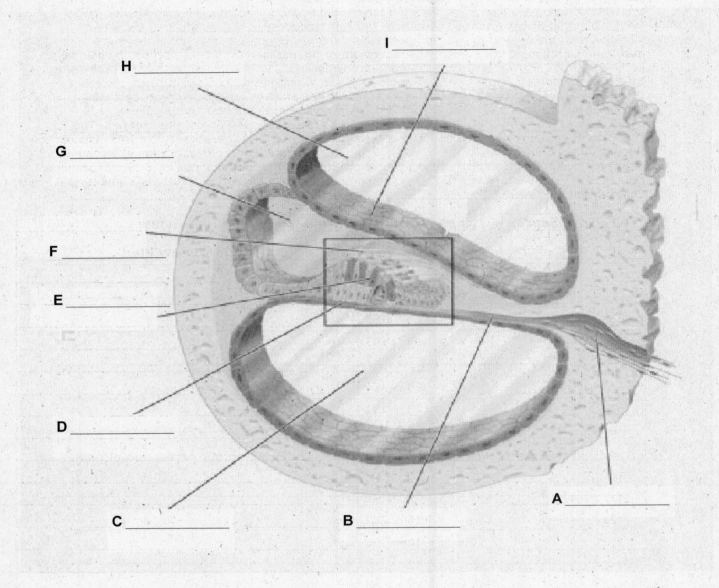

H _____

I _____

G _____

F _____

E _____

D _____

C _____

B _____

A _____

EXERCISE 7.3 ANSWER KEY

True-False: 1. T; 2. T; 3. F. **Multiple Choice:** 4. D) 5. B) 6. C) 7. A) 8. B) 9. D) 10. C) 11. D) 12. A) 13. B). **Fill In:** 14. malleus; incus; stapes. 15. vestibular canal; cochlear duct; tympanic canal. 16. utricle; saccule. 17. substantia gelatinosa; ventral posterior (VP); intralaminar; anterior cingulate cortex; parietal. 18. glomeruli; olfactory bulbs. 19. gustatory; ventral posterior medial (VPM); parietal. **Short Answer/Labeling:** 20. High frequency sounds produce maximum vibration near the base of the basilar membrane, whereas lower frequency sounds produce maximum vibration near the apex. The movement of the basilar membrane is sensed by hair cells in the organ of Corti, which rests on the basilar membrane. 21. The somatosensory cortex retains the ability to reorganize itself in response to its input. When information decreases or increases the amount of somatosensory cortex associated with the affected body part adapts accordingly. 22. Ascending pain messages and descending pathways from the frontal lobe, thalamus, hypothalamus, and amygdala converge on the periaqueductal gray (PAG) of the midbrain. The PAG is a site for large numbers of opiate receptors, and electrical stimulation of the PAG reduces the perception of pain. As a result, the PAG is perfectly situated for the modification of incoming messages about pain by higher-level cognitive processes. 23. A. Spiral ganglion; B. Spiral ganglion cell fibers; C. Tympanic canal; D. Basilar membrane; E. Organ of Corti; F. Tectorial membrane; G. Cochlear duct; H. Vestibular canal; I. Reissner's membrane.

Tally Your Score

Test Item	Point Value	Your Score
1.	1	
2.	1	
3.	1	
4.	4	
5.	4	
6.	4	
7.	4	
8.	4	
9.	4	
10.	4	
11.	4	
12.	4	
13.	4	
14.	5	
15.	5	
16.	5	
17.	5	
18.	5	
19.	5	
20.	6	
21.	6	
22.	6	
23.	9	
TOTAL	100	

Analyze Your Performance/Plan Your Review

LO	Test Item	Text Page	Your Review Plan
7.1	1	190	
	4	190	
7.2	14	192	
	15	193	
	5	194	
	20	194	
	23	194	
	6	198	
7.3	7	199	
7.4	8	201	
7.5	9	202	
	16	202	
7.6	10	205	
	2	206	
	11	206	
	21	210	
	17	212	
	22	214	
7.7	18	218	
	12	219	
7.8	13	219	
	3	220	
	19	221	

Chapter 8. Movement

EXERCISE 8.1 IDENTIFYING KEY TERMS AND THEIR DEFINITIONS

A. Terms for Types of Muscles

1. Striated	A type of muscle named for its striped appearance; including cardiac and skeletal muscles.
2. cardiac	A type of striated muscle found in the heart.
3. Skeletal	A type of striated muscle that is attached to bones and is responsible for the majority of body movements.
4. Smooth	A type of muscle found in the lining of the digestive tract, within arteries, and in the reproductive system; controlled by the autonomic nervous system.

- cardiac muscle
- skeletal muscle
- smooth muscle
- striated muscle

B. Terms of Muscle Anatomy and Contraction

1. Sar	A myofibril segment bound on either side by a Z line and spanned by thin filaments.
2. flexor	A muscle that acts to bend a joint.
3. actin	A protein that makes up the thin filaments of the myofibril.
4. myosin x myofibril	A long fiber strand running the length of a muscle fiber that is responsible for contraction.
5. extensor	A muscle that acts to straighten a joint.
6. Z line	A boundary line for each sarcomere within a myofibril.
7. troponin	The protein covering of an actin molecule that prevents the molecule from binding with myosin when a muscle is in the resting state.
8. fast twitch	A muscle fiber containing Type IIa or Type IIb myosin filaments that contains few mitochondria, uses anaerobic metabolism, and contracts rapidly; primarily responsible for movement requiring explosive strength.
9. myosin	A protein that makes up the thick filaments of the myofibril.
10. twitch	The contraction of a single muscle fiber.
11. Slow twitch	A muscle fiber containing Type I myosin filaments and large numbers of mitochondria that contracts slowly using aerobic metabolism; primarily responsible for movement requiring endurance.

- twitch
- actin
- myofibril
- myosin
- sarcomere
- troponin
- Z line
- fast-twitch fiber
- slow-twitch fiber
- extensor
- flexor

C. Terms Related to Neural Control of Muscles

1. _muscle spindle_	A sensory structure that provides feedback regarding muscle stretch.
2. _extrafusal muscle fiber_	One of the fibers outside the muscle spindle that is responsible for contracting the muscle.
3. _polysynapse reflex_	A spinal reflex that requires interaction at more than one synapse.
4. _recruitment_	The process of gradually activating more motor units as an increasing load is placed on a muscle.
5. _alpha motor neron_	A spinal motor neuron directly responsible for signaling a muscle fiber to contract.
6. _Supplementary motor area_	Motor area located in the gyrus rostral to the precentral gyrus; involved with managing complex sequences of movement.
7. _gamma motor neron_	A small spinal neuron that innervates the muscle spindles.
8. _motor neron_	A special motor neuron that responds to a particular action, whether that action is performed or simply observed.
9. _pre-SMA_	A motor area located in the gyrus rostral to the precentral gyrus; this area participates in holding a motor plan until it can be implemented; formerly referred to as the premotor area (PMA).
10. _intrafusal muscle fiber_	One of the fibers that make up a muscle spindle.
11. _motor unit_	The combination of a single alpha motor neuron and all the muscle fibers that it innervates.
12. _monosynaptic reflex_	A spinal reflex, such as the patellar reflex, that requires the action of only one synapse between sensory and motor neurons.

- alpha motor neuron
- motor unit
- recruitment
- extrafusal muscle fiber
- gamma motor neuron
- intrafusal muscle fiber
- muscle spindle
- monosynaptic reflex
- polysynaptic reflex
- pre-SMA
- mirror neuron
- supplementary motor area

EXERCISE 8.1 ANSWER KEY

A. Terms for Types of Muscles
1. striated muscle (p. 225)
2. cardiac muscle (p. 225)
3. skeletal muscle (p. 225)
4. smooth muscle (p. 225)

B. Terms of Muscle Anatomy and Contraction
1. sarcomere (p. 226)
2. flexor (p. 231)
3. actin (p. 226)
4. myofibril (p. 226)
5. extensor (p. 231)
6. Z line (p. 226)
7. troponin (p. 226)
8. fast-twitch fiber (p. 227)
9. myosin (p. 226)
10. twitch (p. 225)
11. slow-twitch fiber (p. 227)

C. Terms Related to Neural Control of Muscles
1. muscle spindle (p. 233)
2. extrafusal muscle fiber (p. 233)
3. polysynaptic reflex (p. 236)
4. recruitment (p. 232)
5. alpha motor neuron (p. 232)
6. supplementary motor area (SMA) (p. 241)
7. gamma motor neuron (p. 233)
8. mirror neuron (p. 244)
9. pre-SMA (p. 241)
10. intrafusal muscle fiber (p. 233)
11. motor unit (p. 232)
12. monosynaptic reflex (p. 236)

EXERCISE 8.2 LEARNING BY COLORING

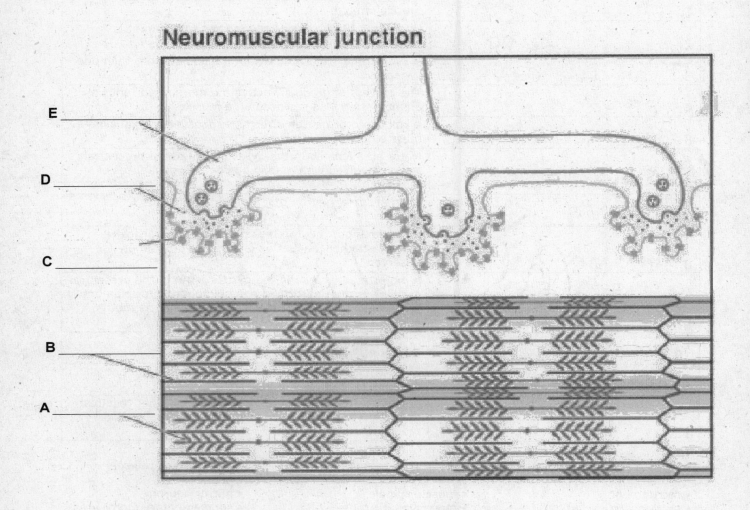

Figure 8.2 The Neuromuscular Junction

Select a different color for each labeled structure or molecule, and color all instances.

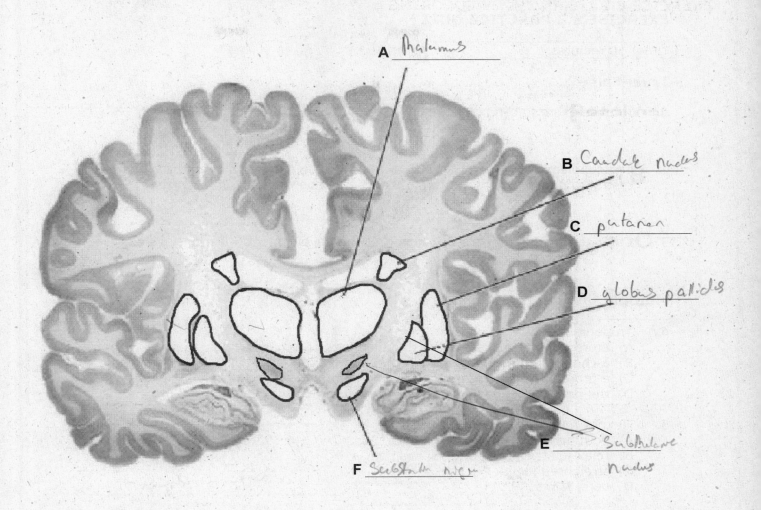

A — Thalamus
B — Caudate nucleus
C — putamen
D — globus pallidis
E — Subthalamic nucleus
F — Substantia nigra

0 Thalamus A
0 Caudate nucleus B
0 Putamen C
0 Globus pallidus D
0 Subthalamic nucleus E
0 Substantia nigra F

Figure 8.14 The Basal Ganglia

Select a different color for each of the labeled structures, and color the structures in both hemispheres.

EXERCISE 8.3 PRACTICE QUIZ

Time: 50 minutes

True–False

1. Intense exercise can convert slow-twitch fibers into fast-twitch fibers.

    T   F

2. The supplementary motor area (SMA) and pre-SMA are located in the gyrus just rostral to primary motor cortex in the frontal lobe of the cerebral cortex.

    T   F

3. Caffeine consumption is a risk factor for the development of Parkinson's disease.

    T   F

Multiple Choice

4. Troponin is
    A) a protein that makes up the thin filaments of a muscle fiber.
    B) a chemical that covers actin in the absence of calcium.
    C) a protein that makes up the thick filaments of a muscle fiber.
    D) the primary neurotransmitter at the neuromuscular junction.

5. Flexors
    A) both bend and straighten joints.
    B) relax joints to their original position.
    C) straighten joints.
    D) bend joints.

6. Alpha motor neurons
    A) process information about muscle stretch.
    B) produce muscle relaxation.
    C) produce contractions in extrafusal fibers.
    D) produce contractions in intrafusal fibers.

7. Feedback about muscle length is provided by
    A) muscle spindles
    B) Golgi tendon organs
    C) alpha motor neurons
    D) gamma motor neurons

8. Which of the following is an example of a monosynaptic reflex?
    A) reciprocal inhibition
    B) the patellar, or "knee-jerk" reflex
    C) pulling your hand away from a hot stove
    D) balancing our weight on two legs

9. Which of the following is one of the lateral pathways?
    A) vestibulospinal tract
    B) tectospinal tract
    C) reticulospinal tract
    D) rubrospinal tract

10. Normal functioning of the cerebellum is disrupted by
    A) consumption of alcohol.
    B) Parkinson's disease.
    C) Huntington's disease.
    D) obsessive-compulsive disorder.

11. Pre-SMA
    A) inhibits the activity of the thalamus.
    B) holds a plan for movement until it can be initiated.
    C) stimulates alpha motor neurons.
    D) inhibits the activity of the basal ganglia.

12. Which of the following substances acts as a cholinergic agonist?
    A) cobra venom
    B) botulinum toxin
    C) black widow spider venom
    D) curare

13. Muscular dystrophy is characterized by
    A) the degeneration of cholinergic receptors.
    B) the destruction of alpha motor neurons.
    C) the presence of an abnormal dominant gene.
    D) abnormalities in muscle fiber proteins.

Fill-ins

14. Striated muscle includes both _____ and _____ muscle.

15. A _____ forms a boundary between two adjacent _____ in a _____, which is a long strand of protein running the length of a muscle fiber.

16. The lateral pathways include the _____ and _____; whereas the ventromedial pathways include the _____, _____, _____, and _____.

17. The basal ganglia include the _____, _____, _____, and _____.

18. _____ and _____ manage movement strategies, while the _____ contributes to the selection of voluntary movements based on previous reward.

19. Malfunctions in the basal ganglia lead to difficulty moving in _____
     disease and to involuntary, uncontrolled movement in _____ disease.

Short Answer/Labeling

20. Describe the processes leading to muscle contraction.

     _____

     _____

     _____

     _____

     _____

     _____

21. What is a mirror neuron?

     _____

     _____

     _____

     _____

     _____

22. Why is myasthenia gravis treated with antagonists for acetylcholinesterase?

     _____

     _____

     _____

     _____

     _____

23. Complete the labels in the figure that follows.

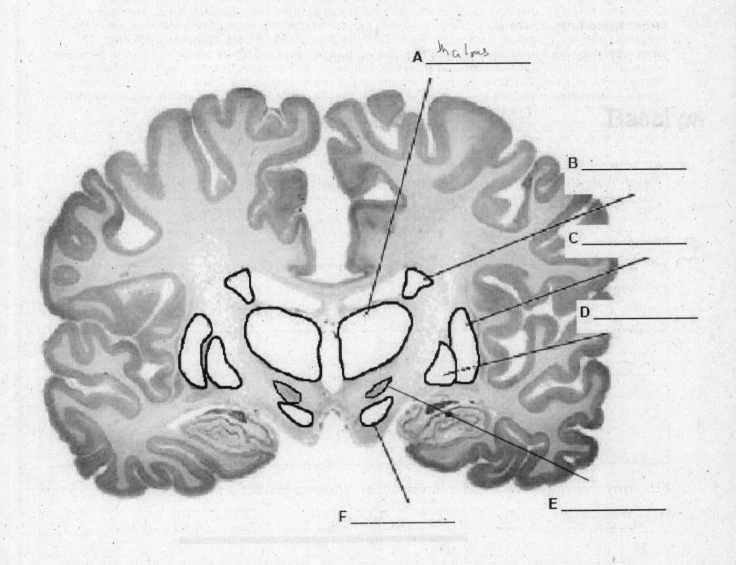

A ___thalmus___

B _____

C _____

D _____

E _____

F _____

EXERCISE 8.3 ANSWER KEY

True-False: 1. F; 2. T; 3. F. **Multiple Choice:** 4. B) 5. D) 6. C) 7. A) 8. B) 9. D) 10. A) 11. B) 12. C) 13. D). **Fill In:** 14. cardiac; skeletal. 15. Z-line; sarcomeres; myofibril. 16. corticospinal tract; rubrospinal tract; tectospinal tract; vestibulospinal tract; pontine reticulospinal tract; medullary reticulospinal tract. 17. caudate nucleus; globus pallidus; putamen; subthalamic nucleus. 18. SMA; pre-SMA; anterior cingulate cortex. 19. Parkinson's; Huntington's. **Short Answer/Labeling:** 20. When acetylcholine interacts with receptors on the muscle fiber, sodium channels open, and an action potential is initiated. Calcium released from internal organelles binds with troponin, freeing actin to interact with myosin. The myosin fibers rotate and the muscle contracts. 21. A mirror neuron is a special neuron that responds to a particular action, regardless of whether the action was performed by the individual or simply observed in another. 22. Myasthenia gravis is characterized by the degeneration of cholinergic receptors. By treating the patient with an AChE inhibitor, more ACh will be available to interact with the remaining receptors, improving movement. 23. A. Thalamus; B. Caudate nucleus; C. Putamen; D. Globus pallidus; E. Subthalamic nucleus.

Tally Your Score			Analyze Your Performance/Plan Your Review			
Test Item	Point Value	Your Score	LO	Test Item	Text Page	**Your Review Plan**
1.	1		8.1	14	225	
2.	1			20	225	
3.	1			4	226	
4.	4			15	226	
5.	4			1	229	
6.	4		8.2	5	231	
7.	4		8.3	6	232	
8.	4		8.4	7	233	
9.	4		8.5	8	236	
10.	4		8.6	9	238	
11.	4			16	238	
12.	4		8.7	2	240	
13.	4			10	240	
14.	5			17	240	
15.	5			23	241	
16.	5		8.8	11	242	
17.	5			18	242	
18.	5			21	244	
19.	5		8.9	12	245	
20.	6		8.10	22	245	
21.	6			13	246	
22.	6			19	248	
23.	9			3	249	
TOTAL	100					

Chapter 9. Temperature Regulation, Thirst, and Hunger

EXERCISE 9.1 IDENTIFYING KEY TERMS AND THEIR DEFINITIONS

A. General Terms Related to Body Regulatory Functions

1.	A value that is defended by regulatory systems, such as core temperature or a particular body weight.
2.	A physiological state of equilibrium or balance.
3.	A part of the hypothalamus involved in a number of regulatory functions.
4.	The process of activating and directing behavior.

- homeostasis
- motivation
- set point
- preoptic area (POA)

B. Terms Related to Regulation of Body Fluids

1.	A receptor in the heart and kidneys that measures blood pressure.
2.	An area of the hypothalamus that is involved with drinking behavior.
3.	Another name for antidiuretic hormone (ADH).
4.	A hormone that promotes retention of fluid by signaling the kidneys to reduce urine production and by stimulating the release of renin. Also known as vasopressin.
5.	The movement of water to equalize concentration on two sides of a membrane.
6.	A structure in the medulla that processes information from baroreceptors, osmoreceptors, glucoreceptors, and taste receptors.
7.	An area of the brain, located near the junction of the two lateral ventricles, that regulates drinking.
8.	An area of the midbrain that participates in the initiation of drinking behavior.
9.	A part of the hypothalamus that participates in behavioral responses to thirst and in the initiation of feeding behavior.
10.	A receptor that detects cellular dehydration.
11.	A chemical dissolved in solution.
12.	Thirst that results from a decrease in the volume of the extracellular fluid.
13.	An area located around the third ventricle in the brain that detects cellular dehydration.
14.	Thirst produced by cellular dehydration.

- solute
- osmosis
- hypovolemic thirst
- organum vasculosum of the lamina terminalis (OVLT)
- osmoreceptor
- osmotic thirst
- antidiuretic hormone (ADH)

- baroreceptor
- vasopressin
- lateral hypothalamus (LH)
- median preoptic nucleus
- nucleus of the solitary tract (NST)
- subfornical organ (SFO)
- zona incerta

C. Terms Related to Regulation and Intake of Body Nutrients

1.	A peptide neurochemical produced in the lateral hypothalamus that stimulates eating. Also known as hypocretin.
2.	A peptide neurochemical secreted by the arcuate nucleus of the hypothalamus that initiates eating.
3.	A hormone produced in the stomach that stimulates feeding behavior.
4.	A substance secreted by fat cells that helps the body regulate its fat stores.
5.	A small protein secreted by the arcuate nucleus that initiates eating.
6.	A cluster of neurons involved with feeding located within the hypothalamus.
7.	A portion of the hypothalamus involved with the regulation of hunger.
8.	A receptor that is sensitive to the presence of glucose.
9.	A hormone that interacts with leptin and plays a role in the regulation of eating.

- agouti-related protein (AgRP)
- arcuate nucleus
- glucoreceptor
- leptin
- neuropeptide Y (NPY)

- paraventricular nucleus (PVN)
- ghrelin
- melanin-concentrating hormone (MCH)
- orexin

D. Terms Related to Cessation of Eating and Eating Disorders

1.	The state of being extremely overweight, with a body mass index of 30 to 39.9, or a weight that is 20 percent higher than typical.
2.	An eating disorder characterized by cycles of bingeing and purging.
3.	A neurochemical originating in the arcuate nucleus, believed to inhibit feeding behavior.
4.	An area within the hypothalamus that participates in satiety.
5.	The sensation of being full, cessation of eating.
6.	An eating disorder characterized by voluntary self-starvation and a grossly distorted body image.
7.	A neurochemical, originating in the arcuate nucleus, believed to inhibit feeding behavior.

- satiety
- ventromedial hypothalamus (VMH)
- alpha melanocyte stimulating hormone (αMSH)

- cocaine- and amphetamine-regulated transcript (CART)
- obesity
- anorexia nervosa
- bulimia nervosa

EXERCISE 9.1 ANSWER KEY

A. General Terms Related to Body Regulatory Functions
1. set point (p. 256)
2. homeostasis (p. 256)
3. preoptic area (POA) (p. 261)
4. motivation (p. 256)

B. Terms Related to Regulation of Body Fluids
1. baroreceptor (p. 266)
2. median preoptic nucleus (p. 268)
3. vasopressin (p. 266)
4. antidiuretic hormone (ADH) (p. 266)
5. osmosis (p. 263)
6. nucleus of the solitary tract (NST) (p. 268)
7. subfornical organ (SFO) (p. 268)
8. zona incerta (p. 268)
9. lateral hypothalamus (LH) (p. 268)
10. osmoreceptor (p. 265)
11. solute (p. 262)
12. hypovolemic thirst (p. 265)
13. organum vasculosum of the lamina terminalis (OVLT) (p. 265)
14. osmotic thirst (p. 265)

C. Terms Related to Regulation and Intake of Body Nutrients
1. orexin (p. 276)
2. neuropeptide Y (NPY) (p. 274)
3. ghrelin (p. 275)
4. leptin (p. 274)
5. agouti-related protein (AgRP) (p. 274)
6. arcuate nucleus (p. 274)
7. paraventricular nucleus (PVN) (p. 274)
8. glucoreceptor (p. 274)
9. melanin-concentrating hormone (MCH) (p. 275)

D. Terms Related to Cessation of Eating and Eating Disorders
1. obesity (p. 278)
2. bulimia nervosa (p. 281)
3. alpha melanocyte stimulating hormone (αMSH) (p. 277)
4. ventromedial hypothalamus (VMH) (p. 276)
5. satiety (p. 276)
6. anorexia nervosa (p. 280)
7. cocaine- and amphetamine-regulated transcript (CART) (p. 277)

EXERCISE 9.2 LEARNING BY COLORING

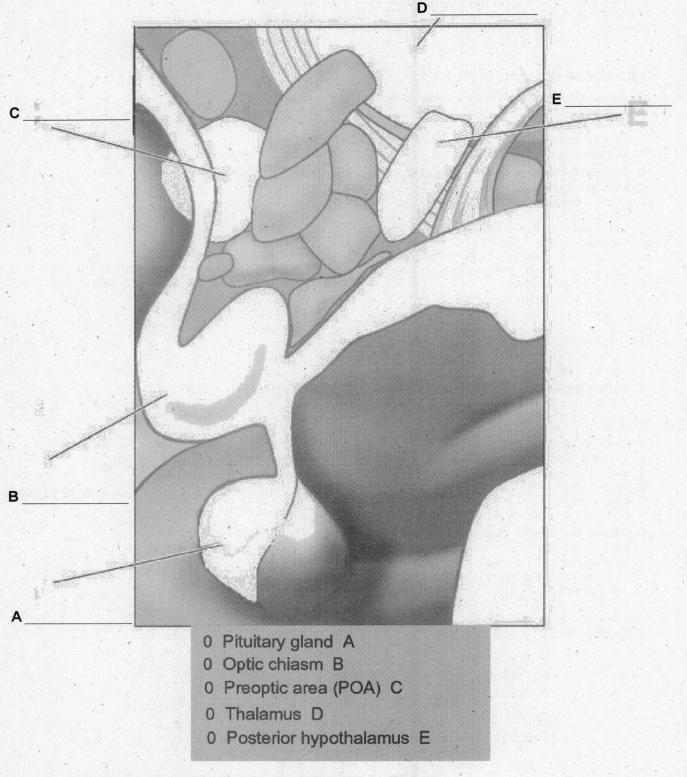

0 Pituitary gland A
0 Optic chiasm B
0 Preoptic area (POA) C
0 Thalamus D
0 Posterior hypothalamus E

Figure 9.7 Hypothalamic Control of Temperature

Select a different color for each of the labeled structures.

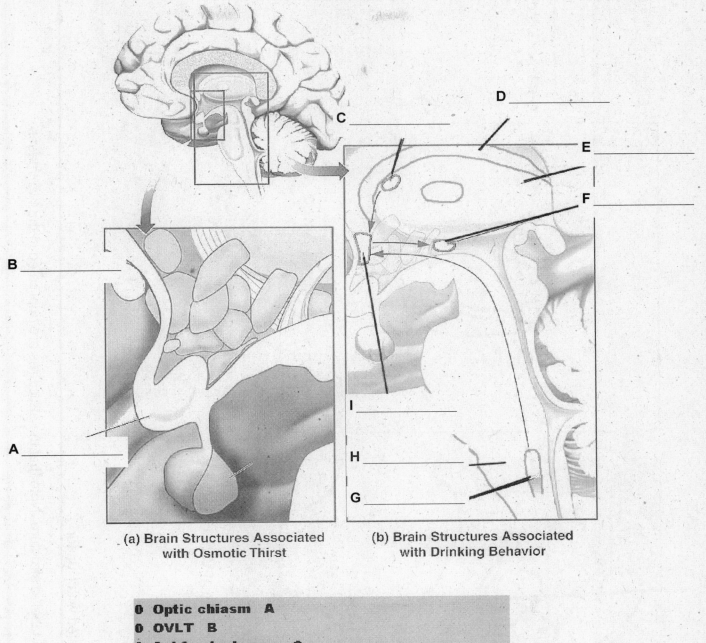

(a) **Brain Structures Associated with Osmotic Thirst**

(b) **Brain Structures Associated with Drinking Behavior**

0 **Optic chiasm   A**
0 **OVLT   B**
0 **Subfornical organ   C**
0 **Fornix   D**
0 **Thalamus   E**
0 **Zona incerta   F**
0 **Nucleus of the solitary tract   G**
0 **Medulla   H**
0 **Median preoptic nucleus of the hypothalamus   I**

Figure 9.10 Brain Structures Association with Thirst

Select a different color for each of the labeled structures.

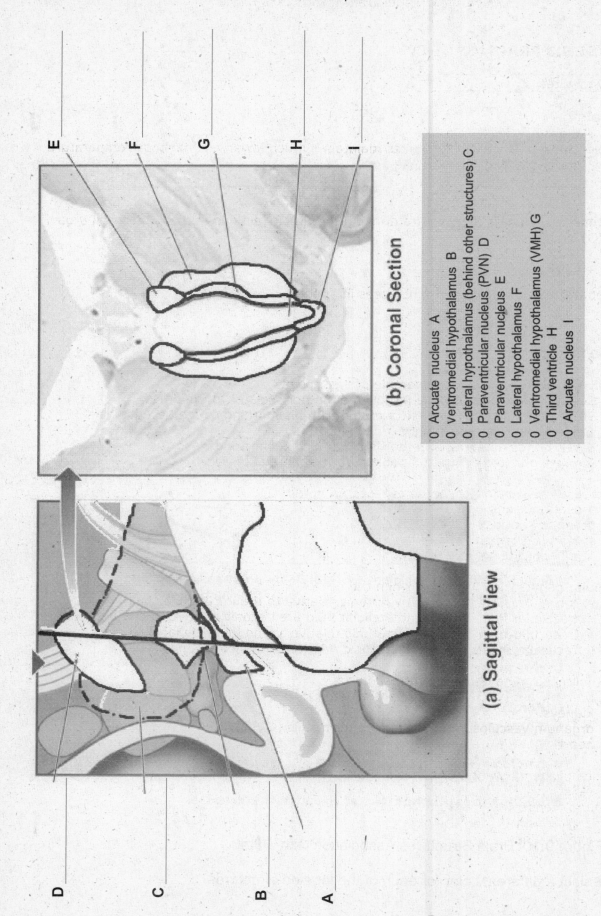

(b) Coronal Section

(a) Sagittal View

- 0 Arcuate nucleus A
- 0 Ventromedial hypothalamus B
- 0 Lateral hypothalamus (behind other structures) C
- 0 Paraventricular nucleus (PVN) D
- 0 Paraventricular nucleus E
- 0 Lateral hypothalamus F
- 0 Ventromedial hypothalamus (VMH) G
- 0 Third ventricle H
- 0 Arcuate nucleus I

Figure 9.17 Structures Associated with Hunger

Select a different color for each labeled structure. Note that the structures are duplicated in the two images.

EXERCISE 9.3 PRACTICE QUIZ

Time: 50 minutes

True–False

1.   "Cold-blooded" animals like snakes maintain a much lower internal body temperature than "warm-blooded" animals like dogs.

                    T   F

2. Angiotensin II appears to stimulate drinking through its actions at the subfornical organ (SFO).

                    T   F

3. Low leptin levels usually lead to increases in appetite.

                    T   F

Multiple Choice

4.   Which of the following is an example of a set point?
     A) Susan shivers because she forgot to bring her sweater to the office.
     B) Steve decides to have an extra muffin with his morning coffee because he's suddenly feeling very hungry.
     C) Karen brings an extra large bottle of water to kickboxing class.
     D) John weighs just about 150 pounds at each annual physical.

5.   Temperature-sensitive neurons are located in the
     A) arcuate nucleus.
     B) preoptic nucleus.
     C) subfornical organ.
     D) nucleus of the solitary tract.

6.   Cellular dehydration will occur when the
     A) extracellular fluid becomes hypertonic relative to the intracellular fluid.
     B) extracellular fluid and the intracellular fluid are isotonic relative to one another.
     C) extracellular fluid becomes hypotonic relative to the intracellular fluid.
     D) intracellular fluid becomes hypertonic relative to the extracellular fluid.

7.   Osmoreceptors have been identified in the
     A) preoptic area (POA) of the hypothalamus.
     B) kidneys.
     C) organum vasculosum of the lamina terminalis (OVLT).
     D) heart.

8.   Which of the following hormones signals the kidneys to retain sodium?
     A) renin
     B) angiotensis I
     C) angiotensin II
     D) aldosterone

9. Electrical stimulation of which of the following structures will lead to the initiation of drinking?
    A) the organum vasculosum of the lamina terminalis (OVLT)
    B) the paraventricular nucleus of the hypothalamus
    C) the zona incerta
    D) the preoptic nucleus (POA) of the hypothalamus

10. Which of the following hormones rises immediately following a meal?
    A) leptin
    B) insulin
    C) vasopressin
    D) aldosterone

11. Feeding behavior is stimulated by the activation of
    A) NPY and AgRP.
    B) αMSH and CART.
    C) TSH and ACTH.
    D) aldosterone and angiotensin II.

12. Lesions in which of the following structures produces large weight gains in rats?
    A) the preoptic area (POA) of the hypothalamus
    B) the zona incerta
    C) the ventromedial hypothalamus
    D) the lateral hypothalamus

13. Unusually elevated CART levels have been observed in people with
    A) obesity.
    B) bulimia nervosa.
    C) a history of weight loss surgery.
    D) anorexia nervosa.

Fill In

14. A _____ is a controlled increase of body temperature in response to infection, whereas _____ results from an uncontrolled increase in body temperature.

15. Solutions that are lower in concentration than a reference solution are referred to as _____, solutions that are higher than a reference solution are _____, and solutions with equal concentrations are _____.

16. _____ thirst results from cellular dehydration, whereas _____ thirst results from decreases in the volume of extracellular fluid, as in the loss of blood due to an injury.

17. When the kidneys release renin, _____ is converted into

_____ then _____, which in turn signals the

kidneys to release _____.

18. High leptin levels activate _____ and _____, leading to

_____ nervous system activity and _____

metabolism.

19. _____ is an eating disorder characterized by very low weight

and a disturbed body image; whereas _____ is an eating

disorder characterized by binging and purging activities.

Short Answer/Labeling

20. Describe the processes leading to hyponatremia.

_____

_____

_____

_____

_____

_____

21. What role do the orexins play in appetite?

_____

_____

_____

_____

_____

22. Complete the labels in the figure that follows.

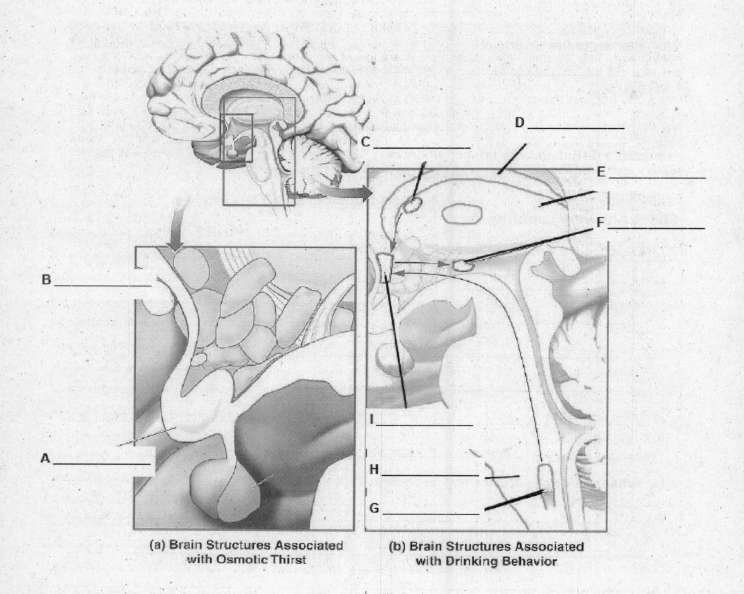

(a) Brain Structures Associated
with Osmotic Thirst

(b) Brain Structures Associated
with Drinking Behavior

EXERCISE 9.3 ANSWER KEY

True-False: 1. F; 2. T; 3. T. **Multiple Choice:** 4. D) 5. B) 6. A) 7. C) 8. D) 9. C) 10. B) 11. A) 12. C) 13. D). **Fill In:** 14. fever; hyperthermia. 15. hypotonic; hypertonic; isotonic. 16. Osmotic; hypovolemic. 17. angiotensinogen; angiotensin I; angiotensin II; aldosterone. 18. αMSH; CART; sympathetic; higher. 19. Anorexia nervosa; bulimia nervosa. **Short Answer/Labeling:** 20. Normally, we observe a negative correlation between fluid and sodium levels. When one is high, the other is low. In hyponatremia, both fluid and sodium levels are low at the same time, which sends conflicting messages to the body's fluid control mechanisms. Because preserving blood volume is a higher priority than cell fluid volume, ADH will continue to be released, leading to a dangerous retention of fluids. 21. Orexins (hypocretins) are produced in the lateral hypothalamus. Levels of orexins are high following fasting and when leptin levels are low. Injection of orexins into the hypothalamus leads to feeding. Neurons releasing orexins project widely in the cortex and brainstem, and possibly link patterns of activity, arousal, and feeding. 22. A. Optic chiasm; B. Organum vasculosum of the lamina terminalis (OVLT); C. Subfornical organ; D. Fornix; E. Thalamus; F. Zona incerta; G. Nucleus of the solitary tract; H. Medulla; I. Median preoptic nucleus of the hypothalamus.

Tally Your Score

Test Item	Point Value	Your Score
1.	2	
2.	2	
3.	2	
4.	4	
5.	4	
6.	4	
7.	4	
8.	4	
9.	4	
10.	4	
11.	4	
12.	4	
13.	4	
14.	6	
15.	6	
16.	6	
17.	6	
18.	6	
19.	6	
20.	6	
21.	6	
22.	6	
TOTAL	100	

Analyze Your Performance/Plan Your Review

LO	Test Item	Text Page	Your Review Plan
9.1	4	256	
9.2	1	257	
	14	260	
	5	261	
9.3	15	263	
	6	265	
	7	265	
	16	265	
	22	266	
9.4	8	267	
	17	267	
	2	268	
	9	268	
	20	269	
9.5	10	273	
9.6	3	274	
	11	274	
	12	276	
	21	276	
	18	277	
9.7	19	280	
	13	282	

Chapter 10. Sexual Behavior

EXERCISE 10.1 IDENTIFYING KEY TERMS AND THEIR DEFINITIONS

A. Terms Involved in Sexual Development

1.	One of two types of sex chromosomes; individuals with a Y chromosome will usually develop into males.
2.	The internal system that develops into a uterus, fallopian tubes, and the upper two thirds of the vagina in the absence of anti-Müllerian hormone.
3.	The internal organs, ovaries in females and testes in males, that produce reproductive cells (eggs and sperm) and secrete sex hormones.
4.	One of two types of sex chromosomes; individuals with two X chromosomes will usually develop into females.
5.	The internal system that develops into seminal vesicles, vas deferens, and the prostate gland in males.
6.	Male gonads; source of sperm and sex hormones.
7.	The external sexual organs, including the penis and scrotum in males and the labia, clitoris, and lower third of the vagina in females.
8.	Female gonads; the source of ova and sex hormones.
9.	Characteristics related to sex that appear at puberty, including deepening voice and facial hair growth in males and widening hips and breast development in females.

- X chromosome
- Y chromosome
- external genitalia
- gonads
- ovaries

- testes
- Müllerian system
- Wolffian system
- secondary sex characteristics

B. Terms for Sexual Hormones

1.	A steroid hormone that develops and maintains typically female characteristics.
2.	A hormone produced in the corpus luteum that prevents the development of additional follicles and promotes the growth of the uterine lining.
3.	An androgen produced primarily in the testes.
4.	A hormone released by the hypothalamus that stimulates the release of luteinizing hormone (LH) and follicle-stimulating hormone (FSH) by the anterior pituitary gland.
5.	A steroid hormone that develops and maintains typically masculine characteristics.
6.	A hormone released by the anterior pituitary that stimulates the development of eggs in the ovaries and sperm in the testes.
7.	A hormone released by the anterior pituitary that signals the male testes to produce testosterone and that regulates the menstrual cycle in females.

8.	An estrogen hormone synthesized primarily in the ovaries.

- androgen
- testosterone
- estradiol
- estrogen

- follicle-stimulating hormone (FSH)
- gonadotropin-releasing hormone (GnRH)
- luteinizing hormone (LH)
- progesterone

C. Terms Related to Sexual Behavior and Orientation

1.	A hormone, released by the posterior pituitary gland, that stimulates uterine contractions, releases milk, and participates in social bonding, including romantic love and parenting behavior.
2.	A collection of four small nuclei in the anterior hypothalamus, two of which (INAH-2 and INAH-3) appear to be sexually dimorphic. The size of INAH-3 might be associated with male sexual orientation.
3.	The custom of having one mate at a time or for life.

- interstitial nuclei of the anterior hypothalamus (INAH)
- monogamy
- oxytocin

EXERCISE 10.1 ANSWER KEY

A. Terms Involved in Sexual Development
1. Y chromosome (p. 286)
2. Müllerian system (p. 289)
3. gonads (p. 288)
4. X chromosome (p. 285)
5. Wolffian system (p. 289)
6. testes (p. 288)
7. external genitalia (p. 288)
8. ovaries (p. 288)
9. secondary sex characteristics (p. 291)

B. Terms for Sexual Hormones
1. estrogen (p. 291)
2. progesterone (p. 295)
3. testosterone (p. 289)
4. gonadotropin-releasing hormone (GnRH) (p. 291)
5. androgen (p. 289)
6. follicle-stimulating hormone (FSH)(p. 291)
7. luteinizing hormone (LH) (p. 291)
8. estradiol (p. 291)

C. Terms Related to Sexual Behavior and Orientation
1. oxytocin (p. 308)
2. interstitial nuclei of the anterior hypothalamus (INAH) (p. 301)
3. monogamy (p. 309)

EXERCISE 10.2 LEARNING BY COLORING

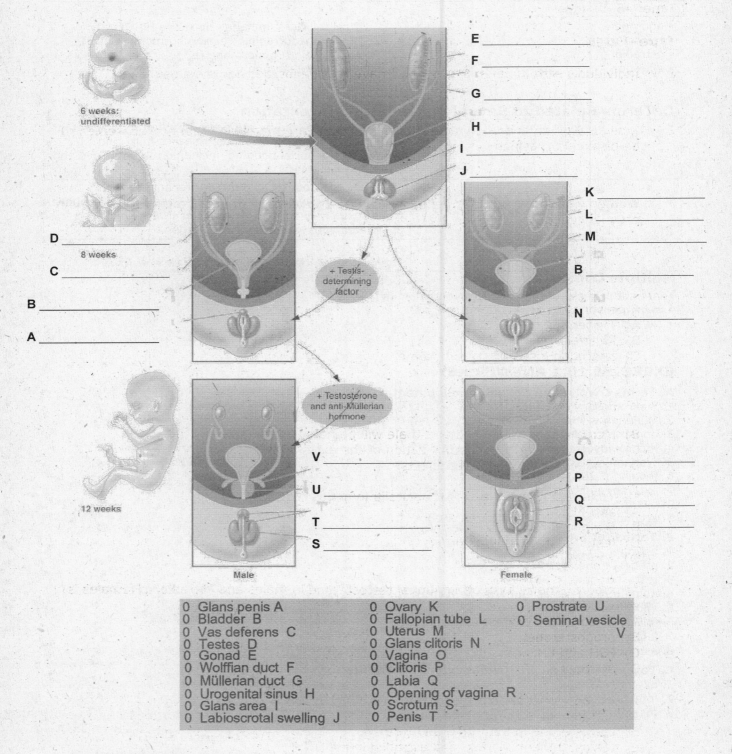

Figure 10.4 Differentiation

Select a different color for each of the labeled structures. Note that the bladder

EXERCISE 10.3 PRACTICE QUIZ

Time: 45 minutes

True–False

1. Individuals with Klinefelter syndrome have XXY genotypes and male sex.

    T   F

2. Individuals with androgen insensitivity syndrome are more likely than other women to be bisexual or lesbian.

    T   F

3. Women's maternal bonding behaviors can be predicted by their oxytocin levels early in pregnancy.

    T   F

Multiple Choice

4. A person with an XO genotype has
    A) Turner syndrome
    B) Klinefelter syndrome
    C) androgen insensitivity syndrome
    D) congenital adrenal hyperplasia

5. In males, congenital adrenal hyperplasia (CAH)
    A) results in unusually aggressive behavior.
    B) increases the chances that a male will be homosexual.
    C) interferes with the masculinization of the external genitalia.
    D) produces few observable effects.

6. Masculinization of the external genitalia in males requires
    A) anti-Müllerian hormone.
    B) 5-alpha-dihydrotestosterone.
    C) testis-determining factor.
    D) anti-Wolffian hormone.

7. At puberty, the release of additional testosterone in males and estradiol in females is stimulated by
    A) 5-alpha-dihydrotestosterone.
    B) progesterone.
    C) FSH and LH.
    D) estrogens.

8. Improved verbal skills are correlated with higher levels of
    A) estradiol in both men and women.
    B) testosterone in both men and women.
    C) testosterone in women and estradiol in men.
    D) estradiol in women and testosterone in men.

9. Sexual interest is correlated with levels of
   A) estradiol in both men and women.
   B) testosterone in both men and women.
   C) testosterone in women and estradiol in men.
   D) estradiol in women and testosterone in men.

10. The highest testosterone levels observed occurred in
    A) men and women who had multiple committed relationships.
    B) men in multiple committed relationships and women in monogamous relationships.
    C) women in multiple committed relationships and men in monogamous relationships.
    D) men and women who were single.

11. Different sizes in INAH-3 have been correlated with
    A) male sexual orientation.
    B) sexual frequency.
    C) female sexual orientation.
    D) premenstrual syndrome.

12. Men with facial features indicating high testosterone are
    A) never preferred by women.
    B) preferred by women seeking long-term, committed relationships.
    C) preferred by women seeking one night stands.
    D) preferred by women for either one night stands or long-term relationships.

13. In the human brain,
    A) oxytocin and vasopressin are expressed equally in men and women.
    B) oxytocin is expressed more by women, and vasopressin is expressed more by men.
    C) vasopressin is expressed more by women, and oxytocin in expressed more by men.
    D) oxytocin is expressed equally in men and women, but vasopressin is expressed more by men.

Fill In

14. Individuals with an XO genotype have _____ syndrome, and those with an XXY genotype have _____ syndrome.

15. The Müllerian system will develop into the _____, upper portion of the _____, and the _____.

16. At the onset of puberty, the hypothalamus releases _____, which in turn stimulates release of _____ and _____ from the _____ pituitary.

17. Just prior to ovulation, levels of _____ peak; following ovulation, levels of _____ increase and then drop if fertilization does not occur.

18. A _____ structure appears to be different in males and females, like the _____ in rats and the _____ in humans.

19. Romantic love probably involves the hormone _____, whereas sexual desire is more related to the hormone _____.

Short Answer/Labeling

20. What are some of the possible reasons for the dropping age at puberty?

_____

_____

_____

_____

_____

_____

21. What odors appear to influence human attraction?

_____

_____

_____

_____

_____

_____

EXERCISE 10.2 ANSWER KEY

True-False: 1. T; 2. F; 3. T. **Multiple Choice:** 4. A) 5. D) 6. B) 7. C) 8. D) 9. B) 10. A) 11. A) 12. C) 13. B). **Fill In:** 14. Turner; Kleinfelter. 15. uterus; vagina; fallopian tubes. 16. gonadotropin-releasing hormone; follicle-stimulating hormone; luteinizing hormone; anterior. 17. estrogen; progesterone. 18. sexually dimorphic; SDN-POA; INAH-3. 19. oxytocin; testosterone. **Short Answer/Labeling:** 20. Among the hypotheses put forward to explain earlier puberty are increased obesity among youth. Accumulation of fat may be one trigger for puberty, so as the population becomes heavier at earlier ages, puberty may begin earlier. Exposure to estrogen-like compounds in food, shampoos, and plastics might also contribute to earlier puberty, as children are especially sensitive to these hormones. 21. Odors reflecting different major histocompatibility complex (MHC) genes contribute to female preferences for different males. Because it is in the best interests of our children to have parents with diverse MHC genes, women are less attracted to men whose smell reflects a genetic makeup different from their own.

Tally Your Score			Analyze Your Performance/Plan Your Review			
Test Item	Point Value	Your Score	LO	Test Item	Text Page	Your Review Plan
1.	2		10.1	4	286	
2.	2			14	286	
3.	2			1	287	
4.	4		10.2	15	289	
5.	4			5	290	
6.	4		10.3	2	290	
7.	4			6	290	
8.	4		10.4	7	291	
9.	4			16	291	
10.	4			20	291	
11.	4			17	294	
12.	4		10.5	8	298	
13.	4			9	298	
14.	6			10	299	
15.	6		10.6	18	300	
16.	6			11	304	
17.	6		10.7	12	306	
18.	6			13	308	
19.	6			19	308	
20.	9			21	308	
21.	9			3	310	
TOTAL	100					

Chapter 11. Sleep and Waking

EXERCISE 11.1 IDENTIFYING KEY TERMS AND THEIR DEFINITIONS

A. Terms Related to Sleep Rhythms and Biochemistry

1.	An area of the hypothalamus located above the optic chiasm; responsible for maintaining circadian rhythms.
2.	An external cue for setting biological rhythms.
3.	A hormone released by the adrenal glands that promotes arousal.
4.	A repeating cycle of about 24 hours.
5.	An indoleamine secreted by the pineal gland that participates in the regulation of circadian rhythms.

- circadian rythm
- zeitgeber
- suprachiasmatic nucleus (SCN)
- melatonin
- cortisol

B. The Terminology of Wakefulness and Sleep

1.	A cycle that occurs several times in a single day.
2.	A brain waveform having 9 to12 cycles per second, associated with less alertness and more relaxation than beta activity during wakefulness.
3.	Having identical periods and phases; in EEG, represents relatively low levels of brain activity.
4.	A brain waveform having 1 to 4 cycles per second that occurs during Stages 3 and 4 of NREM sleep.
5.	A period of sleep characterized by slow, synchronous brain activity, reductions in heart rate, and muscle relaxation.
6.	A period of sleep characterized by desynchronous brain activity, muscle paralysis, eye movement, and storylike dream behavior.
7.	A brain waveform having 15 to 20 cycles per second, associated with high levels of alertness during wakefulness.
8.	An electrical waveform observed during REM sleep, originating in the pons and traveling to the thalamus and occipital cortex. Each PGO wave is associated with an eye movement.
9.	Having different periods and phases; in EEG, represents high levels of brain activity.
10.	A brain waveform having 4 to 7 cycles per second found primarily in lighter stages of NREM sleep.

- desynchronous
- synchronous
- alpha wave
- beta wave
- ultradian cycle
- delta wave
- non-REM sleep (NREM)
- rapid-eye-movement (REM) sleep
- theta wave
- PGO spike

C. Terms for Sleep Disorders

1.	A sleep disorder characterized by the intrusion of REM sleep, and occasionally REM paralysis, into the waking state.
2.	The inability to sleep a normal amount of time.
3.	A sleep disorder that involves difficulty initiating or maintaining sleep.
4.	A feature of narcolepsy in which REM muscle paralysis intrudes into the waking state.
5.	A sleep disorder that involves the intrusion of unusual behaviors into sleep.

- dyssomnia
- insomnia
- parasomnia

- cataplexy
- narcolepsy

EXERCISE 11.1 ANSWER KEY

A. Terms Related to Sleep Rhythms and Biochemistry
1. suprachiasmatic nucleus (SCN) (p. 315)
2. zeitgeber (p. 313)
3. cortisol (p. 319)
4. circadian rythm (p. 313)
5. melatonin (p. 318)

B. The Terminology of Wakefulness and Sleep
1. ultradian cycle (p. 321)
2. alpha wave (p. 321)
3. synchronous (p. 320)
4. delta wave (p. 322)
5. non-REM sleep (NREM) (p. 322)
6. rapid-eye-movement (REM) sleep (p. 322)
7. beta wave (p. 321)
8. PGO spike (p. 331)
9. desynchronous (p. 320)
10. theta wave (p. 322)

C. Terms for Sleep Disorders
1. narcolepsy (p. 335)
2. insomnia (p. 334)
3. dyssomnia (p. 334)
4. cataplexy (p. 335)
5. parasomnia (p. 334)

EXERCISE 11.2 LEARNING BY COLORING

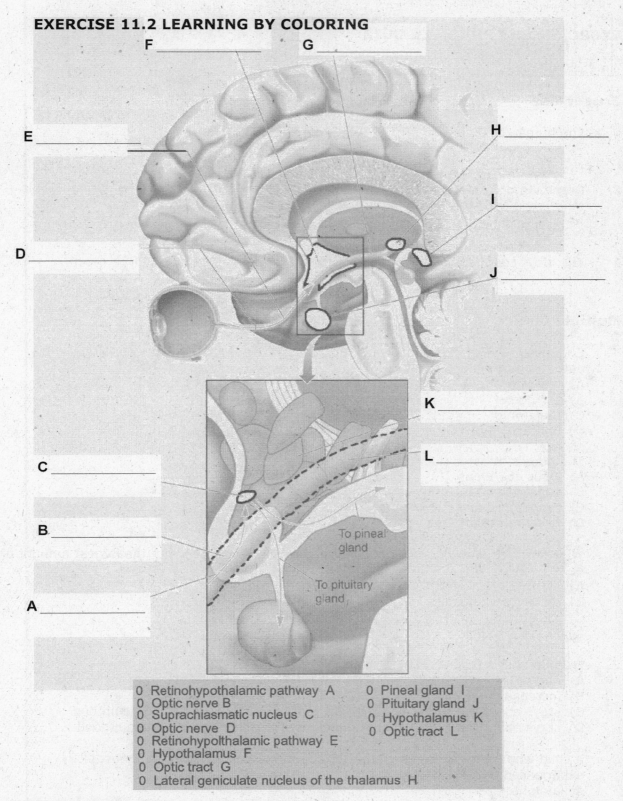

F _____   G _____

E _____

H _____

I _____

D _____

J _____

K _____

L _____

C _____

B _____

To pineal gland

To pituitary gland

A _____

0 Retinohypothalamic pathway A	0 Pineal gland I
0 Optic nerve B	0 Pituitary gland J
0 Suprachiasmatic nucleus C	0 Hypothalamus K
0 Optic nerve D	0 Optic tract L
0 Retinohypolthalamic pathway E	
0 Hypothalamus F	
0 Optic tract G	
0 Lateral geniculate nucleus of the thalamus H	

Figure 11.15 Structures Associated with Sleep

Select a different color for each of the labeled structures. Note that the retinohypothalamic pathway appears twice, and it should be colored the same in both images.

EXERCISE 11.3 PRACTICE QUIZ

Time: 50 minutes

True–False

1.   The human circadian rhythm is exactly 24 hours long.

T   F

2.   Dreaming occurs during both REM and NREM sleep, but the dreaming during REM is more vivid and story-like.

T   F

3.   The locus coeruleus and the raphe nucleus are most active during REM sleep.

T   F

Multiple Choice

4.   Changes in which of the following substances are associated with changing sleep patterns during adolescence?
A) testosterone
B) estrogens
C) melatonin
D) follicle-stimulating hormone (FSH)

5.   The body's "master clock" is the
A) locus coeruleus.
B) suprachiasmatic nucleus (SCN).
C) raphe nucleus.
D) basal forebrain.

6.   Which of the following states of consciousness is associated with the largest amount of delta waves?
A) alertness
B) drowsy wakefulness
C) REM
D) Stage 4 NREM

7.   From infancy to puberty, REM sleep
A) decreases.
B) increases.
C) stays about the same, and then decreases in adolescence and adulthood.
D) stays about the same, and then increases in adolescence and adulthood.

8.   A child who wakes up screaming after about one hour of sleep has most likely experienced
A) a nightmare.
B) a night terror.
C) lucid dreaming.
D) sleep apnea.

9. Complaints of joint and muscle pain follow
    A) deprivation of REM sleep.
    B) night terrors.
    C) a narcoleptic attack.
    D) deprivation of NREM sleep.

10. The preoptic nucleus of the hypothalamus
    A) does not participate in the management of sleep and wakefulness.
    B) is essential for REM sleep.
    C) keeps track of "sleep debt."
    D) is only active during NREM sleep.

11. PGO spikes are usually observed during
    A) wakefulness.
    B) REM sleep.
    C) Stage 2 NREM.
    D) Stages 3 and 4 NREM.

12. Michael observes that levels of serotonin and norepinephrine activity in his laboratory cat are quite low. It is most likely that Michael's cat is
    A) awake.
    B) in REM sleep.
    C) in NREM sleep.
    D) in a coma.

13. Katie's dog falls asleep whenever it gets excited. It is likely that the dog has
    A) sleep apnea.
    B) REM behavior disorder.
    C) insomnia.
    D) narcolepsy.

Fill In

14. The suprachiasmatic nucleus receives input from cells of the retina containing
    _____ via the _____ pathway.

15. Genes in fruit flies that participate in cellular clocks are known as _____,
    _____, and _____.

16. _____ is released early in the morning, whereas _____ is
    released a few hours before sleep.

17. Wakefulness is associated with _____ and _____ waves, whereas
    NREM sleep is characterized by _____ and _____ waves.

18. The locus coeruleus and raphe nuclei are _____ during wakefulness,
    _____ during NREM, and _____ during REM.

19. Neurochemicals showing high activity during wakefulness include

_____, _____, _____,

and _____.

Short Answer/Labeling

20. What hypotheses attempt to explain the functions of sleep?

_____

_____

_____

_____

_____

_____

21. What is the difference between dyssomnias and parasomnias?

_____

_____

_____

_____

_____

_____

22. Complete the labels in the figure that follows.

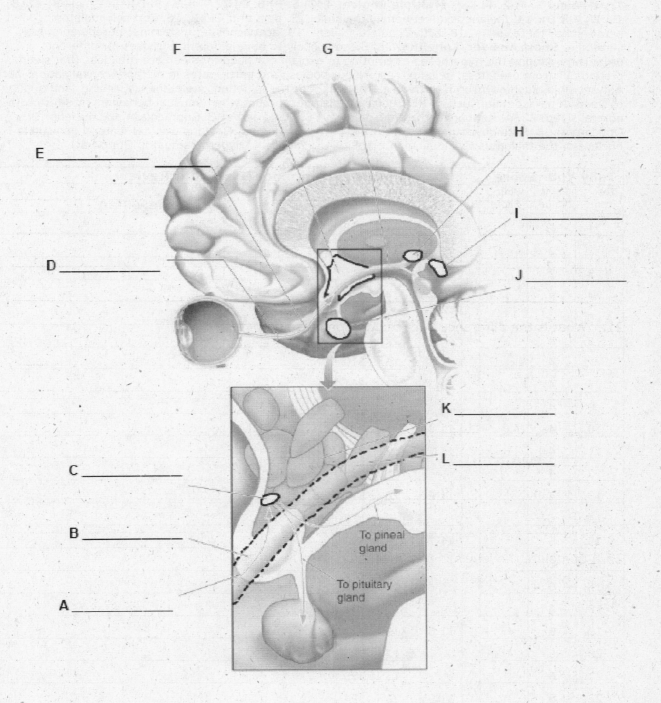

To pineal gland

To pituitary gland

EXERCISE 11.3 ANSWER KEY

True-False: 1. F; 2. T; 3. F. **Multiple Choice:** 4. C) 5. B) 6. D) 7. A) 8. B) 9. D) 10. C) 11. B) 12. B) 13. D) **Fill In:** 14. melanopsin; retinohypothalamic. 15. per; tim; Clock. 16. Cortisol; melatonin. 17. beta; alpha; theta; delta. 18. active; quieter; silent. 19. acetylcholine; histamine; norepinephrine; serotonin. **Short Answer/Labeling:** 20. Sleep is likely to have different purposes for different organisms. Among the hypotheses attempting to explain our need for sleep are the ideas that sleep protects us from predators, helps us restore our bodies, and participates in memory consolidation. 21. A dyssomnia, such as insomnia, involve problems with the initiation, maintenance, timing, and quality of sleep. A parasomnia, such as REM behavior disorder, occurs when unusual behaviors interfere with normal sleep. 22. A. Retinohypothalamic pathway; B. Optic nerve; C. Suprachiasmatic nucleus; D. Optic nerve; E. Retinohypothalamic pathway; F. Hypothalamus; G. Optic tract; H. Lateral geniculate nucleus of the thalamus; I. Pineal gland; J. Pituitary gland; K. Hypothalamus; L. Optic tract.

Tally Your Score			Analyze Your Performance/Plan Your Review			
Test Item	Point Value	Your Score	LO	Test Item	Text Page	**Your Review Plan**
1.	2		11.1	1	313	
2.	2			4	314	
3.	2		11.2	5	315	
4.	4			14	315	
5.	4			15	317	
6.	4			22	317	
7.	4			16	319	
8.	4		11.3	17	321	
9.	4			6	322	
10.	4		11.4	7	323	
11.	4		11.5	2	324	
12.	4			8	325	
13.	4		11.6	20	327	
14.	6			9	328	
15.	6		11.7	3	330	
16.	6			10	330	
17.	6			18	330	
18.	6			11	331	
19.	6		11.8	19	332	
20.	6			12	333	
21.	6			13	335	
22.	6		11.9	21	334	
TOTAL	100					

Chapter 12. Learning and Memory

EXERCISE 12.1 IDENTIFYING KEY TERMS AND THEIR DEFINITIONS

A. Terms Related to Learning

1.	A type of learning in which the experience of one stimulus heightens response to subsequent stimuli.
2.	A type of learning in which the response to a repeated, harmless stimulus becomes progressively weaker.
3.	In classical conditioning, an initially neutral event that takes on the ability to signal other biologically significant events.
4.	A type of associative learning in which a neutral stimulus acquires the ability to signal the occurrence of a second, biologically significant event.
5.	In classical conditioning, an event that elicits a response without prior experience.
6.	In classical conditioning, a spontaneous unlearned reaction to a stimulus without prior experience.
7.	A relatively permanent change in behavior or the capacity for behavior due to experience.
8.	An involuntary response to a stimulus.
9.	In classical conditioning, a learned reaction to the conditioned stimulus.
10.	A stereotyped pattern of behavior elicited by particular environmental stimuli.

- instinct
- learning
- reflex
- classical conditioning
- conditioned response (CR)

- conditioned stimulus (CS)
- habituation
- sensitization
- unconditioned response (UCR)
- unconditioned stimulus (UCS)

B. Terms Related to Memory

1.	Memory loss for information processed following damage to the brain.
2.	An intermediate memory store in which limited amounts of data can be held for a limited amount of time; without further processing, such information is permanently lost.
3.	A type of declarative, explicit memory for personal experience.
4.	A type of implicit memory for performing learned skills and tasks.
5.	An initial stage in memory formation in which large amounts of data can be held for very short periods.
6.	A physical memory trace in the brain.
7.	A type of synaptic plasticity in which the application of a rapid series of electrical shocks to an input pathway increases the postsynaptic potentials recorded in target neurons

8.	A memory store in which apparently unlimited amounts of data can be held for an unlimited amount of time.
9.	A type of declarative, explicit memory for facts and verbal information.
10.	An explicit memory for semantic and episodic information that can easily be verbalized, or "declared."

- declarative memory
- episodic memory
- long-term memory
- procedural memory
- semantic memory

- sensory memory
- short-term memory
- anterograde amnesia
- engram
- long-term potentiation (LTP)

EXERCISE 12.1 ANSWER KEY

A. Terms Related to Learning
1. sensitization (p. 342)
2. habituation (p. 342)
3. conditioned stimulus (CS) (p. 342)
4. classical conditioning (p. 342)
5. unconditioned stimulus (UCS) (p. 342)

6. unconditioned response (UCR) (p. 342)
7. learning (p. 341)
8. reflex (p. 341)
9. conditioned response (CR) (p. 342)
10. instinct (p. 341)

B. Terms Related to Memory
1. anterograde amnesia (p. 354)
2. short-term memory (p. 353)
3. episodic memory (p. 353)
4. procedural memory (p. 353)
5. sensory memory (p. 353)

6. engram (p. 354)
7. long-term potentiation (LTP) (p. 359)
8. long-term memory (p. 353)
9. semantic memory (p. 353)
10. declarative memory (p. 353)

EXERCISE 12.2 LEARNING BY COLORING

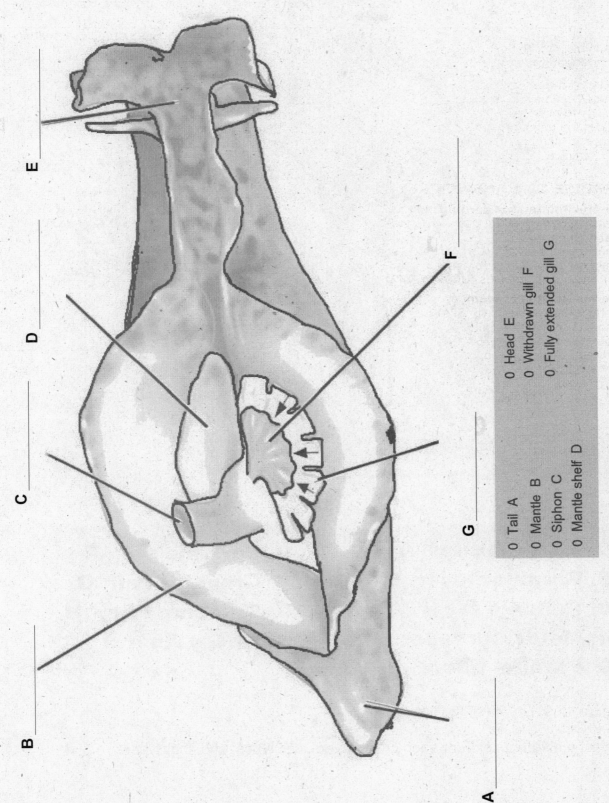

0 Tail A   0 Head E
0 Mantle B   0 Withdrawn gill F
0 Siphon C   0 Fully extended gill G
0 Mantle shelf D

Figure 12.3 The Anatomy of *Aplysia*

Select different colors for each of the labeled structures.

Layers of the
cerebellar cortex

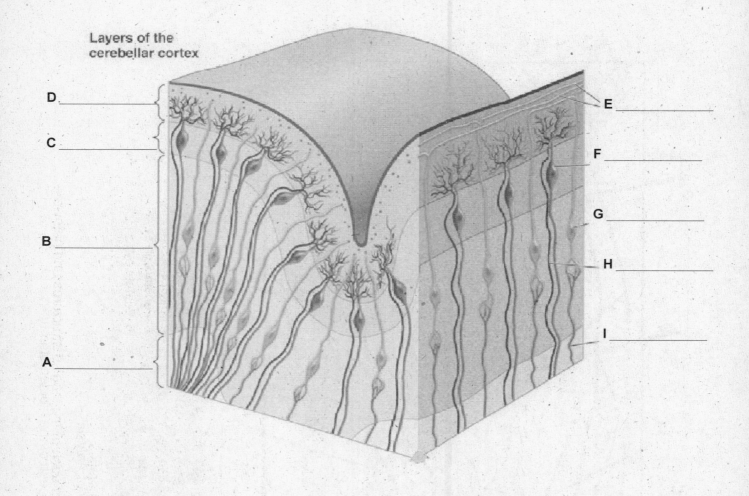

Figure 12.9 Layers of the Cerebellum

Select a different color for each of the layers, cell types, and fiber types.

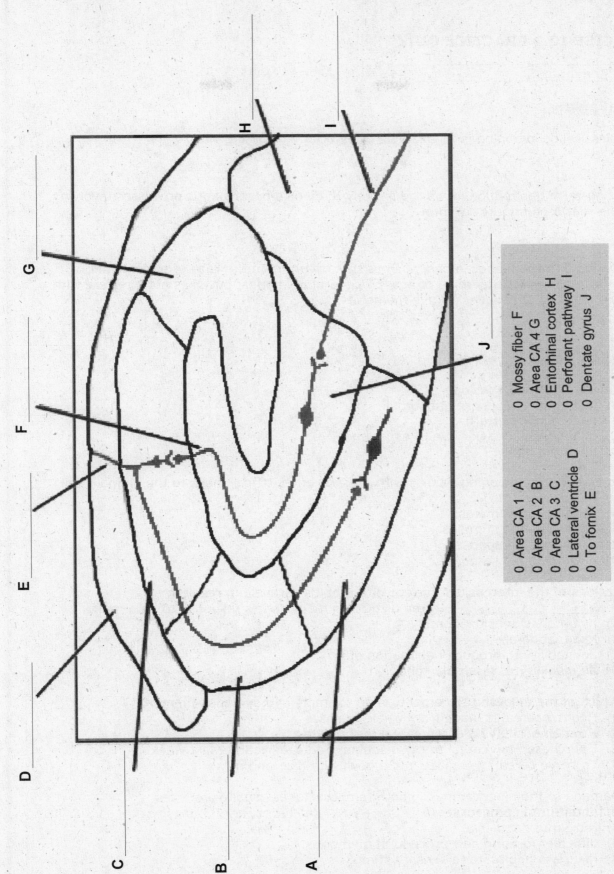

Figure 12.17 The Hippocampus

Select a different color for each of the labeled structures and pathways.

0 Area CA 1 A   0 Mossy fiber F
0 Area CA 2 B   0 Area CA 4 G
0 Area CA 3 C   0 Entorhinal cortex H
0 Lateral ventricle D 0 Perforant pathway I
0 To fornix E   0 Dentate gyrus J

EXERCISE 12.3 PRACTICE QUIZ

Time: 50 minutes

True–False

1. Classical conditioning is an example of associative learning.

        T   F

2. Long-term habituation in *Aplysia* is likely to involve postsynaptic processes involving the NMDA glutamate receptor.

        T   F

3. Damage to the hippocampus, such as that occurring in the case of patient H.M., interferes with the learning of new procedural memories, but does not interfere with the learning of new declarative memories.

        T   F

Multiple Choice

4. Learned behaviors include
    A) involuntary responses to stimuli.
    B) fixed action patterns.
    C) changes in behavior due to experience.
    D) all of the above.

5. In classical conditioning studies with *Aplysia*, an electrical shock to the animal's tail serves as the
    A) conditioned stimulus.
    B) unconditioned stimulus.
    C) conditioned response.
    D) unconditioned response.

6. Lesions of the interpositus nucleus of a rabbit's cerebellum result in _____ the nictitating membrane's response to an airpuff.
    A) heightened sensitization of
    B) habituation of
    C) an inability to produce habituation of
    D) an inability to classically condition

7. Which of the following statements is an example of a semantic memory?
    A) Healthy cereal is made from whole grains.
    B) I remember having eaten cereal for breakfast.
    C) I purchased my cereal at my neighborhood supermarket last week.
    D) To serve cereal, you place it in a bowl with fruit and milk.

8. Damage to the hippocampus in both temporal lobes usually produces
    A) anterograde amnesia.
    B) retrograde amnesia.
    C) difficulty forming new procedural memories.
    D) failure to habituate to sensory stimuli.

9. Areas CA1 and CA3 are connected by
    A) the perforant pathway.
    B) mossy fibers.
    C) the Schaffer collateral pathway.
    D) the fornix.

10. Spatial learning in mice appears to be very similar to
    A) long-term depression.
    B) long-term potentiation.
    C) delay conditioning.
    D) trace conditioning.

11. The striatum appear to be important in the formation of _____ memories.
    A) episodic
    B) short-term
    C) semantic
    D) procedural

12. Fruit flies formed memories more easily than usual when they were engineered to produce extra amounts of
    A) PKA.
    B) C/EPB.
    C) CREB-1.
    D) CREB-2.

13. High levels of glucocorticoids are correlated with more frequent
    A) false memories.
    B) anterograde amnesia.
    C) retrograde amnesia.
    D) flashbulb memories.

Fill In

14. _____ is an example of associative learning, and
    _____ and _____ are examples of non-associative learning.

15. In Kandel's work on classical conditioning in *Aplysia*, touching the mantle serves as the _____ stimulus, shocking the tail serves as the _____ stimulus, and gill withdrawal following a mantle touch serves as the _____ response.

16. Purkinje cells in the cerebellum receive input from granule cells via _____ fibers and from the inferior olive via _____ fibers.

17. The three stages of memory in the Atkinson-Shiffrin model are the _____, _____, and _____.

18. The _____ and the _____ appear
    to provide the executive attentional functions needed in short-term memory.

19. The biochemical sequence in sensitization in *Aplysia* begins with the binding of
    _____ by a sensory neuron, which activates _____, leading to the
    conversion of ATP to _____, which then activates _____.

Short Answer/Labeling

20. What is a Hebbian synapse?

    _____

    _____

    _____

    _____

    _____

    _____

21. Describe the Yerkes-Dodson Law.

    _____

    _____

    _____

    _____

    _____

    _____

22. Complete the labels in the figure that follows.

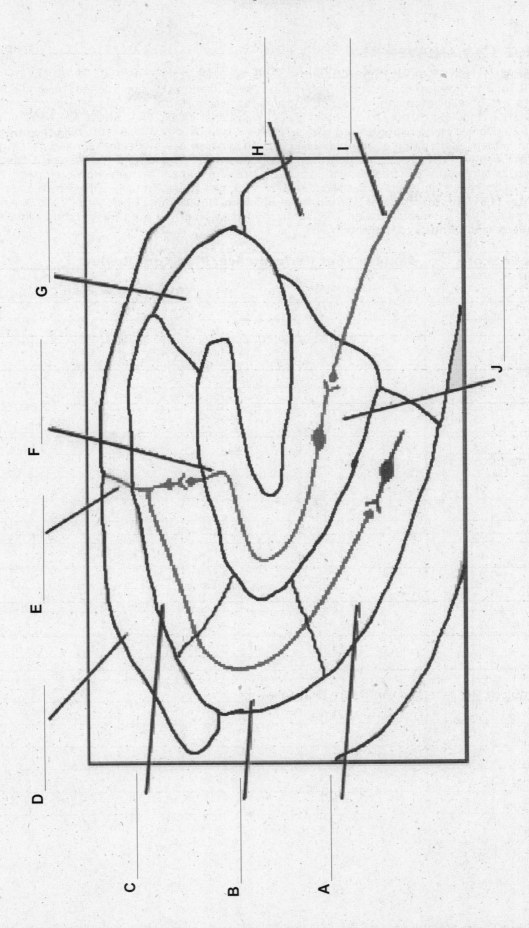

EXERCISE 12.3 ANSWER KEY

True-False: 1. T; 2. T; 3. F. **Multiple Choice:** 4. C) 5. B) 6. D) 7. A) 8. A) 9. C) 10. B) 11. D) 12. C) 13. A). **Fill In:** 14. Classical conditioning; habituation; sensitization. 15. conditioned; unconditioned; conditioned. 16. parallel; climbing. 17. sensory; short-term; long-term. 18. dorsolateral prefrontal cortex; anterior cingulate cortex. 19. serotonin; adenyl cyclase; cAMP; PKA. **Short Answer/ Labeling:** 20. Donald Hebb hypothesized that synapses would become more efficient if the firing of one neuron influences the firing of another. The Hebbian synapse is a model for learning at the neural level that fits well with the process of long-term potentiation. 21. According to Yerkes and Dodson, performance of simple tasks increases with increased stress in a linear fashion. However, performance of complex tasks shows an inverted U-shaped relationship with stress. Initially, stress increases performance, but with greater stress, performance begins to deteriorate. 22. A. Area CA1; B. Area CA2; C. Area CA3; D. Lateral ventricle; E. To fornix; F. Mossy Fiber; G. Area CA4; H. Entorhinal cortex; I. Perforant pathway; J. Dentate gyrus.

Tally Your Score		
Test Item	Point Value	Your Score
1.	2	
2.	2	
3.	2	
4.	4	
5.	4	
6.	4	
7.	4	
8.	4	
9.	4	
10.	4	
11.	4	
12.	4	
13.	4	
14.	6	
15.	6	
16.	6	
17.	6	
18.	6	
19.	6	
20.	6	
21.	6	
22.	6	
TOTAL	100	

Analyze Your Performance/Plan Your Review			
LO	Test Item	Text Page	**Your Review Plan**
12.1	1	341	
	4	341	
	14	341	
12.2	2	345	
	5	346	
	15	346	
12.3	6	349	
	16	350	
12.4	7	353	
	17	353	
12.5	3	356	
	8	356	
	9	358	
12.6	20	359	
	22	359	
	10	360	
	18	364	
	11	365	
12.7	19	366	
	12	368	
12.8	21	368	
	13	370	

Chapter 13. Lateralization, Language, and Intelligence

EXERCISE 13.1 IDENTIFYING KEY TERMS AND THEIR DEFINITIONS

A. Terms Involved in Hemispheric Localization of Function

1. *Lateralization*	The localization of a function in one hemisphere or the other.
2. *Split lesion*	A treatment for seizure disorder in which the commissures linking the two cerebral hemispheres are severed.
3. *Savant behavior*	Extraordinary skills and talents found in those whose overall level of intellectual functioning usually falls in the mentally retarded range.
4. *prosody*	The use of pitch and intonation in language to convey emotional tone and meaning.

- savant behavior
- lateralization
- split-brain operation
- prosody

B. Terms for Language Disorders

1. *Wernicke*	A condition in which speech is fluent, but comprehension, repetition, and naming are quite poor.
2.	A condition in which comprehension is poor, but the ability to repeat is retained.
3. *transcortical*	A condition in which all language functions are lost, including both language production and comprehension.
4.	A condition characterized by fluent speech and good comprehension but poor repetition and naming, believed to result from damage to the arcuate fasciculus and underlying structures.
5. *global aphasia*	A language disorder resulting from damage to the connections and cortical areas associated with the major language centers.
6.	A condition in which language is not fluent, but the ability to repeat is retained.
7. *Broca*	A condition marked by the production of slow, laborious speech accompanied by good comprehension, poor repetition, and poor naming.

- Broca's aphasia
- Wernicke's aphasia
- conduction aphasia
- global aphasia
- transcortical aphasia
- transcortical motor aphasia
- transcortical sensory aphasia

C. Terms for Reading and Writing Disorders

1.	A condition in which a person can spell phonetically but experiences difficulty spelling words that are spelled irregularly, such as *rough.*
2.	The inability to write in a person who previously had the ability.
3.	To abnormally repeat or prolong speech sounds when speaking.
4.	The inability to write by sounding out words.
5.	A condition characterized by difficulty learning to read in spite of normal intelligence and exposure to standard instruction.
6.	The inability to read in a person who previously had the ability.
7.	The ability to discriminate between rapidly presented speech sounds.

- agraphia
- alexia
- dyslexia
- orthographic agraphia
- phonological agraphia
- phonological awareness
- stutter

D. Terms Related to the Ability to Learn

1.	The capacity to acquire and apply knowledge.
2.	A single trait believed by some to determine a person's overall level of intelligence.

- intelligence
- general intelligence (g) factor

EXERCISE 13.1 ANSWER KEY

A. Terms Involved in Hemispheric Localization of Function
1. lateralization (p. 376)
2. split-brain operation (p. 377)
3. savant behavior (p. 374)
4. prosody (p. 382)

B. Terms for Language Disorders
1. Wernicke's aphasia (p. 391)
2. transcortical sensory aphasia (p. 392)
3. global aphasia (p. 392)
4. conduction aphasia (p. 392)
5. transcortical aphasia (p. 392)
6. transcortical motor aphasia (p. 392)
7. Broca's aphasia (p. 390)

C. Terms for Reading and Writing Disorders
1. orthographic agraphia (p. 394)
2. agraphia (p. 394)
3. stutter (p. 396)
4. phonological agraphia (p. 394)
5. dyslexia (p. 394)
6. alexia (p. 394)
7. phonological awareness (p. 395)

D. Terms Related to the Ability to Learn
1. intelligence (p. 396)
2. general intelligence (g) factor (p. 398)

EXERCISE 13.2 LEARNING BY COLORING

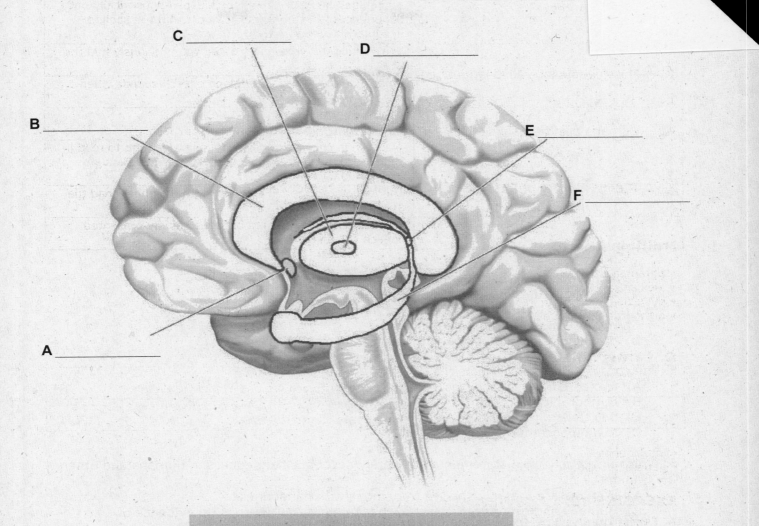

C_____   D_____

B_____   E_____

                                       F_____

A_____

0	Anterior commissure A
0	Corpus callosum B
0	Thalamus C
0	Massa intermedia D
0	Hippocampal commissure E
0	Hippocampus F

Figure 13.3 Commissures

Select a different color for each of the labeled fiber pathways and structures.

EXERCISE 13.3 PRACTICE QUIZ

Time: 50 minutes

True–False

1. Most people lateralize language to the left hemisphere.

    T   F

2. Humans are the only species with mirror neurons.

    T   F

3. The heritability of intelligence is estimated to be between 60 and 80 percent.

    T   F

Multiple Choice

4. Savant behaviors typically affect functions that are
    A) lateralized to the left hemisphere in most people.
    B) lateralized to the right hemisphere in most people.
    C) not lateralized in most people.
    D) managed by caudal parts of the cerebral cortex.

5. The corpus callosum connects the
    A) two cerebral hemispheres.
    B) temporal lobes.
    C) two thalamic nuclei.
    D) two hippocampi.

6. Which of the following statements accurately describes handedness in humans and other animals?
    A) Humans are the only species to demonstrate handedness.
    B) Humans and other primates show handedness, but there is no evidence of lateralization in non-primate species.
    C) Humans and many other animals use a preferred hand, and the ratio of right-to-left handers is about the same in all species.
    D) Humans and many other animals use a preferred hand, but the ratio of right-to-left handers is much larger in humans than in other species.

7. Language is lateralized to the right hemisphere in
    A) nearly all right-handed people, but in a very small minority of left-handed people.
    B) nearly all left-handed people, but in a very small minority of right-handed people.
    C) about a fourth of left-handed people and in a very small minority of right-handed people.
    D) about half of both right- and left-handed people.

8. A mutation in which of the following genes might have led to the development of language?
    A) FOXP2
    B) FMR-1
    C) BRCA
    D) CREB-1

9. The ability of some apes to learn signs by watching the training of others meets which of the following criteria for language?
   A) semanticity
   B) duality
   C) cultural transmission
   D) creativity

10. Imaging studies of people using ASL show that ASL
    A) is managed by the right hemisphere and spoken English by the left in most people.
    B) is managed by the left hemisphere and spoken English by the right in most people.
    C) is managed by the parietal lobe and spoken English in the frontal and temporal lobes in most people.
    D) and spoken English activate the same areas in the brain in most people.

11. A patient who can comprehend most language but who experiences difficulty speaking will likely be diagnosed with
    A) Wernicke's aphasia.
    B) Broca's aphasia.
    C) conduction aphasia.
    D) global aphasia.

12. The excellent verbal skills found in children with Williams syndrome supports
    A) Spearman's general intelligence (g) factor.
    B) a strong role for the environment in intelligence.
    C) the existence of multiple types of intelligence.
    D) the possibility that savant behaviors can be taught to children.

13. Individuals with IQs over 130 are _____ and make up _____ percent of the population.
    A) gifted; about 2
    B) savant; less than 1
    C) above average; about 14
    D) average, nearly 70

Fill In

14. Spatial relations and intuition are normally managed by the _____ hemisphere, whereas language and logic are normally managed by the _____ hemisphere in most people.

15. According to Aitchison, true language is characterized by the ability to produce novel utterances, or _____, the use of symbols, or _____, and the ability to use language without training, or _____.

16. Conduction aphasia results from damage to the _____,

    transcortical motor aphasia results from damage to the _____,

    and transcortical sensory aphasia results from damage to the

    _____.

17. In the language model proposed by Dronkers et al., the language implementation

    system includes _____, _____,

    _____, and _____.

18. People with _____ cannot read at all, whereas people with _____

    have difficulty learning to read in spite of normal intelligence and instruction.

19. Typical readers and readers with dyslexia show different levels of activity in the

    _____, _____, and _____.

Short Answer/Labeling

20. Describe the implications of dichotic listening tasks for our understanding of
    hemisphere lateralization for language.

    _____

    _____

    _____

    _____

    _____

21. What are some of the brain correlates associated with stuttering?

    _____

    _____

    _____

    _____

    _____

22. Complete the labels in the figure that follows.

C _____

D _____

B _____

E _____

F _____

A _____

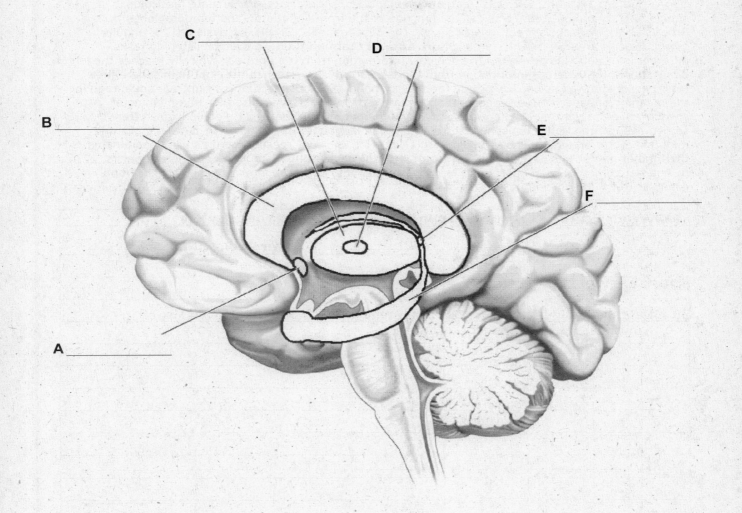

Exercise 13.3 ANSWER KEY

True-False: 1. T; 2. F; 3. T. **Multiple Choice:** 4. B) 5. A) 6. D) 7. C) 8. A) 9. C) 10. D) 11. B) 12. C) 13. A). **Fill In:** 14. right; left. 15. creativity; semanticity, spontaneity. 16. arcuate fasciculus; supplementary motor area; cortex at the junction of the frontal, parietal, and temporal lobes. 17. Broca's area; Wernicke's area; insular cortex; the basal ganglia. 18. alexia; dyslexia. 19. angular gyrus; Broca's area; Wernicke's area. **Short Answer/Labeling:** 20. In dichotic listening tasks, different information is presented to each ear. Information from the right ear typically reaches the left hemisphere first, whereas information from the left ear typically reaches the right hemisphere first. Most people show a left-ear advantage for the emotional tone of speech and a right-ear advantage for the meaning of speech. This suggests that the left hemisphere is specialized for the meaning of speech while the right hemisphere processes emotional tone in speech. 21. People who stutter sometimes use the right hemisphere to process some language. In addition, the basal ganglia and midbrain motor areas are also involved in this behavior. Because these structures use dopamine as their major neurotransmitter, some cases of stuttering can be improved with dopamine agonists. 22. A. Anterior commissure; B. Corpus callosum; C. Thalamus; D. Massa intermedia; E. Hippocampal commissure; F. Hippocampus.

Tally Your Score

Test Item	Point Value	Your Score
1.	2	
2.	2	
3.	2	
4.	4	
5.	4	
6.	4	
7.	4	
8.	4	
9.	4	
10.	4	
11.	4	
12.	4	
13.	4	
14.	6	
15.	6	
16.	6	
17.	6	
18.	6	
19.	6	
20.	6	
21.	6	
22.	6	
TOTAL	100	

Analyze Your Performance/Plan Your Review

LO	Test Item	Text Page	Your Review Plan
13.1	4	375	
	5	377	
	22	377	
13.2	14	379	
	6	380	
13.3	1	377	
	7	381	
	20	381	
13.4	8	385	
13.5	15	385	
	2	387	
	9	387	
13.6	10	389	
13.7	11	390	
	16	390	
	17	393	
	18	394	
	19	396	
	21	396	
13.8	12	398	
13.9	3	398	
	13	400	

Chapter 14. Emotion, Reward, Aggression, and Stress

EXERCISE 14.1 IDENTIFYING KEY TERMS AND THEIR DEFINITIONS

A. Terms Related to Emotional Expression

1.	The ability to relate to the feelings of another person.
2.	A theory of emotion in which general arousal leads to cognitive assessment of the context, which in turn leads to the identification of an emotional state.
3.	The relief of tension through the expression of emotion.
4.	A theory of emotion in which the simultaneous activation of physical responses and the recognition of subjective feelings occur independently.
5.	A theory of emotion in which a person's physical state provides cues for the identification of an emotional state.
6.	A combination of physical sensations and the conscious experience of a feeling.

- emotion
- James-Lange theory
- catharsis
- empathy
- Cannon-Bard theory
- Schachter-Singer theory

B. Terms Related to Positive Emotions, Negative Emotions, and Health

1.	The intentional initiation of a hostile or destructive act.
2.	A three-stage model for describing the body's response to stress developed by Hans Selye.
3.	A fiber pathway that is a major site for electrical self-stimulation. The MFB connects the substantia nigra and ventral tegmental area with higher forebrain structures, including the hypothalamus and nucleus accumbens.
4.	The first stage of Selye's General Adaptation Syndrome, characterized by activation of the sympathetic nervous system and mental alertness.
5.	A source of stress.
6.	A behavior engaged in willingly by research subjects that leads to electrical stimulation of certain parts of the brain.
7.	An unpleasant and disruptive state resulting from the perception of danger or threat.
8.	The second stage in Selye's General Adaptation Syndrome, characterized by the person's efforts to maintain normal activities while coping with stress.
9.	The final stage of Selye's General Adaptation Syndrome, characterized by extremely low reserves of strength and energy.

- electrical self-stimulation of the brain (ESB) (p. 419)
- medial forebrain bundle (MFB) (p. 419)
- aggression (p. 421)
- alarm reaction (p. 425)

- exhaustion stage (p. 425)
- General Adaptation Syndrome (GAS) (p. 425)
- resistance stage (p. 425)
- stress (p. 425)
- stressor (p. 425)

EXERCISE 14.1 ANSWER KEY

A. Terms Related to Emotional Expression
1. empathy (p. 410)
2. Schachter-Singer theory (p. 411)
3. catharsis (p. 410)
4. Cannon-Bard theory (p. 411)
5. James-Lange theory (p. 409)
6. emotion (p. 403)

B. Terms Related to Positive Emotions, Negative Emotions, and Health
1. aggression (p. 421)
2. General Adaptation Syndrome (GAS) (p. 425)
3. medial forebrain bundle (MFB) (p. 419)
4. alarm reaction (p. 425)
5. stressor (p. 425)
6. electrical self-stimulation of the brain (ESB) (p. 419)
7. stress (p. 425)
8. resistance stage (p. 425)
9. exhaustion stage (p. 425)

EXERCISE 14.2 LEARNING BY COLORING

C _____

D _____

E _____

B _____

A _____

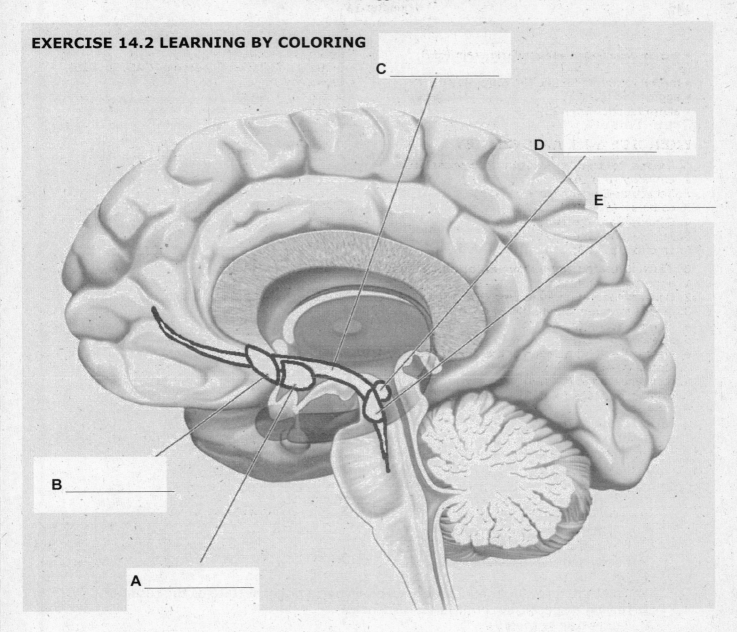

0 Lateral hypothalamus A
0 Nucleus accumbens B
0 Medial forebrain bundle (MFB) C
0 Substantia nigra D
0 Ventral tegmental area E

Figure 14.16 The Dopamine Reward Circuit

Use a different color for each of the labeled structures and pathways.

EXERCISE 14.3 PRACTICE QUIZ

Time: 50 minutes

True–False

1. Infants who respond strongly to environmental stimuli have a greater risk for anxiety and depression later in life.

    T   F

2. People with damage to their amygdalas have trouble identifying facial expressions of fear.

    T   F

3. Each major emotion produces a distinct and non-overlapping pattern of activation in the brain.

    T   F

Multiple Choice

4. The general positive or negative qualities of an emotion make up its
    A) subjectivity.
    B) objectivity.
    C) ability to produce catharsis.
    D) valence.

5. Increased activity in the amygdala is correlated with
    A) a generally positive mood.
    B) a generally negative mood.
    C) increased catharsis.
    D) decreased aggressiveness.

6. Which of the following theories views a subjective emotional state as the result of perceiving a specific set of physical responses?
    A) James-Lange theory
    B) Cannon-Bard theory
    C) Schachter-Singer theory
    D) somatic marker theory

7. Individuals with which of the following disorders show exaggerated responses in the amygdala when shown facial expressions of fear?
    A) autism
    B) schizophrenia
    C) social phobia
    D) antisocial personality disorder

8. People with damage to their right cerebral hemisphere
    A) often experience depression.
    B) are less likely to be depressed than patients with left hemisphere damage.
    C) experience little change in their emotional lives.
    D) are more violent than people with left hemisphere damage.

9. Electrical stimulation of the medial forebrain bundle usually results in
    A) increased fear.
    B) aggression.
    C) decreased fear.
    D) pleasure and reward.

10. Drugs that boost the activity of which of the following neurotransmitters are most likely to be addictive?
    A) glutamate
    B) acetylcholine
    C) dopamine
    D) serotonin

11. Damage to the orbitofrontal cortex is correlated with increases in
    A) impulsive aggression.
    B) premeditated aggression.
    C) social phobia.
    D) pleasure and reward.

12. Which of the following experiences is consistent with Selye's "resistance" stage?
    A) You experience a close call on the freeway, and you are aware of your heart racing.
    B) You are working hard on your senior thesis over a period of several months.
    C) You have to be taken by your roommates to the health center because you just refuse to get out of bed and attend class or go to work anymore.
    D) You are diagnosed with major depressive disorder, and decide to withdraw from classes this term.

13. At times of stress, corticotrophin-releasing hormone (CRH) is released by the
    A) hippocampus.
    B) adrenal glands.
    C) anterior pituitary gland.
    D) hypothalamus.

Fill In

14. The _____ nerves controlling the muscles responsible for facial expression receive input from the _____ nuclei, which in turn receive input from _____ cortex via the _____ tract.

15. The three classic theories of emotion are the _____, _____, and _____ theories.

16. The medial forebrain bundle (MFB) connects the _____ and _____ to forebrain structures, including the _____ and _____.

17. Aggression is correlated with high levels of the hormone _____ and low activity by the neurotransmitter _____.

18. The three stages of the general adaptation syndrome are _____,
    _____, and _____.

19. The "HPA" in the HPA axis stands for the _____,
    _____, and _____.

Short Answer/Labeling

20. What are the drawbacks regarding the use of polygraphs for lie detection?

    _____

    _____

    _____

    _____

    _____

    _____

21. Describe the "fear circuit" discussed by Joseph LeDoux and his colleagues.

    _____

    _____

    _____

    _____

    _____

    _____

22. Complete the labels in the figure that follows.

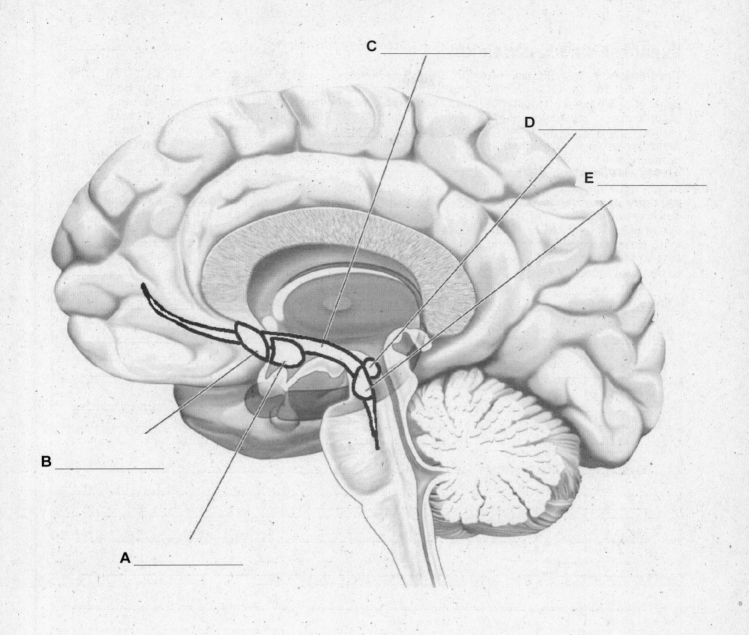

EXERCISE 14.3 ANSWER KEY

True-False: 1. T; 2. T; 3. F. **Multiple Choice:** 4. D) 5. B) 6. A) 7. C) 8. B) 9. D) 10. C) 11. A) 12. B) 13. D). **Fill In:** 14. facial; facial; primary motor; corticobulbar. 15. James-Lange; Cannon-Bard; Schachter-Singer. 16. substantia nigra; ventral tegmental area; lateral hypothalamus; nucleus accumbens. 17. testosterone; serotonin. 18. alarm; resistance; exhaustion. 19. hypothalamus; pituitary gland; adrenal glands. **Short Answer/Labeling:** 20. Standard polygraph equipment measures arousal. Consequently, about one third of innocent people will "fail" a polygraph test, probably due to arousal resulting from being accused of wrongdoing. About one quarter of guilty people will "pass" a polygraph test, as some antisocial people are not capable of feeling remorse or other emotional states as a result of wrongdoing. Overall, polygraphs are accurate only 65 percent of the time. 21. LeDoux described a circuit connecting the thalamus and the amygdala as providing a quick, automatic focus of attention on potentially dangerous stimuli, such as a snake in the road. This circuit operates relatively independently of any cortical input, as evidenced by the ability of rats to learn classically conditioned fear even following damage to the sensory areas of the cortex. 22. A. Lateral hypothalamus; B. Nucleus accumbens; C. Medial forebrain bundle (MFB); D. Substantia nigra; E. Ventral tegmental area.

Tally Your Score				Analyze Your Performance/Plan Your Review			
Test Item	Point Value	Your Score		LO	Test Item	Text Page	Your Review Plan
1.	2			14.1	4	403	
2.	2			14.2	14	404	
3.	2				1	407	
4.	4				5	407	
5.	4				20	408	
6.	4			14.3	15	408	
7.	4				6	409	
8.	4			14.4	2	415	
9.	4				21	415	
10.	4				7	416	
11.	4				8	417	
12.	4				3	418	
13.	4			14.5	9	419	
14.	6				10	419	
15.	6				16	419	
16.	6				22	420	
17.	6			14.6	11	423	
18.	6				17	423	
19.	6			14.7	12	425	
20.	6				18	425	
21.	6				13	426	
22.	6				19	426	
TOTAL	100						

Chapter 15. Neurological Disorders

EXERCISE 15.1 IDENTIFYING KEY TERMS AND THEIR DEFINITIONS

A. Terms Related to Brain Damage

1.	A head injury in which the brain is penetrated, as in a gunshot wound.
2.	An area of brain damage at the site of the blow to the head.
3.	A head injury that results from a blow to the head without penetration of the brain or from a blow to another part of the body that results in force transmitted to the brain.
4.	A condition caused by bleeding in the brain.
5.	A type of brain damage caused by an interruption of the blood supply to the brain.
6.	A condition in which inadequate blood flow results in insufficient quantities of oxygen being delivered to tissue.
7.	A therapeutic process designed to restore function after illness or injury.
8.	A type of brain damage caused by repeated concussions.
9.	An independent growth of tissue that lacks purpose.
10.	An area of brain damage that occurs on the opposite side of the head from the original site of the blow, or coup.

- cerebral hemorrhage
- ischemia
- concussion
- countercoup
- stroke
- coup
- tumor
- rehabilitation
- open head injury
- chronic traumatic brain injury (CTBI)

B. Terms for Electrical Disturbances

1.	A seizure that affects the brain symmetrically without a clear point of origin.
2.	A seizure with symptoms that relate to the functions of the focal area.
3.	A disorder characterized by repeated seizure activity in the brain.
4.	A mild type of generalized seizure in which the patient experiences a brief period of unconsciousness.
5.	A type of partial seizure originating in the temporal lobes.
6.	A seizure that has a clear area of origin, or focus.
7.	A generalized seizure that results in violent convulsions; also known as a tonic-clonic seizure.

8.	The initial stage of a grand mal seizure, in which the patient experiences a loss of consciousness, cessation of breathing, and muscular contraction.
9.	An uncontrolled electrical disturbance in the brain.
10.	The second phase of a grand mal seizure, characterized by violent, repetitious muscle contractions.

- epilepsy
- generalized seizure
- partial seizure
- seizure
- complex partial seizure

- petit mal seizure
- simple partial seizure
- clonic phase
- tonic phase
- grand mal seizure

C. Terms Related to Other Brain Disorders

1.	A condition characterized by inflammation of the brain.
2.	A human TSE resembling classic CJD that results from consumption of beef products contaminated by BSE.
3.	A disease that can be transferred from one animal to another and that produces a fatal, degenerative condition characterized by dementia and motor disturbance.
4.	A condition characterized by brain cysts resulting from parasitic infection by the pork tapeworm, *T. solium*.
5.	A collection of neurological symptoms that result either directly from the actions of the HIV virus itself or from other opportunistic infections overlooked by the impaired immune system of the HIV patient.
6.	A genetically related condition, usually featuring a severe form of headache, nausea, and sensory distortions.
7.	An autoimmune disorder that targets the central nervous system, resulting in demyelination and damage to axons.
8.	A human TSE that results in a progressively degenerative condition characterized by movement and cognitive disorder.
9.	A form of TSE that primarily affects cattle; mad-cow disease.
10.	A protein particle that lacks nucleic acid and is believed to be responsible for TSEs.

- multiple sclerosis
- neurocysticercosis
- encephalitis
- prion
- migraine
- AIDS dementia complex (ADC)
- bovine spongiform encephalopathy (BSE)
- transmissible spongiform encephalopathy (TSE)
- Creutzfeldt-Jakob disease (CJD)
- new variant Creutzfeldt-Jakob disease (vCJD)

EXERCISE 15. 1 ANSWER KEY

A. Terms Related to Brain Damage
1. open head injury (p. 433)
2. coup (p. 433)
3. concussion (p. 433)
4. cerebral hemorrhage (p. 431)
5. stroke (p. 431)
6. ischemia (p. 431)
7. rehabilitation (p. 452)
8. chronic traumatic brain injury (CTBI) (p. 434)
9. tumor (p. 434)
10. countercoup (p. 433)

B. Terms for Electrical Disturbances
1. generalized seizure (p. 436)
2. simple partial seizure (p. 437)
3. epilepsy (p. 436)
4. petit mal seizure (p. 437)
5. complex partial seizure (p. 437)
6. partial seizure (p. 436)
7. grand mal seizure (p. 437)
8. tonic phase (p. 438)
9. seizure (p. 436)
10. clonic phase (p. 438)

C. Terms Related to Other Brain Disorders
1. encephalitis (p. 441)
2. new variant Creutzfeldt-Jakob disease (vCJD) (p. 446)
3. transmissible spongiform encephalopathy (TSE) (p. 443)
4. neurocysticercosis (p. 440)
5. AIDS dementia complex (ADC) (p. 442)
6. migraine (p. 447)
7. multiple sclerosis (p. 439
8. Creutzfeldt-Jakob disease (CJD) (p. 444)
9. bovine spongiform encephalopathy (BSE) (p. 443)
10. prion (p. 445)

EXERCISE 15.2 PRACTICE QUIZ

Time: 45 minutes

True-False

1. Further brain damage following a stroke is more likely due to excitotoxicity than to a lack of oxygen.

      T   F

2. Having the *E4* variant of the *APOE* gene appears to increase a person's risk of chronic traumatic brain injury (CTBI).

      T   F

3. Encephalitis is a brain infection caused by parasites and bacteria, but not by viruses.

      T   F

Multiple Choice

4. Ischemia refers to
   A) a balloon-like bulge in an artery.
   B) a blockage that does not move from its point of origin.
   C) low oxygen levels in the brain.
   D) a blockage that travels from its place of origin.

5. A coup and countercoup may occur during a
   A) closed head injury.
   B) open head injury.
   C) stroke.
   D) thrombosis.

6. A benign tumor
   A) frequently sheds cells that travel to other parts of the body.
   B) is usually encapsulated.
   C) is likely to reoccur after surgical removal.
   D) is usually infiltrating.

7. Degeneration of myelin is characteristic of
   A) neurocysticercosis.
   B) transmissible spongiform encephalopathy.
   C) meningitis.
   D) multiple sclerosis.

8. Infection with mosquito-borne viruses and *Herpes* viruses can lead to
   A) multiple sclerosis.
   B) encephalitis.
   C) meningitis.
   D) neurocysticercosis.

9. Human forms of transmissible spongiform encephalopathies include
   A) kuru.
   B) scrapie.
   C) bovine spongiform encephalopathy.
   D) neurocysticercosis.

10. Migraine headaches involve abnormalities in the activity of which of the following chemicals?
    A) dopamine
    B) estrogens
    C) serotonin
    D) testosterone

11. A patient with weak muscle tone and poor reflexes is likely to have
    A) encephalitis.
    B) AIDS dementia complex.
    C) frontal lobe damage.
    D) spinal damage.

12. A hypothesis stating that recovery from brain damage is a function of developmental age is known as the
    A) crowding hypothesis.
    B) Kennard principle.
    C) mental muscle approach.
    D) specific skills approach.

13. Which of the following tasks is an example of the "mental muscle" approach to therapy for brain damage?
    A) practicing "driving" in a virtual reality simulator
    B) practicing walking using various levels of support
    C) practicing "attention" by hitting a buzzer every time the patient sees the number 3
    D) practicing life skills, such as bathing and feeding

Fill In

14. A _____ is material that blocks a blood vessel without moving from its place of origin, and an _____ is material that blocks a blood vessel after moving through the circulation from its place of origin.

15. Closed head injuries produce damage at the _____, or point of impact, and at the _____ on the opposite side of the head from the original point of impact.

16. Two types of partial seizures are _____ seizures and _____ seizures, and two types of generalized seizures are _____ seizures and _____ seizures.

17. _____ results from an infection with the pork tapeworm, and usually results in _____ seizures.

18. A sheep version of TSE is known as _____; the TSE affecting cattle is _____; and human TSEs include _____, _____, and _____.

19. During a migraine headache, information travels through the _____ nerve to the meninges and blood supply of the brain in the _____ system, resulting in the release of _____ and _____.

Short Answer/Labeling

20. What are the dangers associated with repeated concussion?

_____

_____

_____

_____

_____

_____

21. What are the symptoms of AIDS dementia complex?

_____

_____

_____

_____

_____

_____

_____

EXERCISE 15.2 ANSWER KEY

True-False: 1. T; 2. T; 3. F. **Multiple Choice:** 4. C) 5. A) 6. B) 7. D) 8. B) 9. A) 10. C) 11. D) 12. B) 13. C). **Fill In:** 14. thrombosis; embolism. 15. coup; countercoup. 16. simple partial; complex partial; grand mal; petit mal. 17. Neurocysticercosis; partial. 18. scrapie; bovine spongiform encephalopathy; kuru, Creutzfeldt-Jakob disease; new variant Creutzfeldt-Jakob disease. 19. trigeminal; trigeminovascular; glutamate; calcitonin gene related peptide. **Short Answer/Labeling:** 20. Repeated concussions can have negative effects on cognition that last for years. In some cases, chronic traumatic brain injury (CTBI) can occur, leading to degeneration that is similar to that found in Alzheimer's disease. CTBI can cause slurred speech, memory impairment, personality changes, lack of coordination, and movement difficulties similar to Parkinson's disease. 21. In its initial stages, AIDS dementia complex produces symptoms similar to major depressive disorder, including difficulty concentrating, low sex drive, apathy, and social withdrawal. As the disease progresses, loss of memory, language impairment, and motor coordination difficulties may occur.

Tally Your Score		
Test Item	Point Value	Your Score
1.	2	
2.	2	
3.	2	
4.	4	
5.	4	
6.	4	
7.	4	
8.	4	
9.	4	
10.	4	
11.	4	
12.	4	
13.	4	
14.	6	
15.	6	
16.	6	
17.	6	
18.	6	
19.	6	
20.	9	
21.	9	
TOTAL	100	

Analyze Your Performance/Plan Your Review			
LO	Test Item	Text Page	Your Review Plan
15.1	4	431	
	1	432	
	14	432	
15.2	2	432	
	5	433	
	15	433	
	20	434	
15.3	16	437	
	6	435	
15.4	7	439	
15.5	17	440	
	3	441	
	8	441	
15.6	21	442	
	18	443	
	9	445	
15.7	10	448	
	19	448	
15.8	11	450	
15.9	12	451	
15.10	13	453	

Chapter 16. Psychological Disorders

EXERCISE 16.1 IDENTIFYING KEY TERMS AND THEIR DEFINITIONS

A. General Terms Related to Mental Illness

1.	The statistical probability that one individual will share a trait with another individual, typically a twin or other related person
2.	An unusual pattern of thinking, feeling, and behaving that is harmful to the self or to others.

- psychological disorder
- concordance rate

B. Terms For Psychological Disorders

1.	A severe lifetime disorder characterized by impairments in social interaction, range of interests, and communication.
2.	An anxiety disorder characterized by repetitive, intrusive thoughts and the need to engage in certain behaviors to control anxiety.
3.	A mood disorder characterized by alternating cycles of mania and depression.
4.	A group of disorders characterized by hallucination, delusion, cognitive impairment, mood disturbance, and social withdrawal.
5.	A personality disorder diagnosed in adults, characterized by a failure to conform to social and legal codes of behavior and the violation of the rights of others.
6.	A disorder first diagnosed in childhood, characterized by inattention, hyperactivity, or both.
7.	A condition characterized by an abnormal lack of remorse and empathy, often leading to the exploitation of others to meet personal goals.
8.	A disorder in which intense feelings of sadness, hopelessness, and worthlessness persist a minimum of two weeks.
9.	An anxiety disorder arising in response to an extremely stressful event, characterized by intrusive memories, recurrent dreams, avoidance of stimuli associated with the stressful event, and heightened arousal.
10.	A condition characterized by repeated panic attacks and worries about having panic attacks.

- schizophrenia
- bipolar disorder
- major depressive disorder
- obsessive-compulsive disorder (OCD)
- panic disorder
- posttraumatic stress disorder (PTSD)

- autism
- antisocial personality disorder (APD)
- psychopathy
- attention deficit/hyperactivity disorder (ADHD)

C. Terms for Symptoms of Psychological Disorders

1.	A false belief or opinion that is strongly held in spite of conclusive, contradictory evidence.
2.	A false or distorted perception of objects or events.
3.	The experience of intense feelings of impending doom and the need to escape accompanied by strong sympathetic arousal, including heart palpitations, sweating, trembling, and shortness of breath.
4.	A normal and expected behavior that is absent due to schizophrenia.
5.	An abnormal behavior, such as hallucination and delusion, that does not occur in healthy individuals but occurs in people with schizophrenia.
6.	An emotional state characterized by abnormally elevated, expansive, or irritable mood.

- delusion
- hallucination
- negative symptom
- positive symptom
- mania
- panic attack

EXERCISE 16.1 ANSWER KEY

A. General Terms Related to Mental Illness
1. concordance rate (p. 458)
2. psychological disorder (p. 457)

B. Terms for Psychological Disorders
1. autism (p. 476)
2. obsessive-compulsive disorder (OCD) (p. 474)
3. bipolar disorder (p. 466)
4. schizophrenia (p. 457)
5. antisocial personality disorder (APD) (p. 480)
6. attention deficit/hyperactivity disorder (ADHD) (p. 478)
7. psychopathy (p. 480)
8. major depressive disorder (p. 466)
9. posttraumatic stress disorder (PTSD) (p. 475)
10. panic disorder (p. 475)

C. Terms for Symptoms of Psychological Disorder
1. delusion (p. 457)
2. hallucination (p. 457)
3. panic attack (p. 475)
4. negative symptom (p. 457)
5. positive symptom (p. 457)
6. mania (p. 471)

EXERCISE 16.2 PRACTICE QUIZ

Time: 45 minutes

True–False

1.   Among the negative symptoms of schizophrenia are social withdrawal and emotional disturbances.

        T   F

2.   Men and women are equally likely to be diagnosed with major depressive disorder.

        T   F

3.   Medications provide an effective means for treating autism spectrum disorder.

        T   F

Multiple Choice

4.   Individuals who experience hallucinations and delusions are likely to be diagnosed with
     A) schizophrenia.
     B) bipolar disorder.
     C) autism.
     D) posttraumatic stress disorder.

5.   Compared to healthy control participants, patients with schizophrenia show decreased activity in the _____ lobes of the brain.
     A) occipital
     B) temporal
     C) parietal
     D) frontal

6.   Dopamine antagonists are used to treat
     A) bipolar disorder.
     B) major depressive disorder.
     C) schizophrenia.
     D) panic disorder.

7.   Decreased activity in the left frontal lobe accompanied by increased activity in the right frontal lobe frequently occurs in people diagnosed with
     A) schizophrenia.
     B) major depressive disorder.
     C) autism.
     D) antisocial personality disorder.

8.   Compared to major depressive disorder, bipolar disorder is
     A) less common.
     B) more common.
     C) about as common.
     D) more common among men, but less common among women.

9.   Consumption of fish is negatively correlated with national prevalences of
     A) autism.
     B) schizophrenia.
     C) bipolar disorder.
     D) major depressive disorder.

10. A smaller-than-normal hippocampus has been implicated in cases of
     A) antisocial personality disorder.
     B) schizophrenia.
     C) obsessive-compulsive disorder.
     D) posttraumatic stress disorder.

11. Smaller cortical minicolumns have been observed in the brains of people with
     A) posttraumatic stress disorder.
     B) autism.
     C) antisocial personality disorder.
     D) obsessive-compulsive disorder.

12. Methylphenidate (Ritalin), which is used to treat attention deficit/hyperactivity disorder
     (ADHD), is most similar to which of the following drugs?
     A) phenothiazines, such as Thorazine
     B) SSRIs, such as Prozac and Zoloft
     C) emphetamines
     D) benzodiazepines, such as Valium

13. Damage to the orbitofrontal cortex is associated with
     A) autism.
     B) attention deficit/hyperactivity disorder (ADHD).
     C) obsessive-compulsive disorder.
     D) antisocial behavior.

Fill In

14. _____ antipsychotic medications serve as dopamine antagonists,
     whereas _____ antipsychotic medications target serotonin and other
     neurotransmitters instead.

15. Bipolar disorder is characterized by periods of inflated mood known as _____,
     which alternate with periods of _____.

16. Obsessive-compulsive disorder is associated with abnormalities in circuits connecting
     the _____, _____, and _____.

17. Abnormalities in the brains of individuals with autism have been observed in the
     _____ and _____.

18. Attention deficit/hyperactivity disorder (ADHD) might result from immaturity in the
     _____ and _____.

19. Antisocial behavior may be correlated with abnormalities in the _____,
     _____, and _____.

Short Answer/Labeling

20. Describe the differences between the brain development of typical teens and those
     who will be later diagnosed with schizophrenia.

     _____

     _____

     _____

     _____

     _____

     _____

21. What is the relationship between major depressive disorder and circadian rhythms?

     _____

     _____

     _____

     _____

     _____

     _____

EXERCISE 16.2 ANSWER KEY

True-False: 1. F; 2. F; 3. F. **Multiple Choice:** 4. A) 5. D) 6. C) 7. B) 8. A) 9. C) 10. D) 11. B) 12. C) 13. D). **Fill In:** 14. Typical; atypical. 15. mania; depression. 16. thalamus; basal ganglia; orbitofrontal cortex. 17. amygdala; cerebellum 18. basal ganglia; prefrontal cortex. 19. amygdala, orbitofrontal cortex; anterior cingulate cortex. **Short Answer/Labeling:** 20. At puberty, gray matter in the brain first increases sharply, and then is thinned during adolescence into the early twenties. Individuals who ultimately will be diagnosed with schizophrenia experience significantly more thinning than healthy teens during this period. 21. Major depressive disorder might result from a phase advance in a person's circadian rhythms that interrupts normal patterns of sleep. Normally, cortisol release peaks around dawn, but people with depression show an earlier peak. Although people with depression may sleep too little or too much, many show frequent wakefulness throughout the night. REM sleep is initiated too early in the sleep cycle, and an abnormally large amount of sleep is REM.

Tally Your Score

Test Item	Point Value	Your Score
1.	2	
2.	2	
3.	2	
4.	4	
5.	4	
6.	4	
7.	4	
8.	4	
9.	4	
10.	4	
11.	4	
12.	4	
13.	4	
14.	6	
15.	6	
16.	6	
17.	6	
18.	6	
19.	6	
20.	9	
21.	9	
TOTAL	100	

Analyze Your Performance/Plan Your Review

LO	Test Item	Text Page	Your Review Plan
16.1	1	457	
	4	457	
16.2	5	462	
	6	462	
	20	462	
	14	464	
16.3	2	466	
	7	468	
	8	471	
	15	471	
16.4	21	468	
	9	471	
16.5	16	474	
	10	475	
16.6	11	477	
	17	477	
	3	478	
16.7	12	479	
	18	479	
16.8	13	481	
	19	481	

Appendix: Latin Pronunciation Guide

One of the factors that can make learning biological psychology terms difficult is the large number of Latin terms. Most college students have had little if any exposure to Latin.

Remembering a term will be much easier if you try to pronounce it. Even if you get it "wrong," it's better than not trying. Biological Latin terms are often pronounced differently than classic Latin. For example, we pronounce the term *virus* as "VYE russ," whereas the classical Latin pronunciation would be "WEE russ."

Many of the margin definitions of key terms in your textbook include pronunciation guides. Ray Cui provides a really good tutorial on Latin pronunciation, including sound files of letters and words: http://la.raycui.com/index.html.

Here are some additional guidelines (with many thanks to Paul Shickle, my Latin teacher at San Marino High School, and Tom Weinschenk, Latin teacher at San Luis Obispo High School.)

PRONOUNCING LETTERS AND LETTER COMBINATIONS

Latin is very phonetic. Nearly all letters are pronounced, and very few are silent, making Latin a much easier language to pronounce than English!

Vowels may be long ("a" as in cake, "i" as in ice) or short ("a" as in cat, "i" as in it). For unfamiliar words, it is difficult to know when a vowel is short or long, so consult your pronunciation guides or Ray Cui's website. Vowels other than "a" appearing at the end of a word are usually long. When an "a" appears at the end of the word, it is pronounced "uh" as in amoeba.

A diphthong is a combination of two vowels that are pronounced as having one sound. The diphthongs include: ae, au, eu, oe, and ui.

Dipthong	Pronounced Like:
ae	a long "i," as in kite
au	"ou" in our
eu	"eu" in feud
oe	"oi" in oil
ui	"we"

Consonants are usually pronounced in very similar ways as in English. Ch is pronounced as "k" as in "chiasm." "C" is usually pronounced as "k," but exceptions occur. For example, the c in sulci is usually pronounced as an "s." In words beginning with two consonants, like pterodactyl, you do not pronounce the first consonant.

Accents are usually on the first syllable of a two-syllable word, like SUL ci. In a word having more than two syllables, we have to make a distinction between "heavy" and "light" syllables. Light syllables contain a short vowel. A heavy syllable, sometimes called a long syllable, contains either a long vowel or a diphthong, or ends in a consonant, like me DUL la or ce RE brum. If the next-to-last syllable is heavy, that's where the accent will be. Otherwise, the accent will be on the antepenult, or the syllable ahead of the penult, as in PO di um. In very long words, a secondary accent might occur on an earlier syllable, such as SU pra chi as MA tic.

MAKING PLURALS

Words ending with "um" are singular, and are usually made plural by dropping the "um" and adding an "a."

> Example: the frequently misused datum (singular) and data (plural). (It is incorrect to say, "the data shows" or "the data is." Correct usage would be "the data show" or "the data are.")

Words ending with an "a" are usually made plural by adding an "e" to form "ae."

> Example: agricola (singular) and agricolae (plural). (Agricola means farmer and is the root of the English "agriculture.") The "ae" is pronounced like a long "i."

Words ending with "us" are made plural by dropping the "us" and adding am "i."

> Example: sulcus (singular) and sulci (plural), nucleus (singular) and nuclei (plural), and colliculus (singular) and colliculi (plural). The "i" at the end of the plurals may be pronounced as long "i" (nuclei) or long "e" (colliculi).

Words ending with "is" are made plural by changing the "i" to "e." The "es" is pronounced with a long "e" sound.

> Example: axis (singular) and axes (plural).

iMac®
3rd Edition

by Guy Hart-Davis

Visual
A Wiley Brand

Teach Yourself VISUALLY™ iMac® 3rd Edition

Published by
John Wiley & Sons, Inc.
10475 Crosspoint Boulevard
Indianapolis, IN 46256

www.wiley.com

Published simultaneously in Canada

Wiley publishes in a variety of print and electronic formats and by print-on-demand. Some material included with standard print versions of this book may not be included in e-books or in print-on-demand. If this book refers to media such as a CD or DVD that is not included in the version you purchased, you may download this material at http://booksupport.wiley.com. For more information about Wiley products, visit www.wiley.com.

Library of Congress Control Number: 2013949551

ISBN: 978-1-118-76806-8

Manufactured in the United States of America

10 9 8 7 6 5 4 3 2 1

Trademark Acknowledgments

Wiley, the Wiley logo, Visual, the Visual logo, Teach Yourself VISUALLY, Read Less - Learn More and related trade dress are trademarks or registered trademarks of John Wiley & Sons, Inc. and/or its affiliates. iMac is a registered trademark of Apple, Inc. All other trademarks are the property of their respective owners. John Wiley & Sons, Inc. is not associated with any product or vendor mentioned in this book. *Teach Yourself VISUALLY™ iMac®, 3rd Edition* is an independent publication and has not been authorized, sponsored, or otherwise approved by Apple, Inc.

Contact Us

For general information on our other products and services please contact our Customer Care Department within the U.S. at 877-762-2974, outside the U.S. at 317-572-3993 or fax 317-572-4002.

For technical support please visit www.wiley.com/techsupport.

Credits

Acquisitions Editor
Aaron Black

Project Editors
Jade L. Williams
Lynn Northrup

Technical Editor
Dennis R. Cohen

Copy Editors
Scott Tullis
Lauren Kennedy

Director, Content Development & Assembly
Robyn Siesky

Vice President and Executive Group Publisher
Richard Swadley

About the Author

Guy Hart-Davis is the author of *Teach Yourself VISUALLY MacBook Pro Second Edition, Teach Yourself VISUALLY MacBook Air, Teach Yourself VISUALLY iMac, iMac Portable Genius Fourth Edition,* and *iWork Portable Genius.*

Author's Acknowledgments

My thanks go to the many people who helped create the highly graphical book you are holding. In particular, I thank Aaron Black for asking me to write the book; Jade Williams and Lynn Northrup for keeping me on track and guiding the editorial process; Scott Tullis and Lauren Kennedy for skillfully editing the text; Dennis Cohen for reviewing the book for technical accuracy and contributing helpful suggestions; and EPS for laying out the book.

How to Use This Book

Who This Book Is For

This book is for the reader who has never used this particular technology or software application. It is also for readers who want to expand their knowledge.

The Conventions in This Book

① Steps

This book uses a step-by-step format to guide you easily through each task. **Numbered steps** are actions you must do; **bulleted steps** clarify a point, step, or optional feature; and **indented steps** give you the result.

② Notes

Notes give additional information — special conditions that may occur during an operation, a situation that you want to avoid, or a cross reference to a related area of the book.

③ Icons and Buttons

Icons and buttons show you exactly what you need to click to perform a step.

④ Tips

Tips offer additional information, including warnings and shortcuts.

⑤ Bold

Bold type shows command names, options, and text or numbers you must type.

⑥ Italics

Italic type introduces and defines a new term.

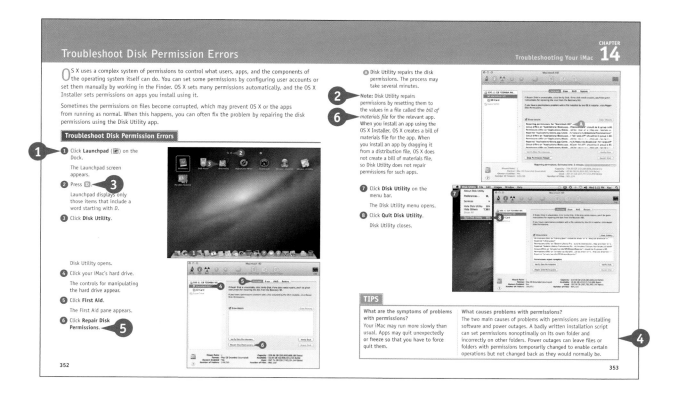

Table of Contents

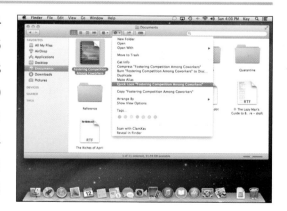

Table of Contents

Chapter 5 — Surfing the Web

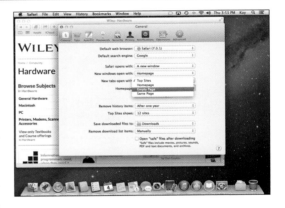

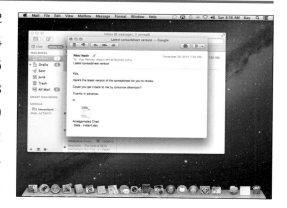

Table of Contents

Table of Contents

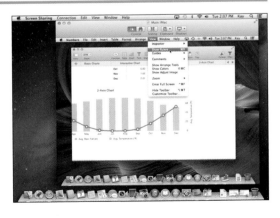

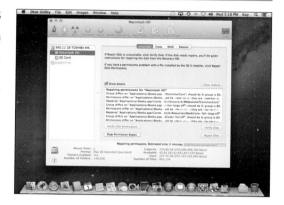

CHAPTER 1

Getting Started with Your iMac

The iMac is a beautifully designed computer and comes with the powerful, easy-to-use OS X operating system. In just a few minutes, you can set up your iMac and begin using it. This chapter shows you how to get started with your iMac, use the OS X interface, and connect extra devices to the iMac.

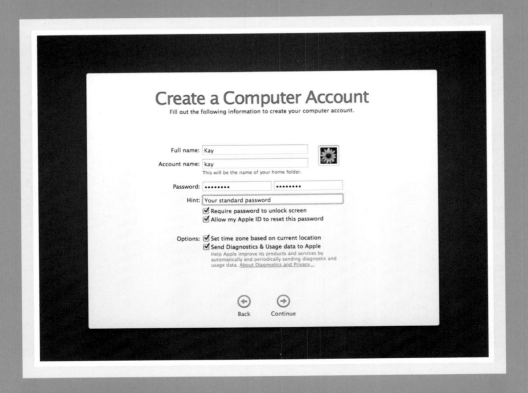

Set Up Your iMac and User Account

I f you have just bought your iMac, you need to connect its hardware, set up OS X, and create your user account before you can use it. Your user account is where you store your files and settings on the iMac.

The first user account you create is an administrator account, which can create other accounts later for other users. You may also choose to create a personal account for yourself, leaving the administrator account strictly for administration.

Set Up Your iMac and User Account

Set Up Your iMac's Hardware

1 Position the iMac on your desk and connect it to power.

2 If your keyboard is wireless, press its power button to turn it on. If you have a wired keyboard, connect its cable to a USB port on the iMac.

3 Turn on your Magic Mouse or Magic Trackpad.

4 Press the power button on the back of your iMac.

The Welcome screen appears.

5 Click your country.

Ⓐ Click **Show All** (☐ changes to ☑) if your country does not appear.

6 Click **Continue** (⊙).

The Select Your Keyboard screen appears.

7 Click your keyboard layout; for example, **U.S.**

Ⓑ Click **Show All** (☐ changes to ☑) if your keyboard layout does not appear.

8 Click **Continue** (⊙).

Ⓒ You can click **Back** (⊙) at any stage in the setup process if you need to go back and change a choice you made.

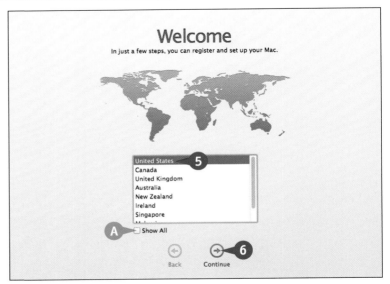

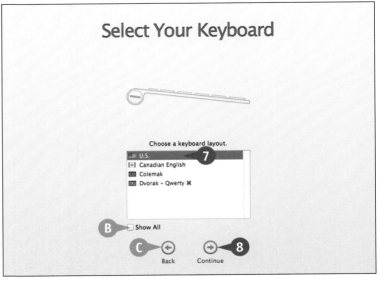

4

The Transfer Information to This Mac screen appears.

9 Click **Don't transfer any information now** (◯ changes to ◉).

Note: If you need to transfer data from another Mac or a backup, click **From a Mac, Time Machine backup, or startup disk** (◯ changes to ◉) and click **Continue** (➡). If you need to transfer data from Windows, click **From a Windows PC** (◯ changes to ◉) and click **Continue** (➡).

10 Click **Continue** (➡).

The Sign In with Your Apple ID screen appears.

11 Click **Sign in with your Apple ID** (◯ changes to ◉) and type your Apple ID and password.

D You can click **Create new Apple ID** to create a new Apple ID.

Note: If you neither have nor want an Apple ID, click **Don't sign in** (◯ changes to ◉).

12 Click **Continue** (➡).

The Allow iCloud to use the location of this Mac for Find My Mac? dialog opens.

13 Click **Allow** or **Not Now**, as appropriate.

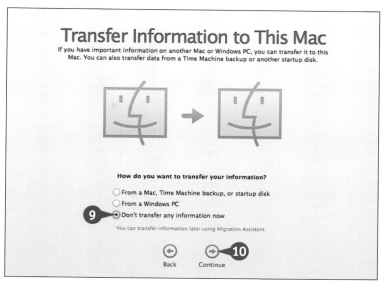

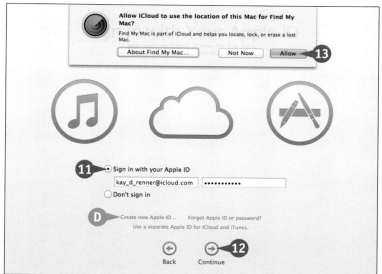

continued ▶

TIPS

Can I use a USB mouse with my iMac?
Yes. You can use any USB mouse for which OS X has a software driver. To use a USB mouse, connect it to one of your iMac's USB ports. If you can move the mouse pointer on the screen, the mouse is working.

What is an Apple ID?
An Apple ID is a free online identity that you use for Apple services such as iCloud, the Mac App Store, and the iTunes Store. To get the most out of your iMac, you should get an Apple ID.

When creating an account, you can use either your full name or a shortened version. You can edit the user name that OS X suggests based on that name. You can choose whether to set a password hint to help yourself remember your password. You can also choose whether to use the iCloud Keychain feature, which enables you to store your passwords and credit-card details securely online. You can then use this information from any Mac, Windows PC, or iOS device with which you use the same Apple ID.

Set Up Your iMac and User Account (continued)

The Create a Computer Account screen appears.

14 Type your name as you want it to appear.

15 Change the account name that OS X suggests as needed.

16 Click the default picture and choose the picture you want. You can also use your iMac's camera to take a photo of yourself.

17 Type a password twice.

18 Optionally, type a password hint.

19 Choose other settings as discussed in the following tip.

20 Click **Continue** (⊙).

The first iCloud Keychain screen appears.

21 Click **Set up iCloud Keychain** (○ changes to ⊙).

22 Click **Continue** (⊙).

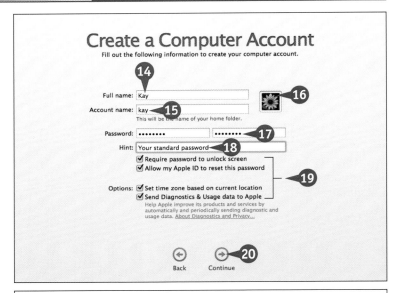

The second iCloud Keychain screen appears.

㉓ Type your iCloud security code.

㉔ Click **Continue** (⊙).

The Register Your Mac screen appears.

㉕ Click **Register this Mac** (◯ changes to ⊙) and type your e-mail address if you want to register your iMac. Otherwise, click **Don't register** (◯ changes to ⊙).

Note: If you choose to register your iMac, click **Keep me up to date with Apple news, and the latest information on products and services** (☑ changes to ☐) if you do not want to receive e-mail messages from Apple.

㉖ Click **Continue** (⊙).

The Setting Up Your Mac screen appears while OS X sets up your iMac.

The OS X desktop appears, and you can start using your iMac as explained in the rest of this book.

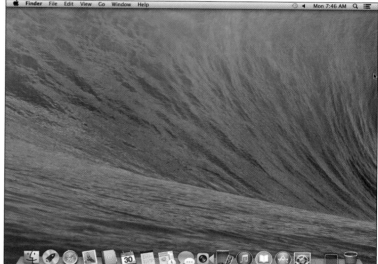

TIP

Which settings should I choose on the Create a Computer Account screen?
Click **Require password to unlock screen** (☐ changes to ☑) to help secure your iMac. Click **Allow my Apple ID to reset this password** (☐ changes to ☑) if you want to be able to use your Apple ID and its password to reset your account password if you forget it. Click **Set time zone based on current location** (☐ changes to ☑) to enable OS X to set the time and date automatically. Click **Send Diagnostics & Usage data to Apple** (☐ changes to ☑) if you want to send anonymized diagnostics and usage data to Apple's servers.

Start Your iMac and Log In

When you are ready to start a computing session, start your iMac and log in to OS X with the credentials for the user account you have set up or an administrator has created for you. After you start your iMac, OS X loads and automatically displays the login screen by default or logs you in automatically. You can then select your user name and type your password.

When you log in, OS X identifies you as the owner of your user account, and displays the OS X desktop with your apps and settings.

Start Your iMac and Log In

1 Press the power button on the back of your iMac.

A screen showing the list of users appears.

Note: Your iMac may not display the list of users and login window. Instead, it may simply log you in automatically or show a different login screen. Chapter 2 shows you how to change this behavior.

Note: You may need to swipe right with two fingers on the Magic Trackpad or Magic Mouse to display your username. Alternatively, start typing the username to display it.

2 Click your username.

The login window appears.

3 Type your password in the Password field.

A If you cannot remember your password, click **Hint** ().

Ⓑ OS X displays your password hint below the password box.

④ Type your password.

⑤ Click **Log In** (⊡).

Note: Instead of clicking **Log In** (⊡), you can press Return.

The iMac displays your desktop, the menu bar, and the Dock. You can now start using the iMac.

TIPS

Why does my iMac go straight to the desktop instead of displaying the list of usernames?
Your iMac is set to log in automatically. Logging in automatically is convenient when you are the only one using your iMac, but it means that anyone who can start your iMac can use it without providing credentials. Chapter 2 shows you how to turn off automatic login.

Why does my iMac not show the list of usernames?
Hiding the list of usernames provides extra security and is widely used in companies, but it is usually not necessary for iMacs used at home. Type your username in the Name field and your password in the Password field, and then click **Log In** (⊡).

Connect to a Wired Network

To get the most out of your iMac, you can connect it to the Internet via either a wired network or a wireless network. By connecting your iMac to a network, you enable it to use the network's Internet connection, such as a cable broadband connection or a Digital Subscriber Line (DSL) connection.

When it is connected to a network, your iMac can also share files and printers with other computers on the network.

Connect to a Wired Network

① Connect one end of a network cable to the Ethernet port on the back of your iMac.

② Connect the other end of the network cable to an Ethernet port on your network switch or network router.

Note: If your Internet router includes a network switch, you can plug the network cable into an Ethernet port on the Internet router.

Your iMac automatically detects the network connection and tries to apply suitable settings.

③ Click **Apple** (🍎).

The Apple menu opens.

④ Click **System Preferences**.

The System Preferences window opens.

⑤ Click **Network**.

The Network preferences pane opens.

6 Click **Ethernet**.

7 Verify that your iMac has an IP address.

8 Click **Close** (⊗).

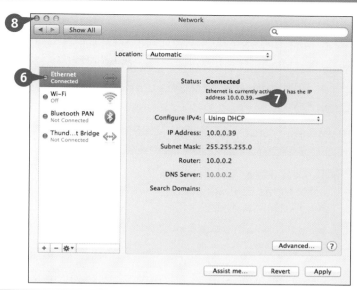

The System Preferences window closes.

9 Click **Safari** (🧭) on the Dock.

A Safari browser window opens and displays your iMac's home page, the page Safari opens automatically.

You have now connected your iMac to the network and the Internet.

TIP

What is an IP address and what is DHCP?

An Internet Protocol address, or IP address, is a number that identifies a computer on a network. An IP address consists of four groups of one, two, or three digits, such as 10.10.0.100 or 192.168.1.10. DHCP stands for Dynamic Host Configuration Protocol and is a way of providing IP addresses to computers on the network. When a computer joins the network, it requests an IP address and other connection information from the DHCP server. Most cable and DSL routers act as DHCP servers.

Connect to a Wireless Network

If you have set up a wireless network, you can connect your iMac to it. Wireless networks are convenient for both homes and businesses because they require no cables and are fast and easy to set up.

Your iMac includes a wireless network card that OS X refers to as Wi-Fi. You can control wireless networks directly from the Wi-Fi menu at the right end of the menu bar. To connect to a Wi-Fi network, you need to know its name and password.

Connect to a Wireless Network

Note: If you connected your iMac to a wireless network during setup, you do not need to set up the connection again.

1. Click the **Wi-Fi status** icon (▽) on the menu bar.

2. Click **Turn Wi-Fi On**.

Note: If the list of wireless networks appears, go to step 4.

OS X turns Wi-Fi on.

3. Click the **Wi-Fi status** icon (🛜) on the menu bar.

The menu opens and displays a list of the wireless networks your iMac can detect.

Ⓐ The No network selected list shows networks that connect using wireless access points. These are called *infrastructure wireless networks*.

Ⓑ The Devices list shows networks created by individual computers or devices such as mobile phones. These are called *ad hoc wireless networks* or *peer-to-peer wireless networks*.

Ⓒ A lock icon (🔒) indicates that the network is secured with a password.

Ⓓ The signal strength icon (🛜) indicates the relative strength of the network's signal.

4. Click the network to which you want to connect your iMac.

If the wireless network uses a password, your iMac prompts you to enter it.

5 Type the password in the Password box.

E If you want to see the characters of the password to help you type it, click **Show password** (☐ changes to ☑).

F If you do not want your iMac to remember this wireless network for future use, click **Remember this network** (☑ changes to ☐).

6 Click **Join**.

Your iMac connects to the wireless network, and you can start using network resources.

G The number of arcs on the Wi-Fi status icon (📶) indicates the strength of the connection, and ranges from one arc to four arcs.

7 To see more details about the wireless network, press Option and click the **Wi-Fi status** icon (📶) on the menu bar.

H The network's details appear, including the physical mode, the wireless channel, and the security type.

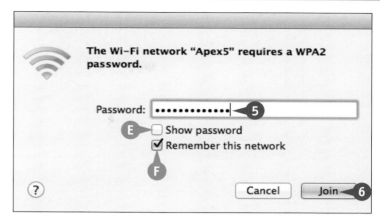

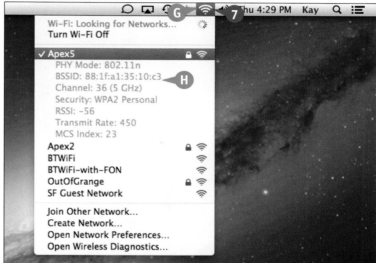

How do I disconnect from a wireless network?

When you have finished using a wireless network, you can disconnect from it by turning Wi-Fi off. Click the **Wi-Fi status** icon (📶) on the menu bar and then click **Turn Wi-Fi Off**.

What kind of wireless network do I need for my iMac?

Wireless networks use several different standards. The latest standard is 802.11ac, which provides the fastest data rates. The best choice for a Mac wireless network is one of Apple's wireless access points, such as an AirPort Extreme or an AirPort Time Capsule; the latter includes backup capabilities.

Set Up iCloud and iCloud Keychain

Apple's iCloud service adds powerful online sync features to your iMac. With iCloud, you can sync your e-mail accounts, contacts, calendars and reminders, Safari bookmarks, Photo Stream photos, and iWork documents and data. You can also use the Find My Mac feature to locate your iMac if it goes missing.

To use iCloud, you set your user account to use your Apple ID, and then choose which features to use. If you added your iCloud account when first setting up your iMac, iCloud is already configured, but you may want to select different settings for it.

Set Up iCloud and iCloud Keychain

1 Press **Ctrl**+click **System Preferences** (⚙) on the Dock.

The contextual menu opens.

2 Click **iCloud**.

System Preferences opens and displays the iCloud pane.

3 Type your Apple ID.

4 Type your password.

Ⓐ You can click **Create new Apple ID** if you need to create an Apple ID.

5 Click **Sign In**.

Another iCloud pane opens.

6 Click **Use iCloud for mail, contacts, calendars, reminders, notes, and Safari** (☐ changes to ☑) if you want to use iCloud for these items.

Note: You can fine-tune your selection of iCloud items after setting up iCloud.

7 Click **Use Find My Mac** (☐ changes to ☑) if you want to use iCloud's Find My Mac feature to locate your iMac if it strays.

8 Click **Next**.

The Enter your Apple ID password to set up iCloud Keychain dialog opens.

9 Type your password.

10 Click **OK**.

Note: If a dialog opens warning you that enabling Find My Mac for your account will disable it for another account, click **Continue** or **Cancel**, as appropriate.

The Enter your iCloud Security Code dialog opens.

11 Type your iCloud security code.

12 Click **Next**.

The Enter the verification code dialog opens.

13 Type the verification code sent to the cellular phone. Click **Don't have access to this phone?** if you need an alternative approach.

14 Click **OK**.

System Preferences enables iCloud Keychain.

Note: You can now enable or disable iCloud features by selecting the check boxes in the iCloud pane.

15 Click **Close** (▣).

TIP

How do I control which apps can store documents and data in iCloud?

Press <kbd>Ctrl</kbd> and click **System Preferences** (▣) on the Dock, and then click **iCloud** on the contextual menu to open the iCloud pane in System Preferences. Click **Options** to the right of Documents & Data to display the dialog for choosing which apps can store documents and data in iCloud. Click an app's check box (☐ changes to ☑) to enable the app to use iCloud. Click **Done** to close the dialog, and then click **Close** (▣) to close the System Preferences window.

Set Up Your Social Networking Accounts

OS X includes built-in support for the major social networks, including Facebook, LinkedIn, Twitter, and Flickr. OS X makes it easy to post updates, photos, and videos to your accounts on these social networks. For example, you can quickly create a Facebook post or a Twitter tweet from the Notifications panel. Similarly, you can easily share a photo from iPhoto or a movie from iMovie.

Before you can use a particular social network, you must set up the social networking account in your user account. To do this, you use System Preferences.

Set Up Your Social Networking Accounts

1 Press **Ctrl** and click **System Preferences** (🖼) on the Dock.

The contextual menu opens.

2 Click **Internet Accounts**.

System Preferences opens and displays the Internet Accounts pane.

3 In the right pane, click the account type you want to add. This example uses **Facebook**.

A If an account is selected in the left pane, click **Add** (➕) to display the list of account types.

A dialog for entering the account information opens. This example shows the Facebook dialog.

4 Type your e-mail address, phone number, or username.

5 Type your password.

6 Click **Next**.

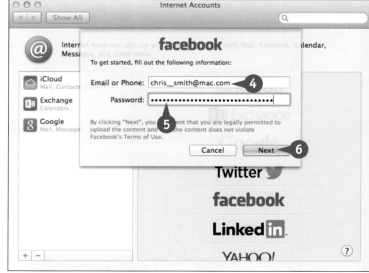

A dialog opens showing further information.

7 Click **Sign In**.

System Preferences signs you into the social networking service.

B The account appears in the left pane of the Internet Accounts pane.

8 Click **Contacts** (☐ changes to ☑) if you want Facebook to be able to use your data in the Contacts app.

9 Click **Calendars** (☐ changes to ☑) if you want Facebook to be able to add events to the Calendar app.

10 Click **Close** (⊗).

The System Preferences window closes.

TIP

What does the Details button for an Internet account do?
Clicking the Details button opens the Details dialog for the selected Internet account. In this dialog, you can type a new password that you have set for the account. You can also change the description that the Internet Accounts pane displays for the account. For example, the Internet Accounts pane displays your e-mail address as the identifier for your LinkedIn account, but you might prefer to use descriptive text such as "Personal Account" or "Work Account." Click **OK** when you are ready to close the Details dialog.

Connect a Printer

To print from your iMac, you need to connect a printer and install a *driver*, the software for the printer. OS X includes many printer drivers, so you may be able to connect your printer and simply start printing. But if your printer is a new model, you may need to locate and install the driver for it.

The most straightforward way to connect a printer to your iMac is with a USB cable. To connect to a printer on your network or shared by another computer, see Chapter 13.

Connect a Printer

1 Connect the printer to the iMac with a USB cable.

Note: If the printer is connected to another Mac or an AirPort wireless device, connect to it as explained in Chapter 13.

2 Plug the printer into an electrical socket and switch it on.

3 Click **System Preferences** (⚙) on the Dock.

The System Preferences window opens.

4 Click **Printers & Scanners**.

The Printers & Scanners pane appears.

Ⓐ If your printer appears in the list, you have connected it successfully. Go to step **11**.

5 If your printer does not appear, click **Add** (⊞).

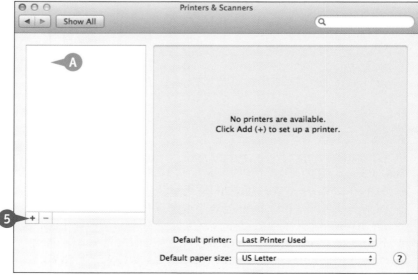

The Add dialog opens.

6 Click **Default**.

The Default pane appears.

7 Click the printer.

8 If you want, change the printer's name.

Note: It is often helpful to use the name to make clear what kind of printer this is — for example, whether it prints in color or black and white.

9 Also optionally, change the description of the printer's location.

10 Click **Add**.

11 Click the **Default printer** pop-up menu (⬍) and then select the printer to use. You can select any installed printer or Last Printer Used.

12 Click the **Default paper size** pop-up menu (⬍) and then select the default paper size, such as **US Letter**.

13 Click **Close** (⬤).

The System Preferences window closes.

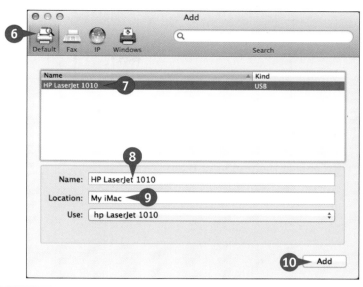

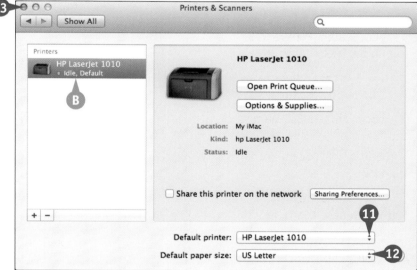

TIPS

What should I type in the Name field and Location field when adding a printer?

You can type anything you want in the Name field and the Location field. This information is to help you identify the printer. If you have many printers, and some are attached to different computers, making each printer's name and location descriptive helps you keep the printers straight.

My printer has the wrong sort of connector — like an oversize phone jack. How can I connect it?

This connector is an Ethernet connector, also known as an RJ-45 connector. You can connect the printer directly to your iMac or to your network switch or router by using an Ethernet cable.

Connect an iPhone, iPad, or iPod

OS X includes iTunes, Apple's app for playing music and video and managing iPhones, iPads, and iPods. If you have an iPhone, iPad, or iPod, you can connect it to your iMac and sync music, videos, and podcasts.

To connect the iPhone, iPad, or iPod, you need the cable that comes with the device. The cable has a USB connector at one end and a Lightning connector or a Dock connector at the other end, depending on the model of iPhone, iPad, or iPod.

Connect an iPhone, iPad, or iPod

1 Plug the cable's USB connector into a USB port on your iMac.

2 Plug the connector on the other end of the cable into the Lightning port or Dock connector port on the iPhone, iPad, or iPod.

Your iMac detects the device and launches iTunes for synchronizing it.

3 Click **iPhone**, **iPad**, or **iPod** on the navigation bar.

The screens for managing the device appear.

Note: If you connect an iPhone, iPad, or iPod touch that contains photos you have not synchronized with iPhoto, iPhoto opens. You can then import the photos.

4 Click **Summary**.

The Summary screen appears.

5 In the Backups box, select backup settings. For example, click **iCloud** (◯ changes to ◉) to back up your device to iCloud.

6 Scroll down the iTunes window.

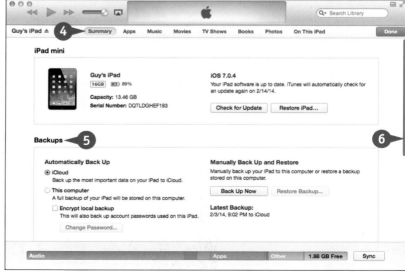

The remaining settings appear.

7 Click **Open iTunes when this** *device* **is connected** (☐ changes to ☑) if you want iTunes to open automatically.

8 Click **Sync with this** *device* **over Wi-Fi** (☐ changes to ☑) if you want to sync via Wi-Fi instead of USB.

9 Click **Sync only checked songs and videos** (☐ changes to ☑) if you want to omit any items you have deselected.

10 Click another tab on the navigation bar.

The screen associated with the tab appears.

11 Choose settings on the tab.

12 Click other tabs as needed and choose settings on their screens.

13 Click **Apply**.

iTunes syncs the data.

14 After the sync finishes, click **Eject** (⏏).

The main iTunes screen appears.

You can disconnect your iPhone, iPad, or iPod from your iMac.

TIP

I am running out of USB ports on my iMac. Is there an alternative to unplugging cables and plugging them back in?

Buy a USB hub, a device that plugs into your iMac and provides extra ports. You can position the hub conveniently for your USB devices. You can find USB hubs at any good computer store, online or offline, including the Apple Store. Buy a USB 3 hub to make sure you get good speeds. It is best to get a powered hub to ensure that your devices receive plenty of power and that battery-powered devices can charge. Use an unpowered hub only for devices that plug into electric sockets.

Connect External Drives

To give yourself more disk space, you can connect an external drive to your iMac by using a Thunderbolt port for top speed or a USB port for everyday speeds. After connecting the external drive, you can partition it using Disk Utility if necessary and access it through the Finder and other apps.

Connect External Drives

Connect and Format an External Drive

1. Connect the external drive to the appropriate port on the back of your iMac.

2. If the external drive needs a power supply, plug it in.

3. If the external drive has a power switch, turn it on.

4. Click **Launchpad** (⟆).

   The Launchpad screen appears.

5. Type **di**.

   Launchpad displays apps that include a word starting with *di*.

6. Click **Disk Utility**.

   The Disk Utility app opens.

7. Click the external drive.

Note: Partitioning a drive removes all its data. Partition a drive only if it is new or if you no longer need any data it contains.

8. Click **Partition**.

9. Click the **Partition Layout** pop-up menu (⟠) and select the number of partitions.

10. Click a partition.

11. Click the **Format** pop-up menu (⟠) and click the format, such as **Mac OS Extended (Journaled)**.

12. Type the partition's name.

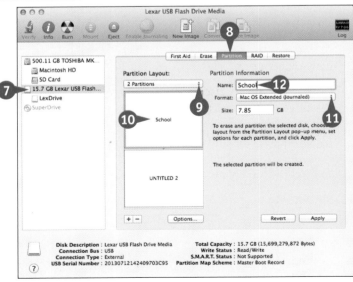

13 Repeat steps **10** to **12** for each other partition.

Note: If you need to be able to start your iMac from this drive, click **Options**, click **GUID Partition Table** (◯ changes to ◉), and then click **OK**. Do this for any drive you use for Time Machine backups.

14 Click **Apply**.

A confirmation dialog opens.

15 Click **Partition**.

Disk Utility partitions the drive.

16 Press ⌘+Q.

Disk Utility closes.

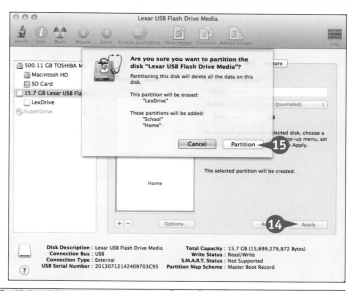

Use and Eject an External Drive

1 Double-click the external drive volume on the desktop.

A Finder window opens showing the contents of the external drive volume.

A You can then copy or move files to or from the drive or create new folders on it.

2 When you want to disconnect the drive, click **Eject** (⏏).

The drive disappears from the Devices list.

You can then disconnect the drive.

TIP

How do I access a drive that does not appear on the desktop?
Click **Finder** (▣) on the Dock to open a Finder window. If the Devices list is collapsed, move the mouse pointer over the Devices heading, and then click the word **Show** that appears. In the list of devices, click the drive to display its contents.

Give Commands

The easiest ways to give commands in OS X are by using the menus and the toolbar. You can also give commands by pressing keyboard shortcuts.

The menu bar at the top of the window shows the Apple menu (🍎) on the left followed by the menus for the active app. Any open window can have a toolbar, usually across its top but sometimes elsewhere in the window.

Give Commands

Give a Command from a Menu

① On the Dock, click the app you want to activate — the Finder (🗂) in this example.

Note: You can also click the app's window if you can see it.

② On the menu bar, click the menu you want to open.

The menu opens.

③ Click the command you want to give.

The app performs the action associated with the command.

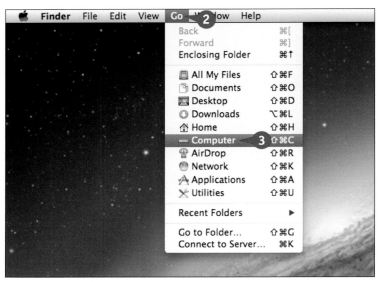

Choose Among Groups of Features on a Menu

① On the Dock, click the app you want to activate — the Finder (🗂) in this example.

② On the menu bar, click the menu you want to open.

The app opens the menu.

③ Select the option you want to use.

The app activates the feature you selected.

Give a Command from a Toolbar

1 On the Dock, click the app you want to activate — the Finder (🖼) in this example.

2 Click the button on the toolbar, or click a pop-up menu and then click the menu item for the command.

The app performs the action associated with the toolbar button or menu item.

Choose Among Groups of Features on a Toolbar

1 On the Dock, click the app you want to activate — the Finder (🖼) in this example.

2 In the group of buttons, click the button you want to choose.

A The app highlights the button you clicked to indicate that the feature is turned on.

B The app removes highlighting from the button that was previously selected.

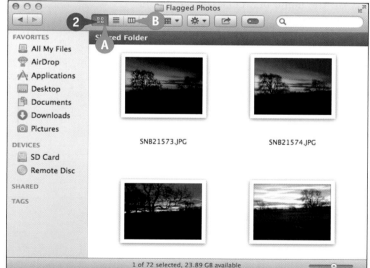

TIP

Is it better to use the menus or the toolbar?
If the toolbar contains the command you need, using the toolbar is usually faster and easier than using the menus. You can customize the toolbar in many apps by opening the **View** menu, choosing **Customize Toolbar**, and then working in the dialog that opens. Use this command, or other similar commands, to place the buttons for your most-used commands just a click away.

Open, Close, Minimize, and Hide Windows

M ost OS X apps use windows to display information so that you can see it and work with it. You can resize most windows to the size you need or expand a window so that it fills the screen. You can move windows and position them so that you can see those windows you require, minimize other windows to icons on the Dock, or hide an app's windows from view.

Open, Close, Minimize, and Hide Windows

Open a Window

1 Click anywhere on the desktop.

OS X activates the Finder and displays the menu bar for it.

Note: Clicking anywhere on the desktop activates the Finder because the desktop is a special Finder window. You can also click **Finder** (▣) on the Dock.

2 Click **File**.

The File menu opens.

3 Click **New Finder Window**.

A Finder window opens, showing your files in your default view.

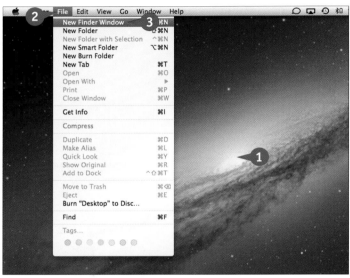

Move, Resize, and Zoom a Window

1 Click the window's title bar and drag the window to where you want it.

2 Click a border or corner of the window and drag until the window is the size and shape you want.

3 Click **Zoom** (⊕).

The window zooms in or out to its optimal size.

4 Click **Zoom** (⊕) again.

The window zooms back to its previous size.

Close a Window

1 Click **Close** (⊗).

The window closes.

Note: You can also close a window by pressing ⌘+W. To close all the windows of the app, press Option+ click **Close** (⊗) or press ⌘+Option+W.

Minimize or Hide a Window

1 Click **Minimize** (⊖).

OS X minimizes the window to an icon on the right side of the Dock.

Note: You can also minimize a window by pressing ⌘+M.

2 Click the icon for the minimized window.

OS X expands the window to its original size and position.

Note: Press and hold Shift while minimizing or restoring a window to see the animation in slow motion.

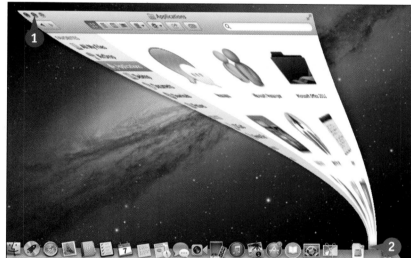

TIPS

What does zooming a window do?
Clicking **Zoom** (⊕) on a window changes its size to the size that OS X judges best shows the window's contents. If this size does not show what you want to see, drag a border or corner of the window to change the size. Clicking **Zoom** (⊕) again returns the window to its previous size.

How can I find out where a window is located?
To quickly see what folder contains a file or folder, press ⌘+click the window's name in the title bar. The window displays a pop-up menu showing the path of folders to this folder. Click a folder in the path to display that folder in the Finder, or click the title bar to hide the pop-up menu again.

Using Notifications

OS X's Notification Center feature keeps you up to date with what is happening in your apps. Notification Center puts all your alerts, from incoming e-mail messages and instant messages to calendar requests and software updates, in a single place where you can easily access and manage them.

You open Notification Center by clicking the icon at the right end of the menu bar. Notification Center opens as a pane on the right side of the screen, and it contains sections you can expand or collapse as needed.

Using Notifications

View a Notification

Ⓐ When you receive a notification, a notification banner appears in the upper-right corner of the screen for a few seconds.

Note: Notification Center can display either banners or alerts. A *banner* appears for a few seconds, and then disappears. An *alert* remains on screen until you dismiss it.

① If you want to see the item that produced the notification, click the banner.

Display Notification Center When Your Desktop Is Visible

① Click **Notification Center** (▤).

Notification Center opens.

② Optionally, click a notification to display the related item in its app.

③ When you are ready to close Notification Center, click **Notification Center** (▤).

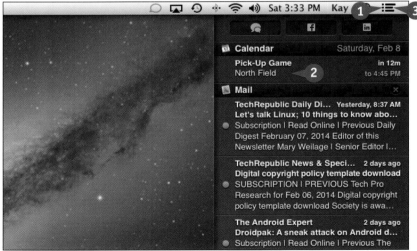

Choose What Types of Notifications to Display and Set Your Do Not Disturb Hours

1 Press **Ctrl** and click **System Preferences** (⚙) on the Dock.

The contextual menu opens.

2 Click **Notifications**.

System Preferences opens and displays the Notifications pane.

3 Click **Do Not Disturb**.

The Do Not Disturb settings appear.

4 Click **From** (☐ changes to ☑) and then set the hours.

5 Choose which calls to accept during Do Not Disturb times.

6 Click an app or feature.

The controls for the app or feature appear.

7 Click **None**, **Banners**, or **Alerts** to set the alert style.

8 Choose other options for the app or feature.

9 Repeat steps **6** to **8** for other apps and features.

10 Click the **Sort Notification Center** pop-up menu (⬍) and select **Manually** or **By time**, as needed.

11 Click **Close** (⊗).

System Preferences closes.

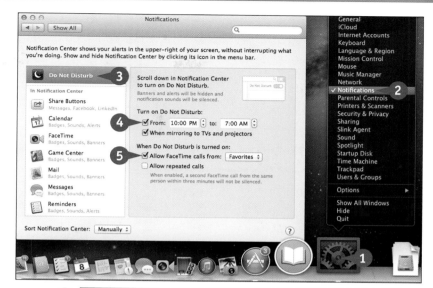

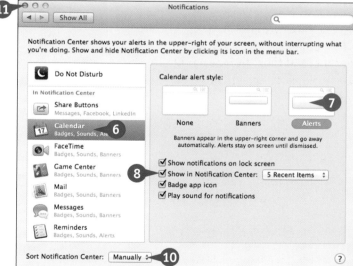

TIP

How do I display Notification Center in a full-screen app?

When a full-screen app is active, swipe to the left on the Magic Mouse or Magic Trackpad to display Notification Center.

If you do not have a Magic Mouse or Magic Trackpad, move the mouse pointer up to the top of the screen to display the menu bar. You can then click **Notification Center** (☰) toward the right end of the menu bar to display Notification Center.

Put Your iMac to Sleep and Wake It Up

OS X enables you to put your iMac to sleep easily and wake it up quickly. So when you are ready for a break but you do not want to end your computing session, put the iMac to sleep instead of shutting it down.

Sleep keeps all your apps open and lets you start computing again quickly. When you wake your iMac up, your apps and windows are where you left them, so you can swiftly resume what you were doing.

Put Your iMac to Sleep and Wake It Up

Put Your iMac to Sleep

1 Click **Apple** (🍎).

The Apple menu opens.

2 Click **Sleep**.

The iMac turns its screen off and puts itself to sleep.

Note: You can also put your iMac to sleep by pressing its power button for a moment.

Wake Your iMac

1 Click the mouse button or the trackpad, or press any key except **Fn** on the keyboard.

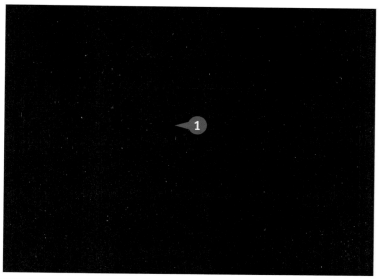

The iMac wakes up and turns on the screen. All the apps and windows that you were using are open where you left them.

The iMac reestablishes any network connections that it normally uses and performs regular tasks, such as checking for new e-mail.

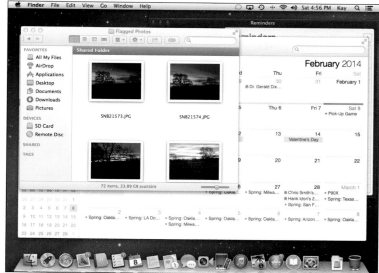

TIPS

What happens if a power outage occurs while my iMac is asleep?

Your iMac loses power and crashes, and you lose any unsaved work. Save any unsaved work before putting your iMac to sleep, and consider buying an uninterruptible power supply, a battery-based device that enables a computer to ride out power outages.

When should I use sleep and when should I shut down my iMac?

Put your iMac to sleep when you want to be able to resume using it quickly. Sleep uses only a minimal amount of power. Shut down your iMac when you plan not to use it for several days.

Log Out, Shut Down, and Resume

When you have finished using your iMac for now, end your computing session by logging out. From the login screen, you can log back in when you are ready to use your iMac again. When you have finished using your iMac and plan to leave it several days, shut it down.

Whether you log out or shut down your iMac, you can choose whether to have OS X reopen your apps and documents when you log back on. This helpful feature can help you get back to work — or play — quickly and easily.

Log Out, Shut Down, and Resume

Log Out from Your iMac

1 Click **Apple** (🍎).

The Apple menu opens.

2 Click **Log Out**.

The iMac shows a dialog asking if you want to log out.

3 Click **Reopen windows when logging back in** (☐ changes to ☑) if you want to resume your apps and documents.

4 Click **Log Out**.

Note: Instead of clicking **Log Out**, you can wait for one minute. After this, the iMac closes your apps and logs you out automatically. To log out quickly, bypassing the dialog, click **Apple** (🍎), press and hold Option, and click **Log Out**.

The iMac displays the window showing the list of users. You or another user can click your name to start logging in.

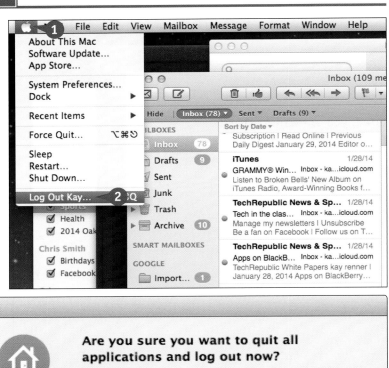

Shut Down Your iMac

1 Click **Apple** (⬛).

The Apple menu opens.

2 Click **Shut Down**.

The iMac shows a dialog asking if you want to shut down.

3 Click **Reopen windows when logging back in** (☐ changes to ☑) if you want to resume your apps and documents.

4 Click **Shut Down**.

Note: Instead of clicking Shut Down, you can wait for one minute. After this, the iMac shuts down automatically. To shut down quickly, bypassing the dialog, click ⬛, press and hold **Option**, and click **Shut Down**.

The screen goes blank, and the iMac switches itself off.

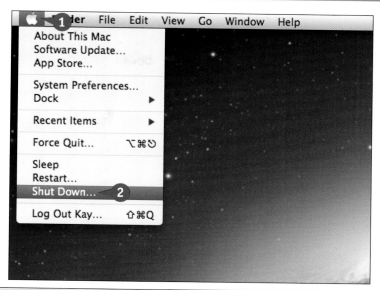

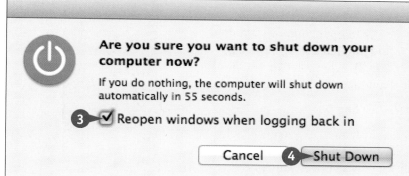

TIP

Do I need to save my documents before logging out?
If the apps you are using are designed to use OS X's automatic-saving features, your iMac automatically saves any unsaved changes to your documents before logging you out. But because not all apps use these features, it is better to save all your documents yourself before you log out. Otherwise, an app may display a dialog prompting you to save unsaved changes, and this dialog may prevent logout or shutdown.

CHAPTER 2

Sharing Your iMac with Others

OS X makes it easy to share your iMac with other people. Each user needs a separate user account for documents, e-mail, and settings.

Create a User Account

A user account is a group of settings that controls what a user can do in OS X. By setting up a separate user account for each person who uses your iMac regularly, you can enable users to have their own folders for documents and to use the settings they prefer. You can also use the Parental Controls feature to apply limitations to the actions a user can take.

When initially setting up your iMac, you create an administrator account that you can use to configure OS X. You can also create a non-administrator account for yourself for day-to-day use.

Create a User Account

1 Click the **Apple** menu (🍎).

2 Click **System Preferences**.

The System Preferences window opens.

3 In the System category, click **Users & Groups**.

Note: You must use administrator credentials to create another account. The easiest way to do this is to use an administrator account; you can also provide an administrator name and password from another account. To check whether you are an administrator, see if your account shows Admin in the Users & Groups pane.

The Users & Groups pane opens.

④ Click the **lock** icon (🔒) to unlock System Preferences.

System Preferences displays a dialog asking you to type your password or an administrator name and password.

⑤ Type your password in the Password field.

⑥ Click **Unlock**.

System Preferences unlocks the preferences (🔒 changes to 🔓).

⑦ Click **Add** (➕).

The New Account dialog opens.

⑧ Click the **New Account** pop-up menu and then click **Standard**.

⑨ Type the username, such as Bee or Bee Jones, and short name, such as bee.

⑩ Type the user's initial password in the Password field and the Verify field.

⑪ Click **Create User**.

The New Account dialog closes, and the new account appears in the Other Users list.

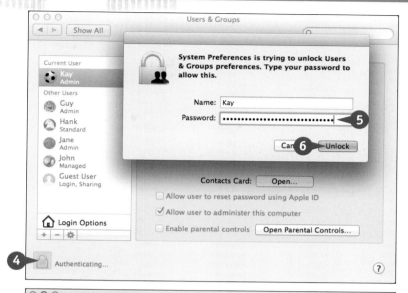

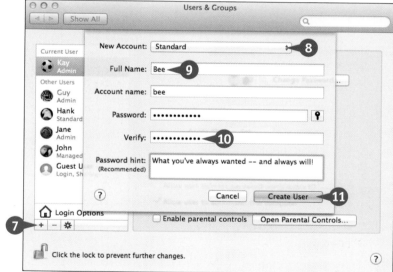

TIP

How do I choose a good password for a user?
For security, each user should choose his password after logging in. As an administrator, after you create a new user account, set a password to secure the account against hackers. Tell the user the password, and ask the user to create a new password the first time he uses the account. To change the password, the user clicks the **Change Password** button in the Users & Groups pane. The Change Password dialog opens, and the user types the new password. The user can click **Password Assistant** (🔑) in the Change Password dialog to open the Password Assistant, which produces hard-to-break passwords.

Configure Your iMac for Multiple Users

OS X includes a feature called Fast User Switching that enables multiple users to remain logged in to your iMac at the same time. So instead of you having to log out of OS X before another user can log in, another user can log in either directly from your OS X session or from the login screen. Your OS X session keeps running in the background, ready for you to resume it.

Before you and others can use Fast User Switching, you must turn on the feature. You can also choose how to display the list of usernames.

Configure Your iMac for Multiple Users

1 Press **Ctrl**+click **System Preferences** (🖼️) on the Dock.

Note: You can click **Apple** (🍎) and then click **System Preferences** to open the System Preferences window.

The contextual menu opens.

2 Click **Users & Groups**.

The System Preferences app opens and displays the Users & Groups pane at the front.

3 Click the **lock** icon (🔒).

System Preferences displays a dialog asking you to type your password.

Note: If you are using a standard account or managed account, the dialog prompts you to provide administrator credentials.

4 Type your password or credentials.

5 Click **Unlock**.

System Preferences unlocks the preferences (🔒 changes to 🔓).

6 Click **Login Options**.

The login options pane appears.

⑦ Click the **Automatic login** pop-up menu (⬍) and click **Off**.

⑧ Click the **Show fast user switching menu as** option (☐ changes to ☑).

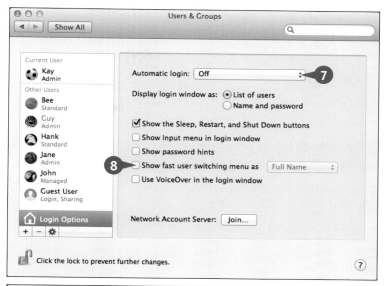

⑨ Click the **Show fast user switching menu as** pop-up menu (⬍).

⑩ Click **Full Name** to show usernames, click **Account Name** to use account names, or click **Icon** to use icons.

Note: Using full names for the Fast User Switching menu is clearest but takes the most space on the menu bar. Account names are more compact. Icons are very compact, but can be visually confusing.

Fast User Switching is now enabled.

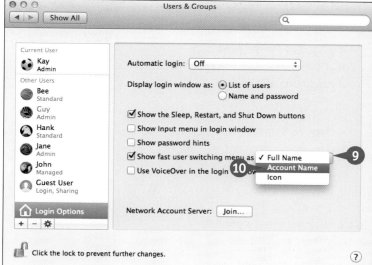

Why should I not use automatic login with Fast User Switching?
Automatic login lets anyone who can turn on your iMac use the account set for automatic login. To turn on Fast User Switching, click the **Automatic login** pop-up menu and then click **Off** to ensure that whoever logs in to the iMac uses his own user account.

Are there any disadvantages to Fast User Switching?
Fast User Switching can make your iMac run more slowly because applications are open in both the current user's session and any background sessions. If your iMac runs too slowly, try turning Fast User Switching off or adding RAM.

Share Your iMac with Fast User Switching

After you enable the Fast User Switching feature, multiple users can remain logged in to OS X on your iMac at the same time. Only one user can use the keyboard, pointing device, and screen at any given time, but each other user's computing session keeps running in the background, with all of her applications still open.

OS X automatically stops multimedia playing when you switch users. For example, if another user is still playing music in iTunes when you switch the iMac to your user account, iTunes stops playing the music.

Share Your iMac with Fast User Switching

Log In to the iMac

1 On the login screen, click your username.

OS X prompts you for your password.

Ⓐ You can click **Back** (◀) to return to the login screen if you need to log in using a different account.

2 Type your password.

3 Click **Log In** (◎).

Your desktop appears.

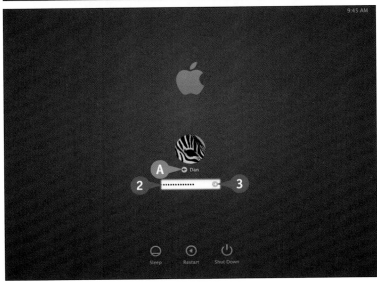

Display the Login Window

1 When you are ready to stop using the iMac for now, but do not want to log out, click your name, account name, or icon on the menu bar.

The Fast User Switching menu opens.

2 Click **Login Window**.

The login window appears.

B Your username shows a check mark icon (), indicating that you have a session open.

Any of the iMac's users can log in by clicking his username.

TIP

How can I log another user out so that I can shut down?

From the Fast User Switching menu, you can see what other users are logged in to the iMac. If possible, ask each user to log in and then log out before you shut down. If you must shut down the iMac, and you are an administrator, click **Shut Down** in the login window. OS X warns you that there are logged-in users. Type your name and password, and click **Shut Down**.

Turn On Parental Controls for an Account

OS X's parental controls enable an administrator to limit the actions that a particular user can take on the iMac. For example, assuming you have an administrator account, you can prevent a user from running certain applications, allow her to chat only with specific people, or prevent her from using the iMac at night.

You can apply parental controls to any standard account. When you apply parental controls, System Preferences changes the standard account to a managed account. You can then choose the specific settings the account needs. Later, you can review logs of the actions the user has taken.

Turn On Parental Controls for an Account

① Press **Ctrl**+click **System Preferences** (🖼️) on the Dock.

Note: You can click **Apple** (🍎) and then click **System Preferences** to open the System Preferences window.

The contextual menu opens.

② Click **Users & Groups**.

The System Preferences app opens the Users & Groups pane at the front.

③ Click the **lock** icon (🔒).

System Preferences displays a dialog asking you to type your password.

Note: If you are using a standard account or managed account, the dialog prompts you to provide administrator credentials.

④ Type your password or an administrator's credentials.

⑤ Click **Unlock**.

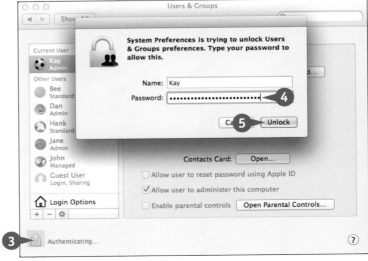

System Preferences unlocks the preferences (🔒 changes to 🔓).

6 Click the account to which you want to apply parental controls.

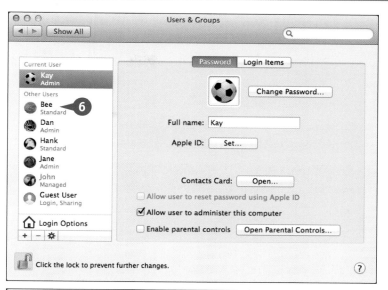

The settings for the account appear.

7 Click the **Enable parental controls** option (☐ changes to ☑).

You can now choose parental control settings.

Note: When you select the Enable parental controls check box, the user type under the username in the list of users changes from standard to managed.

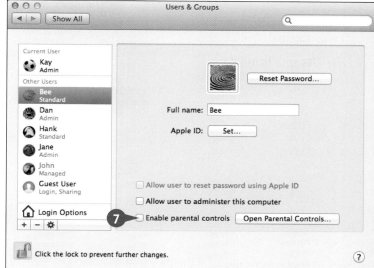

TIP

Can I apply parental controls to any user account?
You can apply parental controls to any standard user account. To apply parental controls to an account, you must use an administrator account or provide administrator credentials. You cannot apply parental controls to an administrator account, but you can downgrade an administrator account to a standard account, and then apply the controls to the standard account. Your iMac must always have at least one administrator account to manage the other user accounts.

Choose What Apps a User Can Run

OS X's parental controls enable an administrator to limit the apps a managed user can run. For example, if you are an administrator, you can control which apps are available to a user. If you do not allow the user to play certain games, you can make those games unavailable.

For users who find the OS X interface too complex, you can turn on Simple Finder. Simple Finder presents a stripped-down interface that makes the most important items easier to find and use.

Choose What Apps a User Can Run

① Click **Apple** (🍎).

The Apple menu opens.

② Click **System Preferences**.

The System Preferences window opens.

③ Click **Users & Groups**.

The Users & Groups pane appears.

Note: If the lock is closed (🔒), click the lock, type your password when prompted, and then click **Unlock** to unlock the preferences.

④ Click the account for which you want to apply app restrictions.

The settings for the account appear.

⑤ Click **Open Parental Controls**.

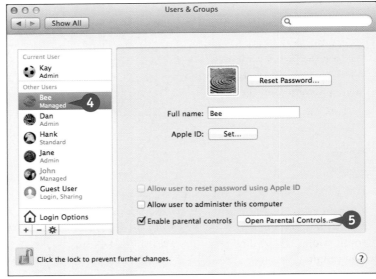

The Parental Controls preferences pane opens.

6 Click the **Apps** tab.

The Apps pane appears.

7 Click the **Use Simple Finder** option (☐ changes to ☑) to make the user use Simple Finder.

8 Click the **Limit Applications** option (☐ changes to ☑).

9 Click the **Allow App Store Apps** pop-up menu (◻) and then click the level of apps to allow.

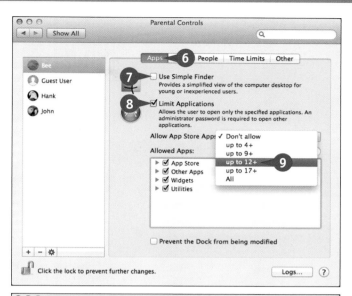

10 In the Allowed Apps list, click the disclosure triangle next to a category of applications (▶ changes to ▼).

The list of applications appears.

11 Click ☑ for each application you want to prevent the user from using (☑ changes to ☐).

12 Click the **Prevent the Dock from being modified** option (☐ changes to ☑) to prevent the user from rearranging the Dock icons, adding icons, or removing icons.

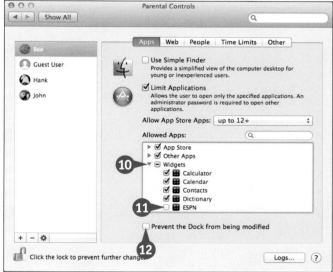

TIP

What is Simple Finder and when should I make a user use it?

Simple Finder is a simplified version of the Finder designed for use by younger, older, or less-experienced computer users. Simple Finder provides a more streamlined look with fewer choices, making it easier to find applications and folders, and prevents the user from changing important settings. Some users benefit from using Simple Finder in the long term, whereas for others it is a step toward using the regular Finder after more computing experience. When a user needs to take actions beyond the bounds of Simple Finder, an administrator can give temporary permission by entering an administrative password.

Limit Website Access for a User

OS X's parental controls enable an administrator to limit the websites a managed user can access. As an administrator, you can allow a user access to only the websites on an approved list. Alternatively, you can set parental controls to limit access to adult websites; you can also customize the list of permitted websites and blocked websites. This limiting of access works only for Safari, not for any other browsers, so you should use the Apps parental controls to make Safari the only web browser the user can run. You should also prevent the user from installing apps.

Limit Website Access for a User

1 In the Users & Groups preferences pane in System Preferences, click the user account you want to change.

Note: You can click **Apple** (🍎) and then click **System Preferences** to open the System Preferences window. Then click **Users & Groups**.

2 Click **Open Parental Controls**.

The Parental Controls preferences pane opens.

3 Click the **Web** tab.

The Web pane appears.

4 In the Website Restrictions area, click the **Try to limit access to adult websites automatically** option to prevent access to adult websites (☐ changes to ◉).

5 Click **Customize**.

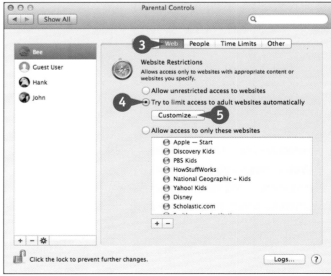

6 In the Customize dialog, click **Add** (⊞).

7 Type or paste the web address to disallow and press **Return**.

Note: You can also add permitted addresses to the Always Allow These Websites field.

8 Click **OK**.

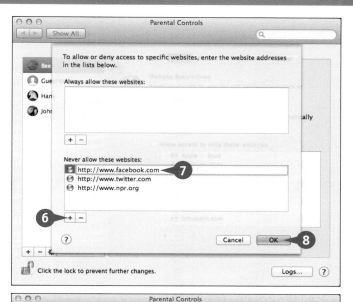

9 To allow only certain websites, click the **Allow access to only these websites** option (◯ changes to ◉).

10 To add a site, click **Add** (⊞) and then click **Add Bookmark**.

11 In the dialog that appears, type a descriptive name for the website.

12 Type the website's address.

13 Click **OK**.

A To remove a site, click it and then click **Remove** (⊟).

Note: When you permit a user to visit only certain websites, those sites appear on the Bookmarks bar in Safari.

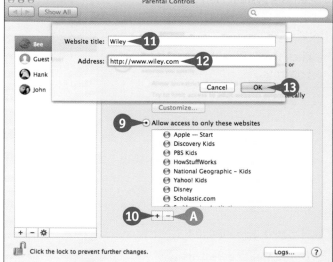

TIP

How effective is the blocking of adult websites?
The blocking of adult websites is only partly effective. OS X can block sites that identify themselves as adult sites using standard rating criteria, but many adult sites either do not use ratings or do not rate their content accurately. Because of this, do not rely on OS X to block all adult material. It is much more effective to choose **Allow access to only these websites** and provide a list of permitted sites. You can add to the list by vetting and approving extra sites when the user needs to access them.

Limit E-Mail, Chat, and Game Center Access

OS X's parental controls enable an administrator to limit a managed user's access to e-mail, chat, and some Game Center features. As an administrator, you can limit a user's contacts for e-mail using the Mail app and for chat using the Messages app. In Game Center, you can control whether the user can join multiplayer games and add friends.

These capabilities are useful for protecting children and other vulnerable individuals from unsuitable e-mail messages, chat, and game players. You can add contacts to the approved list for Mail and Messages as needed.

Limit E-Mail, Chat, and Game Center Access

1 In the Users & Groups preferences pane in System Preferences, click the user account you want to change.

Note: You can click **Apple** (🍎) and then click **System Preferences** to open the System Preferences window. Then click **Users & Groups**.

2 Click **Open Parental Controls**.

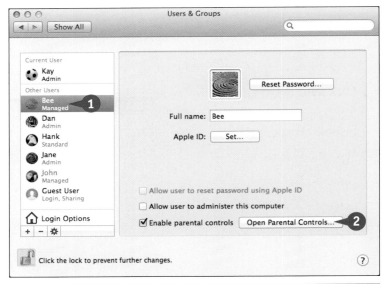

The Parental Controls preferences pane opens.

3 Click the **People** tab.

The People pane appears.

4 Click the **Allow joining Game Center multiplayer games** option (☑ changes to ☐) to prevent the user from joining multiplayer games.

5 Click the **Allow adding Game Center friends** option (☑ changes to ☐) to prevent the user from adding friends in Game Center.

6 Click the **Limit Mail to allowed contacts** option (☐ changes to ☑) to allow e-mail to only the addresses you specify.

7 Click the **Send requests to** option if you want messages sent to prohibited addresses to trigger a message to you.

8 Type your e-mail address for the permission requests.

9 Click the **Limit Messages to allowed contacts** option (☐ changes to ☑) to allow chat only with addresses you specify.

10 Click **Add** (⊞).

A dialog for adding allowed addresses appears.

11 Type the first name.

12 Type the last name.

13 Type the address.

14 Click the pop-up menu (⬍) and click the address type: **Email**, **AIM**, or **Jabber**.

15 Click **Add person to my address book** (☐ changes to ☑).

16 Click **Add**.

The name appears in the Allowed Contacts list.

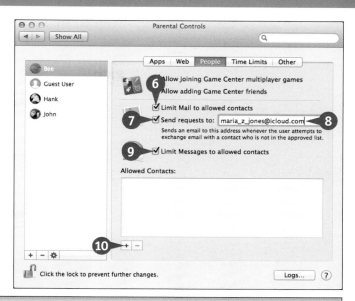

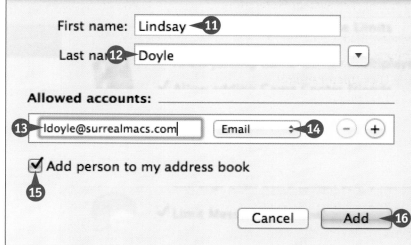

TIP

How effective is the blocking of e-mail and chat?

OS X's blocking of e-mail and chat requests is highly effective for the Mail app and the Messages app. As long as you create a suitable list of allowed e-mail and chat addresses, you can give the user solid protection against unwanted messages and chat requests. OS X does not block other e-mail and instant-messaging apps, however, so you must make sure that none are available for the user to circumvent the blocking. You must also prevent access to websites that provide e-mail or chat functionality.

Set Time Limits for a User

OS X's parental controls enable an administrator to set time limits for a managed user's access to the iMac. As an administrator, you can set the permitted number of hours for weekdays and the number of hours for weekends. You can also specify "bedtime" hours when the user may not use the iMac.

You can set different limits for the nights before school days, Sunday through Thursday, and then for Friday and Saturday nights. You can also override the time limits as needed by typing your administrator username and password.

Set Time Limits for a User

1 Press **Ctrl**+click **System Preferences** (🖥) on the Dock.

The contextual menu opens.

Note: You can click **Apple** (🍎) and then click **System Preferences** to open the System Preferences window.

2 Click **Users & Groups**.

The System Preferences app opens and displays the Users & Groups pane at the front.

Note: If you need to unlock the preferences, click the **lock** icon (🔒), type your password, and click **Unlock** when prompted.

3 Click the user account you want to change.

4 Click **Open Parental Controls**.

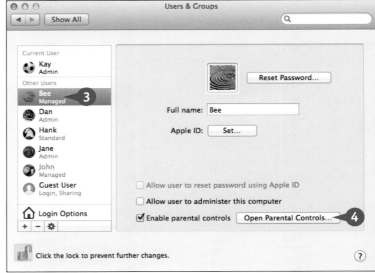

The Parental Controls preferences pane opens.

5 Click the **Time Limits** tab.

The Time Limits pane appears.

6 To set a weekday time limit, click the **Limit weekday use to** option (☐ changes to ☑).

7 Click and drag the slider to set the limit.

8 To set a weekend time limit, click the **Limit weekend use to** option (☐ changes to ☑).

9 Click and drag the slider to set the limit.

10 To set a block of time when the iMac is not available on school nights, click the **School nights** option (☐ changes to ☑).

11 Set the start and end time for school nights.

12 To set a block of time when the iMac is not available on weekend nights, click the **Weekend** option (☐ changes to ☑).

13 Set the start and end time for weekend nights.

TIPS

How can I allow a managed user access to the iMac at other times?

Parental controls make no exception for holidays and vacations, but an administrator can override parental controls. For example, when OS X displays the Your Computer Time Is Almost Up dialog, you can enter your administrator name and password to authorize an extra period of time, from 15 minutes to the rest of the day.

How can I allow a managed user to use the iMac only during the evening?

You can use the Bedtime feature to block any time. For example, set School nights as 9:00 PM to 6:00 PM to permit the user to use the iMac from 6–9 PM.

Apply Other Restrictions to a User

Beyond the controls on apps, website access, contacts and Game Center, and usage times, OS X's parental controls enable an administrator to apply six other types of restrictions to a managed user.

First, you can disable your iMac's built-in camera. Second, you can disable the Dictation feature. Third, you can hide profanity in the Dictionary app. Fourth, you can prevent the user from changing printer settings and adding or removing printers. Fifth, you can prevent the user from changing her password. Sixth, you can prevent the user from burning CDs and DVDs with the Finder or iTunes on a connected optical drive.

Apply Other Restrictions to a User

① Click **Apple** (🍎).

The Apple menu opens.

② Click **System Preferences**.

The System Preferences window opens.

③ Click **Users & Groups**.

The Users & Groups pane appears.

Note: If the lock is closed (🔒), click the lock, type your password when prompted, and then click **Unlock** to unlock the preferences.

④ Click the user account you want to affect.

⑤ Click **Open Parental Controls**.

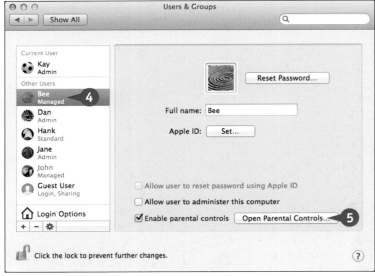

The Parental Controls preferences pane opens.

⑥ Click the **Other** tab.

The Other pane appears.

⑦ Click the **Disable built-in camera** option (☐ changes to ☑) to disable the camera.

⑧ Click the **Disable Dictation** option (☐ changes to ☑) to prevent the user from using the Dictation feature.

⑨ Click the **Hide profanity in Dictionary** option (☐ changes to ☑) to suppress offensive words in the Dictionary app.

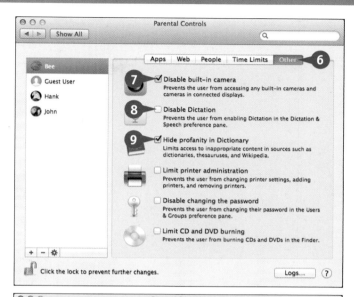

⑩ Click the **Limit printer administration** option (☐ changes to ☑) to prevent the user from administering printers.

⑪ Click the **Disable changing the password** option (☐ changes to ☑) to prevent the user from changing her password.

⑫ Click the **Limit CD and DVD burning** option (☐ changes to ☑) to prevent the user from burning discs using the Finder.

TIP

Why should I prevent a managed user from changing her password?
Normally, it is a good idea for each user to set her own password, and for only that user to know that password. This secrecy helps prevent anybody else from accessing the user's account without the user's consent. When you are dealing with a managed user who tends to forget passwords, you will find it helpful to retain control of the user's password. By clicking the **Disable changing the password** option (☐ changes to ☑), you can avoid the problem of the user changing her password, forgetting about the change, and then needing you to reset the password from an administrator account.

Review a Managed User's Actions

After you, the administrator, enable parental controls for a managed user, OS X logs the actions the user takes with the controlled apps and features. You can review the logs of a user's actions to see what the user has done and what he has tried to do. Using this information, you can decide whether to tighten or loosen the parental controls; for example, you may need to allow access to additional websites, block other websites, or permit the user to run other apps. You can review the parental control logs either from your iMac or from another Mac.

Review a Managed User's Actions

1 In the Users & Groups preferences pane in System Preferences, click the user account you want to change.

Note: You can click **Apple** (🍎) and then click **System Preferences** to open the System Preferences window. Then click **Users & Groups**.

2 Click **Open Parental Controls**.

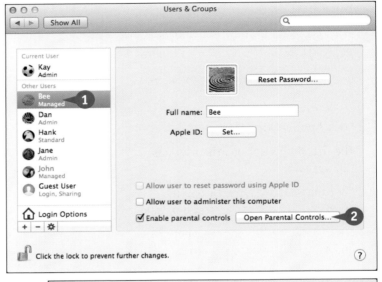

The Parental Controls preferences pane opens.

3 Click **Logs**.

④ Click **Websites Blocked**.

⑤ Click the **Show activity for** pop-up menu (⊟) and select the length of time.

⑥ Click the **Group by** pop-up menu (⊟) and select **Website** or **Date**.

⑦ Click the disclosure triangle (▶) to expand a category.

⑧ Click a site.

Ⓐ Click **Allow** to add the site to the Allowed list.

Ⓑ Click **Open** to open the site in Safari.

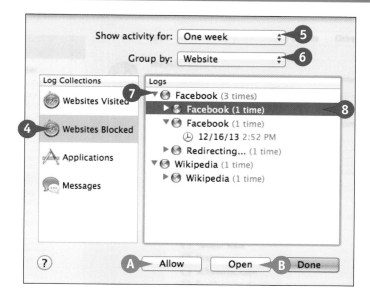

⑨ Click **Applications**.

The list of applications the user has run appears.

⑩ Click the **Show activity for** pop-up menu (⊟) and select the length of time.

⑪ Click the **Group by** pop-up menu (⊟) and select **Application** or **Date**.

⑫ Click the disclosure triangle (▶) to see the times the user used the application.

⑬ Click **Restrict** to restrict an application.

⑭ When you finish reviewing the logs, click **Done**.

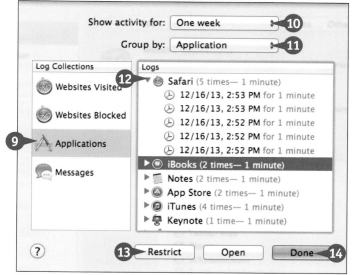

TIP

How do I use the Messages log collection?

Click **Messages** in the Log Collections pane, and then use the **Show activity** pop-up menu (⊟) and the **Group by** pop-up menu (⊙) to choose the activity period and how it appears. Double-click a contact in the Logs pane to view the contact's details. To view the transcript of a text chat, click the chat's date and time, and then click **Open**. To prevent the user from communicating with the contact, click the contact's name, and then click **Restrict**.

CHAPTER 3

Running Apps

OS X includes many apps, such as the TextEdit word processor, the Preview viewer for PDF files and images, and the iTunes player for music and videos. You can install other apps as needed. Whichever apps you run, you can switch among them easily, quit them when you finish using them, and force them to quit if they crash.

Open and Close an App

OS X enables you to open your iMac's apps in several ways. The Dock is the quickest way to launch apps you use frequently. Launchpad is a handy way to see all the apps installed in your iMac's Applications folder and its subfolders. You can also launch an app from the Applications folder, but typically you do not need to do so.

When you finish using an app, you close it by giving a Quit command. You can close an app either from the menu bar or by using a keyboard shortcut.

Open and Close an App

Open an App from the Dock

1 Click the app's icon on the Dock.

Note: If you do not recognize an app's icon, position the mouse pointer over it to display the app's name.

Ⓐ The app opens.

Open an App from Launchpad

1 Click **Launchpad** (🚀) on the Dock.

The Launchpad screen appears.

To scroll to another screen, click and drag left or right, or press ⬅ or ➡. If you have a trackpad, swipe left or right with two fingers.

Ⓑ You can also click a dot to move to another screen.

2 Click the app.

The app opens.

Open an App from the Applications Folder

1 Click **Finder** (⬜) on the Dock.

A Finder window opens.

2 Click **Applications** in the left column.

An icon appears for each app.

3 Double-click the app you want to run.

The app opens.

Note: You can also open an app by clicking **Spotlight** (🔍), starting to type the app's name, and then clicking the appropriate search result.

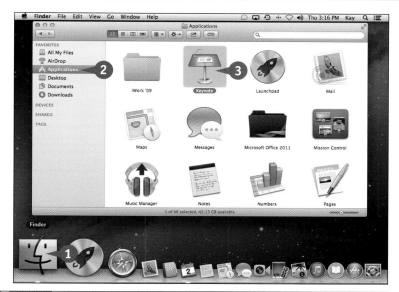

Close an App

1 Click the app's menu, the menu with the app's name — for example, **Keynote**.

The menu appears.

2 Click the Quit command from the menu that has the app's name — for example, **Quit Keynote**.

Note: You can also quit the active app by pressing ⌘+⬜.

Note: To launch an app you have used recently, click **Apple** (), highlight **Recent Items**, and then click the app in the Applications list.

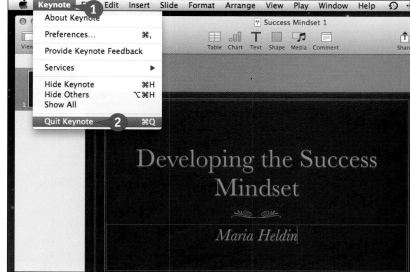

TIPS

How do I add an app to the Dock?

Open the app from Launchpad as usual. Press **Ctrl**+click its Dock icon, highlight **Options** on the contextual menu, and then click **Keep in Dock**. You can also click an app in Launchpad or the Applications folder and drag it to the Dock.

What happens if a document in the app I quit contains unsaved changes?

Some apps automatically save your changes when you quit the app. Other apps display a dialog asking if you want to save the changes. Click **Save** to save the changes or **Don't Save** to discard the changes.

Install an App from the App Store

Your iMac comes with many useful apps already installed, such as Safari for browsing the web, Mail for reading and sending e-mail, and iTunes for enjoying music and video.

To get your work or play done, you may need to install other apps on your iMac. You can install apps in three ways: by downloading them from Apple's App Store, by downloading them from other websites and then installing them, or by installing them from a CD or DVD.

Install an App from the App Store

1 Click **App Store** (◉) on the Dock.

Ⓐ The App Store window opens.

The Featured screen includes sections such as Best New Apps and Best Games.

2 Click **Top Charts**.

The Top Charts screen appears, showing a Top Paid section, a Top Free section, and a Top Grossing section.

Ⓑ You can also click **Categories** to browse apps by categories, such as Business and Entertainment.

3 Click the app you want to view.

The app's screen appears.

④ Click the app's price button, and then click the **Buy App** button that replaces the price button. For a free app, click **Install App**.

The Sign In to Download from the App Store dialog appears.

⑤ Type your Apple ID.

⑥ Type your password.

⑦ Click **Sign In**.

Note: If a dialog opens confirming the purchase, click **Buy**.

The download begins.

⑧ Click **Launchpad** (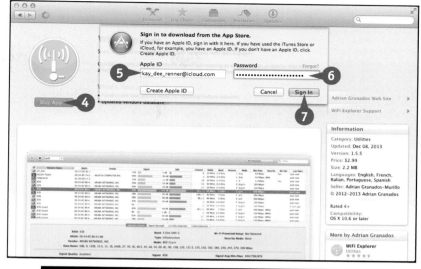).

The Launchpad screen appears, showing stars around the new app's icon.

⑨ Click the app's icon.

The app opens.

TIP

How do I update apps downloaded from the App Store?

Click **App Store** (📲) on the Dock to open the App Store app, and then click **Updates** on the app's toolbar to display the Updates screen. If any updates appear, click to download and install them.

If App Store does not appear on the Dock, click **Apple** (🍎) to open the Apple menu, and then click **Software Update** to check for updates. App Store checks for app updates as well as operating system updates.

Install an App from a Disc or the Internet

If an app is not available on Apple's App Store, you can acquire it either on a CD or DVD or as a file that you download. To install an app from a downloaded file, you open the file. To install an app from a CD or DVD, you must either connect an optical drive to your iMac or use the Remote Disc feature to access an optical drive on another Mac.

Before installing an app in these ways, you may need to change the Gatekeeper setting in Security & Privacy preferences.

Install an App from a Disc or the Internet

Install an App

1 Open the disc or file that contains the app.

If the app is on a CD or DVD, insert the disc in an optical drive.

If the app is in a file, double-click the file.

A Finder window opens showing the contents of the disc or file.

2 If there is a file containing installation instructions, follow the instructions. Otherwise, double-click the Installer icon. If there is no installer, see the first tip in this section.

A dialog opens prompting you to type your password.

Note: To install most apps, you must have an administrator account or provide an administrator's name and password.

3 Type your password.

4 Click **Install Software**.

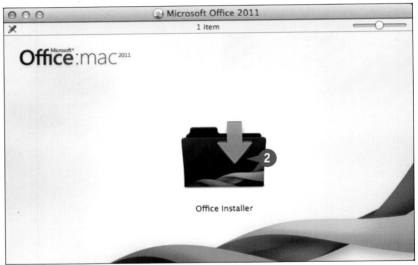

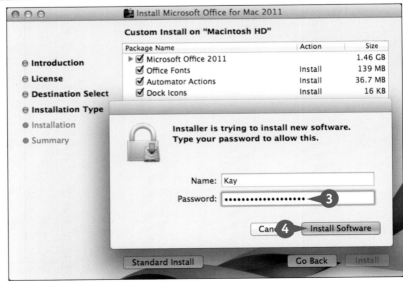

The installation continues. When it completes, Installer displays a screen telling you that the installation succeeded.

5 Click **Close**.

Installer closes.

Note: If OS X prevents you from installing the app, click **Apple** (![apple icon]) and then click **System Preferences**. Click **Security & Privacy**, and then click **General**. Click the **Mac App Store and identified developers** option (![radio button] changes to ![selected radio button]).

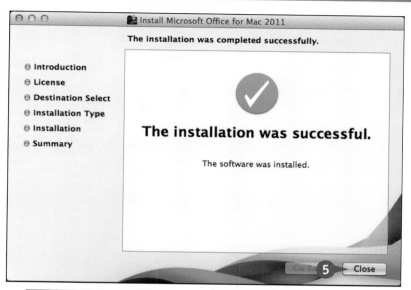

Run the App You Installed

Note: If Installer has added an icon for the app to the Dock, click that icon to run the app.

1 Click **Launchpad** (![launchpad icon]) on the Dock.

A Click the dot to display another Launchpad screen if necessary.

2 Click the app's icon.

The app opens.

TIPS

How do I install an app that has no installer or installation instructions?

If the app does not have an installer or specific installation instructions, click the icon in the Finder window for the app's disc or file, and then drag the app's icon to the Applications folder in the sidebar.

How do I use Remote Disc?

Click **Finder** (![finder icon]) on the Dock to open a Finder window. Position the mouse pointer over Devices in the sidebar and click **Show** to display the Devices list. Click **Remote Disc**, and then click the appropriate optical drive.

Run an App Full Screen

OS X enables you to run an app full screen instead of in a window. Running an app full screen helps you focus on that app, removing the distraction of other open apps.

You can instantly switch the active app to full-screen display. When you need to use another app, you can switch to that app full screen as well — and then switch back to the previous app. When you finish using full-screen display, you can switch back to displaying the app in a window.

Run an App Full Screen

Switch the Active App to Full Screen

① Click **Full Screen** (⬚).

Note: In many apps, you can also switch to full screen by clicking **View** on the menu bar and selecting **Enter Full Screen** or pressing Ctrl + ⌘ + F.

The app expands to take up the full screen.

Switch to Another App

1 Swipe left or right with three fingers on the Magic Mouse or Magic Trackpad.

Note: You can also switch apps by using Application Switcher or Mission Control. Alternatively, press [Ctrl]+[←] or [Ctrl]+[→].

The next app or previous app appears.

2 Swipe in the opposite direction.

The app you were using before you switched appears.

Return from Full-Screen Display to a Window

1 Move the mouse pointer to the top of the screen.

The menu bar appears.

2 Click **View**.

The View menu opens.

3 Click **Exit Full Screen**.

The app appears in a window again.

Note: In many apps, you can also press [⌘]+[Ctrl]+[F] to exit full-screen display.

How do I display the Dock in full-screen view?
Move the mouse pointer to the bottom of the screen; the Dock slides into view. If you have positioned the Dock at the left side or right side of the screen, move the mouse pointer to that side to display the Dock.

Can I exit full-screen display by using the keyboard?
Yes. Press [Esc] twice to return from full-screen view to windowed view.

Switch Quickly Among Apps

When you work with several apps at the same time, it is often useful to switch quickly from one app to another. OS X enables you to switch apps by using either the mouse or the keyboard.

If you have several apps displayed on-screen, you may be able to switch by clicking the window for the app you want to use. If the app is not visible, you can click the app's icon on the Dock. If the app has multiple windows, you can then select the window you need.

Switch Quickly Among Apps

Switch Apps Using the Mouse

1 If you can see a window for the app to which you want to switch, click anywhere in that window.

2 If you cannot see a window to which you want to switch, click the app's icon on the Dock.

All the windows for that app appear in front of the other apps' windows.

3 Click **Window** on the menu bar.

The Window menu opens.

4 Click the window you want to bring to the front.

Note: To bring a specific window to the front, press Ctrl +click the app's icon on the Dock, and then click the window you want to see.

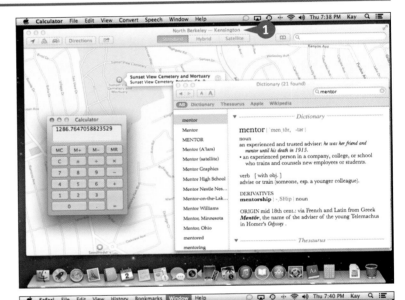

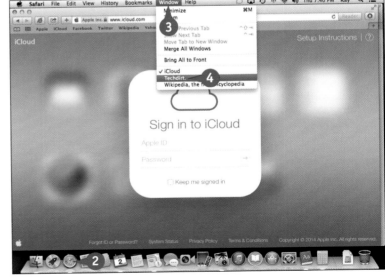

Switch Among Apps Using the Keyboard

1 Press and hold ⌘ and press **Tab**.

A Application Switcher opens, showing an icon for each open app.

2 Still holding down ⌘, press **Tab** one or more times to move the highlight to the app you want.

Note: Press and hold ⌘+**Shift** and press **Tab** to move backward through the apps.

3 When you reach the app you want, release ⌘.

Application Switcher closes, and the selected app comes to the front.

4 If necessary, click **Window** and select the window you want.

Note: You can press ⌘+' to switch among the windows in the current app.

TIPS

Are there other ways of switching among apps?

You can use the keyboard and the mouse together. Press and hold ⌘, press **Tab** once to open Application Switcher, and then click the app you want to bring to the front.

Can I do anything else with Application Switcher apart from switch to an app?

You can also hide an app or quit an application from Application Switcher. Press and hold ⌘, press **Tab** to open Application Switcher, and then select the app you want to affect. Still holding ⌘, press **H** to hide the app or press **Q** to quit the app.

Switch Apps Using Mission Control

OS X provides a powerful feature called Mission Control for managing your desktop and switching among apps and windows. When you activate Mission Control, it shrinks down the open windows so that you can see them all and click the one you want. You can use Mission Control to display all open windows in all apps or just the windows in a particular app.

Mission Control also shows different desktop spaces, enabling you to switch among desktop spaces or move an app window from one desktop space to another.

Switch Apps Using Mission Control

See All Your Open Apps and Windows

1 Press .

Note: On some Mac keyboards, you press `F9` to launch Mission Control. You can also press `Ctrl`+`↑`.

Note: You can also launch Mission Control by using a hot corner. See Chapter 12 for instructions on setting and using hot corners.

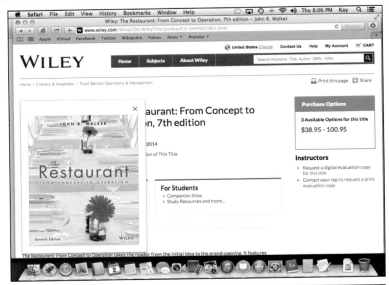

Mission Control opens and displays all open apps and windows.

Ⓐ To preview a window in an app, position the mouse pointer over the window so that a blue outline appears around it. Then press `Spacebar` to preview the window. Press `Spacebar` again to close the preview.

2 Click the window you want to use.

The window appears, and you can work with it.

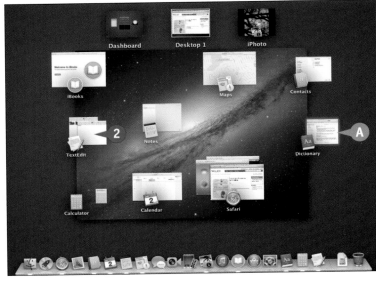

See All the Windows in the Active App

1 Activate the app whose windows you want to see. For example, click the app's Dock icon, or click a window from that app.

2 Press `Ctrl`+`F3`.

Note: On some iMacs, you press `F10` to display the windows of the active app. You can also press `Ctrl`+`↓`.

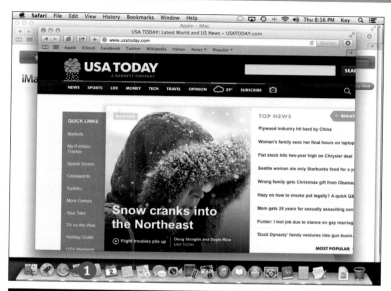

OS X tiles the windows of the app you chose so that you can see them all, and hides the windows of all other apps.

3 Click the window you want to see.

OS X restores all the windows from all the apps, placing the window you clicked at the front.

TIP

What other actions can I take with Mission Control?

After pressing `Ctrl`+`F3` to show all windows of the current app, you can press `Tab` to show all windows of the next app. Press `Shift`+`Tab` to show all windows of the previous app. You can press `⌘`+`F3` to move all open windows to the sides of the screen to reveal the desktop; on some keyboards, you press `F11`. Press `⌘`+`F3` or `F11` when you want to see the windows again.

Set Up Dictation and Text to Speech

OS X's Dictation feature enables you to dictate text, which can be a fast and accurate way of inputting text into documents. The Text to Speech feature enables you to have the system voice read on-screen items to you.

Before using Dictation and Text to Speech, you use Dictation & Speech preferences to enable the features. You can choose options such as whether to use the Enhanced Dictation feature, select your dictation language and the system voice, and define keyboard shortcuts for starting dictation and speaking.

Set Up Dictation and Text to Speech

1 Press **Ctrl**+click **System Preferences** (⚙) on the Dock.

The contextual menu opens.

2 Click **Dictation & Speech**.

The System Preferences window opens and displays the Dictation & Speech pane.

3 Click **Dictation**.

The Dictation pane appears.

4 Click **Input** (▾) and select the correct input.

5 Click **Dictation** (◯ changes to ◉).

A dialog opens explaining how Dictation works without Enhanced Dictation.

6 Click **Enable Dictation**.

The dialog closes.

7 Click **Use Enhanced Dictation** (☐ changes to ☑).

8 Click the **Language** pop-up menu (◉) and select your language.

9 Click the **Shortcut** pop-up menu (◉) and select the shortcut for starting dictation.

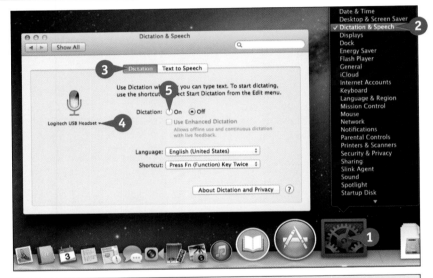

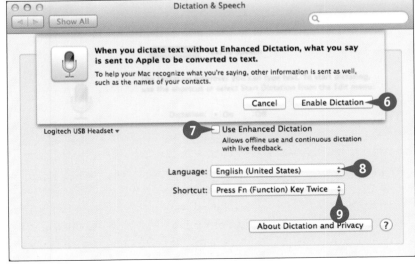

10 Click **Text to Speech**.

The Text to Speech pane opens.

11 Click the **System Voice** pop-up menu (⏏) and select the voice you prefer.

Note: You can install other voices by clicking **Customize** on the System Voice pop-up menu.

12 Click **Play** to hear the voice.

13 Drag the **Speaking Rate** slider to adjust the speed if necessary.

14 Click **Announce when alerts are displayed** (☐ changes to ☑) to hear alerts.

Ⓐ You can click **Set Alert Options** to choose the voice, phrase, and delay for alerts.

15 Click **Speak selected text when the key is pressed** (☐ changes to ☑) to make your iMac speak selected text.

Ⓑ You can click **Change Key** to set the keystroke.

16 Click **Close** (⊗).

System Preferences closes.

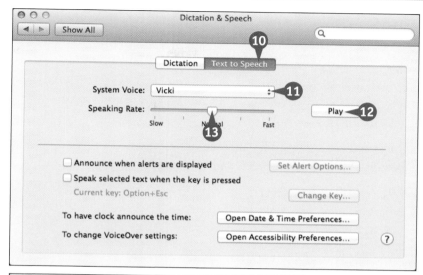

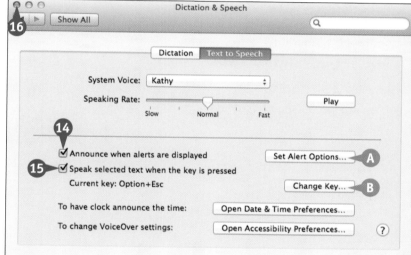

TIP

Should I use Enhanced Dictation?

Using Enhanced Dictation is usually a good idea. Enhanced Dictation uses your iMac to perform the speech recognition instead of sending your speech to Apple servers, and so has three main advantages over standard Dictation. First, you can dictate when your iMac is offline as well as when it is online. Second, you can dictate continuously instead of having to pause between sentences or phrases. Third, you need not worry about the potential privacy implications of sharing your speech with Apple.

Using Dictation and Text to Speech

With the Dictation and Text to Speech features enabled and configured on your iMac, you can use them freely as you work or play. When you are using an app that accepts text input, you can press your keyboard shortcut to turn on Dictation, and then dictate text into a document.

To make Text to Speech read to you, you select the text you want to hear and then press the appropriate keyboard shortcut. If you have enabled the announcing of alerts, your iMac automatically speaks their text as well.

Using Dictation and Text to Speech

Using Dictation

1 Open the app into which you want to dictate text. For example, click **Notes** (🗒) on the Dock to open Notes.

2 Open the document into which you will dictate text. For example, in Notes, click the appropriate note.

3 Position the insertion point.

4 Press the keyboard shortcut you set for starting Dictation.

Note: The default keyboard shortcut is pressing **Fn** twice.

A The Dictation window opens.

5 Speak into your microphone.

B Dictation inserts the text in the document.

6 Click **Done**.

The Dictation window closes.

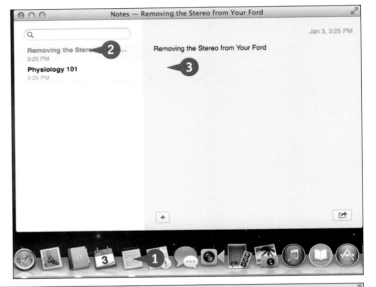

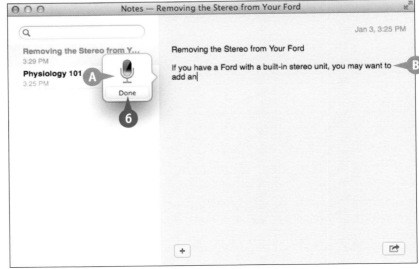

Make Text to Speech Read Text

1 In an app that contains text, select the text you want to hear.

2 Press the keyboard shortcut you set for Text to Speech.

Note: The default keyboard shortcut is `Option`+`Esc`.

Text to Speech reads the selected text to you.

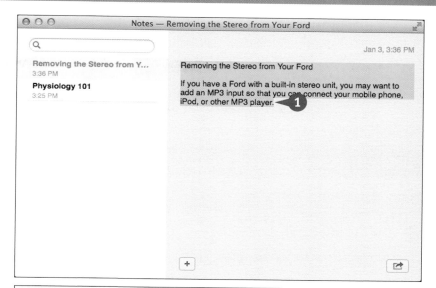

Hear Alerts from Text to Speech

C After an alert appears, Text to Speech waits as long as specified in Dictation & Speech preferences.

If you have not dismissed the alert, Text to Speech announces the app and then reads the text of the alert.

1 Click **Close** or **Snooze**, as appropriate, to dismiss the alert.

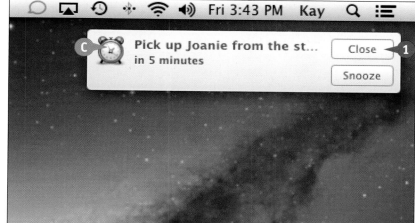

TIP

How accurate is Dictation?
Dictation can be highly accurate, but your results depend on how clearly you speak and how faithfully your microphone transmits the sound. For best results, use a headset microphone and position it to the side of your mouth, outside your breath stream.

When reviewing dictated text, read it for sense to identify incorrect words and phrases. Because all the text is spelled correctly, it can be easy to overlook mistakes caused by Dictation inserting the wrong words or phrases instead of what you said.

Remove Apps

OS X enables you to remove apps you have added, but not apps included with the operating system. If you install apps frequently, you may end up with many apps that you no longer need. These unneeded apps take up disk space and may cause your iMac to run more slowly, so removing them is a good idea.

OS X uses two techniques for removing apps. To remove some apps, you simply place them in the Trash. To remove other apps, you run the uninstall utilities the apps provide.

Remove Apps

Remove an App by Moving It to the Trash

1. Click **Launchpad** (![icon]) on the Dock.

   The Launchpad screen appears.

   Ⓐ If necessary, click a dot to move to another screen in Launchpad. You can also swipe left or right with two fingers on the trackpad or Magic Mouse, or press ⌘+← or ⌘+→.

2. Click the app and drag it to the Trash.

   Finder places the app in the Trash.

Note: You can also drag an app to the Trash from the Applications folder. Alternatively, click the app in the Applications folder, click **Action** (![icon]), and then select **Move to Trash**.

Remove an App by Using an Uninstall Utility

1 Click **Finder** (🙂) on the Dock.

A Finder window opens.

2 Click **Applications**.

Note: With the Finder active, you can press ⌘+Shift+A to open a window showing the Applications folder.

The contents of the Applications folder appear.

3 Navigate to the folder that contains the uninstall utility.

Note: See the tip for instructions on where to find the utility.

4 Press Option+double-click the uninstall utility.

The uninstall utility opens, and the Finder window closes.

5 Follow through the steps of the uninstall utility. For example, click **Continue**.

6 When the uninstall utility finishes running, close it.

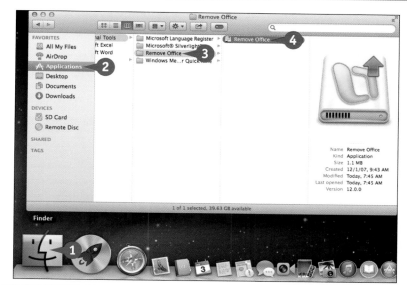

TIP

Where do I find the uninstall utility for an app?

If the app has a folder within the Applications folder, look inside that folder for an uninstall utility. If there is no folder, open the disk image file, CD, or DVD from which you installed the app and look for an uninstall utility there. Some apps use an installer for both installing the app and uninstalling it, so if you do not find an uninstall utility, try running the installer and see if it contains an uninstall option.

Identify Problem Apps

Sometimes you may find that your iMac starts to respond slowly to your commands, even though no app has stopped working. When this occurs, you can use the Activity Monitor utility to see what app is consuming more of the processors' cycles than it should. To resolve the problem, you can quit that app and then restart it.

If you cannot quit the app normally, you can force quit it. You can force quit it either from Activity Monitor or by using the Force Quit Applications dialog.

Identify Problem Apps

1 Click **Launchpad** (🚀) on the Dock.

The Launchpad screen appears.

2 Type **ac**.

Launchpad displays only those items whose names include words starting with *ac*.

3 Click **Activity Monitor** (📊).

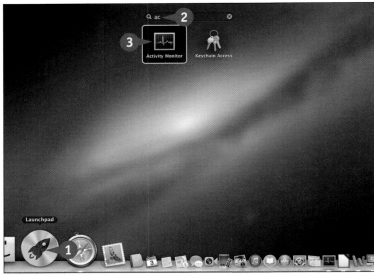

The Activity Monitor window opens, listing all your running apps and processes.

A The title bar shows "(My Processes)" to indicate you are viewing only your processes.

4 Click **View**.

The View menu opens.

5 Click **All Processes**.

Note: You should view all processes because another user's processes may be slowing your iMac.

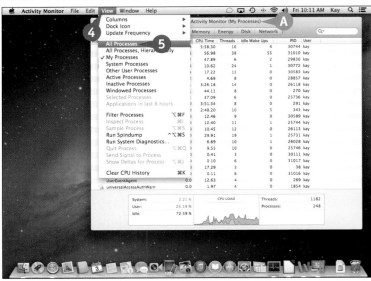

B The title bar shows "(All Processes)."

C Other users' processes appear as well.

6 Click **CPU**.

The details of your iMac's central processing units, or CPUs, appear.

D The CPU Load graph shows how hard the CPU is working.

7 Click **% CPU** once or twice, as needed, so that Descending Sort (▼) appears on the column heading.

Activity Monitor sorts the processes by CPU activity in descending order.

8 Identify the app that is using the most processor cycles.

9 Click that app's Dock icon.

The app appears.

10 Save your work in the app, and then quit it.

11 Click the Activity Monitor window.

12 Click the **Activity Monitor** menu and click **Quit Activity Monitor** to close Activity Monitor.

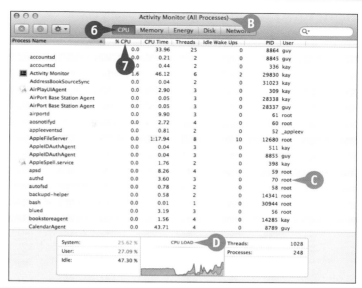

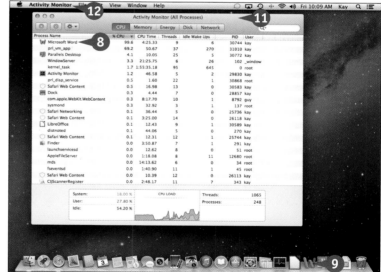

TIPS

What should I do if I cannot quit or force quit the problem app?

If you cannot force quit the app from the Dock or the Force Quit Applications dialog, try force quitting from Activity Monitor. In Activity Monitor, click the app's process name, and then click **Force Quit** (⊗) on the toolbar. A confirmation dialog opens. Click **Force Quit**.

How do I see whether my iMac is running short of memory?

Click **Memory** on the Activity Monitor tab bar and then look at the Memory Pressure readout. Click the **Memory** column heading to sort the processes by the amount of memory they are using.

Force a Crashed App to Quit

When an app is working normally, you can quit it by clicking the Quit command on the app's menu or by pressing ⌘+Q. But if an app stops responding to the mouse and keyboard, you cannot quit it this way. Instead, you use the Force Quit command that OS X provides for this situation.

When an app stops responding, it may freeze, so that the window does not change, or it may display the spinning cursor for a long time, indicating that the app is busy.

Force a Crashed App to Quit

Force Quit an App from the Dock

① Pressing and holding Option, click the app's icon on the Dock. Keep holding down the mouse button until the Dock menu appears.

② Click **Force Quit**.

OS X forces the app to quit.

Force Quit an App from the Force Quit Applications Dialog

① Click **Apple** (🍎).

The Apple menu opens.

② Click **Force Quit**.

Note: You can open the Force Quit Applications dialog from the keyboard by pressing Option + ⌘ + Esc.

The Force Quit Applications dialog opens.

3 Click the app you want to force quit.

4 Click **Force Quit**.

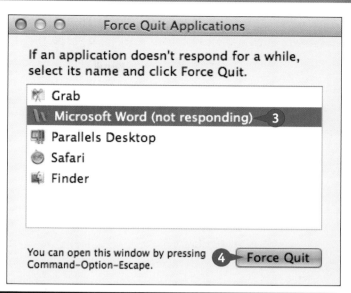

A dialog opens to confirm that you want to force quit the app.

5 Click **Force Quit**.

OS X forces the app to quit.

6 Click **Close** (🔘).

The Force Quit Applications dialog closes.

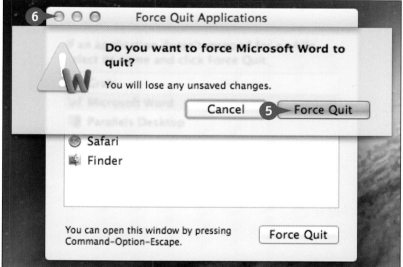

TIP

How do I recover the unsaved changes in a document after force quitting the app?

When you force quit an app, you normally lose all unsaved changes in the documents you were using in the app. However, some apps automatically store unsaved changes in special files called *recovery files*, which the apps open when you relaunch them after force quitting. For some apps, you may also be able to return to an earlier version of the document.

Revert to an Earlier Version of a Document

OS X includes a feature called *versions* that enables apps to save different versions of the same document in the same file. You can display the different versions of the document at the same time and go back to an earlier version if necessary.

Only apps written to work with OS X Lion, 10.7, and subsequent versions of OS X can use the versions feature. Such apps include TextEdit — the text editor and word processor included with OS X — and the apps in Apple's iWork suite.

Revert to an Earlier Version of a Document

1 In the appropriate app, open the document. For example, open a word processing document in TextEdit.

2 Click the app's name on the menu bar.

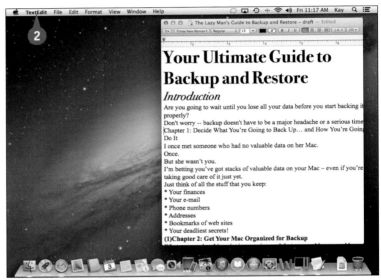

The app's menu opens.

3 Click or highlight **Revert To**.

The Revert To submenu opens.

A You can click a version on the menu to go straight to that version.

4 Click **Browse All Versions**.

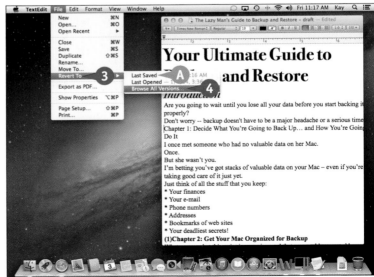

B OS X displays earlier versions of the document on the right, with newer versions at the front, and older versions at the back.

C The current version appears on the left.

5 Position the mouse over the time bars, and then click the version you want.

The version comes to the front.

6 Click **Restore**.

OS X restores the version of the document.

The version opens in the app so that you can work with it.

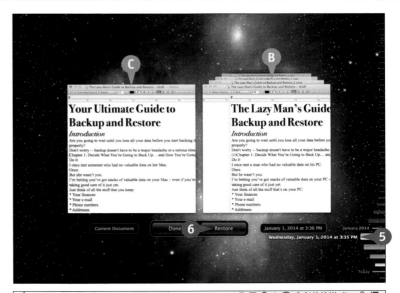

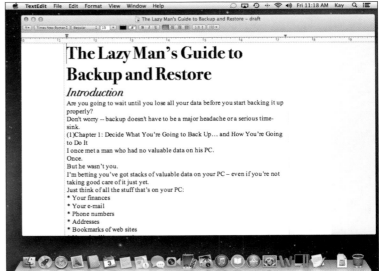

Managing Your Files and Folders

The Finder enables you to manage your files, folders, and drives. You can take many actions in the Finder, including copying, moving, and deleting files and folders.

Understanding Where to Store Files

OS X automatically creates a structure of folders in each user account for storing files. Your home base is your Home folder, which contains folders such as Desktop, Documents, Downloads, and Music. You can navigate easily among your folders by using the sidebar or the Go menu. To help you find your files, the Finder also includes a view called All My Files, which shows your files by their type or another attribute you choose.

Understanding Where to Store Files

① Click **Finder** (🔳) on the Dock.

A Finder window opens to your default folder or view.

② Click **All My Files**.

The Finder window displays the All My Files view, which shows all your files.

③ Click **Documents**.

The contents of the Documents folder appear.

Note: The Documents folder is your storage place for word processing documents, spreadsheets, and similar files.

④ Click **Go**.

The Go menu opens.

⑤ Click **Home**.

The contents of your Home folder appear.

Ⓐ The Desktop folder contains items on your desktop.

Ⓑ The Downloads folder contains files you download via apps such as Safari or Mail.

Ⓒ The Movies folder contains movies, such as iMovie projects.

Ⓓ The Pictures folder contains images.

Ⓔ The Public folder is for sharing files with others.

⑥ Double-click **Music**.

The contents of your Music folder appear.

Ⓕ The iTunes folder contains your music library.

Ⓖ The GarageBand folder appears if you have used GarageBand, the music-composition app.

Ⓗ You can click **Back** (◀) to back along the path of folders you have followed.

⑦ Click **Close** (⊗).

The Finder window closes.

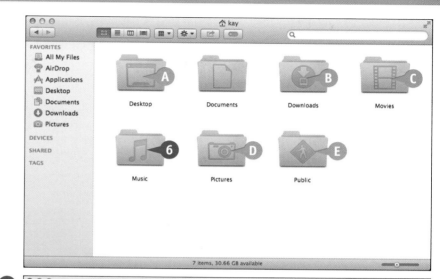

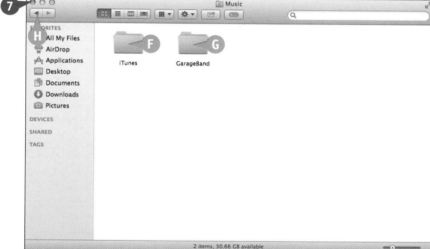

TIP

How do I choose what folder the Finder opens by default?
Click the desktop to activate the Finder. Click **Finder** to open the Finder menu, and then click **Preferences**. Click **General** to display the General pane. Click the **New Finder windows show** pop-up menu (⬍), and then select the folder you want new Finder windows to display. Click **Close** (⊗) to close the Finder Preferences window.

Using the Finder's Views

The Finder provides four views to help you find and identify your files and folders. You can switch from view to view by using the View buttons, the View menu or the contextual menu, or keyboard shortcuts.

Icon view shows each file or folder as a graphical icon. List view shows folders as a collapsible hierarchy. Column view enables you to navigate quickly through folders and see where each item is located. Cover Flow view is great for identifying files visually by looking at their contents.

Using the Finder's Views

Icon View

1 Click **Finder** (■) on the Dock.

A Finder window opens showing your default folder or view.

2 Click the folder you want to display.

The folder — in this case, the Pictures folder — appears.

3 Click **Icons** (▦) on the toolbar.

The files and folders appear in Icon view.

List View

1 Click **List** (▤) on the toolbar.

The files and folders appear in List view.

2 Click **Expand** (▶ changes to ▼) next to a folder.

The folder's contents appear.

Note: If the disclosure triangles do not appear next to folders, click **View**, highlight **Arrange By**, and select **None**.

3 When you need to hide the folder's contents again, click **Collapse** (▼ changes to ▶).

Note: Click a column header in List view to sort by that column.

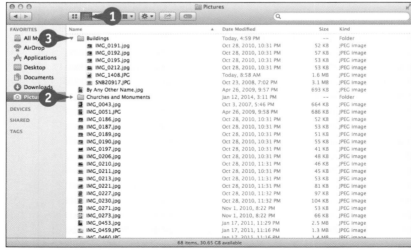

Column View

1 In the Finder window, click **Columns** (▥) on the toolbar.

The files and folders appear in Column view.

2 Click a folder in the first column after the sidebar.

The folder's contents appear in the next column.

3 Click another folder if necessary.

The folder's contents appear.

4 Click a file.

A A preview of the document file appears.

Cover Flow View

1 In the Finder window, click **Cover Flow** (▤) on the toolbar.

The files and folders appear in Cover Flow view.

2 Click a file in the list view.

A preview or icon appears in the Cover Flow area.

B Click to display the previous document.

C Click to display the next document.

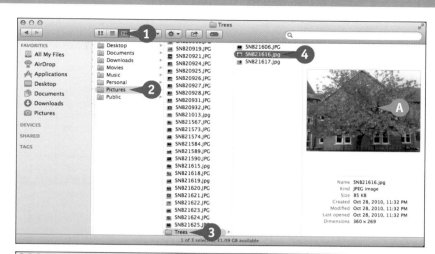

TIP

Can I change the size of icons used in Icon view?

If the status bar and toolbar are displayed, you can change icon size by dragging the slider on the right side of the status bar. If the toolbar is hidden, the status bar appears below the window's title bar. To set a default size in Icon view, choose **View** and **Show View Options**. The View Options window opens, showing the folder's name in the title bar. Click and drag the **Icon size** slider until the icons are the size you want. Click **Use as Defaults**. Click **Close** (⊗) to close the View Options window.

Work with Tabbed Finder Windows

The Finder enables you to open multiple tabs within the same window. This capability is useful when you need to work in multiple folders at the same time. You can navigate quickly among the tabs by using the tab bar.

Finder tabs are especially useful if you switch a Finder window to full-screen mode. You can drag files or folders from one Finder tab to another to copy or move the items.

Work with Tabbed Finder Windows

① Click **Finder** (⬛) on the Dock.

   A Finder window opens.

② Click the folder you want to view in the window.

③ Press ⌘+T or click **File** and **New Tab**.

Note: The Finder hides the tab bar by default when only one tab is open. You can display the tab bar by clicking **View** and clicking **Show Tab Bar** or pressing Shift+⌘+T.

Ⓐ The tab bar appears.

Ⓑ A new tab opens.

④ Click the folder you want to view.

Note: You can use a different view in each tab.

⑤ Click **New Tab** (➕).

Note: To close a tab, position the mouse pointer over it, and then click **Close** (❌). You can also press ⌘+W or click **File** and select **Close Tab**.

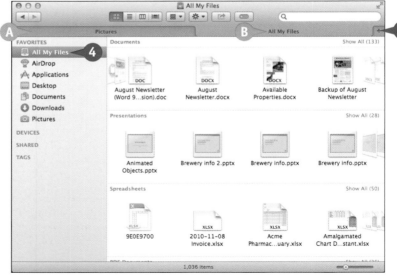

A new tab opens.

6 Drag the tab along the tab bar to where you want it.

Note: You can drag a tab to another Finder window if you want. You can also drag a tab out of a Finder window to turn it into its own window.

7 Click **Full Screen** (⬚).

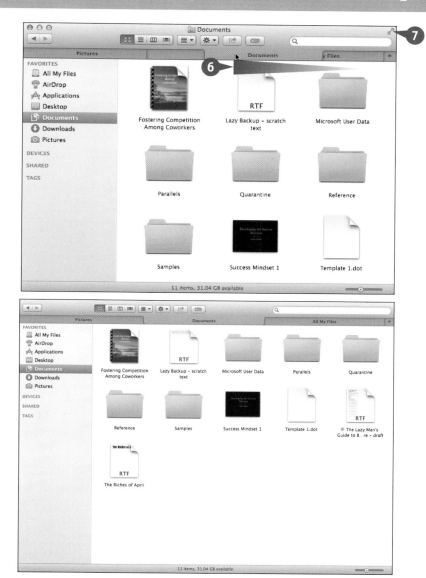

The Finder window appears full screen, giving you more space for working with files, folders, and tabs.

Note: To exit Full Screen view, move the mouse pointer to the top of the screen so that the menu bar appears, and then click **Exit Full Screen** (⬛). Alternatively, press Esc.

TIP

How do I copy or move files using Finder tabs?

Select the files in the source tab, and then drag them to the destination tab on the tab bar. To put the files into the folder open in the destination tab, drop the files on the destination tab in the tab bar. To navigate to a subfolder, position the mouse pointer over the destination tab until its content appears, and then drag the items to the subfolder. If the destination tab does not appear, click **Finder**, click **Preferences**, click **General**, and then click the **Spring-loaded folders and windows** option (☐ changes to ☑). Click **Close** (⬛) and then try again.

View a File with Quick Look

OS X's Quick Look feature enables you to preview files in Finder windows without actually opening the files in their apps. You can use Quick Look to determine what a file contains or to identify the file for which you are looking. You can preview a file full screen with Quick Look or preview multiple files at the same time. Quick Look works for many widely used types of files, but not for all types.

View a File with Quick Look

1 Click **Finder** (🖼) on the Dock.

A Finder window opens to your default folder or view.

2 Click the file you want to look through.

3 Click **Action** (⚙).

The Action pop-up menu opens.

4 Click **Quick Look**.

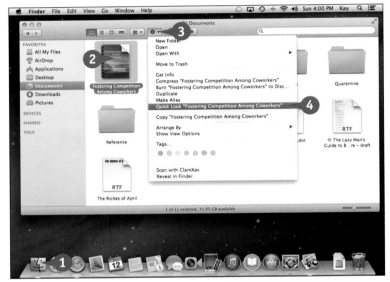

A Quick Look window opens showing a preview of the file or the file's icon.

Note: When you use Quick Look on a video file, OS X starts playing the file.

5 If you need to scroll to see more of the file, scroll down or swipe up.

A You can click **Open with** to open the file in its default app.

6 Click **Full Screen** (🔲).

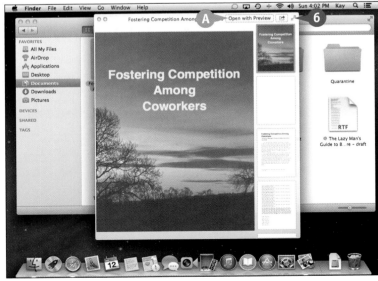

The Quick Look window expands to fill the screen.

Note: To see more of the file in full-screen view, scroll down, swipe up with two fingers, or press Page down.

7 Click **Exit Full Screen** (◻) when you finish using full-screen view.

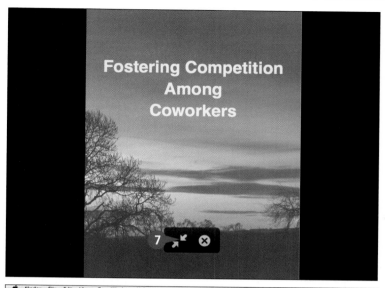

8 Click **Close** (◻) to close the Quick Look window.

Note: Instead of closing the Quick Look window, you can press ➡, ⬅, ⬆, or ⬇ to display another file or folder.

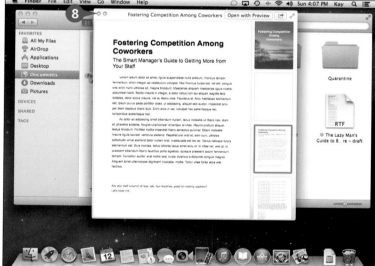

How do I use Quick Look on more than one file at a time?
Select the files you want to view with Quick Look, launch Quick Look, and click **Full Screen** (◻) to enter full-screen view. Click **Play** (▶) to play each preview for a few seconds, or click **Next** (➡) and **Previous** (⬅) to move from preview to preview. Click **Index** (⊞) to see the index sheet showing all previews, and then click the item you want to see.

Search for a File or Folder

OS X includes a powerful search feature called Spotlight that enables you to find the files and folders you need. Spotlight automatically indexes the files on your iMac and connected drives so that it can deliver accurate results within seconds when you search.

You can use Spotlight either directly from the desktop or from within a Finder window. Depending on what you need to find, you can use either straightforward search keywords or complex search criteria.

Search for a File or Folder

Search Quickly from the Desktop

1. Click **Spotlight** (🔍).

   The Spotlight search field opens.

2. Type one or more keywords.

   Spotlight displays a list of matches.

3. Position the mouse pointer over a result.

   Ⓐ A preview of the file appears.

4. Click the file you want to see.

   The file opens in the application associated with it.

Search from a Finder Window

1. Click **Finder** (🖼) on the Dock.

2. Click the folder you want to search.

3. Click in the search field.

4. Type the keywords for your search.

   Ⓑ The Finder window's title bar changes to Searching.

   Ⓒ A list of search results appears.

5. You can click a suggested search criterion on the pop-up menu to restrict the search.

6 To change where Spotlight is searching, click a button on the Search bar.

7 To quickly view a file, press Ctrl+click it and click **Quick Look**.

8 To open a file, double-click it.

9 To refine the search, click **Add** (⊕).

A line of controls appears.

10 Click the pop-up menu (⬍) and click **Kind**, **Last opened date**, **Last modified date**, **Created date**, **Name**, or **Contents**.

11 Click the pop-up menu (⬍) and select search criteria — for example, *Kind is Image*.

Note: To add more search criteria, click **Add** (⊕).

The search results appear.

Note: You can click **Save** to save the search for future use.

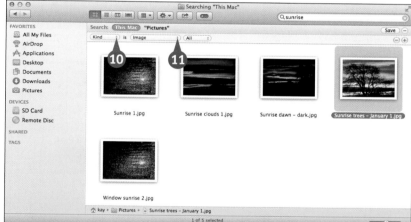

TIPS

What does Spotlight index?

Spotlight indexes both the metadata and the contents of files. Metadata includes information such as the filename, file extension, and file label; the date created, date received, and date last viewed; and the subject, title, and comment assigned to the file. Contents include any text, enabling you to search by keyword in documents that contain text.

Can I change where Spotlight searches for files?

You can customize the list of folders that Spotlight searches. See Chapter 12 for instructions on customizing Spotlight.

Create a New Folder

OS X builds a hierarchy of folders in your user account but also enables you to create as many new folders and subfolders as you need. You can create folders and subfolders in your user account or in other parts of the file system, such as on an external drive connected to your iMac. If the folders are for your personal use, keep them in your user account — as long as your iMac's drive has enough space — or on a removable drive.

Create a New Folder

1 Click **Finder** (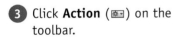) on the Dock.

A Finder window opens to your default folder.

2 Click the folder in which you want to create the new folder.

3 Click **Action** (⚙) on the toolbar.

The Action pop-up menu opens.

4 Click **New Folder**.

Note: You can also create a new folder by pressing ⌘ + Shift + N or clicking **File** on the Finder menu bar and clicking **New Folder**.

Ⓐ A new folder appears in the Finder window.

The new folder shows an edit box around the default name, Untitled Folder.

⑤ Type the name you want to give the folder.

⑥ Press Return.

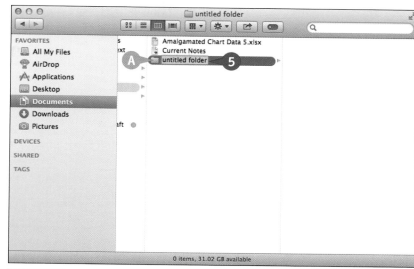

The folder takes on the new name.

⑦ Click or double-click the folder, depending on the view you are using.

The folder opens. You can now add files to the folder or create subfolders inside it.

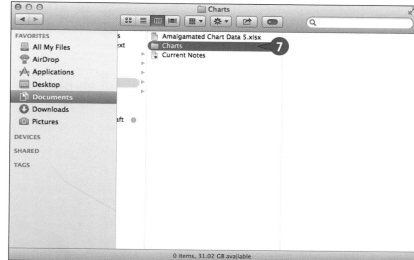

TIP

Why can I not create a new folder inside some other folders?
Most likely, you do not have permission to create a folder in that folder. Each user can create new items in the folders in his user account, and administrators can create folders in some other folders. But OS X protects other folders, such as the System folder and the Users folder, from anybody creating new folders.

Copy a File

The Finder enables you to copy a file from one folder to another. Copying is useful when you need to share a file with other people or when you need to keep a copy of the file safe against harm.

You can copy either by clicking and dragging or by using the Copy and Paste commands. You can copy a single file or folder at a time or copy multiple items.

Copy a File

Copy a File by Clicking and Dragging

1 Click **Finder** (![icon]) on the Dock.

A Finder window opens.

2 Click the folder that contains the file you want to copy.

3 Click **File** and click **New Finder Window**.

A new Finder window opens.

4 In the second Finder window, open the destination folder.

5 Arrange the Finder windows so that you can see both.

6 Select the file or files.

7 Press and hold ⌥Option while you click the file and drag it to the destination folder.

Note: The mouse pointer displays a plus sign (![icon]) to indicate copying.

The copy or copies appear in the destination folder.

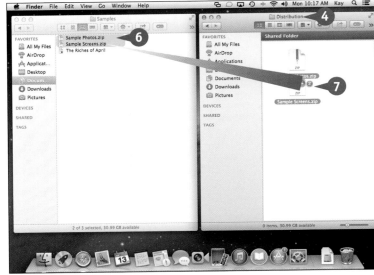

Copy a File by Using Copy and Paste

1 Click **Finder** () on the Dock.

A Finder window opens.

2 Click the folder that contains the file you want to copy.

3 Click the file.

4 Click **Action** (⚙▾).

The Action pop-up menu opens.

5 Click **Copy**.

Finder copies the file's details to the clipboard.

6 Click the folder in which you want to create the copy.

7 Click **Action** (⚙▾).

The Action pop-up menu opens.

8 Click **Paste Item**.

A copy of the file appears in the destination folder.

Note: You can use the Paste command in either the same Finder window or tab or another Finder window or tab — whichever you find more convenient.

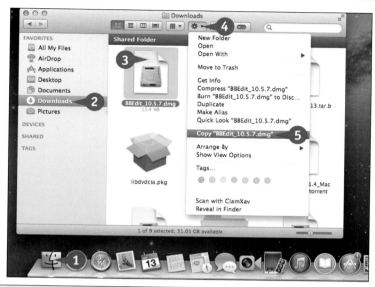

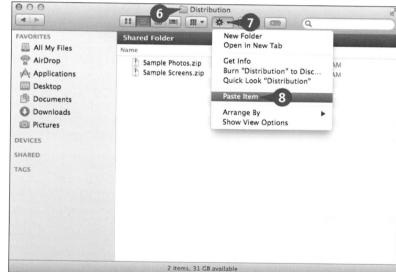

How do I copy a folder?

Use the same techniques as for files: Either press **Option** +click and drag the folder or folders to the destination folder, or use the Copy command to copy the folder and the Paste command to paste it into the destination folder.

Can I make a copy of a file in the same folder as the original?

To make a copy of a file in the same folder as the original, click the file, click **Action** (⚙▾), and then click **Duplicate**. Finder automatically adds *copy* to the end of the copy's filename to distinguish it from the original.

Move a File

The Finder makes it easy to move a file from one folder to another. You can move a file quickly by clicking it in its current folder and then dragging it to the destination folder.

When the destination folder is on the same drive as the source folder, the Finder moves the file to that folder. But when the destination folder is on a different drive, the Finder copies the file by default. To override this and move the file, you press ⌘ as you drag.

Move a File

Move a File Between Folders on the Same Drive

1. Click **Finder** (🗔) on the Dock.

   A Finder window opens.

2. Click the folder that contains the file you want to move.

3. Click **File** and click **New Finder Window**.

A new Finder window opens.

4. In the second Finder window, open the destination folder.

5. Click and drag the Finder windows so that you can see both.

6. Click the file and drag it to the destination folder.

   The file appears in the destination folder and disappears from the source folder.

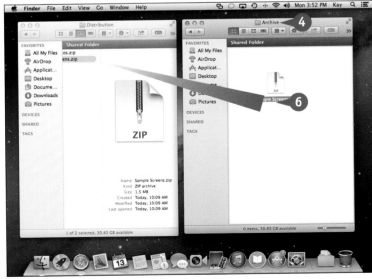

Move a File from One Drive to Another

1 Click **Finder** () on the Dock.

A Finder window opens.

2 Click the folder that contains the file you want to move.

3 Press **Ctrl**+click **Finder** (📁) on the Dock.

The contextual menu opens.

4 Click **New Finder Window**.

A new Finder window opens.

5 In the second Finder window, click the drive to which you want to copy the file.

6 Click the destination folder.

7 Arrange the Finder windows so that you can see both.

8 Press and hold ⌘ while you click the file and drag it to the destination folder.

The file appears in the destination folder and disappears from the source folder.

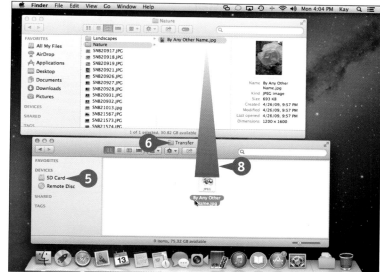

TIP

Can I move files by using menu commands rather than clicking and dragging?

If you find it awkward to click and drag files from one folder to another, you can use menu commands instead. Select the file or files you want to move, and then click **Edit** and **Copy** to copy them. Open the destination folder and click **Edit** to open the Edit menu. Press and hold **Option** and click **Move Item Here** or **Move Items Here**.

Rename a File or Folder

OS X enables you to rename any file or folder you have created. To keep your iMac's file system well organized, it is often helpful to rename files and folders. You can use the Finder to rename files and folders.

It is best not to rename the files and folders that OS X creates in your user account, such as the Desktop and Documents folders. Never rename any of the OS X system folders, such as the System folder itself, the Applications folder, or the Users folder.

Rename a File or Folder

1 Click the desktop.

The Finder becomes active.

2 Click **File**.

The File menu opens.

3 Click **New Finder Window**.

A new Finder window opens.

4 Click the folder that contains the file or folder you want to rename.

5 Click the file or folder.

6 Press **Return**.

Note: You can also display the edit box by clicking the file's name to select it, pausing, and then clicking again. You must pause between the clicks; otherwise, Finder registers a double-click and opens the file.

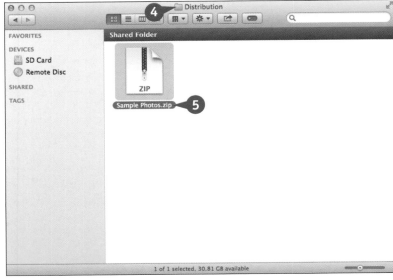

An edit box appears around the file name.

7 Edit the file's current name, or simply type the new name over the current name.

8 Press **Return**.

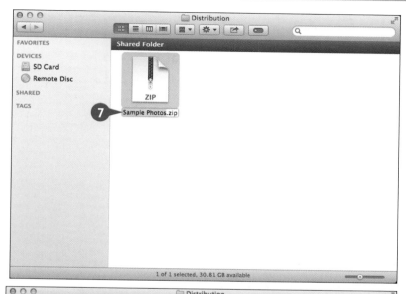

A The file takes on the new name.

You can now open the file by double-clicking it or pressing ⌘+O, or rename another file or folder.

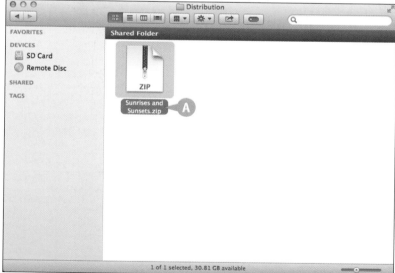

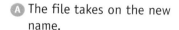

Can I rename several files at the same time?

There is no convenient way to rename several files at the same time from the Finder manually. Each file in a folder must have a unique name, so you cannot apply the same name to two or more files simultaneously. Some applications and scripts have features for renaming multiple files at once, usually by giving them sequential names using numbers appended to a base name — for example, Carlsbad Trip 01, Carlsbad Trip 02, and so on.

View the Information About a File or Folder

OS X keeps a large amount of information about each file and folder. When you view the file or folder in most Finder views, you can see the item's name and some basic information about it, such as its kind, size, and date last modified.

To see further information about the file or folder, you can open the Info window. This window contains multiple sections that you can expand by clicking **Expand** (▶) or collapse by clicking **Collapse** (▼).

View the Information About a File or Folder

1 Click **Finder** (🖼) on the Dock.

A Finder window opens.

2 Click the folder that contains the file whose info you want to view.

3 Click the file.

4 Click **Action** (⚙▾).

5 Click **Get Info**.

The Info window opens.

6 View the preview.

7 Review the tags. Press **Return** to add tags.

8 Review the general information:

Kind shows the file's type. *Size* shows the file's size on disk. *Where* shows the folder that contains the file. *Created* shows when the file was created. *Modified* shows when the file was last changed.

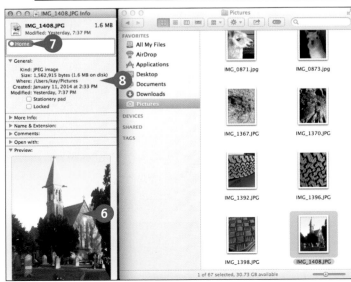

9 Review the details in the More Info section.

Note: The More Info details are especially useful for photos.

A You can change the filename or extension. Normally, it is best not to change the extension.

10 Click **Hide extension** (☐ changes to ☑) if you want to hide the extension.

11 Type any comments to help identify the file.

12 Click the **Open With** pop-up menu (▯) and select the app with which to open this file.

13 Click **Change All** if you want to use the app for all files of this type.

14 Click **Close** (◉).

The Info window closes.

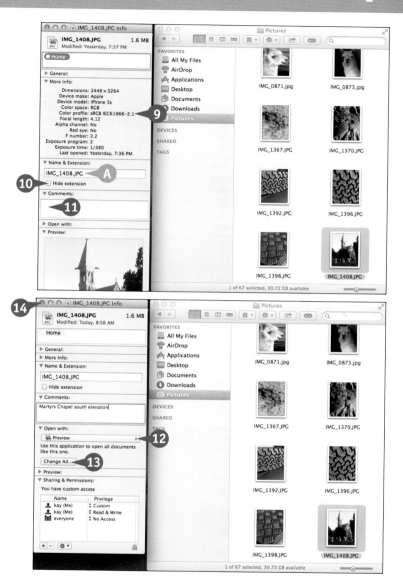

Organize Your Files with Tags

You can organize your files and folders by giving them descriptive names and storing them in appropriate places. But OS X, its apps, and iCloud give you another means of organizing your files and folders: tags.

OS X includes a set of default tags that you can customize to better describe your projects. You can then apply one or more tags to a file to enable you to locate it more easily in the Finder, in iCloud, or in apps. You can use tags to pull together related files from across your iMac's file system and your iCloud account.

Organize Your Files with Tags

Customize Your Tags

1 Click the desktop.

The Finder becomes active.

2 Click **Finder**.

The Finder menu opens.

3 Click **Preferences**.

The Finder Preferences window opens.

4 Click **Tags**.

The Tags pane appears.

5 Click a tag you want to rename, and then type the new name.

6 Click the check box (☐ changes to ☑) to make the tag appear in the list in the Finder.

7 Drag the tags into the order in which you want them to appear.

8 Drag tags to the Favorite Tags list at the bottom to control which tags appear in Finder menus.

9 Click **Close** (◉).

The Finder Preferences window closes.

Apply Tags to Files and Folders

1 If the Tags section of the sidebar is not displayed, position the mouse pointer over Tags and click **Show**.

2 Click the file or folder you want to tag.

3 Click and drag the file or folder to the appropriate tag.

Finder applies the tag.

Note: You can also apply tags from the File menu or from the context menu.

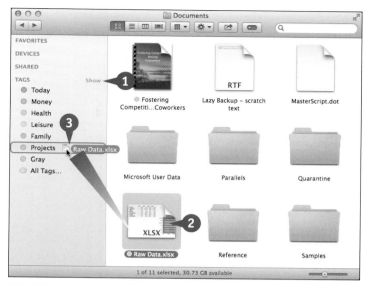

View Files and Folders by Tags

1 If the Tags section of the sidebar is not displayed, position the mouse pointer over Tags and click **Show** when it appears.

2 Click the appropriate tag.

A The Finder window shows the tagged files and folders.

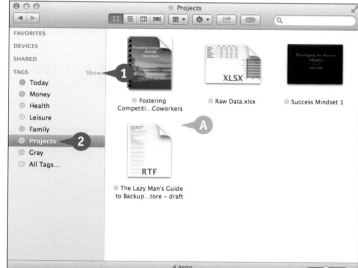

TIP

How do I apply tags to a new document I create?

In the app, click **File** and **Save** or press ⌘+⑤ to display the Save As dialog. Type the filename, then click **Tags** and click each tag you want to apply. You can then choose the folder in which to save the document and click **Save** to save it.

Compress Files

OS X includes a compression tool that enables you to shrink files. Compression is especially useful for files you need to transfer across the Internet, place on a limited-capacity medium such as a USB drive, or archive.

Using the Finder, you can compress a single file or multiple files. Compressing creates a compressed file in the widely used zip format, often called a *zip file,* that contains a copy of the files. The original files remain unchanged.

Compress Files

Compress Files to a Zip File

1 Click **Finder** (🖼) on the Dock.

A Finder window opens.

2 Click the folder that contains the file or files you want to compress.

3 Select the file or files.

4 **Ctrl**+click in the selection.

The contextual menu opens.

5 Click **Compress**.

Ⓐ The compressed file appears in the folder.

Note: If you selected one file, OS X gives the file the same name with the .zip extension. If you selected multiple files, OS X names the zip file Archive.zip.

6 Click the file and press **Return**.

An edit box appears.

7 Type the new name and press **Return**.

The file takes on the new name.

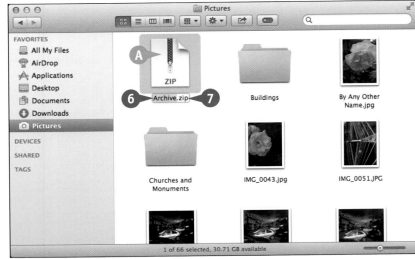

Extract Files from a Zip File

1 Click **Finder** (■) on the Dock.

A Finder window opens.

2 Click the folder that contains the zip file.

Note: If you receive the zip file attached to an e-mail message, save the file as explained in Chapter 6.

3 Double-click the zip file.

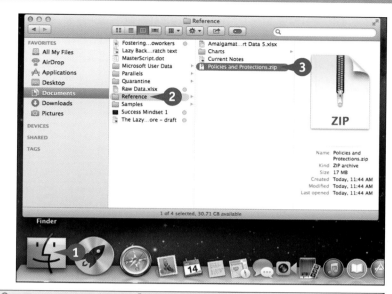

Archive Utility unzips the zip file, creates a folder with the same name as the zip file, and places the contents of the zip file in it.

4 Click the new folder to see the files extracted from the zip file.

TIP

When I compress a music file, the zip file is bigger than the original file. What have I done wrong?
You have done nothing wrong. Compression removes extra space from the file, and can squeeze some graphics and text files down by as much as 90 percent. But if you try to compress an already compressed file, such as an MP3 audio file or an MPEG video file, Archive Utility cannot compress it further — and the zip file packaging adds a small amount to the file size.

Burn Files to a CD or DVD

OS X enables you to copy, or *burn*, files to a CD or DVD using a SuperDrive or a similar optical drive. Some older iMac models have a built-in SuperDrive; if your iMac does not, you can connect an external SuperDrive via USB or connect to a shared optical drive on another Mac.

You use the Finder to burn files to a CD or DVD for general purposes such as backup. You can use iTunes to burn audio CDs or use Disk Utility to burn software disk images to a CD or DVD.

Burn Files to a CD or DVD

① Insert a blank CD or blank DVD in the SuperDrive.

A dialog opens asking what you want to do with the disc.

Note: If you always want to burn this type of disc using the Finder, click **Make this action the default** (☐ changes to ☑).

② Click the **Action** pop-up menu (⬍).

③ Click **Open Finder**.

④ Click **OK**.
The dialog closes.

Ⓐ The blank CD or blank DVD appears on your desktop, with a name such as Untitled CD.

⑤ Double-click the icon for the CD or DVD.

Ⓑ A Finder window opens showing the CD's or DVD's contents — nothing so far.

⑥ Press ⌘+Ⓝ. You can also click **File** and click **New Finder Window**.

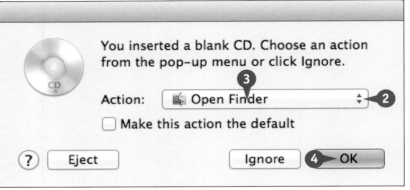

A new Finder window opens.

7 Click the folder that contains the files you want to burn.

8 Click and drag files from the new Finder window to the CD or DVD window.

Note: When you drag files to the CD or DVD, OS X adds aliases, or shortcuts, to the files.

9 Click **Burn**.

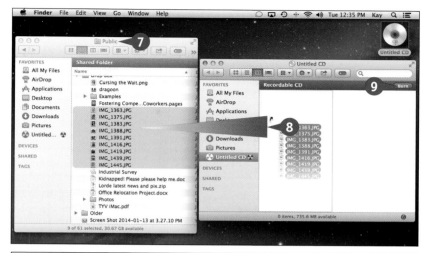

10 Type a name in the dialog that opens.

11 Click the **Burn Speed** pop-up menu (◆) and choose the speed at which to burn the disc. Maximum Possible is usually the best choice.

12 Click **Burn**.

When the burn finishes, the SuperDrive ejects the disc.

Note: Before labeling and storing the disc, reinsert it in the SuperDrive and check that the disc's contents are correct.

TIPS

How much data do CDs and DVDs hold?
Most recordable CDs can hold 640MB or 700MB. A single-layer DVD holds 4.7GB, whereas a dual-layer DVD holds 8.5GB.

Is it better to use rewriteable discs or single-use discs?
Use single-use recordable discs when you want to make a permanent copy of data — for example, on a backup that you intend to keep indefinitely. Use rewriteable discs for data you plan to store for only a short time, such as daily backups you overwrite each week.

Erase a CD or DVD

If you have a SuperDrive connected to your iMac or built into it, you can erase the contents of a rewriteable CD or DVD. Erasing marks all the information on the disc as deleted and restores the disc to a state in which you can burn data onto it again. To erase a rewriteable disc, you use Disk Utility, an app that also works with hard disks and removable disks.

Erase a CD or DVD

1 Insert the CD or DVD in the optical drive.

2 Click **Launchpad** (⬛) on the Dock.

The Launchpad screen appears.

3 Type **di**.

Launchpad displays only the apps whose names include a word starting with *di*.

4 Click **Disk Utility**.

The Disk Utility window opens.

5 Click the CD or DVD in the left pane.

6 Click **Erase**.

7 If the disc has not been working normally, click **Completely** (◯ changes to ◉). Otherwise, click **Quickly** (◯ changes to ◉).

8 Click **Erase**.

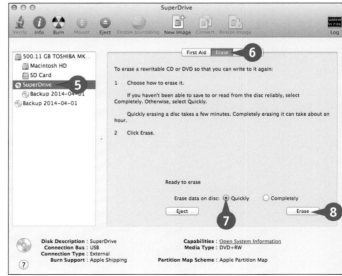

A dialog opens to confirm that you want to erase the disc.

9 Click **Erase**.

Disk Utility erases the disc and shows a readout of its progress.

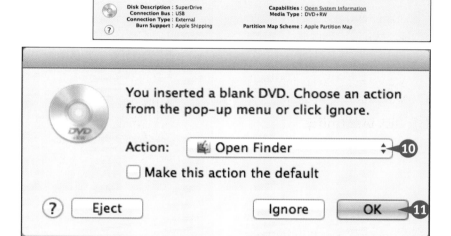

When Disk Utility finishes erasing the disc, a dialog opens.

10 Click the **Action** pop-up menu (⬍) and click the app to open. For example, select **Open Finder** if you want to burn files to the disc.

Note: Click **Eject** if you want to eject the disc, keeping it blank.

11 Click **OK**.

You inserted a blank DVD. Choose an action from the pop-up menu or click Ignore.

Action: 📀 Open Finder

☐ Make this action the default

Eject   Ignore   OK

TIP

How many times can I reuse a rewriteable CD or DVD?
You should be able to reuse a rewriteable CD or DVD several dozen times before needing to replace it. However, if the disc suffers wear and tear, or if it is several years old, it is better to err on the side of caution and replace the disc. Similarly, if the disc gives errors but is not scratched, try using the Completely option in Disk Utility to erase it thoroughly and make it work properly again — but if your data is valuable, replacing the disc instead is safer.

Using the Trash

OS X provides a special folder called the Trash in which you can place files and folders you intend to delete. Like a real-world trash can, the Trash retains files until you actually empty it. So if you find you have thrown away a file that you need after all, you can recover the file from the Trash. The Trash icon appears at the right end of the Dock by default, giving you quick access to the Trash.

Using the Trash

Place a File in the Trash

1 Click **Finder** (⬛) on the Dock.

A Finder window opens to your default folder or view.

2 Click the folder that contains the file you want to throw in the Trash.

3 Click the file you want to delete.

4 Click **Action** (⚙▾).

The Action pop-up menu opens.

5 Click **Move to Trash**.

Ⓐ The file disappears from the folder and moves to the Trash.

Note: You can also place a file in the Trash by clicking and dragging it to the Trash icon on the Dock, or from the keyboard by clicking the file and then pressing ⌘+Del.

Recover a File from the Trash

1. Click **Trash** (🗑) on the Dock.

   The Trash window opens.

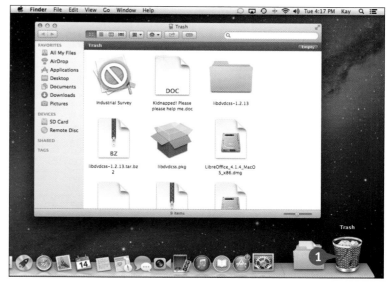

2. Click the file you want to recover.

3. Click **File**.

   The File menu opens.

4. Click **Put Back**.

   The Finder restores the file to its previous folder.

Note: If you want to put the file in a different folder, drag it to that folder. For example, drag the file to the desktop.

5. Press ⌘+W or click **Close** (🔴).

   The Trash window closes.

TIP

What else can I do with the Trash?

When you click a CD, DVD, or removable disk and drag it toward the Trash, the Trash icon changes to an Eject icon (⏏). Drop the item on the Eject icon to eject it. When you click and drag a recordable CD or DVD to which you have added files toward the Trash, OS X displays a Burn icon (☢). Drop the disc on the Burn icon to start burning it.

CHAPTER 5

Surfing the Web

If your iMac is connected to the Internet, you can browse or *surf* the sites on the World Wide Web. For surfing, OS X provides a web browser app called Safari. Using Safari, you can quickly move from one web page to another, search for interesting sites, and download files to your iMac.

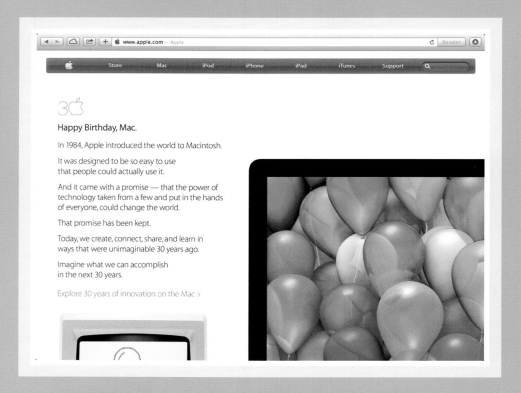

Open a Web Page

The Safari app included with OS X enables you to browse the web in various ways. The most straightforward way to reach a web page is to type or paste its unique address, which is called a *uniform resource locator* or *URL,* into the address box in Safari.

This technique works well for short addresses but is slow and awkward for complex addresses. Instead, you can click a link or click a bookmark for a page you have marked.

Open a Web Page

1 Click **Safari** (●) on the Dock.

Safari opens.

2 Triple-click anywhere in the address box or press ⌘+L.

Safari selects the current address.

3 Type the URL of the web page you want to visit.

Note: You do not need to type the http:// part of the address. Safari adds this automatically for you when you press Return.

4 Press Return.

Safari displays the web page.

Follow a Link to a Web Page

After opening a web page in Safari, you can click a link on it to navigate to another page or another marked location on the same page. Most web pages contain multiple links to other pages, which may be either on the same website or on another website. Some links are underlined, whereas others are attached to graphics or to different-colored text. When you position the mouse pointer over a link, the mouse pointer changes from the standard arrow (🖰) to a hand with a pointing finger (👆).

Follow a Link to a Web Page

1 In Safari, position the mouse pointer over a link (🖰 changes to 👆).

A The address of the linked web page appears in the status bar.

Note: If the Safari window is not showing the status bar, click **View** and select **Show Status Bar** to display it.

2 Click the link.

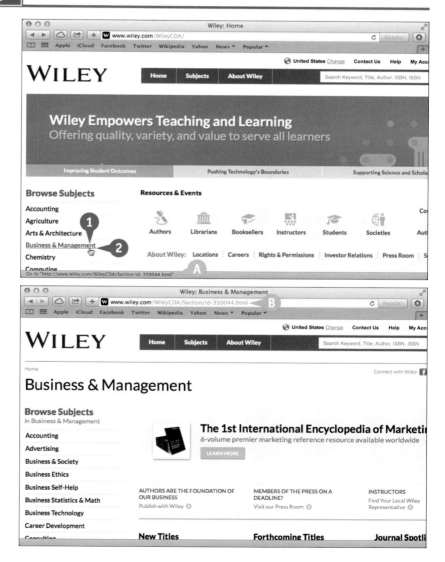

Safari shows the linked web page.

B The address of the linked web page appears in the address box.

Open Several Web Pages at the Same Time

Safari enables you to open multiple web pages at the same time, which is useful for browsing quickly and easily. You can open multiple pages either on separate tabs in the same window or in separate windows. You can drag a tab from one window to another.

Use separate tabs when you need to see only one of the pages at a time. Use separate windows when you need to compare two pages side by side.

Open Several Web Pages at the Same Time

Open Several Pages on Tabs in the Same Safari Window

1 Go to the first page you want to view.

Note: You can also click **Add** (⊞) or press ⌘+T to open a new tab showing your home page. Type a URL in the address box, and then press **Return** to go to the page.

2 Press **Ctrl**+click a link.

The shortcut menu opens.

3 Click **Open Link in New Tab**.

Ⓐ Safari opens the linked web page in a new tab.

Note: You can now repeat steps 2 and 3 to open further pages on separate tabs.

4 To change the page Safari shows, click the tab for the page you want to see.

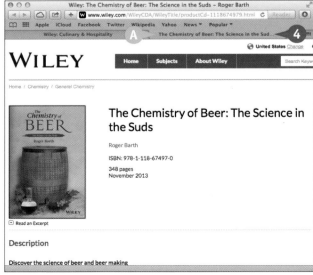

Open Several Pages in Separate Safari Windows

1 Go to the first page you want to view.

2 Press **Ctrl**+click a link.

The shortcut menu opens.

3 Click **Open Link in New Window**.

Note: You can also open a new window by pressing ⌘+**N**.

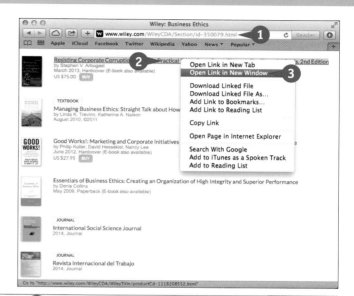

B Safari opens the linked web page in a new window.

4 To move back to the previous window, click it. If you cannot see the previous window, click **Window** and then select the window on the Window menu.

Note: You can also move back to the previous window by closing the new window you just opened.

Note: Press ⌘+**'** to cycle forward through windows and ⌘+**Shift**+**'** to cycle backward.

TIP

Can I change the way that Safari tabs and windows behave?
Click **Safari** and select **Preferences** to open the Preferences window, and then click **Tabs**. Click the **Open pages in tabs instead of windows** pop-up menu (⬍) and then click **Never**, **Automatically**, or **Always**, as needed. Press ⌘+**click to open a link in a new tab** (☐ changes to ☑) to use ⌘ for opening a new tab. Click **When a new tab or window opens, make it active** (☐ changes to ☑) if you want to switch to the new tab or window on opening it. Click **Close** (⊗) to close the Preferences window.

Safari makes it easy to navigate among the web pages you browse. Safari tracks the pages that you visit, so that the pages form a path. You can go back along this path to return to a page you viewed earlier; after going back, you can go forward again as needed.

Safari keeps a separate path of pages in each open tab or window, so you can move separately in each tab or window.

Navigate Among Web Pages

Go Back One Page

1 In Safari, click **Previous Page** (◀).

Safari displays the previous page you visited in the current tab or window.

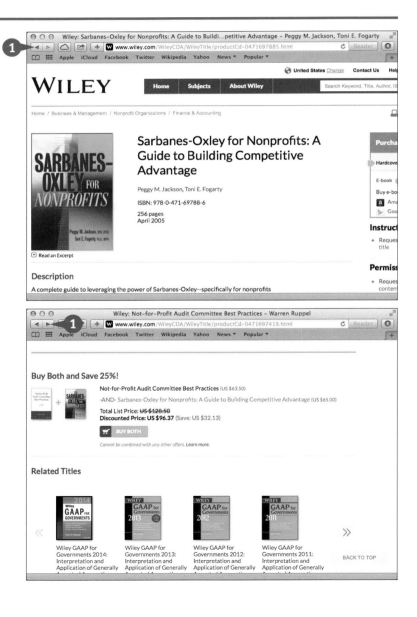

Go Forward One Page

1 Click **Next Page** (▶).

Note: The Next Page button is available only when you have gone back. Until then, there is no page for you to go forward to.

Safari displays the next page for the current tab or window.

Go Back Multiple Pages

1 Click **Previous Page** (◀) and keep holding down the mouse button.

A pop-up menu opens showing the pages you have visited in the current tab or window.

2 Click the page you want to visit.

Safari displays the page.

Go Forward Multiple Pages

1 Click **Next Page** (▶) and keep holding down the mouse button.

A pop-up menu opens showing the pages further along the path for the current tab or window.

2 Click the page you want to visit.

Safari displays the page.

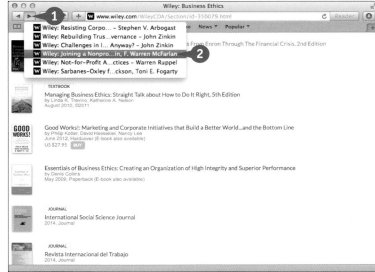

TIP

How can I navigate with the keyboard?

You can use these following keyboard shortcuts:

- Press ⌘+[to display the previous page.
- Press ⌘+] to display the next page.
- Press ⌘+Shift+H to display your home page.
- Press ⌘+Shift+[to display the previous tab.
- Press ⌘+Shift+] to display the next tab.

- Press ⌘+W to close the current tab and display the previous tab. If the window has no tabs, this command closes the window.
- Press ⌘+Shift+W to close the current window and display the previous window, if there is one.

Return to a Recently Visited Page

To help you return to web pages you have visited before, Safari keeps a History list of all the pages you have visited recently.

Normally, each person who uses your iMac has a separate user account, so each person has his own History. But if you share a user account with other people, you can clear the History list to prevent them from seeing what web pages you have visited. You can also shorten the length of time for which History tracks your visits.

Return to a Recently Visited Page

Return to a Page on the History List

1 In Safari, click **History**.

The History menu opens.

A If a menu item for the web page you want appears on the top section of the History menu, before the day submenus, simply click the item.

2 Highlight or click the day on which you visited the web page.

The submenu opens, showing the sites you visited on that day.

3 Click the web page to which you want to return.

Safari displays the web page.

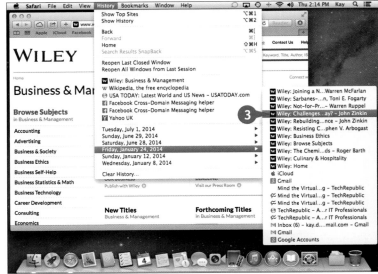

Clear Your Browsing History

1 Click **History**.

The History menu opens.

2 Click **Clear History**.

The Are You Sure You Want to Clear History? dialog opens.

3 Click **Also reset Top Sites** (☐ changes to ☑) if you want to reset the list of sites you visit most frequently.

4 Click **Clear**.

Safari clears the History list.

Note: If you want to browse without History storing the list of web pages you visit, click **Safari** and then click **Private Browsing**. In the Do You Want to Turn on Private Browsing? dialog, click **OK**.

TIP

What does the Show History command do?

Click **History** and select **Show History** to open a History window for browsing and searching the sites you have visited. Type a term in the search box in the lower right corner to search. Click the disclosure triangle (▶ changes to ▼) to expand the list of entries in a day. Double-click a history item to open its page in the same window, or press **Ctrl**+click a history item and click **Open in New Tab** or **Open in New Window** to open the page in a new tab or a new window.

Change Your Home Page

When you open a new window, Safari automatically displays your *home page*, the page it is configured to show at first. You can set your home page to any web page you want, to an empty page, or to the Top Sites screen. You can also control what page Safari shows when you open a new tab or a new window. Your choices are to display the Top Sites screen, your home page, an empty page, or the same page from which you opened the new tab or window.

Change Your Home Page

1 In Safari, navigate to the web page that you want to make your home page.

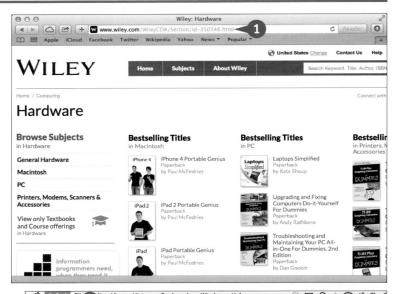

2 Click **Safari**.

The Safari menu opens.

3 Click **Preferences**.

Note: You can also press ⌘+⬚ to open the Preferences window.

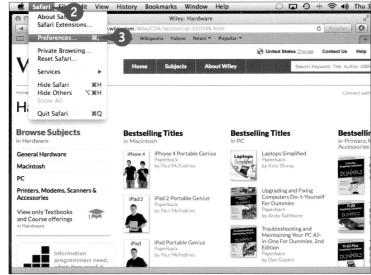

The Preferences window opens.

4 Click **General**.

The General pane opens.

5 Click **Set to Current Page**.

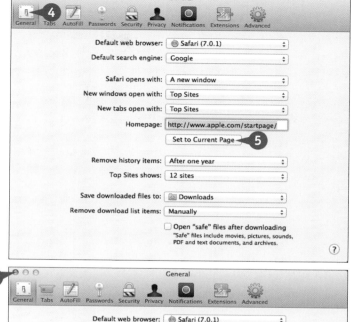

Safari changes the Home Page text field to show the page you chose.

6 Click the **New windows open with** pop-up menu (⬍) and select **Top Sites**, **Homepage**, **Empty Page**, or **Same Page**, as appropriate.

7 Click the **New tabs open with** pop-up menu (⬍) and select **Top Sites**, **Homepage**, **Empty Page**, or **Same Page**, as appropriate.

8 Click **Close** (⊗).

The Preferences window closes.

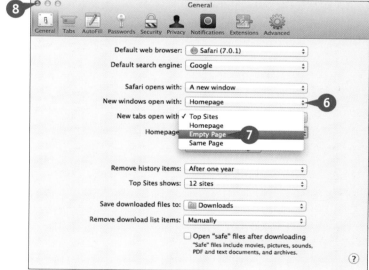

TIPS

How can I display my home page in the current window?
Click **History** and select **Home** or press ⌘+Shift+H.

What setting should I choose for Remove History Items in General preferences?
Choose the setting that best matches the length of time you want to keep history items so you can browse or search them. Your choices are **After one day**, **After one week**, **After two weeks**, **After one month**, **After one year**, or **Manually**. If you select Manually, click **History** and select **Clear History** whenever you want to clear your History items.

Create Bookmarks for Web Pages

Safari enables you to create markers called *bookmarks* for the addresses of web pages you want to be able to revisit easily. When you find such a web page, you can create a bookmark for its address, assign the bookmark a descriptive name, and store it on the Favorites bar, on the Bookmarks menu, or in a Bookmark folder. You can then return to the web page's address by clicking its bookmark. The content of the web page may have changed by the time you return.

Create Bookmarks for Web Pages

Create a New Bookmark

1 In Safari, navigate to a web page you want to bookmark.

2 Click **Bookmarks**.

The Bookmarks menu opens.

3 Click **Add Bookmark**.

Note: You can also press ⌘+D to open the Add Bookmark dialog.

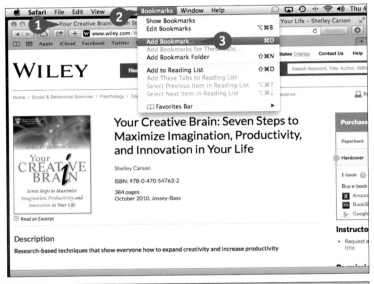

The Add Bookmark dialog opens, with the web page's title added to the upper box.

4 Click the **Add this page to** pop-up menu (⬍) and select the location or folder in which to store the bookmark.

5 Type a descriptive name for the bookmark.

6 Click **Add**.

The Add Bookmark dialog closes.

Safari creates the bookmark.

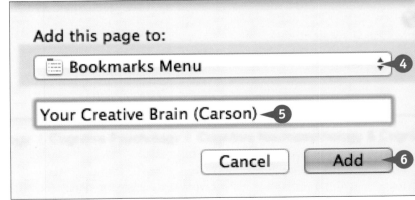

Organize Your Bookmarks

1 Click **Show sidebar** (📖).

Safari displays the sidebar.

2 Click **Bookmarks** (📖).

Safari displays the Bookmarks pane.

3 Click **Add** (➕).

Safari adds a new bookmarks folder to the list.

4 Type the name for the new folder and press **Return**.

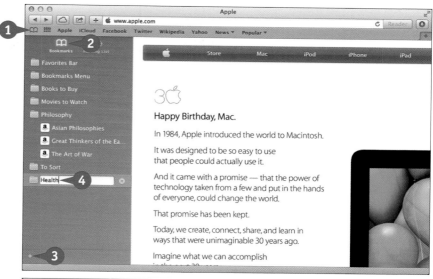

5 Click a collapsed folder to display its contents.

6 Click and drag a bookmark to the new folder.

Note: You can click and drag the bookmark folders into a different order. You can also place one folder inside another folder.

7 Click **Show sidebar** (📖).

Safari hides the sidebar.

How do I go to a bookmark I have created?

If you placed the bookmark on the Favorites bar, click the bookmark. If you put the bookmark on the Bookmarks menu, click **Bookmarks**, and then click the bookmark on the Bookmarks menu or one of its submenus. If you cannot easily locate the bookmark, click **Show sidebar** to display the sidebar, and then click **Bookmarks** to display the bookmarks. Locate the bookmark, and then double-click it.

Maintain a Reading List

ookmarks are a handy way of marking the addresses of web pages you want to be able to visit repeatedly, but you may also want to save some web pages for later reading in their current state. Safari's Reading List feature enables you to save pages like this.

You can quickly add the current web page to Reading List by giving the Add to Reading List command. Once you have added pages, you access Reading List through the sidebar.

Maintain a Reading List

Add a Web Page to Reading List

1 In Safari, navigate to a web page.

2 Click **Add to Reading List** (⊞).

Note: You can also click **Bookmarks** and select **Add to Reading List** or press ⌘+Shift+D.

Note: You can click **Bookmarks** and select **Add These Tabs to Reading List** to add all the tabs in the current window to Reading List.

Open Reading List and Display a Page

1 Click **Show sidebar** (📖).

Safari displays the sidebar.

2 Click **Reading List** (👓).

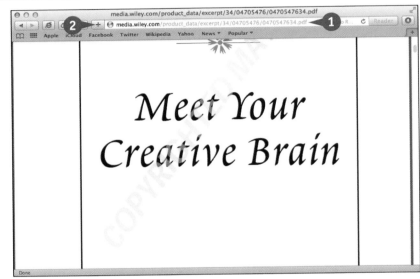

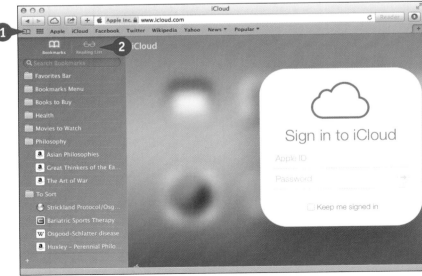

The Reading List pane opens.

3 Click the item you want to read.

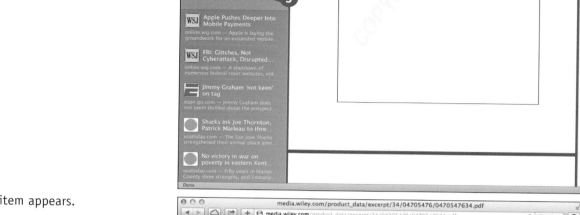

The item appears.

4 When you are ready to remove an item from Reading List, position the mouse pointer over its entry and click **Delete** (⊠).

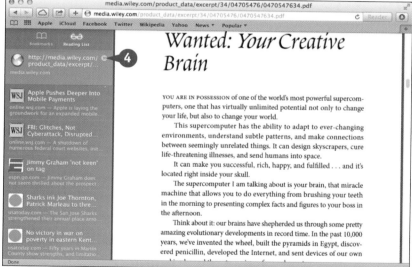

Why does Reading List show me a different version of a web page than a bookmark shows?
Reading List stores the web page as it exists when you give the Add the Reading List command, so when you return to the page, you see it exactly as it was when you stored it. By contrast, clicking a bookmark displays the current version of the web page, which may have changed from the version you saw when you created the bookmark. For example, if you click a bookmark to go to a news site's home page, you will see the latest stories.

Share Web Pages with Other People

Safari enables you to share web pages or their addresses quickly by using the Share button on the toolbar. You can send the page or its URL to someone else via AirDrop, e-mail, or instant messaging. Alternatively, you can share the page more widely by posting it to Twitter or Facebook.

When sharing via Mail, you can send the page as it is, a Reader version of the page, a PDF file showing the page, or a link to the page.

Share Web Pages with Other People

Share a Page via AirDrop

1 Navigate to the web page you want to share.

2 Click **Share** (⬆).

The Share pop-up menu opens.

3 Click **AirDrop**.

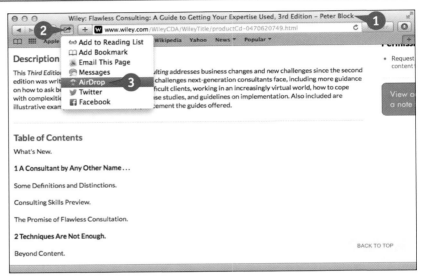

The AirDrop dialog opens.

4 Click the person to whom you want to send the page.

5 Click **Send**.

AirDrop sends an invitation to receive the page. If the person accepts, AirDrop sends the page.

The AirDrop dialog closes.

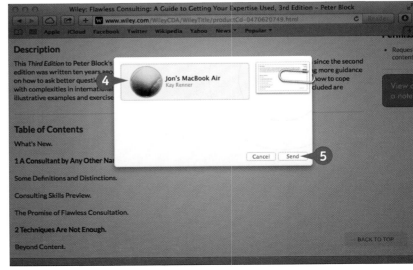

Share a Link via E-Mail

1. Navigate to the web page you want to share.

2. Click **Share** (![icon]).

   The Share pop-up menu opens.

3. Click **Email This Page**.

   Mail creates a new message.

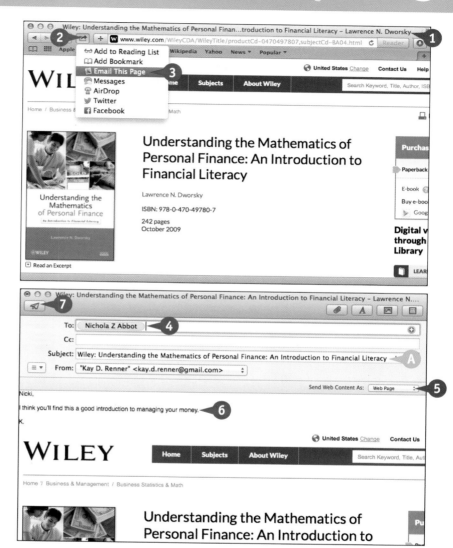

Ⓐ The page's title appears in the Subject box.

4. Add the recipient's address.

5. Click the **Send Web Content As** pop-up menu (![icon]) and select what to send: **Web Page**, **Reader**, **PDF**, or **Link Only**.

Note: Sending a link enables the recipient to view the latest version of the page.

6. Type any message needed.

7. Click **Send** (![icon]).

   Mail sends the message.

Follow Links Others Share with You

OS X and its apps enable you to follow links that other people share with you. When you receive a link in an e-mail message in Mail, you can preview the link to see if you want to follow it. You can then open the link in Safari or add it to Reading List.

If you open an AirDrop window or tab in the Finder, you can receive links via AirDrop. You can save these links and optionally open them in Safari.

Follow Links Others Share with You

Follow a Link Shared via AirDrop

1 Click **Finder** (🖥) on the Dock.

A Finder window opens.

2 Click **AirDrop**.

The AirDrop screen appears.

Note: You can minimize the AirDrop window or open another tab in front of it without deactivating AirDrop.

3 When you receive a link via AirDrop, click **Save and Open**.

A You can click **Save** to save the link without opening it.

Safari displays the linked page.

Follow a Link Shared via E-Mail

1. In Mail, click the message that contains the link.

2. Position the mouse pointer over the link.

3. Click the pop-up button (▼).

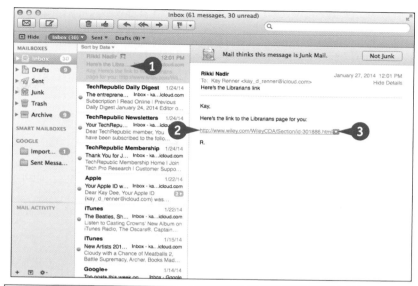

The preview of the page appears.

4. Click **Open with Safari**.

B. You can click **Add to Reading List** to add the web page to Reading List instead of opening it.

Safari displays the page.

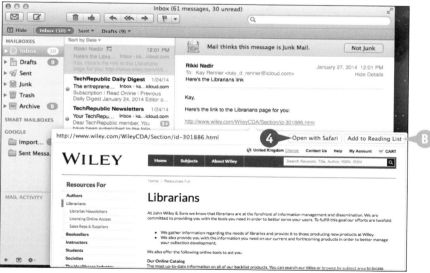

TIP

What other actions can I take with a link in Mail?

In Mail, you can press **Ctrl** +click a link in a message to open the contextual menu, which contains actions you can take with the link. Click **Open Link Behind Mail** to open the link in Safari but keep Mail displayed so that you can finish reading your mail. Click **Copy Link** to copy the link so that you can paste it into a document.

Find Interesting Web Pages

Safari includes a built-in search capability that enables you to search the Internet using some of the largest search engines. You can search automatically with the search engine configured in Safari's General preferences, but you can also easily switch to a different search engine for a particular search.

After searching, you can review the results the search engine returns and open links that seem promising.

Find Interesting Web Pages

Search with Your Default Search Engine

1 In Safari, click in the address box.

2 Start typing your search terms.

A The blue text shows your current search engine.

As you type, Safari displays suggested searches.

3 Click the search you want to use.

Note: If Safari does not display a search you want to use, type your remaining search terms and press **Return**.

Safari displays a page of search results.

4 Click a link to open a web page.

The web page opens.

Note: When examining search results, it is often useful to press **Ctrl**+click a link and select **Open in New Tab** or **Open in New Window**. This way, the page of search results remains open, and you can follow other linked results as needed.

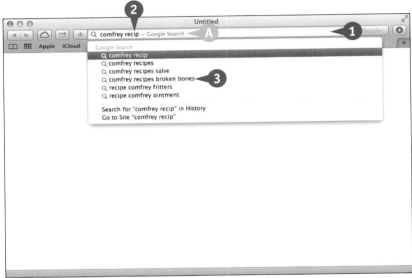

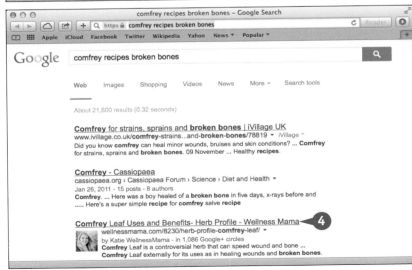

Use a Different Search Engine Temporarily

1 Click the **Search** icon in the address box.

The pop-up menu opens.

2 Click the search engine you want to use.

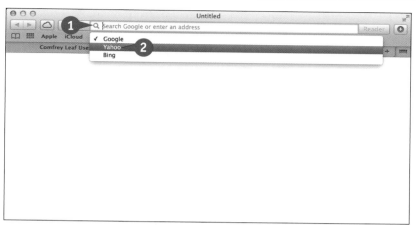

Safari switches to the search engine you select.

3 Type your search terms.

As you type, Safari displays suggested searches.

4 Click the search you want to use.

How can I get more useful search results from Google?
Here are three techniques to improve your search results:

- Enter words in double quotes to keep them together instead of searching for them separately. For example, use "add memory" to search for that phrase instead of for "add" and "memory" separately.

- To exclude a word from a search, put a – sign before it. For example, –mavericks tells Google not to return search results that include the term "mavericks."

- To make sure each search result includes a particular term, put a + sign before it. For example, +upgrade tells Google to return only search results that include the term "upgrade."

Download a File

My any websites provide files to download, and Safari makes it easy to download files from websites to your iMac's file system. For example, you can download apps to install on your iMac, pictures to view on it, or songs to play.

OS X includes apps that can open many file types, including music, graphic, movie, document, and PDF files. To open other file types, you may need to install extra apps or add plug-in software components to extend the features of the apps you already have.

Download a File

1 In Safari, go to the web page that contains the link for the file you want to download.

2 Click the link.

Safari starts the download.

Note: The indicator on the Downloads button (📥) shows the progress of the download.

3 Click **Downloads** (📥) to open the Downloads window.

4 When the download is complete, press Ctrl +click the file in the Downloads window.

The shortcut menu opens.

5 Click **Open**.

Note: Depending on the file type and the preferences you have set, Safari may open the file automatically for you.

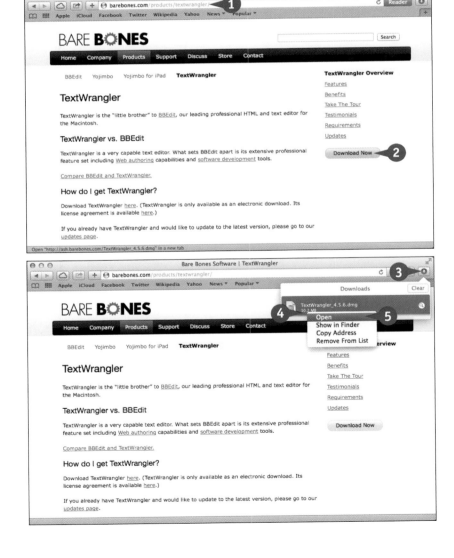

The file opens.

Depending on the file type, you can then work with the file, enjoy its contents, or install it.

Note: If the file is an app, you can install it as discussed in Chapter 3. If the file is a data file, such as a document or a picture, OS X opens the file in the app for that file type.

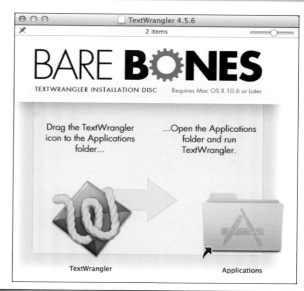

⑥ If the file disappears from the Downloads window and Safari does not open the file for you, click **Downloads** on the Dock.

The Downloads stack opens.

⑦ Click the file you downloaded.

The file opens.

TIP

What should I do when clicking a download link opens the file instead of downloading it?
If clicking a download link on a web page opens the file instead of downloading it, press Ctrl+click the link, and then click **Download Linked File**. Safari saves the file in your Downloads folder. To save the file in a different folder or under a different name of your choice, click **Download Linked File As**. Safari opens a dialog in which you can specify the folder and filename.

Select Essential Security Settings

The web is packed with fascinating sites and useful information, but it is also full of malefactors and criminals who want to attack your iMac and steal your valuable data.

Safari enables you to protect your iMac and your data by configuring security settings. Your options include preventing Safari from automatically opening supposedly safe files you download, refusing unwanted cookie files, and removing stored passwords. You can also block pop-up windows, which malicious websites can use to distribute malevolent software.

Select Essential Security Settings

1 Click **Safari**.

The Safari menu opens.

2 Click **Preferences**.

The Preferences window opens.

3 Click **General**.

The General pane opens.

4 Click **Open "safe" files after downloading** (☑ changes to ☐).

5 Click **Security**.

The Security pane opens.

6 Click **Warn when visiting a fraudulent website** (☐ changes to ☑).

7 Click **Block pop-up windows** (☐ changes to ☑).

Note: Some websites need pop-up windows to function properly. When you visit such a site, click **Safari** and click **Block Pop-up Windows** to temporarily allow pop-ups. Repeat the command afterward to block pop-up windows again.

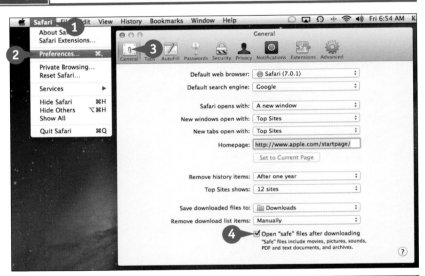

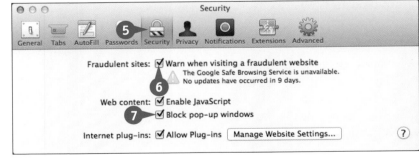

8 Click **Privacy**.

The Privacy pane opens.

9 Click **From third parties and advertisers** (⬜ changes to ⦿).

10 Click **Prompt for each website once each day** (⬜ changes to ⦿).

11 Click **Ask websites not to track me** (⬜ changes to ☑) if you want to request not to be tracked. Websites may not honor this request.

12 Click **Do not preload Top Hit in the background** (☑ changes to ⬜).

13 Click **Passwords**.

The Passwords pane opens.

Ⓐ You can click a stored password and click **Remove**.

14 Click **Allow AutoFill even for websites that request passwords not be saved** (☑ changes to ⬜).

Ⓑ You can click **AutoFill user names and passwords** (☑ changes to ⬜) to prevent Safari automatically entering your usernames and passwords.

15 Click **Close** (⦿).

The Preferences window closes.

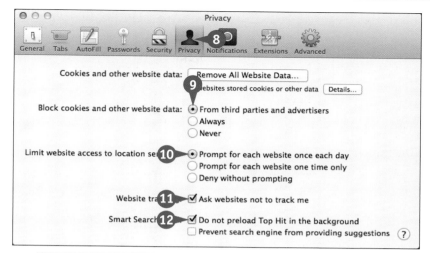

TIP

What are cookies, and should I accept them?
A *cookie* is a small text file that a website uses to store information about what you do on the site — for example, what products you have browsed or added to your shopping cart. Cookies from sites you visit are usually helpful to you. Cookies from third-party sites, such as those that advertise on sites you visit, may threaten your privacy. For this reason, choose **From third parties and advertisers** rather than **Never** in the Block Cookies area of the Privacy pane.

CHAPTER 6

Sending and Receiving E-Mail

OS X includes Mail, a powerful e-mail app. After setting up your e-mail accounts, you can send and receive e-mail messages and files.

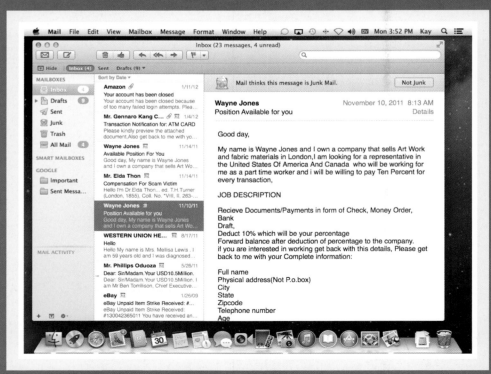

Set Up Your E-Mail Accounts

The Mail app enables you to send and receive e-mail messages easily using your existing e-mail accounts. If you add an iCloud account to your user account during initial setup or in System Preferences, OS X can automatically set up e-mail in Mail. If you have other e-mail accounts, you can add them manually.

To set up some types of e-mail accounts, Mail requires only your e-mail address and password. For other types, you also need to enter the addresses and types of your provider's mail servers.

Set Up Your E-Mail Accounts

1 Click **Mail** (📧) on the Dock.

The Choose a Mail Account to Add dialog opens.

Note: If Mail opens and displays your inbox, your e-mail account is already set up and working.

2 Click the account type. Your choices are **iCloud**, **Exchange**, **Google**, **Yahoo!**, **AOL**, or **Add Other Mail Account**.

3 Click **Continue**.

A dialog opens for entering the details the account needs.

Note: If you select Add Other Mail Account, you must choose between IMAP and POP for your incoming mail server type and enter the mail server's address.

4 Type your name the way you want it to appear on messages you send.

5 Type your e-mail address.

6 Type your password.

7 Click **Set Up**.

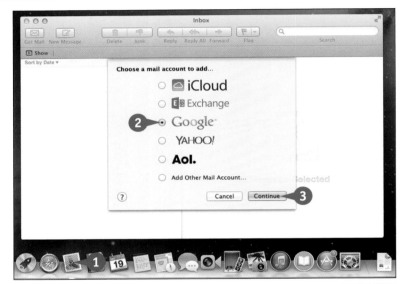

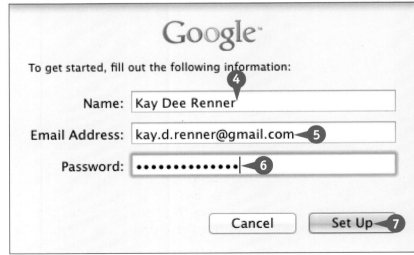

The Select the Apps to Use dialog opens.

8 Click the check box (☐ changes to ☑) for each app you want to use with this account.

9 Click **Done**.

Mail displays your inbox.

You can begin reading and sending e-mail.

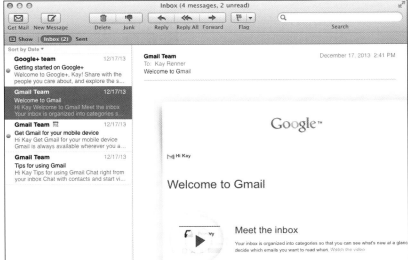

TIPS

How do I add further e-mail accounts?
You can add further e-mail accounts by clicking **File** on the menu bar, clicking **New Account**, and then following the prompts. Alternatively, press `Ctrl`+click **System Preferences** on the Dock, click **Internet Accounts**, click **Add** (`+`), and follow the prompts.

Which account type should I choose for my incoming mail server?
Check your ISP's website or call customer service to find out what type of mail server to use. Most ISPs use either POP (Post Office Protocol) or IMAP (Internet Mail Access Protocol), but others use Exchange or Exchange IMAP.

Send an E-Mail Message

The Mail app enables you to send an e-mail message to anybody whose e-mail address you know. After starting a new message, you can specify the recipient's address either by typing it directly into the To field or by selecting it from your list of contacts in the Contacts app.

You can send an e-mail message either to a single person or to multiple people at the same time. You can send copies to Cc, or carbon-copy, recipients or send hidden copies to Bcc, or blind carbon-copy, recipients.

Send an E-Mail Message

1 In Mail, click **Compose New Message** (🖉).

Note: You can also press ⌘+N or click **File** on the menu bar and then click **New** to start a new message.

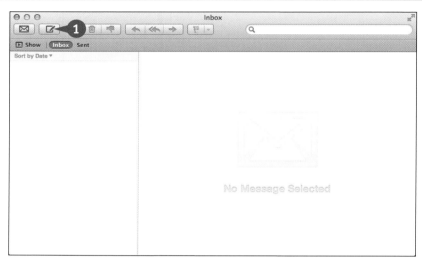

A new message window opens.

A The window's title bar displays New Message until you type the subject. The title bar then displays the subject.

2 Click **Add Contact** (⊕).

The Contacts panel opens.

3 Click the contact.

4 Click the e-mail address.

Note: In the Contacts panel, a name in gray has no e-mail address in the contact record.

The contact name appears as a button in the To field.

Note: You can add other addresses to the To field as needed.

⑤ To add a Cc recipient, click the Cc field.

⑥ Start typing a name or e-mail address.

Mail displays matches from Contacts.

⑦ Click the appropriate match or finish typing.

The name or address appears in the Cc box.

⑧ Type the subject for the message.

⑨ Type the body text of the message.

⑩ Click **Send** (📨).

Mail sends the message and stores a copy in your Sent folder.

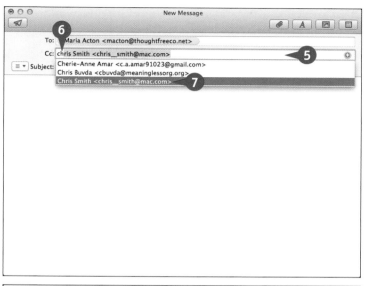

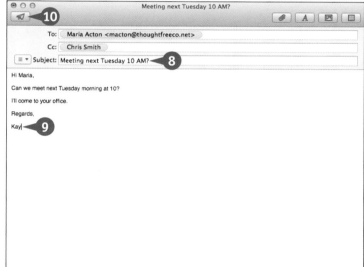

TIP

How can I send Bcc (blind carbon-copy) messages?

Mail hides the Bcc field in the New Message window by default. To display the Bcc field, click **Customize** (▣) and then click **Bcc Address Field** on the pop-up menu. The Bcc field appears below the Cc field, and you can add recipients either by clicking **Add Contact** (◉) or by typing their names or e-mail addresses.

Each Bcc recipient sees only his own address, not the addresses of other Bcc recipients. The To recipients and Cc recipients see none of the Bcc recipients' names and addresses.

Send an E-Mail Message Using Stationery

Mail includes dozens of stationery templates that enable you to create messages easily that have a graphical look and consistent, attractive formatting. Mail divides the stationery templates into five categories — Birthday, Announcements, Photos, Stationery, and Sentiments — but you can use any template for whatever purpose you choose.

To use stationery, you first create a new message. You then open the Stationery pane and apply the appropriate stationery template. You can then place your text in the template's text placeholders and your photos in any photo placeholders.

Send an E-Mail Message Using Stationery

1 In Mail, click **Compose New Message** (![icon]).

Note: You can also press ⌘+N or click **File** on the menu bar and then click **New** to start a new message.

Note: Using stationery, especially including photos, can greatly increase message size, which may cause problems for some recipients. Some e-mail apps cannot display stationery correctly.

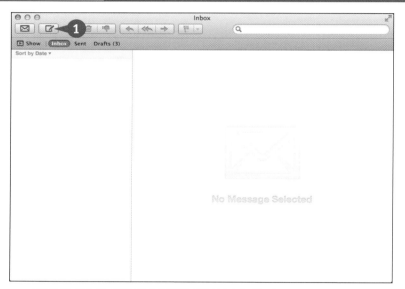

A new message window opens.

2 Add the recipient or recipients to the To box.

Note: You can add a recipient either by clicking **Add Contact** (![icon]) and then clicking the contact in the Contacts panel or by typing the recipient's name or e-mail address.

3 Type the subject.

4 Click **Stationery** (![icon]).

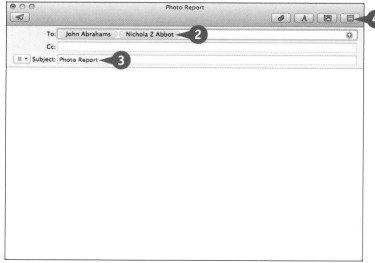

The Stationery pane opens.

5 Click a category of stationery.

6 Click a stationery design.

The design appears in the lower part of the message window.

7 Click **Stationery** (▦).

The Stationery pane closes.

8 Replace the sample text with your own text.

9 Click **Photo Browser** (▣) if the stationery includes photo placeholders.

The Photo Browser opens.

10 Click and drag a photo from the Photo Browser to each placeholder.

11 Click **Photo Browser** (▣) to close the Photo Browser.

12 Click **Send** (✈).

Mail sends the message.

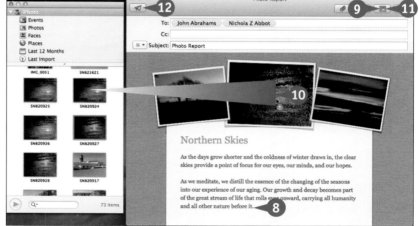

TIP

How can I apply font formatting to a message?

You can apply font formatting by using either the Format bar or the Fonts window. The Format bar, which you display or hide by clicking **Format Bar** (𝐀) on the toolbar, enables you to change the font family, font size, and font color, and apply boldface, italics, or underline. The Fonts window, which you display or hide by pressing ⌘+T, enables you to apply a wider range of font formatting and to change the document color.

Receive and Read Your Messages

Mail enables you to receive your incoming messages easily and read them in whatever order you prefer. A message sent to you goes to your mail provider's e-mail server. To receive the message, you cause Mail to connect to the e-mail server and download the message to your iMac.

When working with e-mail, it often helps to display the mailbox list on the left side of the Mail window. You can use this list to navigate among mailboxes and to see which activities Mail is currently performing.

Receive and Read Your Messages

Display the Mailbox List and Receive Messages

1 In Mail, click **Show** (▣).

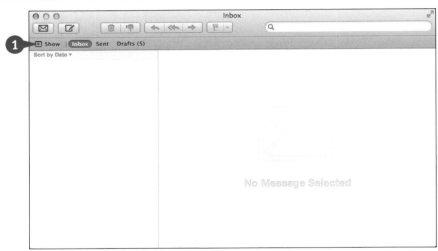

Ⓐ The mailbox list appears.

2 Click **Get Mail** (✉).

Mail connects to the e-mail server and downloads any messages.

Ⓑ A notification banner or alert may appear.

Ⓒ The Mail Activity pane shows what Mail is doing.

Ⓓ The new messages appear in your Inbox.

Ⓔ A blue dot indicates that you have not read a message yet.

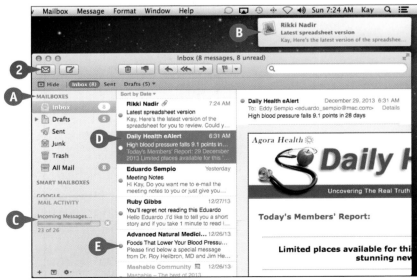

Read Your Messages

1 Click a message in the message list.

F The message appears in the reading pane.

2 Double-click a message in the message list.

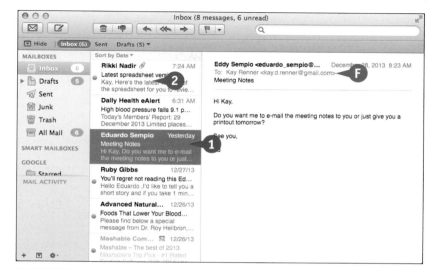

The message's text and contents appear in a separate window.

3 Read the message.

4 Click **Close** (⊗).

The message window closes.

G You can click **Hide** (▣) if you want to hide the mailbox list again.

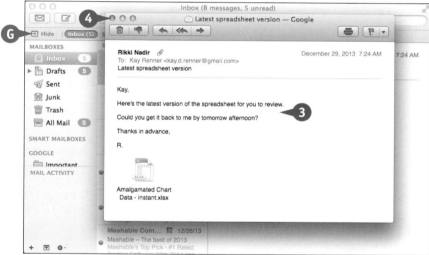

TIPS

Is there an easy way to tell whether I have new messages?

If you have unread messages, the Mail icon on the Dock shows a red circle containing the number of unread messages.

How can I change Mail's frequency of checking for new messages?

Click **Mail** and **Preferences** to open the Preferences window, and then click **General**. Click the **Check for new messages** pop-up menu (⬓), and then select the interval: **Every minute**, **Every 5 minutes**, **Every 15 minutes**, **Every 30 minutes**, **Every hour**, or **Manually**. Click **Close** (⊗) to close the Preferences window.

Reply to a Message

Mail enables you to reply to any e-mail message you receive. When you reply, you can include either the whole of the original message or just the part of it that you select.

If you are one of several recipients of the message, you can choose between replying only to the sender and replying to both the sender and all the other recipients other than Bcc recipients. You can also adjust the list of recipients manually if necessary, removing existing recipients and adding other recipients.

Reply to a Message

1 In the Inbox, click the message to which you want to reply.

Note: You can also double-click the message to open it in a message window, and then start the reply from there.

2 Click **Reply** (⬅).

Note: If the message has multiple recipients, you can click **Reply All** (⬅⬅) to reply to the sender and to all the other recipients except Bcc recipients.

Mail creates the reply and opens it in a window.

A The recipient's name appears as a button. If your contacts list contains multiple e-mail addresses for the contact, the e-mail address appears after the contact's name.

B You can position the mouse pointer over the contact's name, click the pop-up button (▾) that appears, and then click a different address if necessary.

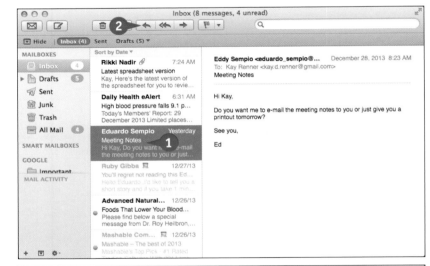

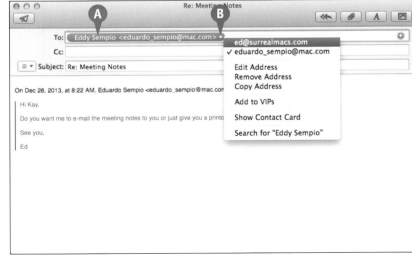

3 Type the text of your reply.

It is usually best to type your text at the beginning of the reply rather than after the message you are replying to.

Note: You can also add other recipients to the message as needed. If you have chosen to reply to all recipients, you can remove any recipients as necessary.

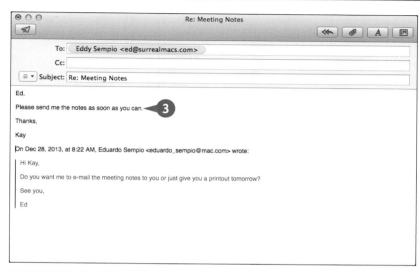

4 Click **Send** ().

Mail sends the reply and saves a copy in your Sent folder.

Note: Click **Message** and then click **Send Again** to send the same message again — for example, because a mail server rejects it. You can change recipients or the message contents as needed.

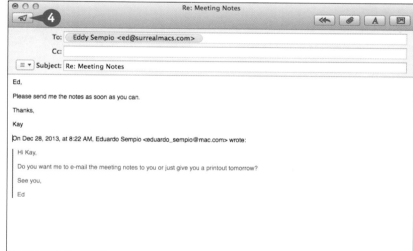

TIP

Can I reply to only part of a message rather than send the whole of it?
Yes. Select the part you want to include, and then click **Reply** (⬅) or **Reply All** (⬅), as appropriate. Mail creates a reply containing only the part you selected. If Mail includes all of the message, click **Mail**, click **Preferences**, click **Composing**, and then click **Include selected text, if any; otherwise include all text** (◯ changes to ◉).

Forward a Message

Mail provides an easy way to forward to other people a message that you receive. You can either forward the entire message or forward only a selected part of it.

When you forward a message, it usually helps to add your own comments to the message. For example, you might want to explain to the recipient which person or organization sent you the original message, why you are forwarding it, and what action — if any — you expect him to take as a result of the message.

Forward a Message

1 Click the mailbox that contains the message you want to forward.

The messages appear.

2 Click the message.

The message's content appears in the reading pane.

Note: You can also forward a message that you have opened in a message window.

3 Click **Forward** (➡️).

Note: You can click **Message** and then click **Redirect** to redirect a message to someone else without the Fwd: indicator appearing.

A window opens showing the forwarded message.

The subject line shows Fwd: and the message's original subject, so the recipient can see it was forwarded.

4 Type the recipient's name or address. You can either type the address or click **Add Contact** (⊙) and then select the address from the Contacts panel.

5 Edit the subject line of the message if necessary.

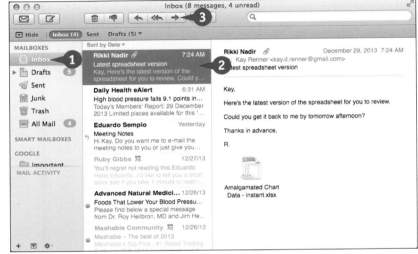

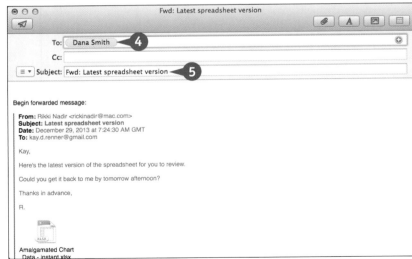

6 Optionally, edit the forwarded message to shorten it or make it clearer to the recipient.

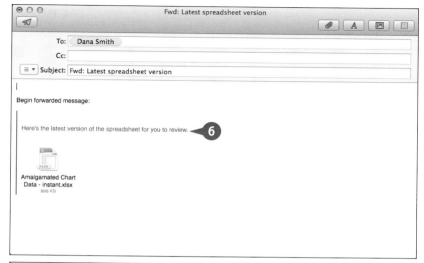

7 Type any message you want to include to the recipient.

8 Click **Send** (🖅).

Mail sends the forwarded message to the recipient.

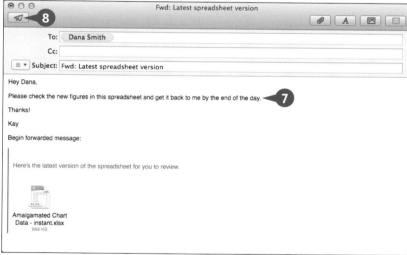

TIPS

What does the Forward as Attachment command on the Message menu do?

The Forward as Attachment command enables you to send a copy of a message as an attachment to a message instead of in the message itself. This command is useful when you want to send a forwarded message that includes formatting in a plain text message.

Can I forward only part of a message rather than all of it?

To forward only part of a message, select the part you want to forward, and then click **Forward** (➡). Mail includes only the part you selected.

Send a File via E-Mail

As well as enabling you to communicate via e-mail messages, Mail gives you an easy way to transfer files to other people. You can attach one or more files to an e-mail message so that the files travel as part of the message.

You can send any kind of file, such as a document or a photo, but avoid sending files larger than several megabytes in size because mail servers may reject them. The recipient can then save the file on her computer and open it.

Send a File via E-Mail

1 In Mail, click **Compose New Message** (▨).

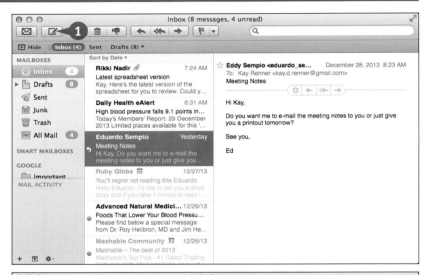

A new message window opens.

2 Add the recipient's name or address. You can either type the address or click **Add Contact** (◉) and then select the address from the Contacts panel.

3 Type the subject for the message.

4 Type any message body that is needed.

5 Click **Attach** (📎).

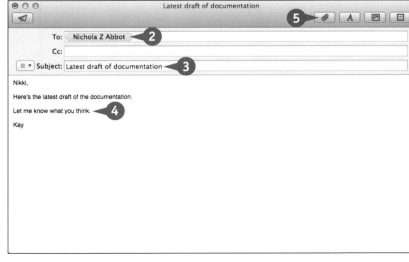

A dialog opens.

6 Click the file you want to attach to the message.

7 Click **Choose File**.

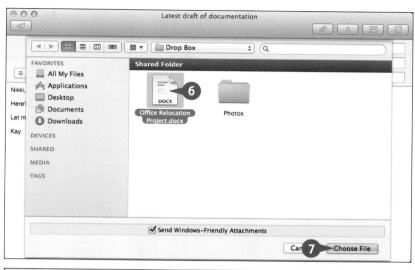

The dialog closes.

A Mail attaches the file to the message.

Note: Depending on the file type, the attachment may appear as an icon in the message or as a picture.

8 Click **Send** (📧).

Mail sends the message with the file attached.

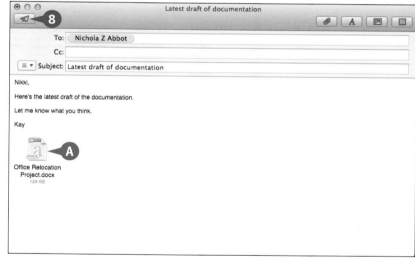

TIP

How big a file can I attach to a message?
The size limit is hard to determine because it depends on your e-mail provider and the recipient's e-mail provider. Generally, limit attachments to 5MB total, either a single file or multiple files. Check the message size that Mail shows, because e-mail encoding makes the message substantially larger than the combined size of the files you attach. If you need to transfer many files, use a file transfer site such as Dropbox (www.getdropbox.com) or an FTP server.

Receive a File via E-Mail

A file you receive via e-mail appears as an attachment to a message in your Inbox. You can use the Quick Look feature to examine the file and decide whether to keep it or delete it. Quick Look can display the contents of many types of files well enough for you to determine what they contain.

To keep an attached file, you can save it to your iMac's hard drive. You can then remove the attached file from the e-mail message to help keep down the size of your mail folder.

Receive a File via E-Mail

1 In your Inbox, click the message.

The message appears in the reading pane.

2 Press `Ctrl`+click the attachment.

The contextual menu opens.

3 Click **Quick Look Attachment**.

A Quick Look window opens showing the attachment's contents.

Note: Click **Full Screen** (⬚) if you want to view the document full screen. Click **Open With** to open the file in a suitable app — for example, click **Open with Microsoft Excel** to open a workbook file in Excel.

4 When you finish previewing the file, click **Close** (⊗).

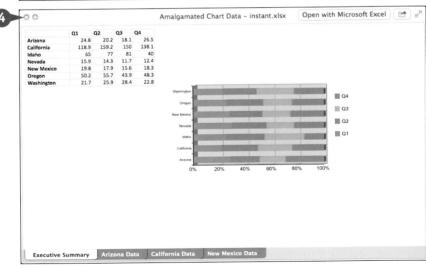

The Quick Look window closes.

5 Press **Ctrl**+click the attachment.

The contextual menu opens.

6 Click **Save Attachment**.

The Save As dialog opens.

Note: If the Save As dialog opens at its small size, click **Expand Dialog** (▼) to expand it.

7 Navigate to the folder in which you want to save the file.

8 Click **Save**.

Mail saves the file.

Note: If you want to remove the attachment from the message, click **Message** and then click **Remove Attachments**.

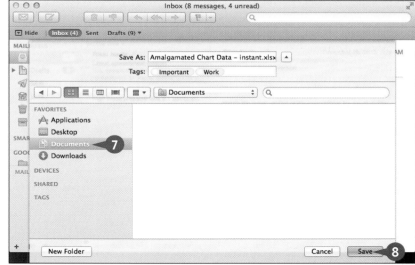

TIPS

Should I check incoming files for viruses and malevolent software?

Yes, you should always check incoming files with antivirus software. Even though OS X generally has fewer problems with viruses and malevolent software than Windows PCs, it is possible for a file to cause damage, steal data, or threaten your privacy.

Is there a quick way to see what messages have attachments?

In the Inbox, click the **Sort by** pop-up menu, and then click **Attachments**. Mail sorts the Inbox so that the messages with attachments appear first.

View E-Mail Messages by Conversations

M ail enables you to view an exchange of e-mail messages as a conversation instead of viewing each message as a separate item. Conversations, also called *threads*, let you browse and sort messages on the same subject more easily by separating them from other messages in your mailboxes.

If you decide to organize your messages by conversations, you can expand or collapse all conversations to see the messages you want.

View E-Mail Messages by Conversations

1 In Mail, click the mailbox that contains the messages you want to view.

Ⓐ The messages in the folder appear.

2 Click **View**.

The View menu opens.

3 Click **Organize by Conversation**.

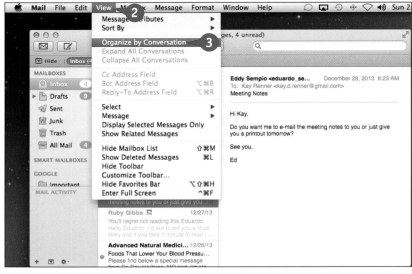

Mail organizes the messages into conversations, so that each exchange appears as a single item rather than as separate messages.

The number to the right of a conversation indicates how many messages it contains.

④ Click the conversation's number.

Note: You can expand all conversations in the folder by clicking **View** and clicking **Expand All Conversations**. Click **View** and click **Collapse All Conversations** to collapse them again.

Ⓑ Mail expands the conversation so that you can see each of the messages it contains.

⑤ Click the message you want to read.

Ⓒ The message appears in the reading pane.

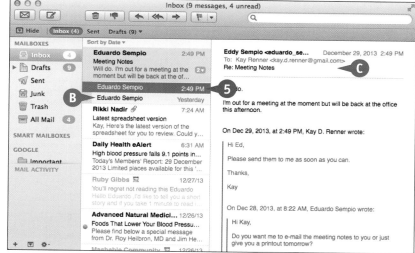

TIP

Are there other advantages to viewing an exchange as a conversation?
When you view an exchange as a conversation, you can manipulate all the messages in a single move instead of having to manipulate each message individually. For example, click the conversation and drag it to a folder to file all its messages in that folder, or click the message and press ⌘ + Delete to delete the entire conversation.

Reduce the Amount of Spam in Your Inbox

*S*pam is unwanted e-mail messages, also called *junk mail*. Spam ranges from messages offering specialized products, such as pharmaceuticals, to attempts to steal your financial details, passwords, or personal information.

Mail includes features that enable you to reduce the amount of spam that reaches your inbox. You can configure Mail to identify junk mail automatically, and you can learn to spot identifying features of spam messages. Unfortunately, it is not yet possible to avoid spam completely.

Reduce the Amount of Spam in Your Inbox

Set Mail to Identify Junk Mail Automatically

1 Click **Mail**.

2 Click **Preferences**.

3 Click the **Junk Mail** tab.

4 Click the **Enable junk mail filtering** option (☐ changes to ☑).

5 Click the **Mark as junk mail, but leave it in my Inbox** option (◯ changes to ◉) to review junk mail in your Inbox.

6 Click each of the three check boxes (☐ changes to ☑).

7 Click the **Trust junk mail headers in messages** option (☐ changes to ☑).

8 Click **Close** (◉).

The Preferences window closes.

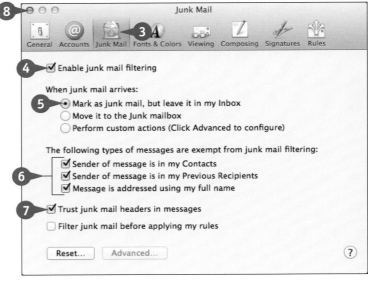

Review Your Junk Mail

1. Click **Inbox** or **Junk Email** — wherever you told Mail to put your junk mail in step **5**.

2. Click a message.

3. See whether Mail has identified the message as junk mail.

4. See if the message is addressed to you.

5. Check whether the message greets you by name or with a generic greeting.

6. Read the message's content for veracity.

7. If the message appears to be spam, and Mail has not identified it as junk, click **Junk** (🖐).

8. Click **Delete** (🗑) to delete the message.

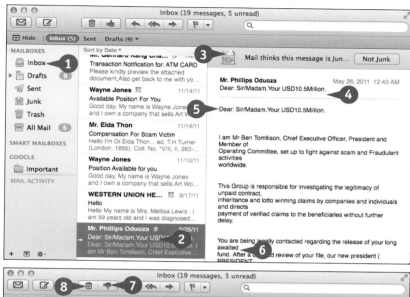

How can I tell whether a message is genuine or spam?

If a message does not show your e-mail address and your name, it is most likely spam. If the message does show your e-mail address and name, read the content carefully to establish whether the message is genuine. If the message calls for action, such as reactivating an online account that you have, do not click a link in the message. Instead, open Safari, type the address of the website, log in as usual, and see if an alert is waiting for you.

CHAPTER 7

Chatting with Messages and FaceTime

OS X includes Messages for instant messaging and FaceTime for video chat with Mac, iPad, iPhone, and iPod touch users.

Set Up Messages

The Messages app enables you to chat with your contacts via instant messaging. Using Messages, you can connect via Apple's iMessage service to contacts on Macs and iOS devices or to contacts on other online messaging services, such as Google Talk, Yahoo! Messenger, and AOL.

The first time you run Messages, you set it up with your Apple ID, which identifies you uniquely on the iMessage service. You can also add other messaging accounts as needed by using the Add Account command or the Accounts pane in Messages Preferences.

Set Up Messages

Set Up Messages with Your Apple ID

1. Click **Messages** (🗨) on the Dock.

2. Type your Apple ID.

Ⓐ You can click **Create an Apple ID** to create an Apple ID if you do not have one.

3. Type your password.

4. Click **Sign In**.

The Messages window opens.

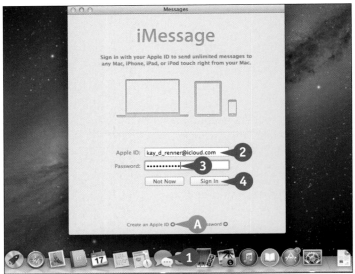

Add Another Messaging Account

1. Click **Messages**.

The Messages menu opens.

2. Click **Add Account**.

The Choose a Messages Account to Add dialog opens.

3. Click a message account option (◯ changes to ◉). Your choices are **Google**, **Yahoo!**, **AOL**, and **Other messages account**.

4. Click **Continue**.

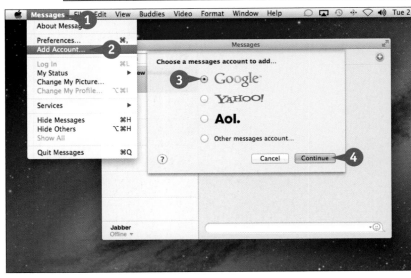

Note: If you selected the Other messages account option, click the **Account Type** pop-up menu (⬍) and click the account type: **AIM**, **Google Talk**, **Jabber**, or **Yahoo!**.

A dialog for entering the account information appears. This example uses Google.

5 Type your name as you want it to appear.

6 Type the e-mail address for the messaging account.

7 Type your password.

8 Click **Set Up**.

A dialog appears enabling you to select what services to use with the messaging account.

9 Click an option, such as **Mail**, **Contacts**, **Calendar**, or **Notes** (☐ changes to ☑).

10 Click **Done**.

Messages sets up the account, and you can start using it.

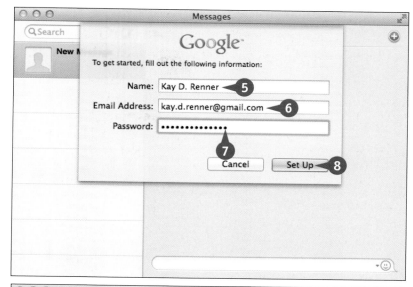

TIPS

What is iMessage?
iMessage is Apple's instant-messaging service. To use iMessage, you need only an Apple ID, such as your iCloud account ID. With iMessage, you can send instant messages to any iPhone user or anyone who uses an Apple ID on a Mac, iPad, or iPod touch.

How can I use Messages with people on my local network?
You can use Bonjour, an Apple communications technology, to communicate with other Mac users and iOS device users on your local network. To set up Bonjour, click **Messages**, and then click **Preferences**. In the Preferences window, click **Accounts**, click **Bonjour**, and then click **Enable Bonjour instant messaging** (☐ changes to ☑).

Chat with a Buddy

Messages enables you to chat with your contacts, or *buddies*, via instant messaging. The easiest way to start using Messages is by sending text messages. Depending on the messaging services and the computers or devices your buddies are using, you may be able to chat via audio or video as well.

To start chatting, you send your buddy an invitation. If your buddy accepts the invitation, the reply appears in the Messages window. You can conduct multiple chats simultaneously, switching from chat to chat as needed.

Chat with a Buddy

1 In Messages, click **Compose New Message** (▢).

A New Message entry appears in the left pane.

2 Click **Add Contact** (●).

The Contacts panel opens.

3 Click the buddy with whom you want to chat.

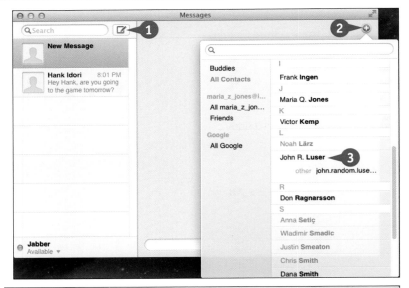

Ⓐ The buddy's name appears in the To area.

Ⓑ A green dot (●) indicates that the buddy is available for chat.

4 Type the text you want to send, and then press Return.

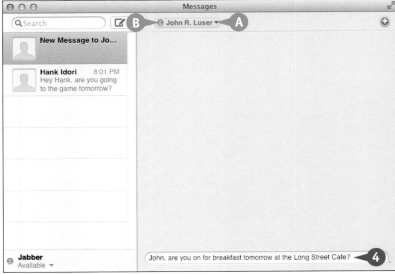

C Your message appears in a bubble on the right side of the right pane.

Note: You can change the way messages appear by clicking **View**, highlighting **Messages**, and then clicking **Show as Balloons**, **Show as Boxes**, or **Show as Compact**.

D A reply from your buddy appears on the left side of the right pane.

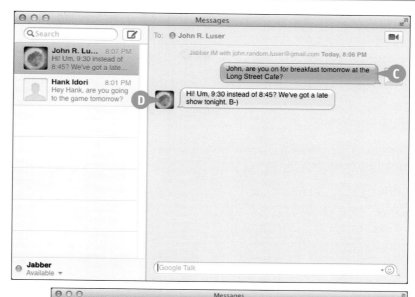

5 Type a reply to your buddy's reply.

6 Click **Special Characters** (☺).

The Special Characters panel opens.

7 Click the category of special characters you want: **Recents and Favorites** (🕐), **People** (☺), **Nature** (❀), **Objects** (🔔), **Places** (🚗), or **Symbols** (🔣).

8 Click the special character.

9 Press Return.

Messages sends the message, including the special character.

How do I change my status in Messages?

When you log in, Messages automatically sets your status to Available so that your contacts can see you are available for chat. If you do not want to receive any messages for a while, you can set your status to Offline by clicking **Messages** on the menu bar, clicking **My Status**, and then clicking **Offline**. Alternatively, press Control + ⌘ + O. When you are ready to go back online, click **Messages**, click **My Status**, and then click **Available**. Alternatively, press Control + ⌘ + A.

Send and Receive Files with Messages

As well as chat, Messages enables you to send files easily to your buddies and receive files they send to you. During a chat, you can send a file either by using the Send File command or by dragging a file from a Finder window into Messages.

When a buddy sends you a file, you can decide whether to receive it. Messages automatically stores the files you receive in the Downloads folder in your user account, but you can change the destination to another folder if you so choose.

Send and Receive Files with Messages

Send a File

1. Start a text chat with the buddy to whom you want to send a file, or accept a chat invitation from that buddy.

2. Click **Buddies**.

   The Buddies menu opens.

3. Click **Send File**.

The Send File dialog opens.

4. Click the file you want to send.

5. Click **Send**.

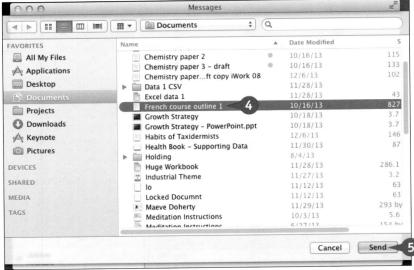

A A button for the file appears in the text box.

6 Type any message needed.

7 Press **Return**.

Messages sends the message, including a button for transferring the file.

If your buddy accepts the file, Messages transfers it.

Receive a File

B When your buddy sends you a file, it appears as a button in the Chat window.

1 Click the file's button to download the file.

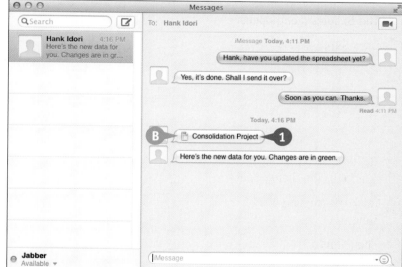

TIP

Can I change the folder in which Messages puts files I download?
Yes, you can change the folder from its default location, the Downloads folder in your user account. To change the folder, click **Messages**, and then click **Preferences**. The Preferences window opens. Click **General** in the upper left corner. The General preferences pane opens. Click the **Save Received Files To** pop-up menu ([⬍]), and then click **Other**. A dialog opens. Click the folder you want to put your downloaded files in, and then click **Select**. Click **Close** ([⊗]) to close the Preferences window.

Set Up FaceTime

Apple's FaceTime technology enables you to make audio and video calls easily across the Internet. FaceTime works with all recent Macs and with the last several generations of the iPhone, iPod touch, and iPad and iPad mini.

Your iMac includes a built-in video camera and microphone, so it is ready to use FaceTime right out of the box. Before you can make calls, you need to set up FaceTime with your Apple ID.

Set Up FaceTime

Open and Set Up FaceTime

1 Click **FaceTime** (🔘) on the Dock.

Note: If the FaceTime icon does not appear on the Dock, click **Launchpad** (🚀) on the Dock, and then click **FaceTime** on the Launchpad screen.

The FaceTime window opens.

2 Type your Apple ID.

Note: If you need to create a new Apple ID, click **Create New Account**.

3 Type your password.

4 Click **Sign In**.

FaceTime signs you in.

5 Click the e-mail address or addresses at which you want people to contact you via FaceTime.

A check mark appears (✔) next to each address you select.

6 Click **Next**.

Your contacts list appears.

A Click **Favorites** to display your list of FaceTime favorites.

B Click **Recents** to display a list of recent calls you have made, received, and missed.

C Click **Contacts** to display your contacts from the Contacts app.

You are now ready to make FaceTime calls.

Close FaceTime

1 When you finish using FaceTime, click **FaceTime**.

The FaceTime menu opens.

2 Click **Quit FaceTime**.

FaceTime closes.

Note: You can also close FaceTime by pressing ⌘+Q.

How do I change the e-mail address FaceTime is using for me?
To change the e-mail address, click **FaceTime** on the menu bar, and then click **Preferences**. The Preferences pane appears on the right side of the FaceTime window. Click **Add Another Email**, type the e-mail address you want to use, and press Return. Then click the e-mail address you want to remove. On the Email screen that appears, click **Remove Email**, and then click **Remove Email Address** in the confirmation dialog. Click **Done**.

Make and Receive FaceTime Calls

When you have set up FaceTime with your Apple ID, you can make and receive FaceTime calls from your iMac. You can call any iPhone user or any user of a Mac or other iOS device who has enabled FaceTime.

To make a call, you open FaceTime, click the contact, and then select the e-mail address or phone number to use for contacting him. To receive a call, you simply answer when FaceTime alerts you to the incoming call.

Make and Receive FaceTime Calls

Make a FaceTime Call

1 Click **FaceTime** (📷) on the Dock.

Note: If no FaceTime icon appears on the Dock, click **Launchpad** (🚀), and then click **FaceTime** (📷).

2 Click **Contacts**.

3 Click the contact you want to call.

Note: You can also place a call from the Favorites list or the Recents list.

4 Click the e-mail address or phone number to call.

FaceTime places the call.

5 When your contact answers, begin chatting.

6 When you are ready to finish the call, move the mouse to display the pop-up control bar, and then click **End**.

Receive a FaceTime Call

When you receive a FaceTime call, a FaceTime window appears.

1 Click **Accept**.

Note: In the Contacts app, you can assign a specific ringtone and a specific text tone to a contact. These tones can help you identify which contact is calling or messaging you.

The call begins.

A You can move the mouse to display the pop-up control bar and then click **Full Screen** (■) to enlarge the FaceTime window to full screen.

2 Chat.

B You can click **Mute** (■) to mute the audio.

C You can click **Rotate** (■) to rotate the view.

3 When you are ready to finish the call, click **End** on the pop-up control bar.

TIP

Must I keep FaceTime running all the time to receive incoming calls?
No. After you set up FaceTime with your Apple ID, FaceTime runs in the background even when the app itself is not open. When FaceTime detects an incoming call, it plays a ringtone and displays a window in front of your other open windows. You can then decide whether to accept the call or reject it.

CHAPTER 8

Organizing Your Life

To help you keep your daily life organized, your iMac includes the Calendar, Contacts, Reminders, and Maps apps.

Navigate the Calendar App

The Calendar app enables you to input your appointments and events and track them easily. After launching the app, you can navigate to the dates with which you need to work.

Calendar has a streamlined user interface that makes it easy to move among days, weeks, months, and years. You can click the **Today** button to display the current day, or use the Go to Date dialog to jump directly to a specific date.

Navigate the Calendar App

Open Calendar and Navigate by Days

1 Click **Calendar** (📅) on the Dock.

Calendar opens.

2 Click **Day**.

Calendar displays the current day, including a schedule of the day's events.

3 Click **Next** (▶) to move to the next day or **Previous** (◀) to move to the previous day.

Calendar displays the day you chose.

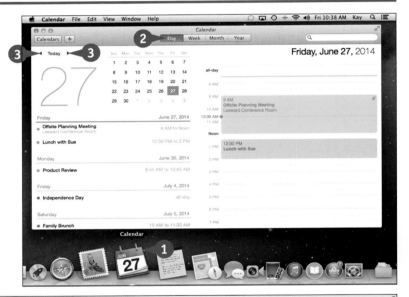

View and Navigate by Weeks

1 Click **Week**.

Calendar displays the week for the date you were previously viewing.

2 Click **Next** (▶) to move to the next week or **Previous** (◀) to move to the previous week.

Calendar displays the week you chose.

View and Navigate by Months

1 Click **Month**.

Calendar displays the current month.

2 Click **Next** (▶) to move to the next month or **Previous** (◀) to move to the previous month.

Calendar displays the month you chose.

View and Navigate by Years

1 Click **Year**.

Calendar displays the year for the date you were last viewing.

2 Click **Next** (▶) to move to the next year or **Previous** (◀) to move to the previous year.

Calendar displays the year you chose.

Note: In Week view, Month view, or Year view, double-click a day to display it in Day view.

A You can click **Today** to display today's date.

TIP

Which keyboard shortcuts can I use to navigate in Calendar?

Press ⌘+**1** to display the calendar by day, ⌘+**2** by week, ⌘+**3** by month, or ⌘+**4** by year. Press ⌘+**→** to move to the next day, week, month, or year, or ⌘+**←** to move to the previous one. Press ⌘+**Shift**+**T** to open the Go to Date dialog, which enables you to jump to a specific date. Press ⌘+**T** to jump to today's date.

Create a New Calendar

Calendar enables you to create as many calendars as you need to separate your appointments into logical categories. Calendar comes with two calendars already created for you: the Home calendar and the Work calendar. You can create new calendars as needed alongside these calendars.

After creating a new calendar, you can create events in it. You can also change existing events from another calendar to the new calendar.

Create a New Calendar

1 In Calendar, click **File**.

The File menu opens.

2 Click **New Calendar**.

Note: If the Calendars pane is open, you can create a new calendar by pressing Ctrl + clicking in open space in the Calendars pane and then clicking **New Calendar** on the contextual menu.

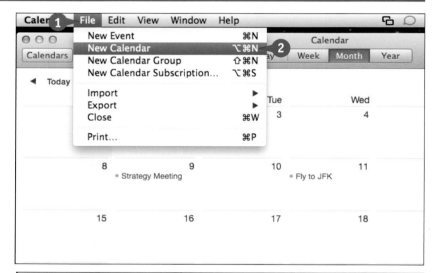

Calendar displays the Calendars pane if it was hidden.

Calendar creates a new calendar and displays an edit box around its default name, Untitled.

3 Type the name for the calendar and press Return.

Calendar applies the name to the calendar.

4 Press **Ctrl**+click the calendar's name.

The contextual menu opens.

5 Click **Get Info**.

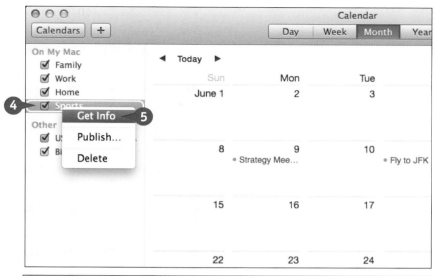

A dialog opens showing information for the calendar.

6 Click the **Color** pop-up menu (▲) and then select the color you want the calendar to use.

7 Type a description for the calendar.

Note: Click **Ignore alerts** (☐ changes to ☑) if you want to suppress alerts for the calendar.

8 Click **OK**.

The dialog closes.

You can now add events to the calendar.

TIPS

What do the check boxes in the Calendars pane do?

The check boxes control what calendars Calendar displays. Click a check box (☑ changes to ☐) to remove a calendar's events from display.

How can I organize my many calendars?

You can organize your calendars by creating calendar groups. Click **Calendars** to open the Calendars pane, and then press **Ctrl**+click or right-click in it and click **New Group**. Type the name for the new group and press **Return**. You can then click a calendar and drag it into the group, so that it appears in a collapsible list under the group.

Create an Event

Calendar makes it easy to organize your time commitments by creating an event for each appointment, meeting, trip, or special occasion. Calendar displays each event as an item on its grid, so you can see what is supposed to happen when.

You can create an event either for a specific length of time, such as one or two hours, or for an entire day. And you can create either an appointment that occurs only once or an appointment that repeats one or more times, as needed.

Create an Event

1 Navigate by days, weeks, months, or years to reach the day on which you want to create the event.

2 If the appointments area is in Month view or Year view, click **Day** to switch to Day view or **Week** to switch to Week view.

3 In the appointments area, click the time the event starts, and then drag to the time at which it ends.

Calendar creates an event where you clicked and applies a default name, New Event.

When you release the mouse button, a pop-up panel appears.

4 Type the name for the event and then press Return.

5 Click the **Color** pop-up menu and select the color for the event.

6 Click **location** and type the location for the event.

7 Click **Add Alert, Repeat, or Travel Time**.

Controls for setting the alert, repeat, and travel time appear.

Ⓐ You can click **all-day** (☐ changes to ☑) to make the event an all-day event.

Ⓑ You can click **travel time** and specify the travel time required.

⑧ If you want a reminder, click **alert** and specify the details of the alert, such as **10 minutes before**.

⑨ To add further information, click **Add Notes, Attachments, or URL**.

⑩ Click **Add Note** and type any notes needed.

⑪ Click **Add Attachment**, click the file in the Open dialog, and then click **Open**.

⑫ Click **Add URL** and type or paste the URL for the event.

⑬ Click outside the event panel.

The panel closes.

The event appears in your calendar.

TIP

How do I create a repeating event?
In the panel showing the event's details, click **repeat** and click **Every day**, **Every week**, **Every month**, or **Every year**. Use the controls that appear for setting the details of the repetition — for example, click **end**, click **After**, and specify **8 times**. For other options, click **Custom** to open the Custom dialog. You can then click the **Frequency** pop-up menu (⬍) and select **Daily**, **Weekly**, **Monthly**, or **Yearly**, and then specify the repetition patterns, such as **Every 2 Weeks**.

Share a Calendar

Calendar enables you to share one or more calendars with other people so that they know when you are busy.

Your calendars stored on iCloud sync automatically to your other Macs and iOS devices. You can share a calendar stored on iCloud either as a private calendar, available only to the people whose names or e-mail addresses you specify, or as a public calendar, available to everyone. If you store your calendar on your iMac, you can share that calendar with others by publishing it to a calendar server on the Internet.

Share a Calendar

Share a Calendar on iCloud

1. In Calendar, click **Calendars**.

2. Position the mouse pointer over the calendar.

   The Share icon (🖾) appears.

3. Click **Share** (🖾).

   The Share dialog opens.

4. Start typing a name or e-mail address.

5. Double-click the e-mail address for the contact.

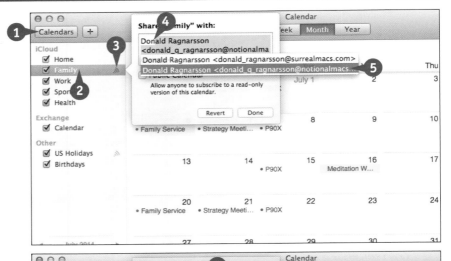

6. Click the pop-up button (✉).

7. Click **View & Edit** to enable the contact to edit the calendar. Click **View Only** to enable the contact to only view the calendar.

8. Add other contacts as needed by repeating steps 4 to 7.

9. Click **Public Calendar** (☐ changes to ☑) if you want to make the calendar public.

10. Click **Done**.

    Calendar shares the calendar.

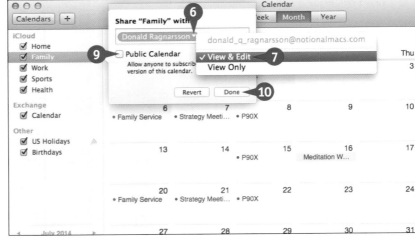

Publish a Calendar Stored on Your iMac

Note: Publishing a calendar makes it public, available to anyone who can access the calendar server that hosts it. Only you can edit your public calendars.

1 In Calendar, click **Calendars**.

The Calendars panel appears.

2 Press Ctrl +click the calendar you want to share.

The contextual menu opens.

3 Click **Publish**.

The Publish calendar dialog opens.

4 Type a descriptive name for the calendar.

5 Type or paste the URL for the calendar server.

6 Type your login name.

7 Type your password.

8 Click **Publish changes automatically** (☐ changes to ☑) to publish calendar changes automatically.

9 Click **Publish titles and notes** (☐ changes to ☑) to publish brief details of your events.

A You can click **Publish to do items** (☐ changes to ☑) to include your to-do items.

10 Click **Publish**.

Calendar publishes the calendar.

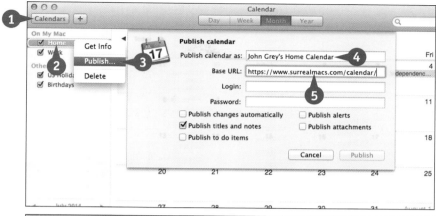

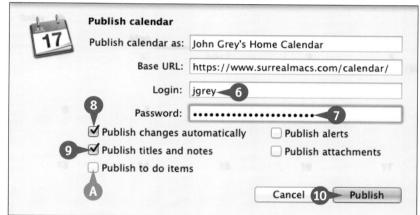

TIPS

How do I stop sharing a calendar?
Click **Calendars** to display the Calendars pane. Press Ctrl +click the shared or published calendar, and then click **Stop Sharing** or **Stop Publishing**, as appropriate. In the confirmation dialog that opens, click **Stop Sharing** or **Stop Publishing**.

Should I publish alerts and attachments with my calendar?
Do not publish alerts or attachments with a calendar unless you are certain that many of the people who subscribe to the calendar want the alerts or attachments.

Subscribe to a Published Calendar

Calendar enables you to subscribe to calendars that others have published on iCloud or the Internet. By subscribing to a calendar, you add it to Calendar so that you can view the events in the calendar along with those in your calendars.

You can subscribe to a calendar either by typing or pasting its URL into Calendar or by clicking a link in a message that you have received.

Subscribe to a Published Calendar

1 In Calendar, click **File**.

The File menu opens.

2 Click **New Calendar Subscription**.

Note: Many organizations, sports teams, and artists make their calendars available on their websites. You can either copy the calendar's URL or download the calendar.

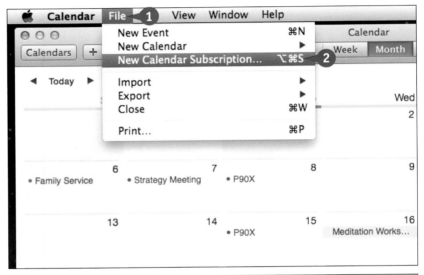

The Enter the URL of the Calendar You Want to Subscribe To dialog opens.

3 Type or paste in the calendar's URL.

Note: If you receive a link to a published calendar, click the link in Mail. Calendar opens and displays the Enter the URL of the Calendar You Want to Subscribe To dialog with the URL inserted. Click **Subscribe**.

4 Click **Subscribe**.

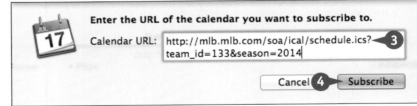

A dialog opens showing the details of the calendar.

5 Type the name to display for the calendar.

6 Click the **Color** pop-up menu (⬚) and select the color to use for the calendar.

7 Click the **Location** pop-up menu (⬚) and choose where to store the calendar. Your choices are **iCloud** or **On My Mac**.

8 Click **Alerts** (☐ changes to ☑) if you want to remove alerts.

9 Click **Attachments** (☐ changes to ☑) if you want to remove attachments.

10 Click the **Auto-refresh** pop-up menu (⬚) and select your preferred option for automatically refreshing the calendar, such as **Every week**.

11 Click **Ignore alerts** (☐ changes to ☑) if you want to ignore alerts set in the calendar.

12 Click **OK**.

Calendar adds the calendar, and its events appear.

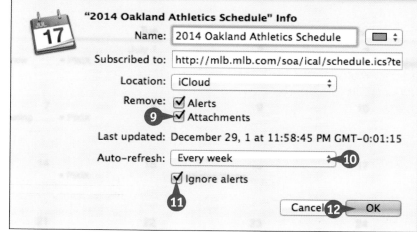

TIPS

How do I update a published calendar?
You can update all your published calendars at the same time by clicking **View** and selecting **Refresh Calendars**. You can also give the Refresh Calendars command by pressing ⌘+R.

How do I unsubscribe from a published calendar?
Instead of unsubscribing, you delete the calendar from the list. Click **Calendars** to display the Calendars pane, press Ctrl+click or right-click the calendar, and then click **Delete** on the contextual menu.

Add a Contact

O S X's Contacts app enables you to track and manage your contacts. Contacts stores the data for each contact on a separate virtual address card that contains storage slots for many different items of information, from the person's name and phone numbers to the e-mail addresses and photo.

To add a contact, you create a new contact card and enter the person's data on it. You can also add contact information quickly from vCard address card files that you receive.

Add a Contact

1 Click **Contacts** (⬛) on the Dock.

The Contacts app opens.

2 Click **File**.

The File menu opens.

3 Click **New Card**.

Note: You can also create a new contact card by pressing ⌘+N or by clicking **Add** (+) and then selecting **New Contact** from the pop-up menu.

Contacts creates a new card and selects the First placeholder.

4 Type the contact's first name.

Note: Press Tab to move the selection from the current field to the next.

5 Type the contact's last name.

6 If the contact works for a company, type the company name.

Ⓐ You can click **Company** (☐ changes to ☑) when creating a card for a company or organization.

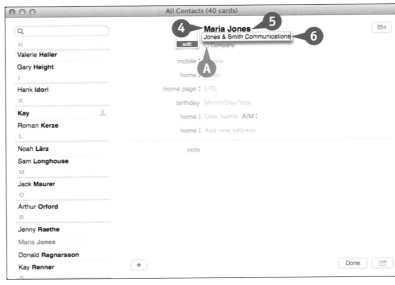

7 Click the pop-up menu (⬍) next to the first Phone field and select the type of phone number, such as **work** or **mobile**.

8 Type the phone number.

9 Add other phone numbers as needed.

10 Click the pop-up menu (⬍) next to the first Email field and select the type of e-mail address, such as **work** or **home**.

11 Type the e-mail address.

12 Add the physical address and other information.

13 Click **Done**.

Contacts closes the card for editing.

The card appears in the contacts list.

Note: Only the fields that contain data appear in the card.

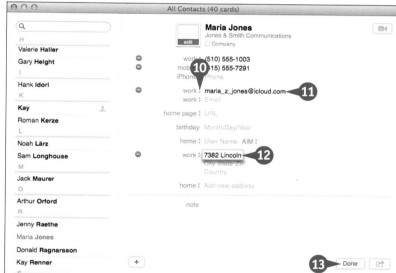

How do I add a vCard to Contacts?

If you receive a vCard file, which has the .vcf file extension and contains a virtual address card, in Mail, press `Ctrl`+click the card, highlight **Open With** on the contextual menu, and then select **Contacts**. A dialog opens prompting you to confirm that you want to import the card into Contacts. Click **Import**.

How do I delete a contact from Contacts?

To delete a contact, click the card, click **Edit**, and then select **Delete Card** or press `Delete`. A confirmation dialog opens. Click **Delete**.

Change a Contact's Information

Contacts makes it easy to change the information for a contact. So when you learn that a contact's details have changed, or you need to add extra information, you can open the contact record and make the changes needed.

Contacts enables you to add a wide variety of different fields to a contact record to store the information about a contact. You can also add a photo to a contact record.

Change a Contact's Information

1 In the left column in the Contacts window, click the contact whose information you want to change.

2 Click **Edit**.

Contacts opens the contact's card for editing.

3 To change an existing field, click it and then type the updated information.

A You can add a field by clicking **Add** (+) and then clicking the field on the contextual menu or the More Fields submenu.

4 To remove an existing field, click **Remove** (−) next to it.

5 To add a photo for the contact, double-click the picture placeholder.

A dialog opens.

6 Click **Faces**.

The faces you have identified in iPhoto appear.

Note: Click **Defaults** to assign one of OS X's user account pictures. Click **iCloud** to use a picture you have stored in iCloud. Click **Camera** to take a photo with your iMac's camera.

7 Click the face you want to use.

8 Click **Edit**.

The photo opens for editing.

9 Click and drag the slider to zoom in or out.

10 Click and drag the photo to change the part that appears.

Ⓑ You can click **Effect** (🔲) to apply an effect to the photo.

11 Click **Done**.

Contacts adds the photo to the contact record.

12 Click **Done**.

Contacts closes the contact record for editing.

TIPS

How can I add information that does not fit in any of Contacts' fields?

You can use the Notes field for any information, but you can also create custom fields. Click the pop-up menu (🔽) next to an empty field, and then click **Custom** to open the Add Custom Label dialog. Type the name for the field and click **OK**. You can then type the data for the field.

Are there other ways of adding photos to contact records?

Yes. You can click and drag a photo from iPhoto, a Finder window, an e-mail message, or a web page to the photo placeholder.

Organize Contacts into Groups

Contacts enables you to organize your contacts into separate groups, making it easier to find the contacts you need. Groups are useful if you have several different categories of contacts, such as family, friends, and colleagues. You can assign any contact to as many groups as needed.

After creating groups, you can view a single group at a time or search within a group. You can also send an e-mail message to all the members of a group.

Organize Contacts into Groups

Create a Group of Contacts

1. In Contacts, click **View**.

   The View menu opens.

2. Click **Show Groups**.

Note: You can also press ⌘+① to display the Groups pane.

The Groups pane opens on the left side of the Contacts window.

3. Position the mouse pointer over the account in which you want to create the group, such as **iCloud**.

   The Add button (⊕) appears.

4. Click **Add** (⊕).

   Contacts adds a group and displays an edit box around the default name, *untitled group*.

5. Type the name and press Return.

   The name appears.

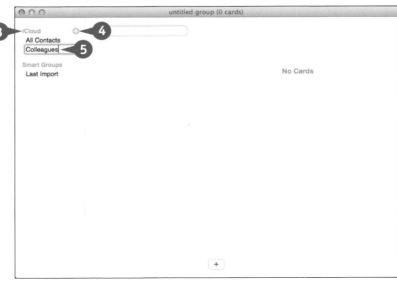

Add Contacts to a Group

1 Click **All Contacts**.

Contacts displays all your contacts.

2 Click and drag a contact to the new group.

Note: To add multiple contacts to the group, click the first, and then press ⌘+click each of the others. Click and drag the selected contacts to the group.

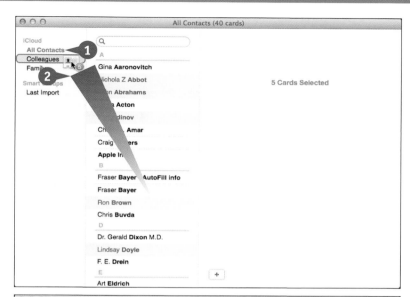

View a Group or Search Within It

1 Click the group.

Contacts displays the contacts in the group.

2 To search within the group, click in the search box and type a search term.

Contacts displays matching contacts.

3 Click the contact you want to view.

A The contact's details appear.

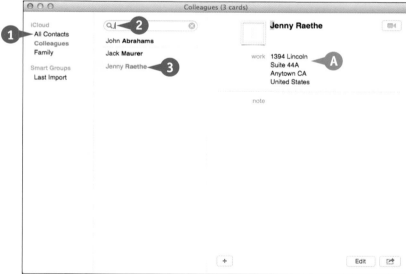

TIPS

How do I remove a contact from a group?
Click the group and then click the contact. Click **Edit** and select **Remove from Group**. Contacts removes the contact from the group but does not delete the contact record.

How do I delete a group?
Click the group, click **Edit**, and then select **Delete Group**. Contacts displays a confirmation message. Click **Delete**. Deleting a group does not affect the contacts it contains; the contacts remain available through the All Contacts group or any other groups to which they belong.

Create Notes

The Notes app included with OS X enables you to take text notes on your iMac. You can format the notes by using italics, boldface, indentation, and other widely used formatting. Notes are text only and cannot contain objects such as images.

If you store the notes in your iCloud account, you can access them from your iOS devices, your other Macs running OS X 10.7 or later versions, a Windows PC with the iCloud Control Panel installed, or any Windows PC or Mac that has a compatible web browser.

Create Notes

1 Click **Notes** (▨) on the Dock.

Note: If Notes (▨) does not appear on the Dock, click **Launchpad** (▨) and then click **Notes** (▨) on the Launchpad screen.

The Notes window opens.

Ⓐ You can click an existing note to display its contents.

2 Click **Add** (⊞).

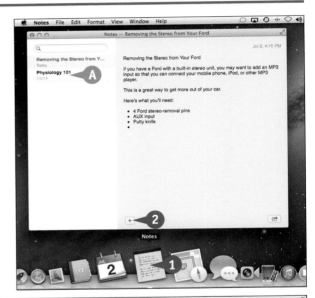

Notes creates a new blank note.

3 Type the title of the note and press Return.

4 Type the text of the note.

Ⓑ Notes automatically applies numbered-list formatting when you start a paragraph by typing a numbering format, such as **1.** followed by a space or tab.

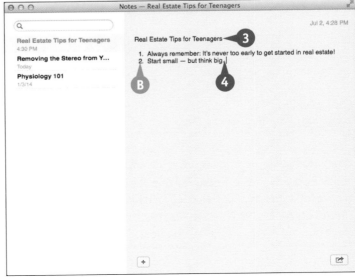

5 Click and drag to select the text that you want to format.

6 Click **Format**.

The Format menu opens.

7 Highlight the submenu for the formatting you want to apply, such as **Font**.

The submenu opens.

8 Click the appropriate command, such as **Italic**.

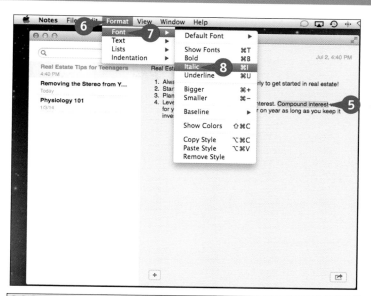

Notes applies the formatting.

C You can quickly share a note by clicking **Share** (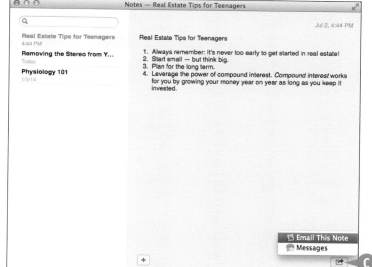) and then clicking **Email This Note** or **Messages**, as appropriate.

9 When you finish creating the note, press ⌘+Q.

Notes closes.

TIP

How do I move my notes from my iMac to iCloud?
Click **System Preferences** (⬚) on the Dock to open the System Preferences window. Click **iCloud** to display the iCloud pane. Click **Notes** (☐ changes to ☑). In the Do You Want to Merge Notes with iCloud? dialog, click **Merge**. System Preferences moves your notes to iCloud, and you can then work on them via the Notes app on your iMac or your iOS devices.

Keep Track of Tasks with Reminders

OS X's Reminders app gives you an easy way to track what you have to do and your progress on your tasks. Reminders enables you to link a reminder to a specific time, a specific location, or both. Linking a reminder to a location is useful when you sync your reminders with a MacBook or with an iPhone, iPad, or iPod touch that you carry from location to location.

Keep Track of Tasks with Reminders

Create a Reminder

1 Click **Reminders** (▣) on the Dock.

Note: If the Reminders icon (▣) does not appear on the Dock, click **Launchpad** (▣), and then click **Reminders** (▣).

The Reminders window opens.

2 Click **Add** (⊞).

Reminders starts a new reminder.

3 Type the description of the reminder.

4 Position the mouse pointer over the reminder.

The Info button (▣) appears.

5 Click **Info** (▣).

The Info panel appears.

6 Click **On a Day** (☐ changes to ☑).

The date and time controls appear.

7 Click the date.

The date panel opens.

8 Double-click the date for the reminder.

The date panel closes, and the date appears in the Info panel.

9 Type the time for the reminder.

Ⓐ You can click **repeat** to set up a repeating reminder.

10 Click the **priority** pop-up menu (⬍) and select the priority: **None**, **Low**, **Medium**, or **High**.

11 Click **note** and type any notes needed for the reminder.

12 Click **Done**.

The Info panel closes.

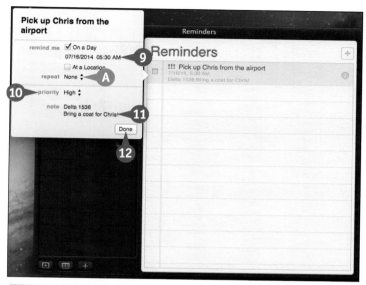

Create a Reminders List

1 In Reminders, click **New List** (➕).

Note: If the sidebar is hidden, click **View** and select **Show Sidebar**.

A new list appears in the sidebar.

2 Type the list's name.

3 Press **Return**.

The list appears, and you can start adding reminders to it.

Note: You can click and drag an existing reminder to the list in the sidebar.

TIP

How do I link a reminder to a location?
In the pop-up panel containing the reminder's details, click **At a Location** (☐ changes to ☑). A new section appears under At a Location. In the text box, type a contact's name or an address. Click **Show List** (⬇) to display a list of matching items, and then click the correct item. Then click either **Departing** (◌ changes to ◉) or **Arriving** (◌ changes to ◉).

Find Directions with Maps

OS X's Maps app enables you to pinpoint your iMac's location by using known wireless networks. You can view your location on a road map, a satellite picture, or a hybrid that shows street annotations on the satellite picture. You can easily switch among map types to find the most useful one for your current needs. You can use Maps to get directions to where you want to go. In some areas, you can also display current traffic congestion to help you identify the most viable route for a journey.

Find Directions with Maps

Open Maps and Find Your Location

1 Click **Maps** (📍) on the Dock.

Note: If Maps (📍) does not appear on the Dock, click **Launchpad** (🚀) on the Dock and then click **Maps** (📍) on the Launchpad screen.

The Maps window opens.

2 Click **Current Location** (➤ changes to ➤).

Ⓐ A blue dot shows your current location. The blue circle indicates that Maps is determining your location.

Change the Map Type and Zoom In or Out

1 Click **Hybrid**.

The map switches to Hybrid view, showing satellite images with place names.

2 Click **Zoom Out** (➖) one or more times.

The map zooms out.

Note: Click **Zoom In** (➕) to zoom in.

Note: You can rotate the map by pressing Option+clicking and dragging. To return the map to its default northward orientation, click the compass arrow (⬆).

Get Directions

1 Click **Directions**.

The Directions pane opens, suggesting Current Location as your starting point.

2 Type your start point.

Note: If Maps displays a panel of suggestions for the start point or end point you type, click the appropriate suggestion.

Note: Click **View** on the menu bar and then click **Show Traffic** to display traffic conditions if they are available.

3 Type your end point.

Maps displays suggested routes.

Ⓑ The green pin marks the start.

Ⓒ The red pin marks the end.

Ⓓ The current route appears in darker blue.

Ⓔ The current route's details appear in the Directions pane.

Ⓕ You can click another route or its time box to display its details.

4 Click a direction to display that part of the route.

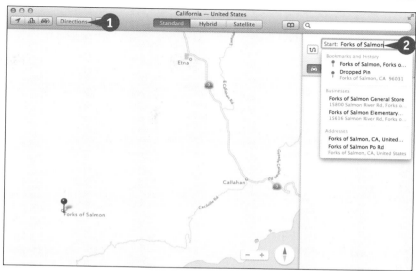

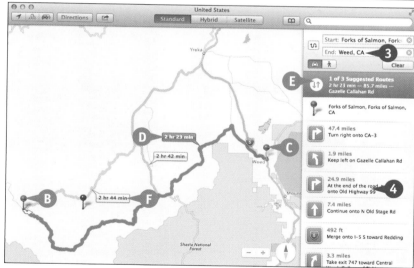

TIPS

How do I use the Magic Trackpad or Magic Mouse for Maps?

Place two fingers on the Magic Trackpad or Magic Mouse. Pinch apart to zoom in. Pinch inward to zoom out. Rotate your fingers to rotate the map.

How do I get directions for walking?

Tap **Walking** (🚶) in the Directions panel to display the distance and time for walking the route. Be aware that walking directions may be inaccurate or optimistic. Before walking the route, verify that it does not send you across pedestrian-free bridges or through rail tunnels.

Explore with Maps

The Maps app enables you not only to find out where you are and get directions to places, but also to explore with 3-D flyovers of the places on the map.

To use 3-D flyovers, you navigate to the place you want to explore, and then switch on the 3D feature. You can then zoom in and out on the map, pan around, and move backward to forward.

Explore with Maps

① Click **Maps** (▨) on the Dock.

Note: If Maps (▨) does not appear on the Dock, click **Launchpad** (▨) on the Dock and then click **Maps** (▨) on the Launchpad screen.

The Maps window opens.

② Display the area of interest in the middle of the screen by browsing or searching.

③ Click **Flyover** (▨ changes to ▨).

The map switches to Flyover view.

④ Click **Zoom In** (⊞) to zoom in.

⑤ Click and drag to scroll the map.

6 Press Option +click and drag clockwise or counterclockwise.

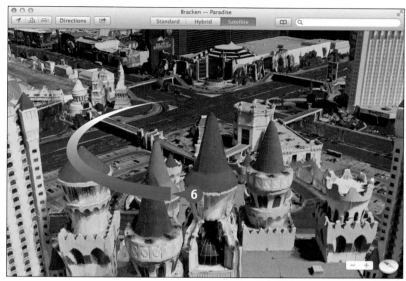

The view rotates, and you can explore.

Note: Pan and zoom as needed to explore the area.

Ⓐ The red end of the compass arrow (▧) indicates north. You can tap this icon to restore the direction to north.

7 Click **Flyover** (▧ changes to ▧).

The map returns to normal view.

TIPS

How do I use the Magic Trackpad or Magic Mouse for Flyover?
Place two fingers on the Magic Trackpad or Magic Mouse. Move your fingers in the direction you want to move the view. Rotate your fingers to rotate the view.

What does Flyover do with the Standard map?
When you tap **Flyover** (▧) to switch on Flyover with the Standard map displayed, Maps tilts the map at an angle, as you might do with a paper map, and displays outlines of buildings if they are available. For most purposes, Flyover is most useful with the Satellite map and the Hybrid map.

CHAPTER 9

Enjoying Music, Video, and Books

Your iMac comes equipped with apps for enjoying music, video, and books. iTunes enables you to copy songs from CDs, play them back, and watch videos, movies, and podcasts. iBooks enables you to build an e-book library on your iMac and read books comfortably.

Set Up Home Sharing

iTunes includes a feature called Home Sharing that enables you to share songs among your Macs, PCs, and iOS devices. Home Sharing saves time and effort over copying song files manually between your computers. To use Home Sharing, you must have an Apple ID — for example, one you create when setting up an account on Apple's iTunes Store. If you do not already have an Apple ID, you can create one in a couple of minutes.

Set Up Home Sharing

1. Click **iTunes** (![icon]) on the Dock.

   iTunes opens.

2. Click **File**.

   The File menu opens.

3. Highlight **Home Sharing**.

   The Home Sharing submenu opens.

4. Click **Turn On Home Sharing**.

The Home Sharing screen appears.

5. Type your Apple ID.

6. Type your password.

7. Click **Turn On Home Sharing**.

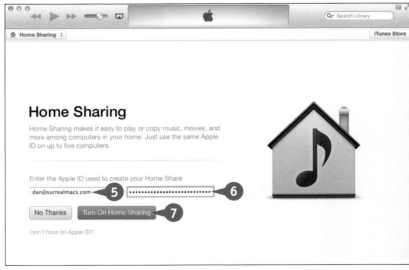

The Home Sharing screen appears.

8 Click **Done**.

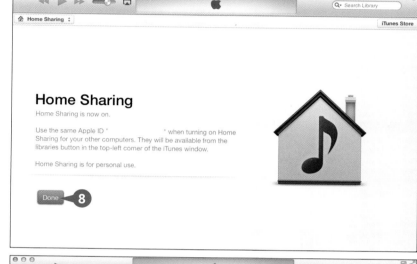

Your library appears again.

9 Click the **Source** pop-up menu (⬍).

10 Click the appropriate shared library in the Home Shares list on the menu.

The shared content appears.

11 Select the items you want to import.

12 Click **Import**.

iTunes imports the items.

TIPS

Can iTunes automatically transfer new items I purchase to my iMac?
Yes. Click the **Source** pop-up menu (⬍), and then select a share in the Home Shares category to display the shared content. Click **Settings** to display the Home Sharing Settings dialog. Click the check box (☐ changes to ☑) for each item you want to transfer automatically, and then click **OK**.

How can I share music without using Home Sharing?
Click **iTunes** and then click **Preferences**. Click **Sharing** to display the Sharing pane. Click the **Share my library on my local network** option (☐ changes to ☑) and then click the **Share entire library** option (◯ changes to ◉) or the **Share selected playlists** option (◯ changes to ◉). Others can then play your shared content but not copy it.

Add Your Music to iTunes

iTunes enables you to build your music library quickly by adding your existing songs to it. You can copy songs from your CDs by using a SuperDrive or other optical drive. You can also import songs that you already have as digital files on your iMac.

When importing songs from CDs, you can choose among different settings to create files using different formats and higher or lower audio quality. The highest-quality files give the best sound but require the most space on your iMac's disk.

Add Your Music to iTunes

1. Click **iTunes** ( ) on the Dock.

   iTunes opens.

2. Insert a CD in the optical drive.

   iTunes looks up the CD's details online and opens a dialog asking if you want to import the CD.

Note: If you want to prevent iTunes from prompting you to import each audio CD you insert, click **Do not ask me again** (changes to) before clicking **No**.

3. Click **No**.

   The dialog closes.

4. Click **CD Info**.

   The CD Info dialog opens.

5. Verify that the information is correct. If it is not, correct it.

Note: Many entries for CDs in the online database that iTunes uses contain misspelled or inaccurate information.

6. Click **Compilation CD** (changes to) if the CD is a compilation by various artists.

7. Click **OK**.

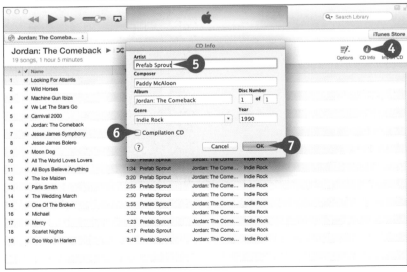

The CD Info dialog closes.

⑧ Click **Import CD**.

The Import Settings dialog opens.

⑨ Click the **Import Using** pop-up menu (⬍) and select the encoder to use.

⑩ Click the **Setting** pop-up menu (⬍) and select the setting.

⑪ Click **Use error correction when reading Audio CDs** (☐ changes to ☑).

⑫ Click **OK**.

The Import Settings dialog closes.

iTunes imports the songs.

⑬ When iTunes finishes importing, click **Eject** (⏏).

The optical drive ejects the CD.

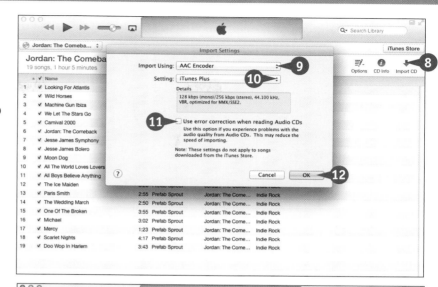

TIPS

How can I create MP3 files rather than AAC files?

In the Import Settings dialog, click the **Import Using** pop-up menu (⬍) and select **MP3 Encoder**. Click the **Setting** pop-up menu (⬍) and select the quality you want: **Higher Quality** gives reasonable quality, but for top quality, select **Custom** and then select the **320 kbps** bitrate in the **Stereo Bit Rate** pop-up menu (⬍).

Should I use error correction?

Using error correction for reading CDs is almost always a good idea. Importing may be a little slower, but not enough to matter.

Buy Songs Online

iTunes enables you to buy songs and other content from the iTunes Store, Apple's online store for music and media. To buy items from the iTunes Store, you must set up an account including either your credit card details or another means of payment, such as an iTunes Gift Card, PayPal, or an allowance account. If you do not already have an account, iTunes prompts you to set one up when you first attempt to buy an item.

Buy Songs Online

1 In iTunes, click **iTunes Store**.

iTunes displays the home page of the iTunes store.

2 Position the mouse pointer over **Music**.

A pop-up menu button (🔻) appears.

3 Click the pop-up menu button.

The pop-up menu opens.

4 Click the type of music you want to browse.

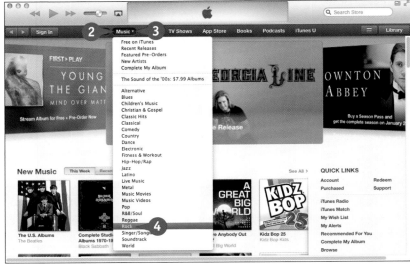

iTunes displays the kind of music you clicked.

5 Click an item to display information on it.

6 Highlight a song and click **Play** (image) to play a sample.

7 Click the price button.

Note: If the Sign In to the iTunes Store dialog opens, type your password, and then click **Buy**.

iTunes downloads the song.

8 Position the mouse pointer over **Library**.

9 Click the pop-up menu button (image).

10 Click **Purchased**.

The Purchased playlist appears, showing your purchase.

TIPS

What other online stores sell songs I can play in iTunes?
Many online stores sell songs in the widely used MP3 format, which you can play in iTunes and on iOS devices. Explore stores such as Amazon.com (www.amazon.com), eMusic (www.emusic.com), and 7digital (www.7digital.com).

How can I restart a download that fails?
Click **Store** and select **Check for Available Downloads**. Sign in if iTunes prompts you to do so. iTunes then automatically restarts any downloads that were not completed.

Play Songs

iTunes makes it easy to play back your songs. You can view your music listed by songs, albums, artists, or genres, which enables you to quickly locate the songs you want to hear. You can also search for songs using artist names, album or song names, or keywords.

After locating the music you want to hear, you can start a song playing by simply double-clicking it. You can then control playback by using the straightforward controls at the top of the iTunes window.

Play Songs

Play a Song in Songs View

1 In iTunes, click **Songs**.

iTunes switches to Songs view.

The column browser appears.

Note: If the column browser does not appear, click **View**, highlight **Column Browser**, and select **Show Column Browser**.

2 Click the genre.

3 Click the artist.

4 Click the album.

5 Double-click the song.

The song starts playing.

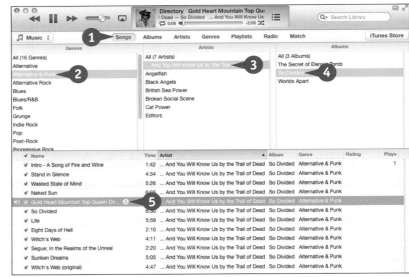

Play a Song in Albums View

1 Click **Albums**.

iTunes switches to Albums view.

2 Click the album you want to open.

The album's contents appear.

3 Double-click the song.

The song starts playing.

Ⓐ You can click **Close** (🔀) to close the album's pane.

Ⓑ You can click **In the Store** to see songs by this artist in the iTunes Store.

Play a Song in Artists View

1 Click **Artists**.

iTunes switches to Artists view.

2 Click the artist whose music you want to see.

3 Scroll up or down to locate the album.

4 Double-click a song to start it playing.

C You can click **Play** (▶) to play the whole album.

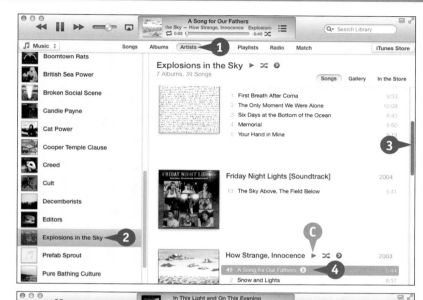

Play a Song in Genres View

1 Click **Genres**.

iTunes switches to Genres view.

2 Click the genre you want to browse.

3 Scroll up or down to locate the album.

4 Double-click a song to start it playing.

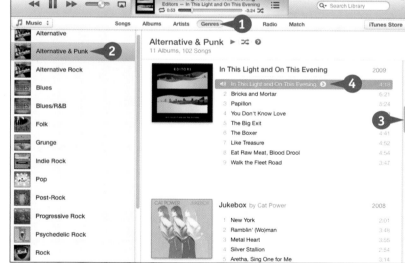

TIP

How can I search for songs?
Click in the search box and start typing your search term. iTunes shows matching items as you type. Click an item to go to it in your current view. Position the mouse pointer over an item and click **Add** (⊕) to add it to the Up Next list of songs to play. Click **More** (▣) to display a menu of other actions, such as adding the song to a playlist or creating a Genius playlist based on it.

Play Videos

iTunes enables you to play videos, including video podcasts. You can buy music videos, TV shows, and movies from the iTunes Store or export files of your own movies from iMovie or other applications. After adding videos to iTunes, you access them by selecting **Movies** in the Source pop-up menu.

You can watch video content either within the iTunes window or full screen. You can also play videos from your iMac to a TV connected to an Apple TV.

Play Videos

1 In iTunes, click the **Source** pop-up menu (⬍) and then click **Movies**.

Note: To watch a TV show, click **TV Shows** on the Source pop-up menu. To watch a music video you have purchased, click **Music**, click **Playlists** on the navigation bar, and then click **Purchased**.

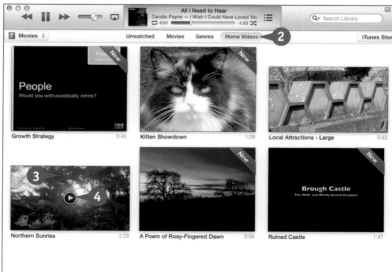

The Movies screen appears.

2 On the navigation bar, click the view to use: **Unwatched**, **Movies**, **Genres**, **Home Videos**, or **List**.

iTunes displays the movies in the view you click.

3 Position the mouse pointer over the movie you want to play.

The Play button appears.

4 Click **Play** (◉).

iTunes starts playing the movie.

⑤ Move the mouse pointer over the video.

The pop-up control bar appears.

⑥ Use the controls on the pop-up bar to control playback.

Ⓐ You can click **Full Screen** (▣) to switch to full-screen viewing.

⑦ Click **Close** (▣) to stop viewing the video.

TIP

How do I play a video from iTunes on the TV connected to my Apple TV?

First, make sure your iMac is connected to the same network as the Apple TV via either a wireless network or a wired network. You can then click **AirPlay** (▣) to the right of the volume control in iTunes to display the AirPlay menu. Click the Apple TV's name on the menu. iTunes sends the video output to the Apple TV, which displays it on the TV's screen.

Create Playlists

iTunes enables you to create playlists that contain the songs you want in your preferred order. Playlists are a great way of getting more enjoyment out of your music. You can listen to a playlist, share it with others, or burn it to a CD for listening on a CD player.

To create a playlist, you drag items to the Playlists pane. In Songs, Albums, Artists, or Genres view, the Playlists pane automatically appears on the right side of the window when you start dragging songs.

Create Playlists

1. In iTunes, navigate to a song you want to put into a new playlist.

2. Click the song and drag it to the right.

The Playlists pane appears.

3. Drop the song in open space in the Playlists pane.

Note: You can drag the song to an existing playlist to add it to that playlist.

iTunes creates a new playlist, assigns it a default name based on the song name, and displays an edit box around the name.

④ Type the name for the playlist.

⑤ Press **Return**.

The playlist takes on the new name.

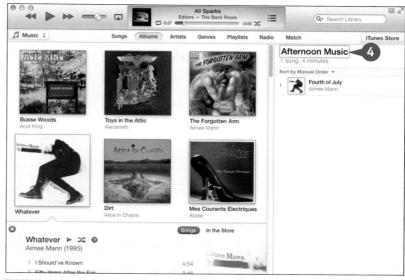

⑥ Click and drag other songs, artists, albums, or genres to the playlist.

Note: You can click and drag songs to the playlist from other views, such as Songs view or Genres view.

⑦ Click and drag the songs in the playlist into the order you want.

⑧ Click **Done**.

iTunes creates the playlist.

You can now play the playlist by clicking **Playlists** and then double-clicking the playlist.

TIP

How can I keep my playlists organized?
You can organize your playlists into playlist folders. Click **File**, highlight **New**, and then select **Playlist Folder**. iTunes creates a folder and displays an edit box around the name. Type the name for the folder and press **Return** to apply it. You can then click and drag playlists to the folder. Click **Expand** (▶) to expand a folder and reveal its playlists; click **Collapse** (▼) to collapse the folder and hide its playlists.

Create Smart Playlists

Instead of creating playlists manually by adding songs to them, you can have iTunes' Smart Playlists feature create playlists automatically for you. A *Smart Playlist* is a playlist iTunes builds based on criteria you specify. You can set iTunes to update a Smart Playlist automatically as well.

To create a Smart Playlist, you set up the criteria, also called *rules*, and name the playlist. iTunes then adds content to the playlist for you.

Create Smart Playlists

1 In iTunes, click **File**.

The File menu opens.

2 Highlight **New**.

The New submenu opens.

3 Click **Smart Playlist**.

Note: You can also start a Smart Playlist by pressing ⌘ + Option + N.

The Smart Playlist dialog opens.

4 Click the first ⬍ and select the item for the first condition — for example, **Genre**.

5 Click the second ⬍ and select the comparison for the first condition — for example, **contains**.

6 Click the text field and type the text for the comparison — for example, **Alternative** — making the condition "Genre contains Alternative."

7 To add another condition, click **Add** (⊕).

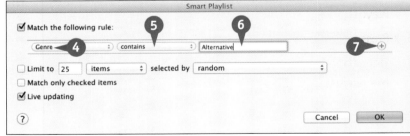

8 Click the **Match** pop-up menu (⬍) and select **any** to match any of the rules or **all** to match all the rules.

9 Set up the second condition by repeating steps **4** to **6**.

Note: You can add as many conditions as you need to define the playlist.

Ⓐ You can limit the playlist by clicking **Limit to** (☐ changes to ☑) and specifying the limit.

10 Click **Live updating** (☐ changes to ☑).

11 Click **OK**.

iTunes creates the Smart Playlist and adds it to the Playlists section of the Source list.

Ⓑ An edit box appears around the suggested name.

12 Type the name for the Smart Playlist.

13 Press Return.

iTunes applies the name to the playlist.

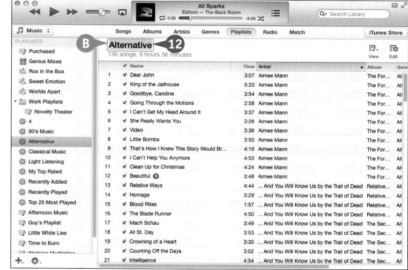

How do I produce a Smart Playlist the right length for a CD?

In the Smart Playlist dialog, first click **Limit to** (☐ changes to ☑). Click the left pop-up menu (⬍) and select **minutes**, and then set the number before it to **74** or **80**, depending on the capacity of the CD.

What does the Match Only Checked Items option do?

Click **Match only checked items** (☐ changes to ☑) to restrict your Smart Playlist to songs whose check boxes are selected. This means you can uncheck the check box for a song to prevent it from appearing in your Smart Playlists.

Create a Custom CD

iTunes enables you to burn a playlist to a CD or DVD. You can create an audio CD that you can play in almost any CD player, an MP3 CD that you can play in only some CD players and DVD players, or a data DVD that contains backups of your media files.

To create CDs or DVDs, you need a SuperDrive or other optical burner either connected to your iMac via USB or built into your iMac. You also need a blank recordable CD or recordable DVD.

Create a Custom CD

1 In iTunes, click **Playlists**.

iTunes switches to Playlists view.

2 Click the playlist you want to burn to CD.

The songs in the playlist appear.

3 Verify that the playlist is short enough to fit on a CD.

Note: An audio CD can hold a maximum of 74–80 minutes of audio. To ensure all the CD will play consistently, do not exceed 74 minutes.

4 Click **File**.

The File menu opens.

5 Click **Burn Playlist to Disc**.

The Burn Settings dialog opens.

6 Click the **Preferred Speed** pop-up menu (⬍) and select **Maximum Possible**.

7 Click **Audio CD** (◯ changes to ◉).

8 Click the **Gap Between Songs** pop-up menu (⬍) and select the gap, such as **2 seconds**.

9 Click **Use Sound Check** (☐ changes to ☑) if you want iTunes to standardize the songs' volume on the CD.

10 Click **Burn**.

iTunes prompts you to insert a CD.

11 Insert a CD in your iMac's optical drive.

iTunes checks the disc and burns the CD.

Ⓐ The display shows the progress of the burn.

iTunes displays the CD's contents when it finishes burning the CD.

12 Play the CD to test it.

13 Click **Eject** (⏏) to eject the CD.

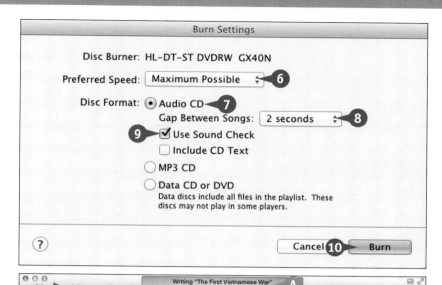

TIP

Is it a good idea to use Sound Check?

This depends on your music and your tastes. Try burning several CDs both with and without Sound Check and see which you prefer.

Without Sound Check, songs originally recorded at different levels play at different volumes from the CD. This can make for awkward listening because you may need to change the playback volume suddenly. Sound Check makes the overall volume more consistent but can rob songs of their dynamic range and power.

Listen to iTunes Radio and Internet Radio

iTunes enables you to listen to online radio stations. The iTunes Radio feature comes set to access a selection of stations on demand, which means you can pause the radio stream and resume it from the same place. You can skip some songs if you do not want to listen to them, and you can create custom stations.

You can also use iTunes to access radio stations that broadcast across the Internet in real time. When listening to such stations, you cannot pause the content or skip songs.

Listen to iTunes Radio and Internet Radio

Listen to a Radio Station

1 In iTunes, click **Radio**.

The Radio screen appears.

Note: If the main window displays an informational message about iTunes Radio, click **Start Listening**.

2 Position the mouse pointer over the station to which you want to listen.

The Play button (▣) appears.

3 Click **Play** (▣).

The station starts playing.

A Details of the current song appear.

B You can click **Skip** (▶▶) to skip to the next track.

C You can click **More** (▣) to display a menu of other actions, such as creating a new station from the artist or song.

D You can click **Add to My Stations** to add this station to your list of stations.

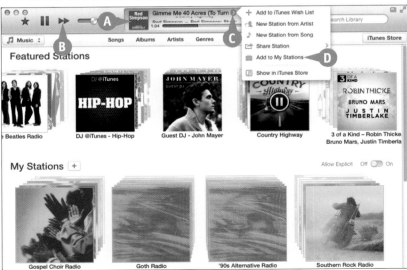

Customize Your List of Stations

1 Click **Add** (⊞).

The Add Station panel opens.

2 Click the genre you want to browse.

Ⓔ You can type an artist's name, a keyword, or a genre.

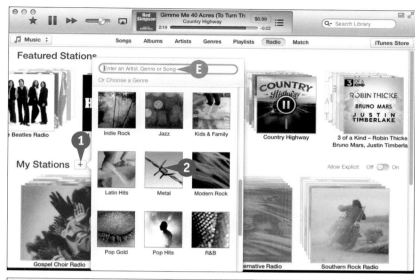

The stations in the genre appear.

3 Click **Play** (▶) to preview the genre.

4 Click **Add**.

iTunes adds the station to your My Stations list.

Note: To remove a station from your My Stations list, press **Ctrl**+click the station and then click **Delete**.

Enjoy Podcasts

A *podcast* is an audio or video file that you can download from the Internet and play on your iMac or a digital player like the iPhone, iPad, or iPod. iTunes enables you to access a wide variety of podcasts on the iTunes Store. The iTunes Store makes a wide variety of podcasts available. You can either download a single podcast episode or subscribe to a podcast so that iTunes automatically downloads new episodes for you.

Enjoy Podcasts

1 In iTunes, double-click **iTunes Store**.

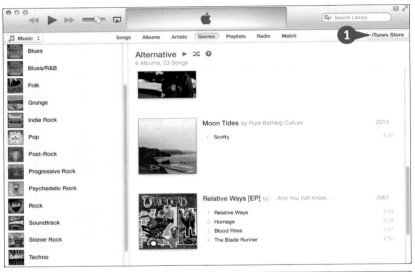

iTunes displays the home page of the iTunes Store.

2 Position the mouse pointer over **Podcasts**.

A pop-up menu button (▼) appears.

3 Click the pop-up menu button.

The pop-up menu opens.

4 Click the category of podcasts you want to browse.

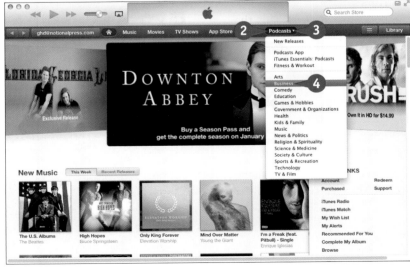

iTunes shows the category you clicked.

5 Click the podcast you want to view.

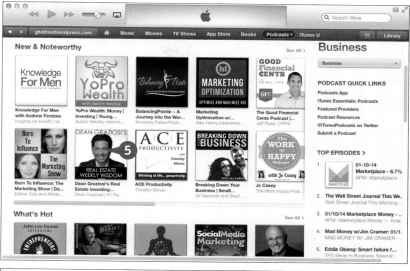

6 Click **Subscribe** if you want to subscribe to the podcast.

A confirmation dialog opens.

A You can click a price button or a Free button to download a single episode.

7 Click **Subscribe**.

iTunes subscribes you to the podcast and downloads the available episodes.

TIP

How do I watch the podcasts I have downloaded?

In iTunes, click **Podcasts** on the navigation bar. The list of podcasts appears. Click **Expand** (▶) to expand a podcast so that you can see the available episodes. You can then double-click the episode you want to listen to or watch. iTunes starts playing the podcast and displays a bar of pop-up controls for managing playback.

Add E-Books to iBooks and Read Them

OS X includes the iBooks app, which enables you to enjoy electronic books, or *e-books*, on your iMac. Using iBooks, you can read e-books that you already have on your iMac, download free or paid-for e-books from online stores, or read PDF files stored on your iMac.

Before you can read e-books that you have on your iMac, you must add them to iBooks. You can then open a book and start reading it.

Add E-Books to iBooks and Read Them

Add Your E-Books to iBooks

1 Click **iBooks** (◻) on the Dock.

Note: If iBooks (◻) does not appear on the Dock, click **Launchpad** (▣) on the Dock and then click **iBooks** (◻) on the Launchpad screen.

The iBooks window opens.

2 Click **File**.

The File menu opens.

3 Click **Add to Library**.

The Add to Library dialog opens.

4 Navigate to the folder that contains the books.

5 Select the books you want to add to iBooks.

6 Click **Add**.

The Add to Library dialog closes.

The books appear in iBooks.

Read E-Books

1 Click **iBooks** (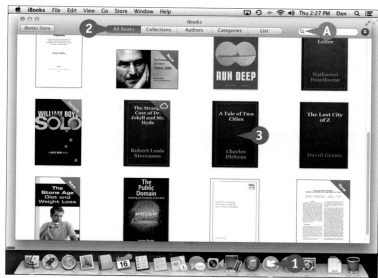) on the Dock.

The iBooks window opens.

2 Click the button for the view by which you want to browse. For example, click **All Books** to view all your books.

Ⓐ You can search for a book by clicking in the search box and typing keywords.

3 Click the book you want to open.

The book opens.

4 Press ➡ to display the next page or ⬅ to display the previous page.

Ⓑ You can click and drag the slider to move quickly through the book.

Ⓒ You can click **Appearance** (🅰🅰) to adjust the appearance of the page and the text.

Ⓓ You can click **Library** (▤) to display your library, leaving the book open.

5 When you finish reading, click **Close** (🔘).

The book closes, and your library appears.

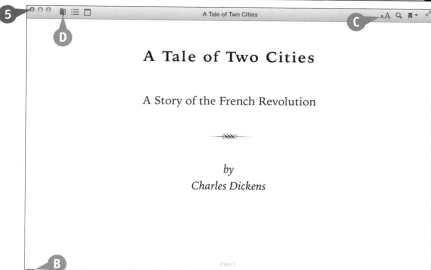

A Tale of Two Cities

A Story of the French Revolution

by
Charles Dickens

TIP

How else can I add my existing e-books to iBooks?

If you have added e-books to iTunes, you can move them to iBooks. This is usually a good idea because iBooks enables you to read the e-books easily. In iBooks, click **File** and select **Move Books from iTunes**. iBooks locates the e-books in your iTunes folders and moves them to its folders. The e-books appear in iBooks, and you can start reading them.

Buy Books on the iBooks Store

The iBooks app connects directly to the online Apple bookstore, which you can browse to find e-books. Some e-books are free; others you have to pay for, but many have samples that you can download to help you decide whether to buy the book.

After you download an e-book, it appears on your iBooks bookshelf. You can then open it and read it as described in the previous section, "Add E-Books to iBooks and Read Them."

Buy Books on the iBooks Store

1. Click **iBooks** (🔲) on the Dock.

Note: If iBooks (🔲) does not appear on the Dock, click **Launchpad** (🚀) on the Dock and then click **iBooks** (🔲) on the Launchpad screen.

   The iBooks window opens.

2. Click **iBooks Store**.

   iBooks displays the home page of the iBooks Store.

3. Scroll down to browse the categories and books on the home page.

Ⓐ The Free section is a great place to build your library without spending money.

4. Click a book you want to view.

224

iBooks displays the book's details.

⑤ Read about the book.

Ⓑ You can click **Get Sample** to download a sample of the book.

⑥ Click the price button or the **Free** button to buy the book.

The Sign In to Download from the iBooks Store dialog opens.

⑦ Type your Apple ID.

⑧ Type your password.

⑨ Click **Buy**.

iBooks downloads the book.

The Read button appears.

⑩ Click **Read**.

The book opens for reading.

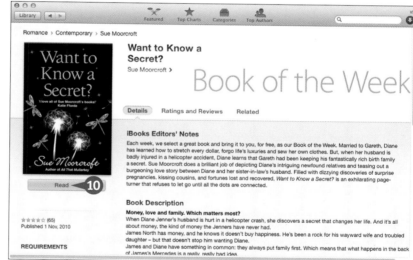

CHAPTER 10

Making the Most of Your Photos

Each new iMac comes with iPhoto, a powerful but easy-to-use application for managing, improving, and enjoying your photos. You can import photos from your digital camera; crop them, straighten them, and improve their colors; and turn them into albums, slideshows, or e-mail messages.

Import Photos

iPhoto enables you to import photos directly from a wide range of digital cameras, phones, and tablets, including the iPhone, iPad, and iPod touch. iPhoto normally recognizes a camera automatically when you connect it to your iMac and switch it on.

If you do not have a suitable cable to connect your digital camera directly to your iMac, you can remove the digital camera's memory card and insert it in a memory card reader connected to the iMac or in the iMac's SDXC slot.

Import Photos

1 Connect your digital camera to your iMac via USB.

2 Turn on the digital camera.

Note: Some digital cameras turn on automatically when you connect them to a powered USB port, but most cameras need to be turned on manually. Phones and tablets usually remain on and wake from sleep.

The iPhoto window appears.

A The digital camera appears in the Devices category in the Source list.

B iPhoto displays thumbnails of the camera's photos.

C You can click and drag the **Zoom** slider to enlarge the thumbnails.

3 Select the photos to import. Click a photo and then either press **Shift**+click to add a range of photos or press **⌘**+click to add individual photos.

Note: If you want to import all the photos, you need not select any.

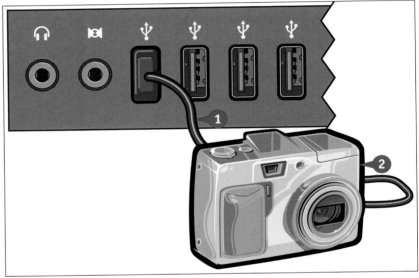

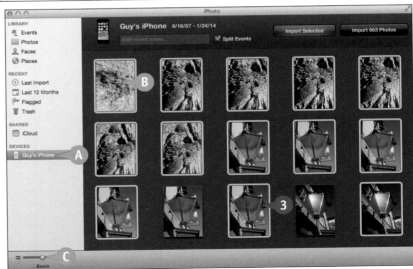

228

④ Type a name for the event that will contain these photos.

⑤ Click **Split Events** (☐ changes to ☑) to make iPhoto put photos into different events based on their dates and times.

⑥ Click **Import Selected** to import the photos you selected. Click **Import Photos** to import all the photos.

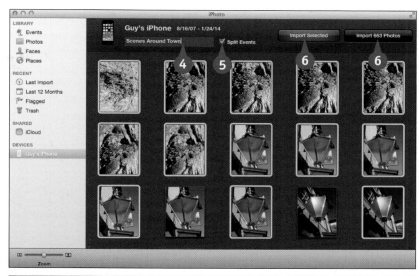

iPhoto copies the photos from the digital camera to your iMac.

The Delete Photos? dialog opens.

⑦ Click **Delete Photos** if you want to delete the photos. To keep the photos, click **Keep Photos**.

Note: For a digital camera, click **Eject** (⏏) next to the camera's name in the Source list to eject the camera before you disconnect it.

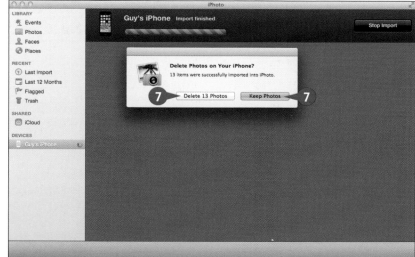

TIP

What is an event, and what names should I give my events?
An event is a way of grouping photos in iPhoto. When you import photos, you assign them to an event, and you can then browse and organize them through the event. An event can be a period of time from a few hours to a week or more, but you can also create events based on ideas or themes as needed. A photo can be in only one event, but you can move photos from one event to another as needed.

Browse Your Photos

To locate the photos you want to view and work with, you browse your photos. iPhoto enables you to browse your photos easily: You first select a category in the Source list on the left side of the iPhoto window, and then use the main part of the window to view the photos in the source.

If you have just imported photos, the best way to begin browsing is by viewing the Last Import category, which contains the photos you most recently imported.

Browse Your Photos

1 Click **iPhoto** (📷) on the Dock.

iPhoto opens.

2 If the Recent category is collapsed, move the mouse pointer over Recent.

The Show icon appears.

3 Click **Show**.

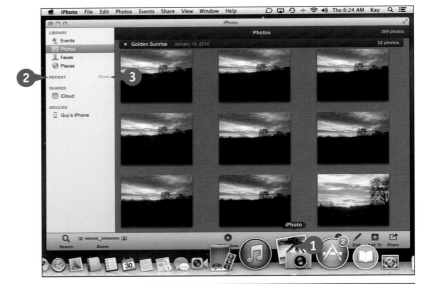

The Recent category expands.

4 Click **Last Import**.

The last batch of photos you imported into iPhoto appears.

5 Scroll through your photos as needed.

6 Double-click the photo you want to view.

iPhoto displays the photo.

Ⓐ You can click **Next** (▶) or press ▶ to display the next photo, or click **Previous** (◀) or press ◀ to display the previous photo.

⑦ Click and drag the **Zoom** slider to zoom in.

The Navigation window opens.

⑧ Click and drag the rectangle to display the part of the photo you want to view.

⑨ Click **Full Screen** (▨).

The iPhoto window expands to fill the screen.

After a few seconds, iPhoto hides the on-screen controls, enabling you to view the photo better.

Ⓑ You can click **Close** (▨) to close the Navigation window.

⑩ Move the mouse pointer anywhere on the screen.

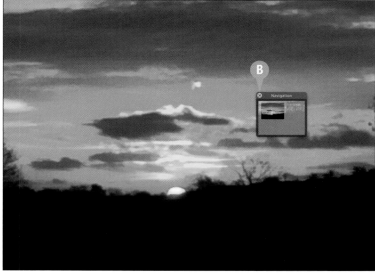

TIP

How can I navigate a zoomed-in photo if I close the Navigation window?
You can navigate a zoomed-in photo by using either a mouse or a trackpad. With the mouse, click and drag to navigate the photo. With the trackpad, scroll with two fingers to move about the photo. With the trackpad, you can also pinch apart with two fingers to zoom in or pinch inward with two fingers to zoom out; both maneuvers display the Navigation window again.

continued ▶

You can browse your photos by the entire collection, by events, by the faces you have identified, or by photo location. You browse by looking at thumbnails of photos, which enables you to view multiple photos on the screen at once. To examine a photo closely, you open it so that it takes up the entire iPhoto window. You can also switch iPhoto into full-screen mode to view your photos at as large a size as possible.

Browse Your Photos (continued)

The on-screen controls appear.

11 Move the mouse pointer over the thumbnail bar at the bottom of the screen.

The thumbnail bar expands, showing larger thumbnails.

12 Click the thumbnail for the photo you want to view.

The photo appears.

13 Move the mouse pointer to the top of the screen.

The menu bar appears.

Note: You can also press Esc to return from full-screen view to a window.

14 Click **Exit Full Screen** (▣).

iPhoto appears in a window instead of full screen.

15 Click another source in the Source list, such as **Photos**.

The contents of that source appear, and you can continue browsing your photos.

TIP

What are Events, Photos, Faces, and Places in the Library category of the Source list?
Click **Events** to browse photos by the events you have created or iPhoto has created for you when importing photos. Double-click an event to display its photos. Click **Photos** to see all the photos in your iPhoto Library. Click **Expand** (▶) to expand a collapsed group of photos or click **Collapse** (▼) to collapse an expanded group. Click **Faces** to open the Faces feature, which uses facial recognition to identify the people in photos. Click **Places** to use the Places feature, which sorts photos by their GPS locations or locations you add manually.

Crop a Photo

To improve a photo's composition and emphasize its subject, you can crop off the parts you do not want to keep. iPhoto enables you to crop to any rectangular area within a photo, so you can choose exactly the part of the photo that you need. You can either constrain the crop area to specific dimensions or crop freely. Constraining an area to specific dimensions is useful for producing an image with a specific aspect ratio, such as 3 × 5 or the ratio of your iMac's display.

Crop a Photo

1 In iPhoto, click the photo you want to crop.

2 Click **Edit** (![]).

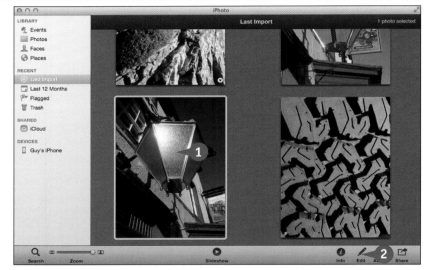

iPhoto opens the photo for editing and displays the editing tools.

3 Click **Quick Fixes**.

The Quick Fixes pane appears.

4 Click **Crop** (![]).

iPhoto displays the cropping tools.

5 If you want to crop to specific proportions or dimensions, click **Constrain** (☐ changes to ☑).

6 Click the **Constrain** pop-up menu (⬍) and choose the size or proportions — for example, **Square** or **3 × 5**.

7 Click inside the cropping rectangle and drag it so that the center square covers the middle of the area you want.

8 Click and drag the corner handles to crop to the area you want.

9 Click **Done**.

iPhoto crops the picture to the area you chose.

10 Click **Edit** (✎).

iPhoto hides the editing tools again.

TIP

I cropped off the wrong part of the photo. How can I get back the missing part?
You can undo an edit by choosing **Edit** and **Undo** or pressing ⌘+Z, but you can also return to a photo's original state. To do so, click the photo, click **Edit** (✎) to display the editing tools, and then click **Revert to Original** at the bottom of the Edit pane. A dialog opens to make sure that you want to revert to the original. Click **Revert**.

Rotate or Straighten a Photo

With digital cameras, and especially with phones and tablets, you can easily take photos with the device sideways or the wrong way up. iPhoto enables you to rotate a photo easily by 90 or 180 degrees to the correct orientation.

iPhoto also enables you to straighten a photo by rotating it up to 10 degrees clockwise or counterclockwise. To keep the resulting picture in its current aspect ratio, iPhoto automatically crops off the parts that no longer fit.

Rotate or Straighten a Photo

Rotate a Photo

1 In iPhoto, move the mouse pointer over the photo you want to rotate.

A pop-up button (▾) appears.

2 Click the pop-up button (▾).

The pop-up control panel appears.

3 Click **Rotate** (↻).

Note: Press Option and click **Rotate** (↻) to rotate the photo clockwise. If you need to rotate photos clockwise frequently, see the first tip in this section.

iPhoto rotates the photo 90 degrees counterclockwise.

4 If you need to rotate the photo further, click **Rotate** (↻) again.

Straighten a Photo

1 Click the photo you want to straighten.

2 Click **Edit** (✎).

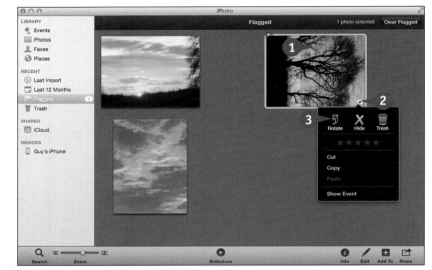

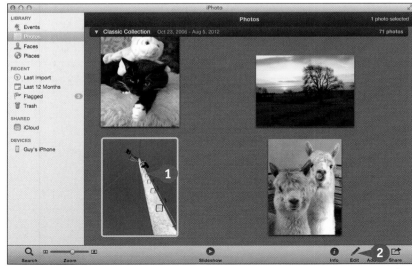

iPhoto opens the photo for editing and displays the editing tools.

3 Click **Quick Fixes**.

The Quick Fixes pane appears.

4 Click **Straighten** (▣).

iPhoto displays the straightening tools.

5 Click and drag the **Angle** slider to straighten the photo.

Note: Use the major and minor gridlines in the straightening grid to judge when lines in the picture have reached the horizontal position or the vertical position.

6 Click **Done**.

iPhoto applies the straightening.

7 Click **Edit** (✎).

iPhoto hides the editing tools again.

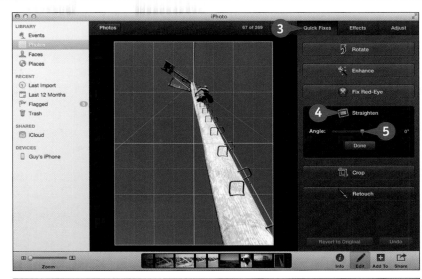

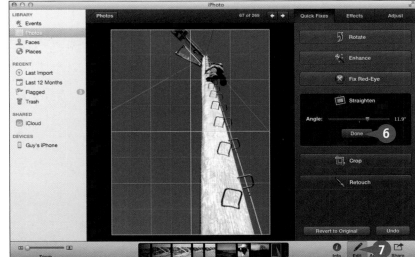

TIPS

How can I set iPhoto to rotate photos clockwise rather than counterclockwise?
If you usually need to rotate clockwise rather than counterclockwise, choose **iPhoto** and then click **Preferences**. The Preferences window opens. Click **General** on the toolbar. The General preferences pane opens. Click the clockwise **Rotate** option (◯ changes to ◉), and then click **Close** (⊗).

How do I rotate a photo with the Magic Trackpad?
Place two fingers on the trackpad, and then rotate them clockwise or counterclockwise.

Remove Red-Eye

A camera's flash can make all the difference when you are taking photos in dark or dull conditions, but flash often gives people *red-eye* — glaring red spots in the eyes. iPhoto's Fix Red-Eye tool enables you to remove red-eye from your photos, making your subjects look normal again.

To use Fix Red-Eye, you open the photo and switch to Edit mode. You can then either have iPhoto detect and fix the red-eye automatically or fix it manually by clicking the eyes.

Remove Red-Eye

1 Click the photo from which you want to remove red-eye.

2 Click **Edit** ( ).

iPhoto opens the photo for editing and displays the editing tools.

3 Click **Quick Fixes**.

The Quick Fixes pane appears.

4 Click and drag the **Zoom** slider to zoom in.

5 Click and drag the highlight in the Navigation window so that the red-eye is visible.

6 Click **Fix Red-Eye** ( ).

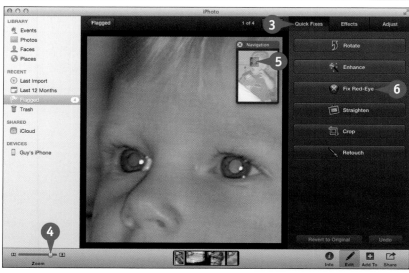

iPhoto displays the red-eye tools.

Ⓐ By default, the Auto-fix red-eye check box is selected, and iPhoto attempts to remove the red-eye.

⑦ If you need to remove red-eye manually, drag the **Size** slider until the circle is the right size to cover the pupil of the eye in the photo.

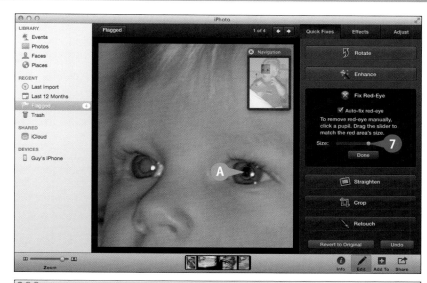

⑧ Click the red-eye.

iPhoto removes the red-eye from the eye.

⑨ Click **Done**.

iPhoto applies the changes to the photo.

⑩ Click **Edit** (🖉).

iPhoto hides the editing tools again.

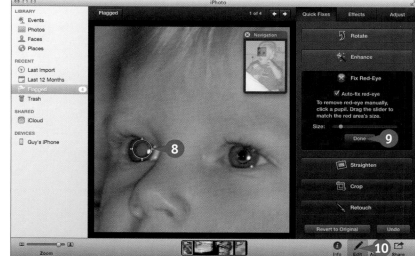

TIP

Should I use the Auto-Fix Red-Eye tool or fix red-eye manually?
This is up to you. The Auto-Fix Red-Eye tool should be the quickest way to remove red-eye from a photo, and in many photos it successfully identifies and removes red-eye. But where the tool cannot remove red-eye automatically, drag the **Size** slider to the right size for the red-eye you need to remove, and then click each affected eye in turn.

Improve a Photo's Colors

Photo includes powerful tools for improving the colors in your photos. If a photo is too light, too dark, or the colors look wrong, you can use these tools to make it look better. Usually, the best way to start is to use the Enhance tool, which boosts flat colors while muting overly bright ones. If Enhance does not give you the results you need, you can use the tools in the Adjust pane to edit settings such as exposure, contrast, and saturation.

Improve a Photo's Colors

Quickly Enhance the Colors in a Photo

1. In iPhoto, click the photo you want to enhance.

2. Click **Edit** (▨).

3. Click **Quick Fixes** to display the Quick Fixes pane.

4. Click **Enhance** (▦).

   iPhoto adjusts the exposure and enhances the colors.

Note: If the Enhance tool does not improve the photo, click **Undo** and use the Adjust window instead.

5. Click **Edit** (▨) again.

Improve the Colors with the Adjust Window

1. Click the photo you want to adjust.

2. Click **Edit** (▨).

3. Click **Adjust**.

4. To add dark tones, click and drag the **Black Point** slider to the right.

5. To add light tones, click and drag the **White Point** slider to the left.

6. To adjust the gray balance, click and drag the **Midtones** slider to the left or right.

⑦ If white in the picture appears gray or pink, click the **eyedropper** () and then click the color that should be white.

⑧ Click and drag the **Exposure** slider to make the photo lighter or darker.

⑨ Click and drag the **Contrast** slider to increase or decrease the contrast.

⑩ Click and drag the **Saturation** slider to increase or decrease the color saturation.

⑪ Click and drag the **Definition** slider to increase definition.

⑫ Click and drag the **Highlights** slider to recover lost detail in the lighter areas.

⑬ Click and drag the **Shadows** slider to bring out detail in the darker areas.

⑭ Click and drag the **Temperature** slider to adjust the color temperature.

⑮ Click and drag the **Tint** slider to adjust the tint.

⑯ Click **Edit** (✎) to finish editing.

TIPS

What do the Sharpness and De-noise sliders in the Adjust pane do?

Sharpness increases the contrast between neighboring pixels that have different colors. De-noise attempts to remove incorrect colors and artifacts from the photo. For both settings, make changes gradually to achieve a better look.

How can I make the same change to several photos?

After making changes to one photo, click **Edit** and then click **Copy Adjustments**. Click a photo you want to paste the adjustments onto, click **Edit**, and then click **Paste Adjustments**. Repeat the command as needed.

Add Effects to Photos

Photo includes 14 preset effects that you can quickly apply to change a photo's look and add life and interest to it. For example, you can change a color photo to black and white or sepia, boost or fade the color, or turn the subject into a vignette in a blacked-out oval.

To add effects, you open the photo for editing and display the Effects panel. You can then experiment with the available effects to get the combination that works best.

Add Effects to Photos

1 In iPhoto, click the photo to which you want to apply effects.

2 Click **Edit** (◩).

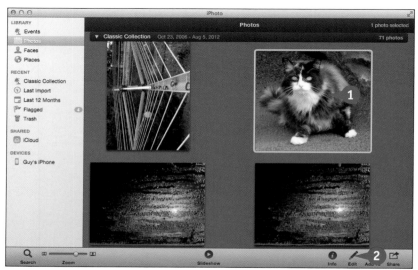

iPhoto opens the photo for editing and displays the editing tools.

3 Click **Effects**.

The Effects pane appears.

4 Click the effect you want to apply. This example uses the B & W effect.

Note: The Photo Booth app provides a similar but more extensive collection of effects.

The photo takes on the effect.

5 Apply another effect. This example uses the Matte effect.

6 If the effect shows a number in the Effects window, click the right arrow to increase the effect or the left arrow to decrease it.

iPhoto adjusts the effect correspondingly.

7 Apply any other effects needed.

8 Click **Edit** ().

iPhoto hides the editing tools again.

TIPS

How can I remove the effects from a photo?

To remove the effects you have applied to a photo, click **None** in the lower-right corner of the Effects tab.

How many effects can I apply to a photo?

You can apply as many effects as you need. Some of the effects are mutually exclusive — for example, you cannot apply both B & W and Sepia to a photo at the same time. But you can apply other combinations of effects, such as applying both Sepia and Vignette to a photo.

Sort Photos into Events

Events in iPhoto enables you to organize the photos in your photo library so that you can browse them quickly. Each event is represented by a key photo in the iPhoto window.

iPhoto automatically creates events when you import photos, but you can move photos from one event to another as needed to keep your photos organized. You can also split one event into two events, or merge two or more existing events into a single event.

Sort Photos into Events

Move Photos from One Event to Another

1 In iPhoto, click **Events**.

The list of events appears.

Note: Each event shows its key photo on top. Move the mouse around over the key photo to see other photos in the event.

2 Click the event that contains the photos you want to move.

3 Press ⌘ and click the destination event.

4 Press **Return**.

iPhoto opens the events.

5 In one event, select the photos you want to move.

6 Click and drag the photos to the other event.

Note: To move all the photos from one event to another event, simply display the Events screen and then click and drag one event on top of the other event.

7 Click **All Events** to return to the Events list.

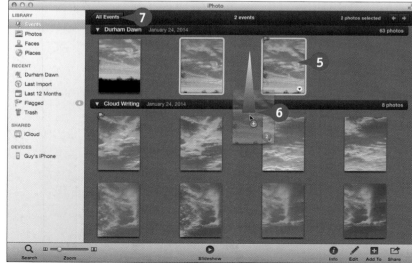

Split an Event into Two Events

1 Click **Events** in the Source list.

The list of events appears.

2 Double-click the event you want to open.

3 Click the photo that marks the beginning of the new event. This photo and those after it will appear in the new event.

4 Click **Events**.

The Events menu opens.

5 Click **Split Event**.

iPhoto creates a new event named Untitled Event, starting with the photo you selected.

6 Click the event name.

7 Type the name you want to give the event.

8 Press Return.

The event takes on the new name.

TIP

Can I change how iPhoto creates events?

You can set iPhoto to create an event for every two hours, every eight hours, every day, or every week. iPhoto uses the times and dates in the photos you import, not your iMac's clock. Choose **iPhoto** and then click **Preferences**. The Preferences window opens. Click **Events** to open the Events preferences pane. Click **Autosplit into Events** and choose **Two-hour gaps**, **Eight-hour gaps**, **One event per day**, or **One event per week**, as needed. Click **Close** (⊗) to close the Preferences window.

Create Photo Albums

When you want to assemble a custom collection of photos, you create a new album. You can then add to it exactly the photos you want from any of the sources available in the Source list. After assembling the collection of photos, you can arrange them in your preferred order.

iPhoto can also create *Smart Albums* that automatically include all photos that meet the criteria you choose. iPhoto updates Smart Albums automatically when you download photos that match the criteria.

Create Photo Albums

1 If you are viewing photos you want to add to the new album, select them.

2 Click **File**.

The File menu opens.

3 Click **New Album**.

The new album appears in the Albums list in the Source list. iPhoto selects the default name, Untitled Album.

4 Type the name for the album and press Return.

iPhoto applies the name to the album.

5 Click **Photos** in the Library category of the Source list.

Note: You can also add photos to the album from events, from Last Import, or from any of the other items in the Source list. This example uses Photos.

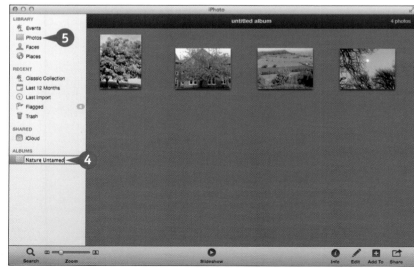

The list of photos appears.

⑥ Select the photos you want to add to the album.

⑦ Click in the selection and drag the photos to the new album.

iPhoto adds the photos to the album.

⑧ Click the album in the Source list.

The photos in the album appear.

⑨ To change the order of the photos, click a photo and drag it to where you want it.

iPhoto arranges the photos.

TIP

What is a Smart Album, and how do I create one?

A Smart Album is an album based on criteria you choose. For example, you can create a Smart Album of photos with the keyword "family" and a rating of four stars or better. iPhoto then automatically adds each photo that matches those criteria to the Smart Album. To create a new Smart Album, click **File** and select **New Smart Album**, and then set your criteria in the New Smart Album dialog. Click **Add** (⊞) to add another row of criteria to the Smart Album.

Create and Play Slideshows

One of the best ways to enjoy your photos and share them with others is to play a slideshow. iPhoto enables you to create two types of slideshows: instant slideshows and saved slideshows. For an instant slideshow, you simply select the collection of photos you want to view and then start the slideshow playing, as explained in the tip in this section. For a saved slideshow, you select the photos for the slideshow, arrange them into your preferred order, and save the show so that you can run it when needed.

Create and Play Slideshows

1 In iPhoto, select the first photo or photos you want to use in the slideshow.

2 Click **File**.

The File menu opens.

3 Click **New Slideshow**.

The new slideshow appears in the Slideshows category in the Source list. iPhoto puts an edit box around the default name.

4 Type the name for the slideshow, and then press **Return**.

5 To add other photos to the slideshow, click **Photos** in the Source list.

Note: You can also add photos from Events, from Last Import, or from any of the other items in the Source list. This example uses Photos.

The list of photos appears.

6 Select the photos you want to use in the slideshow.

7 Click in the selection and drag the photos to the new slideshow.

iPhoto adds the photos to the slideshow.

8 Click the slideshow in the Source list.

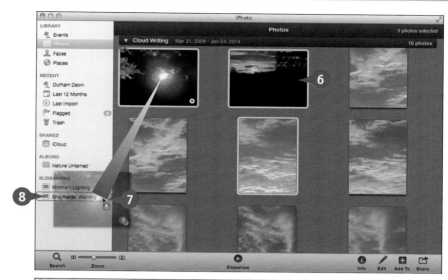

The photos in the slideshow appear.

9 Click and drag the photos into the order in which you want them to appear in the slideshow.

10 Click **Themes** (▣).

continued ▶

TIP

How do I play an instant slideshow?

First, select the photos you want to view. You can either select a whole category, such as Last Import or Flagged, or select individual photos within a category. Next, click **Slideshow** (▣) on the toolbar at the bottom of the iPhoto window. The Slideshow dialog opens, and you can choose a theme, music, and settings as described in the main text. Click **Play** when you are ready to start the slideshow playing.

To make a slideshow look the way you want it to, you can give the slideshow one of iPhoto's themes. The themes include animated transitions between slides that give your slideshow a particular look.

During the slideshow, you can play a particular song or an existing playlist, or you can create a custom playlist to accompany the slideshow. You can also choose whether to play each slide for a minimum length of time or to fit the slideshow to the music you provide for it.

Create and Play Slideshows (continued)

The Choose a Slideshow Theme dialog appears.

11 Click the theme you want to use.

12 Click **Choose**.

The Choose a Slideshow Theme dialog closes, and iPhoto applies the theme to the slideshow.

13 Click **Music** (♫).

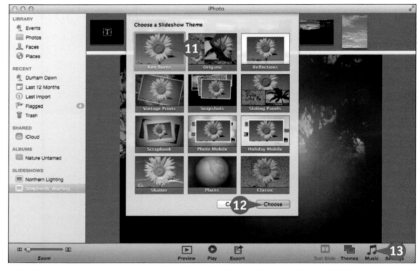

The Music Settings dialog appears.

14 Choose the music to play with the slideshow.

Note: For a silent slideshow, click **Play music during slideshow** (☑ changes to ☐).

15 Click **Choose**.

16 Click **Settings** (⚙).

The Slideshow Settings dialog appears with the All Slides tab displayed.

17 Click **Play each slide for a minimum of *NN* seconds** (⬜ changes to ⦿) and select the number of seconds.

18 Click **Transitions** (⬜ changes to ☑).

19 Click the **Transition** pop-up menu (⬍) and then select the transition to use.

Ⓐ You can click **This Slide** and set options for the current slide.

20 Click **Close** (⊗).

21 Click **Play** (▶).

The slideshow starts playing.

22 Use the controls on the control bar to move from slide to slide or stop the slideshow.

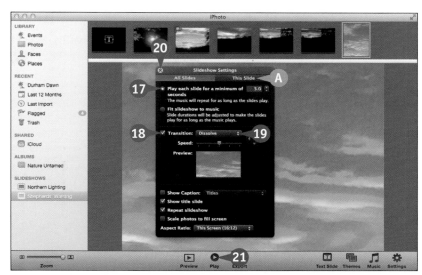

How do I create a custom title slide?
Click the first slide, and then click **Text Slide** (▦) on the toolbar. iPhoto adds a text slide before the first photo slide. Type the text for the title slide on the placeholder. iPhoto then displays this text superimposed on the first slide.

How do I create a custom playlist?
Click **Music** (♫) on the toolbar to display the Music Settings dialog. Click **Custom Playlist for Slideshow** (⬜ changes to ☑). A box appears for creating the playlist. Drag songs into the box, and then drag them into the order you want. Click **Choose**.

Identify Faces in Photos

Photo's Faces feature enables you to use facial recognition to automatically identify the people in your photos. First, you identify a face and teach iPhoto the name for it. Second, iPhoto scans your other photos for other instances of the same face. Third, you review the photos iPhoto has found, confirm the matches, and reject the misses.

After identifying faces, you can browse your photos by them, or use them to create albums, slideshows, or other collections.

Identify Faces in Photos

Identify a Face

① Double-click the photo that contains the face.

iPhoto enlarges the photo to fill the window.

② Click **Info** (ℹ).

The Info pane appears.

③ Move the mouse pointer over the face in the photo.

Note: Facial recognition in real life is slower and less accurate than portrayals in popular media. Faces is an enjoyable feature, but do not expect it to deliver wonders.

A white outline appears around the face.

Note: If the white outline is not around the face, click and drag the outline to the middle of the face. You can then click and drag the sizing handles to resize the outline as needed.

④ Click the **click to name** prompt, type the name, and press (Return).

iPhoto learns the name for the face.

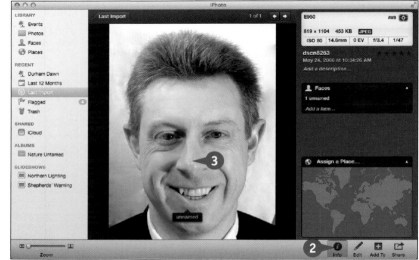

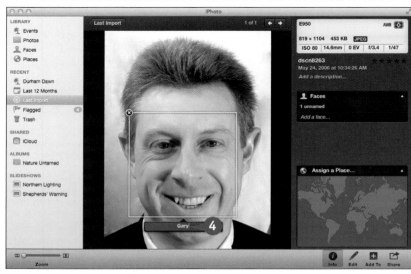

Browse the Faces in Your iPhoto Library

1 In iPhoto's Source list, click **Faces**.

The Faces screen appears.

2 Double-click the face whose pictures you want to see.

The pictures for the face appear.

3 Click the right side of the **Photos/Faces** switch to display the faces. Click the left side to display the whole photos.

You can now work with the photos as normal. For example, double-click a photo to expand it, or click **Edit** (✐) to open it for editing.

4 Click **All Faces** when you want to return to the Faces screen.

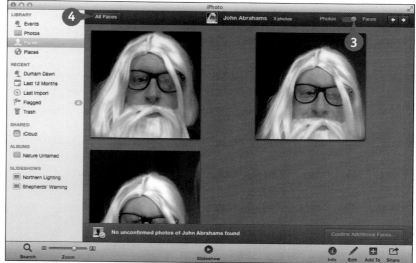

TIP

What does the Confirm Additional Faces button do?
If the Confirm Additional Faces button is available, you can click it to display a screen showing other faces that iPhoto has identified as being similar to the current face. You can then confirm each match or reject each mismatch. Working through the possible matches that iPhoto identifies is quicker and easier than reviewing your photos and identifying each face manually, as explained in the main text.

E-Mail a Photo

From iPhoto, you can quickly create an e-mail message containing one or more photos you want to send to a contact or multiple contacts. You can choose among various graphical designs, add any text message needed to explain what you are sending, and choose between including the full version of the photo and creating a smaller version of it that will transfer more quickly.

E-Mail a Photo

1 In iPhoto, click the photo you want to send via e-mail.

2 Click **Share** (📤) on the toolbar.

The Share panel opens.

3 Click **Mail** (📧).

Note: The first time you give the Mail command, you may need to follow through a procedure to set up iPhoto with your e-mail account.

iPhoto creates a message containing the photo.

4 Click the stationery template you want to use.

Note: Messages that use stationery templates may not display correctly in all e-mail apps.

5 Type the recipient's address.

A If iPhoto displays a pop-up menu of matching contacts, click the correct address.

6 Optionally, edit the subject of the message.

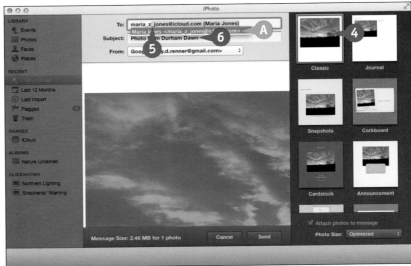

⑦ Type any message text needed to explain why you are sending the photo.

Ⓑ You can use the formatting controls on the pop-up bar to change the font, font size, horizontal alignment, and vertical alignment.

⑧ Click the **Photo Size** pop-up menu (⬚).

The Photo Size pop-up menu opens.

⑨ Click the size of photo to send — for example, **Large (Higher Quality)**. See the tip for recommendations.

⑩ Click **Send**.

iPhoto sends the message.

Which size should I use for sending a photo?
In the Photo Size pop-up menu, choose **Small (Faster Downloading)** if the recipient needs only to view the photos at a small size in the message. Choose **Medium** to let the recipient view more detail in the photos in the message. Choose **Large (Higher Quality)** to send versions of the photos that the recipient can save and use in albums or web pages. Choose **Actual Size (Full Quality)** to send the photos unchanged, so that the recipient can enjoy, edit, and use them at full resolution.

Take Photos or Videos of Yourself

Your iMac includes a built-in FaceTime HD camera that is great not only for video chats with Messages and FaceTime but also for taking photos and videos of yourself using the Photo Booth application. You can use Photo Booth's special effects to enliven the photos or videos. The special effects include distorted views, color changes such as Thermal Camera and X-Ray, and preset backgrounds that you can use to replace your real-world background.

Take Photos or Videos of Yourself

1 Click **Photo Booth** (🖼️) on the Dock.

Note: If Photo Booth (🖼️) does not appear on the Dock, click **Launchpad** (🚀) on the Dock. On the Launchpad screen, click **Photo Booth** (🖼️).

Photo Booth opens.

2 If your face appears off center, either rotate or tilt your iMac's screen or move yourself so that your face is correctly positioned.

3 Choose the type of picture to take:

Ⓐ For four pictures, click **Take four quick pictures** (⊞).

Ⓑ For a single still, click **Take a still picture** (▣).

Ⓒ For a video, click **Take a movie clip** (▦).

4 To add effects to the photo or video, click **Effects**.

The Photo Booth window shows various effects applied to the preview.

Note: To see more effects, click **Next** (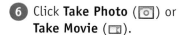). The center effect on each screen is Normal. Use this effect to remove any other effect.

⑤ Click the effect you want to use.

⑥ Click **Take Photo** (📷) or **Take Movie** (🎞️).

Photo Booth counts down from three and then takes the photo or photos, or starts recording the movie.

If you are taking a movie, click **Stop Recording** (⬜) when you are ready to stop.

Photo Booth adds the photo or movie to the photo well.

TIP

How can I use the photos and video I take in Photo Booth?

After taking a photo or video, click it in the photo well, and then click **Share** (📤). Photo Booth displays a panel with buttons for sharing the photo or video. Click **Mail** to send it in a message. Click **iPhoto** to add it to iPhoto. Click **Change Profile Picture** to use it as your account picture. Click **Messages** to make it your picture in Messages.

CHAPTER 11

Creating Your Own Movies

Your iMac includes all the software you need to make top-quality movies from your own video footage. You can import video from a digital camcorder, iOS device, or a digital camera; edit the footage; add titles and credits; and give the movie a soundtrack. You can then share the movie with other apps, export the movie to a file, or post it on YouTube.

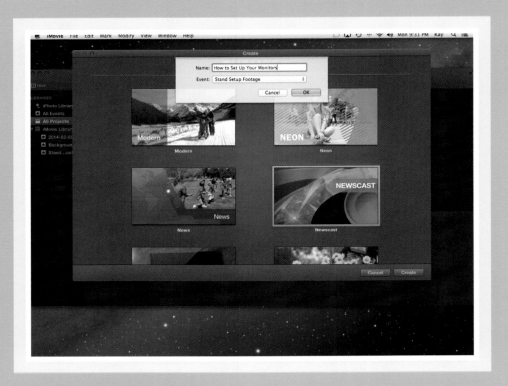

Import Video from a Camcorder or iOS Device

iMovie is a powerful but easy-to-use app for importing video, editing it, and creating movies from it. Normally, your first move is to import video clips into iMovie to give yourself material to work with.

If you have an iPhone, iPad, or iPod touch, or a camcorder that records onto internal memory, you can connect the device to your iMac via USB and import the video. You can choose which video clips to import, or simply import all of them at once.

Import Video from a Camcorder or iOS Device

① Connect the camcorder or iOS device to your iMac with a USB cable.

② Switch the camcorder on and put it in Play mode or VCR mode. With an iOS device, you do not need to take an action.

If your iMac does not activate iMovie, click **iMovie** (▧) on the Dock or on the Launchpad screen.

③ Click **Import** (⬇).

The Import window opens.

④ In the Cameras list, click the camera or iOS device.

⑤ Click the **Category** pop-up menu (▯) and click **Videos**.

⑥ Click the first clip you want to import and press ⌘+click each other clip. If you want to import all the clips, select none.

Ⓐ The preview shows the current clip. Move the mouse pointer over the current clip to scrub through it.

⑦ Click the **Import to** pop-up menu (▯).

⑧ Click **New Event**.

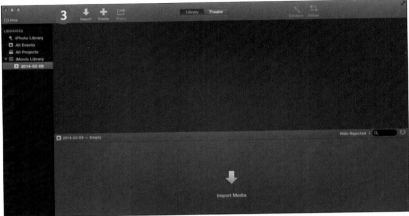

The New Event dialog opens.

Note: Instead of creating a new event, you can select an existing event on the **Import to** pop-up menu.

9 Type the name of the event.

10 Click **OK**.

The New Event dialog closes.

11 Click **Import Selected**. If you selected no clips, click **Import All**.

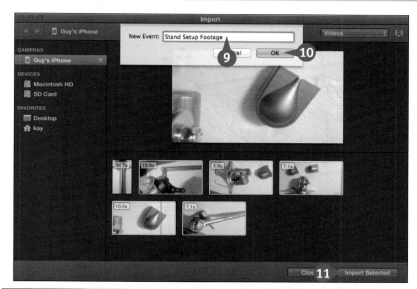

Your iMac imports the clips.

The Import window closes.

B The event appears in your iMovie Library.

C The clips appear in the event, and you can start working with them.

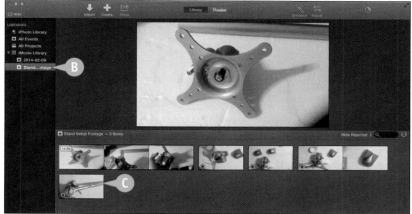

TIP

How can I make iMovie recognize the camera I have connected via USB?
If you have connected your camera via USB, but iMovie does not recognize the camera, try using a different USB port. It is best to use either a USB port on your iMac itself or a USB port on a USB hub that has its own power supply. Avoid connecting your camera to an unpowered USB hub — a hub that draws power from your iMac — or to a USB port on a keyboard unless the camera is also plugged into an external power supply.

Import Video from a Digital Camera

I f you have a digital camera that takes videos as well as still photos, you can bring the videos into iMovie and use them in your movies.

To import videos from a digital camera, you must normally use iPhoto rather than iMovie. You can then access the videos through iMovie's collection called *iPhoto Videos*. To establish whether you need to use iPhoto or iMovie, connect your digital camera and see which app becomes active.

Import Video from a Digital Camera

1 Connect the digital camera to your iMac via USB.

2 Switch the camera on.

iPhoto automatically launches and displays the camera's contents.

Note: If iMovie launches when you connect your digital camera, import the video using iMovie.

A Each photo appears as a thumbnail.

B Each movie appears as a filmstrip icon.

3 Type the name for the event.

4 Click the first video you want to import, and then press ⌘+click to select each other.

5 Click **Import Selected**.

iPhoto imports the videos.

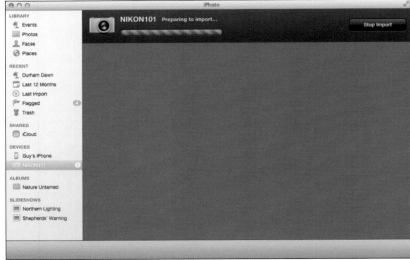

The Delete Photos on Your Camera? dialog opens.

6 Click **Keep Photos**.

Note: The Delete Photos on Your Camera? dialog always mentions photos even if you have imported videos. It is wise to keep the photos or videos on the camera until you have verified that the import was successful.

The dialog closes, and the videos appear in the Last Import list in iPhoto.

7 In iMovie, click **iPhoto Library** in the Libraries list.

8 Click the **View** pop-up menu (▤) and select **Events**.

The list of events appears.

9 Click the event that contains the video clips.

C The details of the event's contents appear.

10 Double-click the event.

The clips in the event appear, and you can use them in your movies.

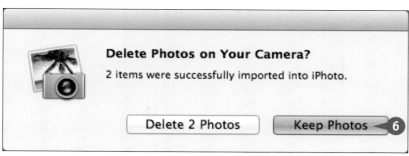

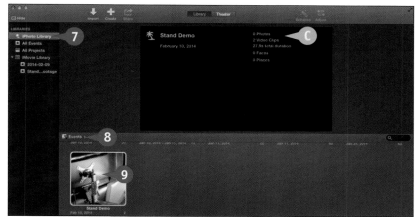

TIP

Why does the event I just added to iPhoto not appear in iMovie?
Sometimes iMovie does not immediately refresh the list of events in the iPhoto Library list. If this happens, click the **View** pop-up menu (▤) and select a different item, such as **Albums.** Then click the **View** pop-up menu (▤) again and select **Events.** If the event still does not appear, press ⌘+Q to quit iMovie, and then restart the app.

Import Video Files from Your iMac

If you have video files stored on your iMac, you can import them into iMovie so that you can use them in your movies. To import the video files, you use the Import window and browse your iMac's storage.

You can also use this technique to import video files from a digital camera whose memory card you can remove from the camera and connect to your iMac. This approach is useful if you cannot connect or manage the camera via USB.

Import Video Files from Your iMac

1. In iMovie, click **Import** (![]).

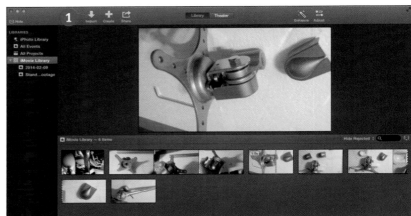

The Import window opens.

2. Navigate to the folder that contains the video files.

A You can click **Macintosh HD** to browse your iMac's drive.

B You can click your username to browse your user account.

3. Click a video file.

C The preview appears.

4. Click **Play** (![]) to view the file.

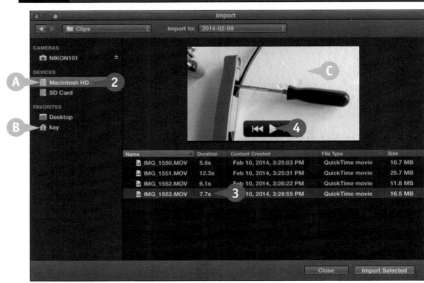

5 Select the video files you want to import. Click the first file and then press ⌘ and click each of the others.

6 Click the **Import to** pop-up menu (▐) and select the event in which to place the files.

Note: You can click **New Event** and create a new event.

7 Click **Import Selected** or **Import All**, as appropriate.

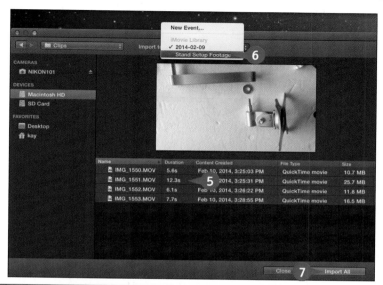

The Import window closes.

D The video clips appear in the event you specified.

You can now use the video clips in your projects.

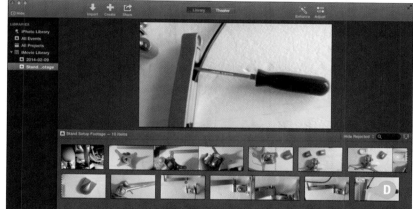

How should I organize my events in iMovie?

Organize your events in whichever way suits you best. You can create a new event at any point by clicking **File** and selecting **New Event** or pressing ⌘+Option+N and then typing the event name; this way you can reorganize your clips easily when you need to. To move a clip to another event, open the event that currently contains the clip, press Option and click to select it, and then click and drag it to the destination event.

Create a Movie Project

To make a movie, you first create a *movie project,* a file that contains the details of the movie. You base the movie project on a *theme,* a preset design. You then add video clips to the movie project, arrange and edit them, and add transitions and titles.

iMovie also enables you to create *trailer projects,* projects that contain movie trailers. iMovie provides different themes for creating trailers, but you use the same techniques to add video clips and work with them as for movie projects.

Create a Movie Project

1 In iMovie, click **Create** (⊞).

The Create panel opens.

2 Click **Movie** (▦).

The Create window opens, showing the available themes for creating movies.

3 Move the mouse pointer over a theme.

The Preview button appears.

4 Click **Preview** (▣).

iMovie plays the theme, so you can see how it looks and hear its sample music.

5 Click the theme you want to use.

6 Click **Create**.

iMovie displays the Save As dialog.

7 Type the name of the movie.

8 Click the event on which you want to base the movie.

9 Click **OK**.

iMovie creates the project and adds it to your iMovie Library.

A iMovie displays the pane in which you can build the movie.

TIPS

How do I rename a movie project?

To rename a movie project, click **Project Library** to display the list of projects. Click the project's name. iMovie displays an edit box around the name. Type the new name and press Return.

How do I delete a movie project?

To delete a movie project, you move it to the Trash. Click **Project Library** to display the list of projects. Press Ctrl+click the project to display the contextual menu, and then click **Move to Trash**. Deleting a movie project deletes only the details of the items it contains. The video clips remain in your iMovie Library, where you can use them in other projects.

Select Video Clips

After importing video from your camcorder or your iMac, you have one or more events in iMovie containing *video clips* — short sections of video. Your next step is to identify the video footage you want to use in your projects. To do so, you play back the clips and select the parts you want to use. You can mark a clip as a Favorite or as a reject for easy sorting.

Select Video Clips

View a Clip

Ⓐ You can click **Adjust Thumbnail Appearance** (▦) and drag the Clip Size slider to make the thumbnails bigger or smaller.

❶ Click the event that contains the clip.

❷ Position the mouse pointer over the clip.

The playhead appears as a vertical orange line.

Ⓑ The viewer displays the frame under the playhead.

❸ Press ⎵Spacebar⎵ to play the clip in the viewer.

❹ Press ⎵Spacebar⎵ again to stop playback.

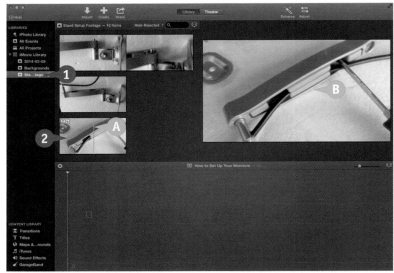

Select Part of a Clip

❶ Click the event that contains the clip.

❷ Position the mouse pointer over the clip.

❸ Move the playhead to where you want the selection to start.

❹ Click and drag to where you want the selection to end.

Ⓒ The bubble shows the selection's length in seconds.

Ⓓ You can click **Add Selection** (➕) to add the selection straight to your movie.

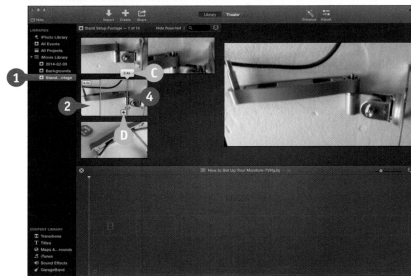

Mark a Selection as a Favorite or a Reject

1 Select the relevant part of a clip.

2 Press **Ctrl**+click in the selection.

3 Click **Favorite**.

iMovie puts a green bar across the top of the selection, indicating it is a favorite.

4 Select part of another clip.

5 Press **Ctrl**+click in the selection.

6 Click **Reject**.

iMovie puts a red bar across the top of the selection, indicating it is a reject.

Note: To remove the marking you have applied to a clip, click **Unrate**.

View Only Your Favorites

1 Click the **Show** pop-up menu (⬚), and select **Favorites**.

iMovie displays only the footage you have marked as favorites.

Note: You can select **Hide Rejected** to view all footage you have not marked as rejected.

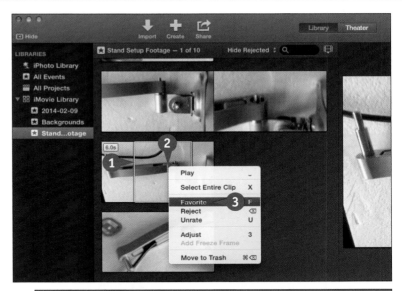

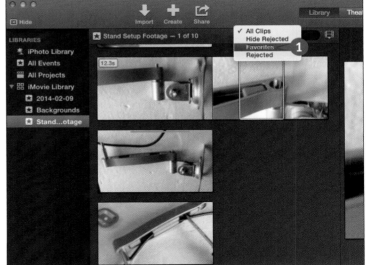

TIP

In what other ways can I rate my clips?

You can rate a selection quickly from the keyboard. Press **F** to mark the selection as a favorite. Press **Delete** to mark the selection as a reject. Press **U** to remove the rating.

You can also apply a rating by clicking **Mark** on the menu bar and then clicking the appropriate menu item: **Favorite**, **Reject**, or **Unrate**.

Build Your Movie Project

After marking your clips as favorites and rejects, you can build your movie by adding the appropriate footage to the movie project. You can add entire clips or selections from clips, as needed. After adding the clips to the movie project's timeline, you can arrange the clips in the order in which you want them to play.

Build Your Movie Project

Note: If your movie project is already open, skip steps **1** and **2**.

1 In iMovie, click **All Projects**.

The All Projects list appears.

2 Double-click the project.

iMovie opens the project.

3 Select the clip or partial clip you want to add to the project.

Note: Click the green Favorite bar at the top of a clip to select the Favorite section quickly. Press `Option` and click to select an entire clip.

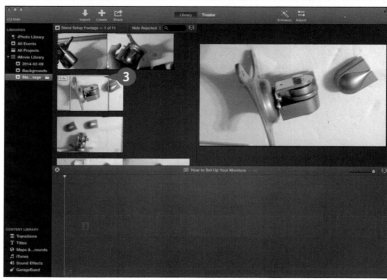

4 Click the selection and drag it to the Project pane.

iMovie adds the selection to the project.

Ⓐ If the theme includes transitions, a transition icon such as 🔀 appears before and after each clip.

Ⓑ If the theme includes titles, they appear at the relevant parts of the timeline.

Ⓒ You can drag the **Zoom** slider to zoom in or out on the clips.

5 Add other clips and selections as needed.

6 To rearrange the clips in the movie, click a clip to select it, and then drag it by its yellow outline to where you want it to appear.

Note: To remove a clip from a project, click the clip in the Project pane and then press Delete .

Note: To delete a title you do not need, click it and press Delete . If the Automatic Titles and Transitions Are Turned On dialog opens, click **Turn Off Automatic Content**.

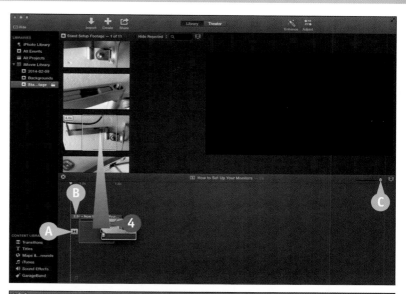

Why does an orange bar appear across the bottom of a clip?
The orange bar simply indicates that you have used the marked part of the clip in your movie.

Can I use the same clip twice in my movie?
Yes, you can use a clip as many times as you want. Simply drag the clip, or the part of it that you want to use, to the relevant place in the movie.

Add Transitions

To make one clip flow better into the next, you can apply an effect called a *transition* between the clips. For example, the widely used Cross Dissolve transition gradually replaces the end of the first clip with the beginning of the second clip.

Depending on the theme you choose for your movie, iMovie may apply transitions automatically as you build the movie. You can leave these transitions in place if they work well, but you retain greater control when you apply transitions manually and adjust them as needed.

Add Transitions

1 With your movie project open, click **Transitions**.

A The Transitions browser pane opens.

2 Position the mouse pointer over a transition.

B The viewer displays a preview of the transition.

Note: Move the mouse pointer across the transition to see the full effect.

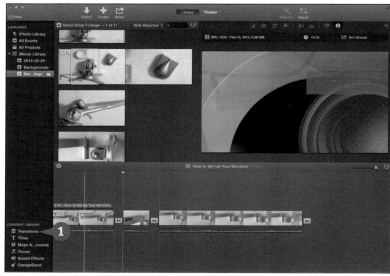

3 Click the transition you want to apply and drag it to the transition icon () or to the space between clips.

iMovie adds the transition.

4 Click the transition icon.

5 Adjust the time for the transition if necessary.

C You can click **Apply to All Transitions** if you want to apply the timing to all transitions. Normally, it is best to set the timing individually for each transition.

TIP

How can I adjust a transition more precisely?

Press Ctrl+click the transition's icon and then click **Show Precision Editor** on the contextual menu. The Precision Editor opens at the bottom of the iMovie window, showing an expanded section of the clips on either side of the transition and a wider button for the transition. Click and drag the transition's button to move the transition forward or back along the clips. Click and drag one of the endpoints of the transition button to adjust the length of the transition so that it is exactly right. Click **Close Precision Editor** to close the Precision Editor.

Add Still Photos

iMovie enables you to use still photos as well as video clips in your movie projects. This capability lets you enrich your movies with photos from your iPhoto library.

You can crop a photo to show exactly the right part in the movie. To prevent the photo from appearing static, you can bring life and movement to it by adding a Ken Burns effect, which pans and zooms across the photo.

Add Still Photos

1 In iMovie, click **iPhoto Library** in the Libraries list.

The Photo browser pane opens.

2 Click the **View** pop-up menu (☐) and then select the item by which you want to browse. This example uses **Events.**

The list of events appears.

3 Double-click the event you want to browse.

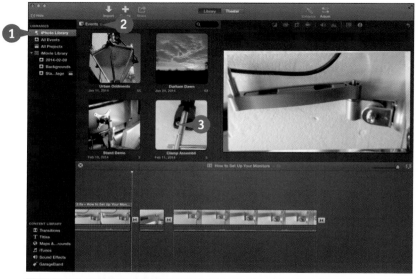

4 Click the photo you want to add and drag it down to the Project pane.

iPhoto adds the photo to the movie.

5 Click the photo.

6 Click **Adjust** (⊟).

The Adjust controls appear.

7 Click **Crop** (◻).

The Crop tools appear.

8 Click **Ken Burns**.

9 Click the Start rectangle, the one with the solid white outline, and drag it to encompass the part of the photo you want to display at first.

10 Click the dotted End rectangle.

The End rectangle becomes solid white.

11 Click the End rectangle and drag it to encompass the part of the photo you want to display at the end of the effect.

Ⓐ The yellow arrow indicates the direction and distance of the pan.

12 Click **Play** (▶).

iMovie plays the effect.

13 Click **Apply** (✓).

iMovie applies the effect to the photo.

TIP

How do I crop or rotate a photo?

Click the photo in the Project pane, click **Adjust** (⊟), and then click **Crop** (◻). Click **Crop** to display the cropping tools, and then click and drag a corner handle to specify the cropping. Click **Rotate Counterclockwise** (◱) or **Rotate Clockwise** (◲) as needed to rotate the photo to the orientation you want. Click **Apply** (✓) to apply your changes to the photo.

Create a Soundtrack

Your movie includes any audio you recorded along with your video clips, but you can suppress the audio for any clip if necessary. You can also create a soundtrack for your movie by adding a song or playlist that plays in the background.

iMovie also enables you to add a sound effect at a particular point in a movie, or add narration to any footage that needs it.

Create a Soundtrack

Add a Background Track

1 Click **iTunes**.

The iTunes browser pane opens.

2 Click the **Source** pop-up menu (▤) and select the source of music, such as **iTunes** itself, **Music**, or a particular smart playlist.

Ⓐ You can click the **Search** box and type a search term to search for music.

3 Click the song you want to add.

The song's waveform appears.

Ⓑ You can click **Play** (▶) to play the song.

Ⓒ You can click and drag to select the part of the waveform you want to use.

4 Click the song and drag it to the background sound well at the bottom of the timeline.

Add a Sound Effect to a Video Clip

1 Click **Sound Effects**.

The Sound Effects browser pane opens.

2 Click the **Source** pop-up menu (▤) and choose the source of the sound effects — for example, **iLife Sound Effects**.

Ⓓ You can click **Play** (▣) to listen to the highlighted effect.

3 Click a sound effect and drag it to the Project pane, dropping it where you want it to play.

iMovie attaches the sound effect to the clip.

Set the Sound Level

1 Move the mouse pointer over the horizontal volume line on the audio clip or background sound item.

2 Click and drag the line up or down to increase or decrease the volume.

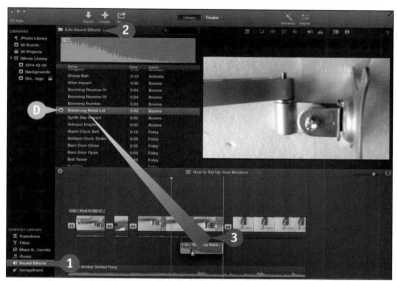

TIP

How do I add narration to a movie?

Click **Window** on the menu bar and then click **Record Voiceover**. The Voiceover control bar appears. Click **Voiceover Options** (▦) to display the Voiceover Options dialog. Click the **Input Source** pop-up menu (▤) and select the audio source, such as your microphone. Click and drag the **Volume** slider to set the volume. Click **Mute Project** (☐ changes to ☑) if you want to mute the project audio. Click **Start Recording** (▮), wait for the countdown to complete, and then speak. Click **Stop Recording** (▮) when you finish.

Add Titles and Credits

To give your movie an identity and a professional look, add a title, subtitle, and credits. iMovie provides a wide variety of title types suitable for different kinds of movies, so you can easily add the text you need.

You can also add title screens to other parts of the movie that need them — for example, to indicate a change of scene to the audience or to explain a sequence of instructions.

Add Titles and Credits

Add a Title

1 Click **Titles**.

Ⓐ The Titles browser pane opens.

Ⓑ You can click **Search** to search for a particular type of title.

2 Click a title and drag it to the beginning of the movie. Drop the title before the first clip.

iMovie adds the title.

3 Click the title.

The title appears in the viewer.

4 Click each placeholder and type your text in its place.

Note: If you do not need one of the placeholders, select it, and then press `Delete` to delete it.

5 Click **Apply** (☑).

iMovie applies the text to the title.

Note: You can change the font by selecting text and the using the Font controls above the Viewer.

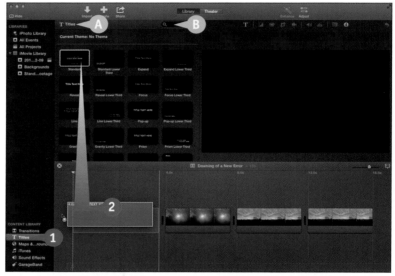

Add Credits

1. Click the clip on which you want to superimpose the credits.

2. Click **Titles**.

   The Titles browser pane opens.

3. Double-click the **Scrolling Credits** title.

   iMovie applies the title to the selected clip.

4. Double-click the title.

   The title appears in the viewer.

5. Click each placeholder and type your text in its place.

Note: If you do not need one of the placeholders, select it, and then press Delete to delete it.

6. Click **Apply** (☑).

   iMovie applies the text to the title.

TIP

Can I change a title from being superimposed to being stand-alone?
Yes. Click the title in the timeline and drag it to a position before the relevant clip. iMovie changes the title from being superimposed on the clip to being a stand-alone title. You can also change a stand-alone title to a superimposed title. Simply click the title in the timeline and drag it to a position above the clip over which you want it to play.

Share the Movie Online

After creating a movie project with iMovie, you can share it easily with others. iMovie includes built-in features for sharing a movie online via services such as iMovie Theater, YouTube, Facebook, or Vimeo. You can also send a copy of a movie to iTunes so that you can either play it in iTunes or sync it to your iOS device or iPod and carry it with you.

Share the Movie Online

Share a Movie on iMovie Theater

1 Click **All Projects**.

The All Projects list appears.

2 Click the movie you want to share.

3 Click **Share** (🔄).

The Share panel opens.

4 Click **Theater**.

Note: iMovie Theater stores your movies online in your iCloud account, enabling you to watch them from any of your Macs or iOS devices.

iMovie exports a copy of the movie and uploads it to your iCloud account.

Ⓐ You can play the movie by clicking **Play** (▶).

Ⓑ For more options, click **More** (▶).

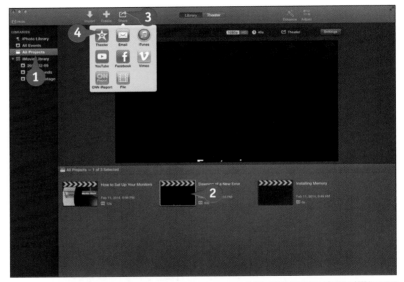

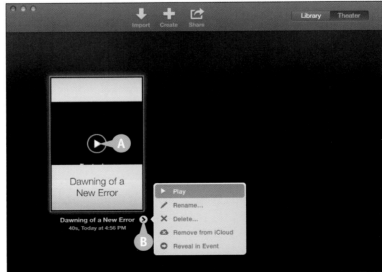

Share a Movie on YouTube

Note: To share a movie on YouTube, you must have a YouTube account or Google account. You can create a Google account at the Google Accounts website, accounts.google.com. Read the restrictions on size and content before posting movies to YouTube.

1 Click **All Projects**.

The All Projects list appears.

2 Click the movie you want to share.

3 Click **Share** (⬚).

The Share panel opens.

4 Click **YouTube**.

The YouTube dialog opens.

5 Type a description.

6 Type tags to identify the movie.

7 Click the **Size** pop-up menu (⬚) and select the size.

8 Click the **Category** pop-up menu (⬚) and select the category.

9 Click the **Viewable By** pop-up menu (⬚) and select the audience.

10 Click **Sign In**, type your username and password, and then click **OK**.

11 Click **Next** and then complete the remaining steps in the procedure.

iMovie uploads the movie to your YouTube account.

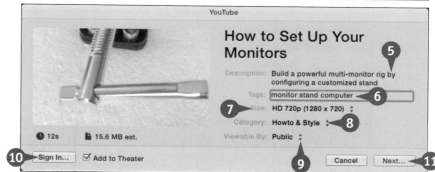

What are tags and why should I use them?

A *tag* is a text term that helps explain concisely what a movie is about. YouTube uses tag information in searches, so the tags help people find movies they are interested in. By adding suitable tags to your movie, you can make your movie easier to find and increase its audience.

CHAPTER 12

Customizing Your iMac

You can customize many aspects of OS X to make it work the way you prefer. You can change the desktop background, personalize the Dock icons, and adjust the keyboard and pointing device. You can also run apps or open specific documents each time you log in or set your iMac to go to sleep automatically when you are not using it.

Change the Desktop Background

OS X enables you to change the desktop background to show the picture you prefer. OS X includes many varied desktop pictures and solid colors, but you can also set any of your own photos as the desktop background. You can tile, stretch, or crop the photo to fill the screen or center it on the screen.

Whether you use the built-in pictures or your own pictures, you can choose between displaying a single picture on the desktop and displaying a series of images that change automatically.

Change the Desktop Background

1 Press **Ctrl**+click the desktop.

The contextual menu opens.

2 Click **Change Desktop Background**.

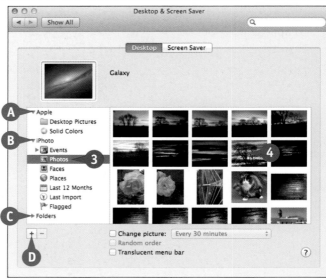

The Desktop pane in System Preferences appears.

3 Click the category of image you want to see.

A Apple contains the built-in desktop backgrounds.

B iPhoto contains your iPhoto library.

C Folders contains your folders.

D Click **Add** (➕) to add a folder.

The images appear in the right-hand pane.

4 Click the image you want to use.

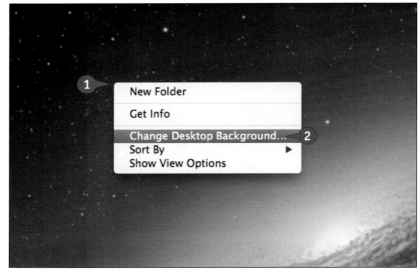

The image appears on the desktop.

5 If you chose a photo or picture of your own, click the pop-up menu (▣) and click the way to fit the image to the screen. See the tip for details.

6 If you want to set a series of background images, click the category.

7 Click the **Change picture** option (☐ changes to ☑).

8 Click the **Change picture** pop-up menu (▣) and click the interval — for example, **Every 30 minutes**.

9 Click the **Random order** option (☐ changes to ☑) if you want the images to appear in random order.

10 Click the **Translucent menu bar** option (☑ changes to ☐) if you want the menu bar to appear solid gray rather than translucent.

11 Click **Close** (▣).

System Preferences closes.

TIP

Which option should I choose for fitting the image to the screen?
In the Desktop & Screen Saver preferences, choose **Fit to Screen** to match the image's height or width — whichever is nearest — to the screen. Choose **Fill Screen** to make an image fill the screen without distortion but cropping off parts that do not fit. Choose **Stretch to Fill Screen** to stretch the image to fit the screen exactly, distorting it as needed. Choose **Tile** to cover the desktop with multiple copies of the image. Choose **Center** to display the image at full size in the middle of the desktop.

Set Up a Screen Saver

OS X enables you to set a screen saver to hide what your screen is showing when you leave your iMac idle. A *screen saver* is an image, a sequence of images, or a moving pattern that appears on the screen. You can choose what screen saver to use and the length of the period of inactivity before it starts.

OS X comes with a variety of attractive screen savers. You can download other screen savers from websites.

Set Up a Screen Saver

1 Press **Ctrl**+click the desktop.

The contextual menu opens.

2 Click **Change Desktop Background**.

The Desktop pane of Desktop & Screen Saver preferences opens.

3 Click **Screen Saver**.

The Screen Savers pane appears.

4 Click a screen saver in the list on the left.

The screen saver you clicked starts playing in the Preview area.

5 Click the **Starts after** pop-up menu (◉).

The pop-up menu opens.

6 Click the length of time to wait until the screen saver starts.

Note: To turn off the screen saver, select **Never** in the Start After pop-up menu.

7 Position the mouse pointer over the preview.

The Preview button appears.

8 Click **Preview**.

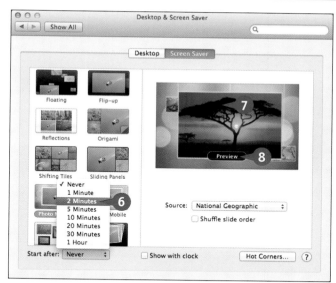

The screen saver preview appears full screen.

9 Click anywhere on the screen saver when you want to stop the preview.

The Screen Saver pane appears.

10 Press ⌘+Q.

System Preferences closes.

TIP

Must I use a screen saver to protect my iMac's screen from damage?

No. Screen savers originally protected cathode ray tube (CRT) displays from having static images "burned in" to their screens. LCD and LED screens, such as that on your iMac, do not suffer from this problem, so you need not use a screen saver. Nowadays you can use a screen saver to protect the information on-screen or to provide visual entertainment.

Customize the Dock

OS X enables you to customize the Dock so that it contains the icons you find most useful and it appears in your preferred position on the screen. You can add apps, files, or folders to the Dock; reposition the Dock's icons; and remove most of the existing items if you do not need them.

To customize the Dock, you drag items to it, from it, or along it. You can also use the Dock's contextual menu to change the Dock's position, configuration, or behavior.

Customize the Dock

Add an App to the Dock

1. Click **Launchpad** (📷) on the Dock.

   The Launchpad screen appears.

2. Click and drag the app to the left side of the divider line on the Dock.

   The app's icon appears on the Dock.

Note: After opening an app, you can press Ctrl +click its Dock icon, highlight or click **Options**, and then click **Keep in Dock**.

Add a File or Folder to the Dock

1. Click **Finder** (🖥) on the Dock.

2. In the Finder window, navigate to the file or folder you want to add to the Dock.

3. Click and drag the file or folder to the right side of the divider line on the Dock.

   The item's icon appears on the Dock.

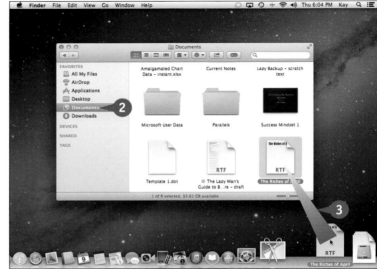

Remove an Item from the Dock

1 If the app is running, press Ctrl + click its Dock icon and select **Quit** from the contextual menu.

Note: The Dock displays an icon for each running app. So if the app is running, you can drag the icon from the Dock, but it will not disappear.

2 Click and drag the icon from the Dock to the desktop. When a puff of smoke appears, release the icon.

The icon vanishes in a puff of smoke.

Configure the Dock

1 Press Ctrl +click the Dock divider bar.

Ⓐ Click **Turn Hiding On** to hide the Dock when the mouse pointer is not over it.

Ⓑ Click **Turn Magnification Off** to turn off magnification.

Ⓒ Click **Position on Screen** and then click **Left**, **Bottom**, or **Right** to reposition the Dock.

Ⓓ Click **Minimize Using** and then click **Genie Effect** or **Scale Effect**.

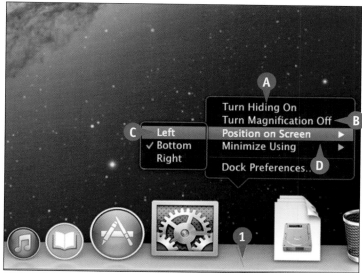

TIP

How else can I customize the Dock?

You can increase or decrease the size of the Dock by clicking the Dock divider bar and dragging it up or down. For more precise control of the Dock, press Ctrl +click the Dock divider bar and then click **Dock Preferences** to display the Dock pane in System Preferences. Here you can change the Dock size, turn on and adjust magnification, set the Dock's position, and choose the effect for minimizing windows. You can also choose other options for controlling the Dock's appearance and behavior.

Add or Remove Desktop Spaces

OS X enables you to create multiple desktop spaces on which to arrange your documents and apps. You can switch from space to space quickly to move from app to app. You can tie an app to a particular space so that it always appears in that space or allow it to appear in any space.

When you no longer need a desktop space, you can remove it in just moments. To configure desktop spaces, you use Mission Control.

Add or Remove Desktop Spaces

Create a Desktop Space and Add Apps to It

1 Press **F3** or **Ctrl**+**⬆**.

Note: On some keyboards, you press **F9** to invoke Mission Control.

The Mission Control screen appears.

2 Move the mouse pointer to the upper-right corner of the screen.

Note: If you have positioned the Dock on the right, the + sign appears in the upper-left corner of the screen.

A panel showing a + sign appears.

3 Click the + panel.

Ⓐ Another desktop space appears at the top of the Mission Control screen.

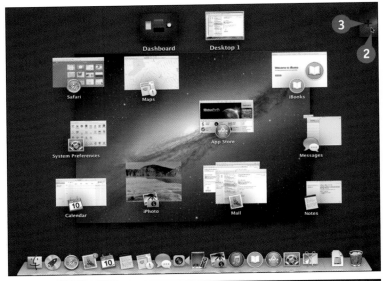

4 Click a window and drag it to the desktop space in which you want it to appear.

5 Click the desktop space you want to display.

The desktop space appears.

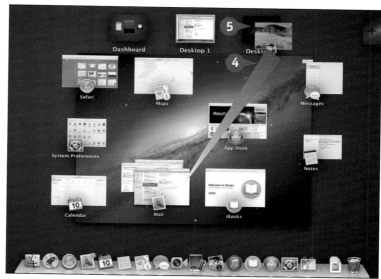

Remove a Desktop Space

1 Press **F3**.

The Mission Control screen appears.

2 Position the mouse pointer over the desktop space you want to close.

The Close button (⊗) appears.

3 Click **Close** (⊗).

The desktop space closes.

4 Click the desktop space you want to display.

Mission Control displays that desktop space.

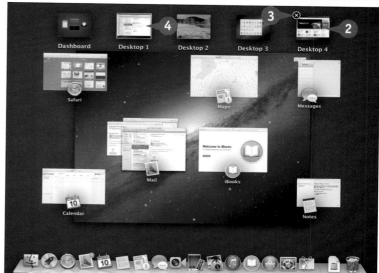

TIP

How can I assign an app to a particular desktop?
First, use Mission Control to activate the desktop to which you want to assign the app. Then press **Ctrl**+click or right-click the app's Dock icon, click **Options**, and click **This Desktop**. If you want to use the app on all desktops, click **All Desktops** in the Assign To section of the Options menu.

Set Up Hot Corners

OS X's Hot Corners feature enables you to trigger actions by moving the mouse pointer to the corners of the screen. You can set up from one to four hot corners. Each hot corner can perform an action such as opening Mission Control, displaying your desktop, or starting the screen saver.

To set up hot corners, you use the Hot Corners dialog. You can open this dialog from the Mission Control pane or the Screen Saver pane in System Preferences.

Set Up Hot Corners

Set Up a Hot Corner

1. Press Ctrl+click **System Preferences** (🖼️) on the Dock.

   The contextual menu opens.

2. Click **Mission Control**.

   System Preferences opens and displays the Mission Control pane.

3. Click **Hot Corners**.

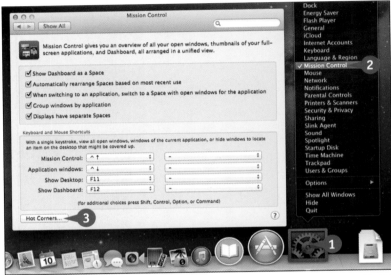

The Hot Corners dialog opens.

4. Click the pop-up menu (🔽) for the hot corner you want to set.

   The pop-up menu opens.

5. Click the action you want to assign to the corner.

6. Choose other hot corner actions as needed.

Note: You can set up multiple hot corners for the same feature.

7. Click **OK**.

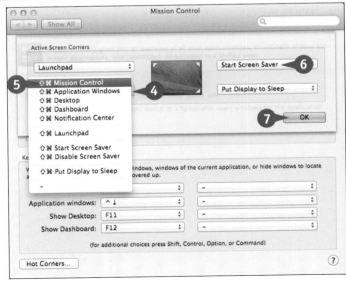

The Hot Corners dialog closes.

8 Press **Ctrl**+click **System Preferences** () on the Dock.

The contextual menu opens.

9 Click **Quit**.

System Preferences closes.

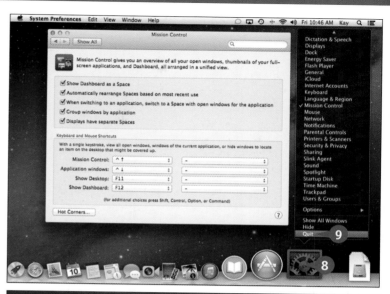

Use a Hot Corner to Run Mission Control

1 Move the mouse pointer to the hot corner you allocated to Mission Control.

The Mission Control screen appears.

2 Click the window you want to display.

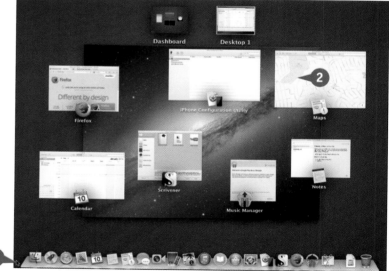

TIP

Are there other ways I can run Mission Control using the Magic Mouse or Magic Trackpad?
You can use the mouse's secondary button or a gesture, or another button or gesture, to run Mission Control. In the Keyboard and Mouse Shortcuts section in Mission Control preferences, click the **Mission Control** pop-up menu (⬍) and select the mouse button or gesture. Press and hold ⌘, **Option**, **Ctrl**, **Shift**, or a combination of the four keys to add them to the keystroke. Use the same technique for the Application Windows pop-up menu, the Show Desktop pop-up menu, and the Show Dashboard pop-up menu.

Add a Second Display

OS X enables you to add an external display to your iMac to give yourself more space for your apps. The easiest type of display to connect is a Thunderbolt display, but you can also connect other types of displays by using suitable converter cables, such as a Mini DisplayPort-to-DVI connector or Mini DisplayPort-to-VGA connector.

After connecting the external display using a suitable cable, you use the Displays pane in System Preferences to set the resolution and specify the arrangement of the displays.

Add a Second Display

1 Connect the display to your iMac.

2 Connect the display to power and turn it on.

3 Click **Apple** (🍎).

The Apple menu opens.

4 Click **System Preferences**.

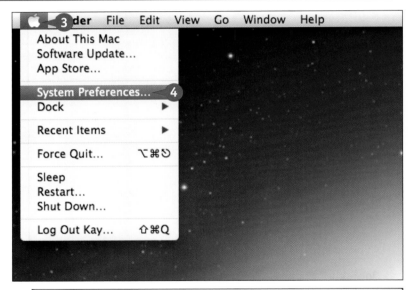

The System Preferences window opens.

5 Click **Displays**.

Note: Your iMac may automatically open the Displays pane of System Preferences after you connect the display and turn it on.

The Displays pane opens on each display.

6 In the Displays pane for the external display, click **Display**.

7 Click **Best for display** (⭕ changes to ⦿) to apply the display's best resolution.

Ⓐ You can click **Scaled** (⭕ changes to ⦿) and then click a different resolution.

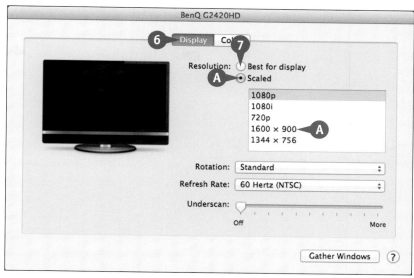

8 In the Displays pane for the iMac's display, click **Arrangement**.

The Arrangement pane appears.

9 Click and drag either display thumbnail to match the displays' physical locations.

10 To move the menu bar and Dock, click and drag the menu bar from the iMac's icon to the external display's icon.

11 Click **Close** (⦿).

System Preferences closes.

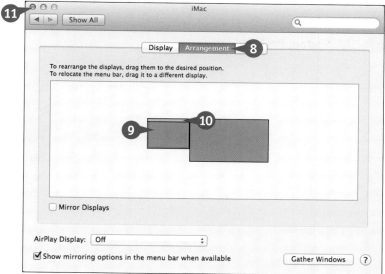

TIPS

Can I add two external displays?

This depends on your iMac's specification and the monitor types. Most iMacs released from 2011 onward support two Thunderbolt displays.

Can I use my iMac as a display for my MacBook?

If your iMac supports Target Display mode, as most recent iMac models do, you can use it as a display. With the iMac running, connect a male-to-male Mini DisplayPort cable to each Mac's Thunderbolt port or Mini DisplayPort. The iMac enters Target Display mode automatically, and the other Mac's screen appears. You can press ⌘+F2 to toggle between Target Display mode and the iMac's own output.

Configure Your Keyboard

OS X enables you to customize the settings for your keyboard. You can change the repeat rate and the delay until repeating starts; you can create text shortcuts; and you can turn on automatic spell checking.

If you have difficulty pressing the keys, you can turn on Sticky Keys or Slow Keys. Sticky Keys enables you to set a modifier key, such as ⌘, without having to hold it down. Slow Keys increases the delay between you pressing a key and OS X registering the keystroke.

Configure Your Keyboard

1 Press **Ctrl**+click **System Preferences** (🖼️) on the Dock.

The contextual menu opens.

2 Click **Keyboard**.

System Preferences opens and displays the Keyboard pane.

3 Click and drag the **Key Repeat** slider to control how quickly a key repeats.

4 Click and drag the **Delay Until Repeat** slider to set the repeat delay.

5 Click **Text**.

The Text pane appears.

6 Click **Add** (⊞).

7 Type the text that will trigger the replacement.

8 Type the replacement text.

9 Click the **Correct spelling automatically** option (☐ changes to ☑) to use automatic spell checking.

10 Click the **Use smart quotes and dashes** option (☐ changes to ☑) if you want OS X to replace regular quotes and dashes with smart quotes and dashes.

11 Click **Show All**.

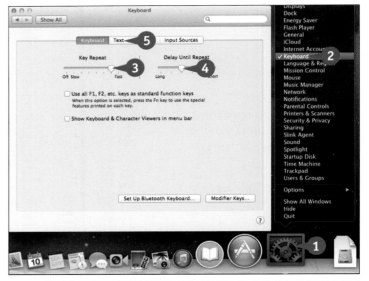

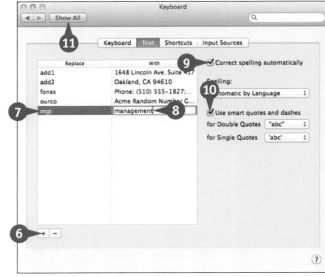

The System Preferences pane appears.

12 If you want to use Sticky Keys or Slow Keys, click **Accessibility**. Otherwise, go to step **16**.

Note: Sticky Keys displays the current modifier keys on-screen. For example, when you press ⌘, the ⌘ symbol appears on-screen.

The Accessibility pane appears.

13 Click **Keyboard**.

14 Click the **Enable Sticky Keys** option (☐ changes to ☑) if you want to press modifier keys separately from the keys they modify.

15 Click **Enable Slow Keys** if you want to slow down OS X's registration of keystrokes.

Note: You can click **Options** to configure Sticky Keys or Slow Keys.

16 Click **Close** (⊗).

System Preferences closes.

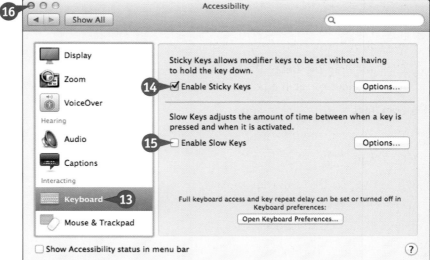

TIP

What is the purpose of the Shortcuts pane and the Input Sources pane in Keyboard preferences?
You use the Shortcuts pane to configure keyboard shortcuts for controlling OS X and apps directly from the keyboard. For example, you can set a keyboard shortcut to show Notification Center or to switch to a particular desktop.

You use the Input Sources pane to load the keyboard layouts you want to use. For example, if you use the Dvorak keyboard layout instead of the U.S. keyboard layout, you can add the Dvorak layout and remove the U.S. layout.

Configure Your Mouse or Trackpad

OS X automatically configures your iMac's pointing device with default settings. You can customize the settings to make the pointing device work the way you prefer. For example, you can select the gestures to use with the Magic Mouse or Magic Trackpad.

You can adjust the speed at which OS X tracks the movement you input with your pointing device. You can also enlarge the cursor to make it easier to see on-screen.

Configure Your Mouse or Trackpad

1 Press **Ctrl**+click **System Preferences** ( ) on the Dock.

The contextual menu opens.

2 Click **Mouse** or **Trackpad**, as appropriate. This example uses Trackpad.

System Preferences opens and displays the Mouse pane or the Trackpad pane.

3 Click and drag the **Tracking speed** slider to adjust the tracking speed.

4 Click each option you want to use (changes to).

5 Click another tab.

The pane associated with the tab appears.

6 Click each option you want to use (changes to).

7 When you finish choosing trackpad options, click **Show All**.

The System Preferences pane appears.

8 Click **Accessibility**.

The Accessibility pane appears.

9 Click **Mouse & Trackpad**.

A You can click the **Enable Mouse Keys** option (☐ changes to ☑) if you want to turn on Mouse Keys. This feature enables you to control the mouse pointer using the keyboard number pad.

10 Click and drag the **Double-click speed** slider to adjust the double-click speed.

11 Click **Close** (⊗).

System Preferences closes.

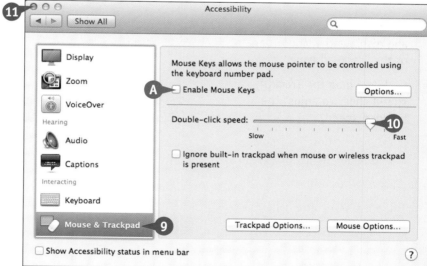

TIP

What are the options on the Scroll & Zoom tab and More Gestures tab in Mouse preferences or Trackpad preferences?

The Scroll & Zoom tab in Trackpad preferences enables you to choose options for scrolling, zooming, and rotating using the trackpad. The More Gestures tab in Mouse preferences and Trackpad preferences lets you choose extra gestures. Click a check box (☐ changes to ☑) to turn a gesture on. If the preference has a pop-up button (▾), click it to display options you can choose — for example, the number of fingers to use for swiping left or right.

Make the Screen Easier to See

OS X's Accessibility features include several options for making the contents of your iMac's screen easier to see. You can invert the colors, use grayscale instead of colors, enhance the contrast, and increase the cursor size. You can also turn on the Zoom feature to enable yourself to zoom in quickly up to the limit you set. To configure these options, you open System Preferences and work in the Accessibility pane.

Make the Screen Easier to See

1 Click **System Preferences** () on the Dock.

The System Preferences pane appears.

2 Click **Accessibility**.

The Accessibility pane appears.

3 Click **Zoom**.

The Zoom options appear.

4 Click the **Use keyboard shortcuts to zoom** option (☐ changes to ☑).

5 Click the **Zoom follows the keyboard focus** option (☐ changes to ☑) if you want the zoomed area to follow the focus of the keyboard.

6 Click **Zoom Style** and select **Fullscreen** or **Picture-in-picture**, as appropriate.

7 Click **More Options**.

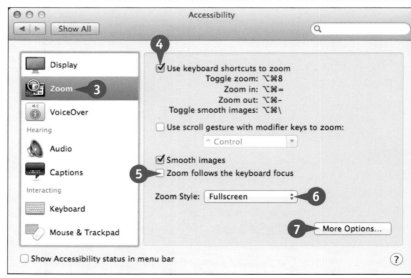

The More Options dialog opens.

8 Click and drag the **Maximum Zoom** slider to set the maximum zoom.

9 Click and drag the **Minimum Zoom** slider to set the minimum zoom.

10 In the "When zoomed in, the screen image moves" area, click the option button for the zoom motion you want (⊙ changes to ◉).

11 Click **Done**.

The More Options dialog closes.

12 Click **Display**.

13 Click the **Invert colors** option (☐ changes to ☑) if you want to invert the video colors.

14 Click and drag the **Enhance Contrast** slider if you want to increase the contrast.

15 Click and drag the **Cursor Size** slider if you want to make the cursor bigger.

16 Click **Close** (⊗).

System Preferences closes.

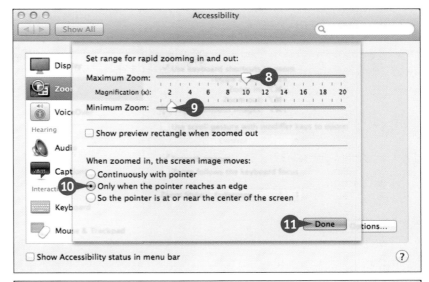

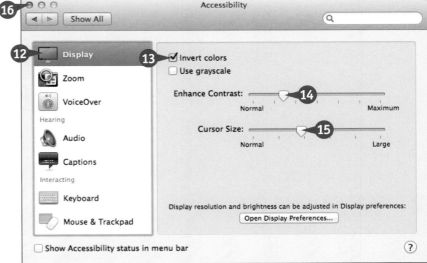

TIP

What is the quickest way to turn on the Universal Access features for seeing the screen?

The quickest way to turn on the Universal Access features for seeing the screen is to use keyboard shortcuts. Press Option+⌘+8 to toggle zoom on or off. With zoom turned on, press Option+⌘+= to zoom in by increments. Press Option+⌘+− to zoom out by increments. If you enable the Smooth Images feature by clicking the **Smooth images** option (☐ changes to ☑) in the Zoom options, you can press Option+⌘+\ to toggle Smooth Images on or off.

Customize Spotlight Searches

OS X's Spotlight feature indexes your iMac's files so that you can easily search them from either the Spotlight icon on the menu bar or from a Finder window. To improve the search results that Spotlight returns, you can customize the folders that Spotlight searches. You can exclude folders you do not want to search and change the order of the other folders to set search priorities. To customize Spotlight, you work in the Spotlight pane in System Preferences.

Customize Spotlight Searches

1 Click **Spotlight** (🔍).

The Spotlight search field opens.

2 Type a few letters in the search field.

The list of search results appears.

3 Click **Spotlight Preferences**.

The System Preferences window opens with the Spotlight pane at the front.

4 Click **Search Results**.

5 Click the check box for any item you want to exclude from searches (☑ changes to ☐).

6 Click and drag the categories into the order in which you want to see search results.

A You can disable or change the keyboard shortcuts for Spotlight.

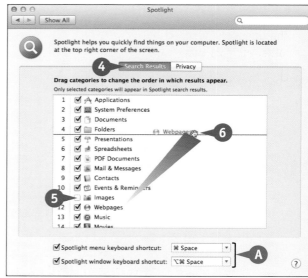

7 Click **Privacy**.

The Privacy pane appears.

8 Click **Add** ([+]).

Note: Adding a folder to the exclusion list prevents even a search in a Finder window showing that folder's contents from finding matches. This can be confusing to users, because the files are right there and clearly match the search criteria.

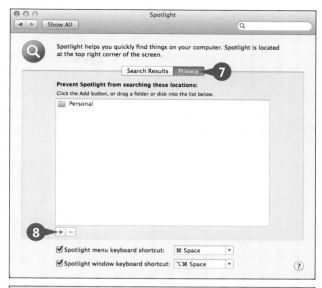

A dialog opens.

9 Click the folder you want to add.

Note: You can select two or more folders by clicking the first and then ⌘+clicking each of the others.

10 Click **Choose**.

The dialog closes, and the folder appears in the list.

11 Click **Close** (⊗).

System Preferences closes.

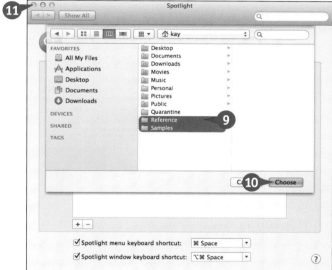

TIP

Is there another way to add folders to the Privacy list?
Instead of using the dialog to build the list of folders you do not want Spotlight to search, you can work from a Finder window. Click **Finder** (🖼) on the Dock to open a Finder window, and position it so that you can see both it and the Spotlight preferences pane. Click and drag from the Finder window to the Spotlight preferences pane the folders you want to protect to add them to the list. You can select multiple folders to save time.

Run Apps at Login

OS X enables you to set apps to open automatically each time you log in to your iMac. By opening your most-used apps automatically, you can save time getting started with your work or play. Opening apps at login does make the login process take longer, so it is best to run only those apps you always use. You can configure an app to open automatically either from the Dock or by using the Login Items pane in Users & Groups preferences.

Run Apps at Login

Use the Dock to Set an App to Run at Login

1. If the app does not have a Dock icon, click **Launchpad** (![icon]) on the Dock and then click the app.

2. Press **Ctrl**+click the app's Dock icon.

   The contextual menu opens.

3. Click or highlight **Options**.

4. Click **Open at Login**.

   A check mark appears next to Open at Login.

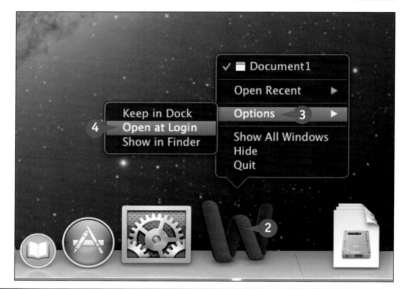

Use System Preferences to Set an App to Run at Login

1. Press **Ctrl**+click **System Preferences** (![icon]) on the Dock.

   The contextual menu opens.

2. Click **Users & Groups**.

   The Users & Groups pane appears, showing your user account.

3. Click **Login Items**.

The Login Items pane
appears.

Note: If you need to run an app
in the background, click the **Hide**
option (☐ changes to ☑) next
to the app.

4 Click **Add** (⊞).

A dialog opens showing a list
of the apps in the Applications
folder.

Note: You can also add documents
to the list for automatic opening.
To do so, navigate to the
document, click it, and click **Add**.
OS X opens the document in its
default app at login.

5 Click the app you want to run
automatically at login.

Note: To select multiple apps, click
the first, and then press ⌘+click
each of the others.

6 Click **Add**.

The dialog closes.

The app appears in the list.

7 Click **Close** (⊗).

System Preferences closes.

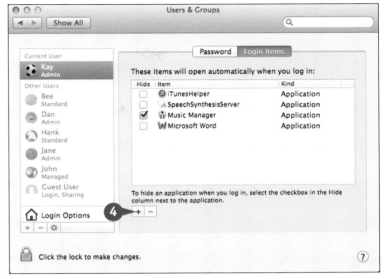

TIP

How else can I add an app to the Login Items pane?
Instead of clicking **Add** (⊞) and using the dialog to pick the apps, you can click and drag the apps from a
Finder window. Click **Finder** (🖼) on the Dock to open a Finder window, and then click **Applications** in the
sidebar. Click the app you want, and then drag it across to the Login Items pane of Account preferences.

Put Your iMac to Sleep

OS X's Energy Saver feature enables you to set your iMac to put itself to sleep after a period of inactivity. You can also configure Energy Saver to put the display to sleep after a shorter period of inactivity, thus saving more power when you are not using your iMac. You can put your iMac to sleep manually at any time by clicking **Apple** (🍎) to open the Apple menu and then clicking **Sleep**.

Put Your iMac to Sleep

1 Click **System Preferences** (⚙️) on the Dock.

The System Preferences pane opens.

2 Click **Energy Saver**.

The Energy Saver pane appears.

3 Click and drag the **Computer sleep** slider to set the period of inactivity before putting the iMac to sleep.

4 Click and drag the **Display sleep** slider to set the period of inactivity before blanking the display.

Note: Set Display Sleep to a shorter time than Computer Sleep.

5 Click **Schedule** if you want to set a schedule for your iMac. Otherwise, go to step **14**.

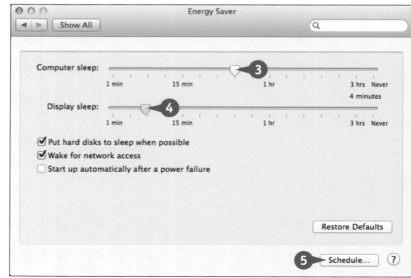

The Schedule dialog opens.

6 Click the **Start up or wake** option (☐ changes to ☑).

7 Click the pop-up menu (⇳) and click a frequency: **Weekends**, **Weekdays**, **Every Day**, or a particular day of the week.

8 Click the stepper control (⇳) to set the wake-up time.

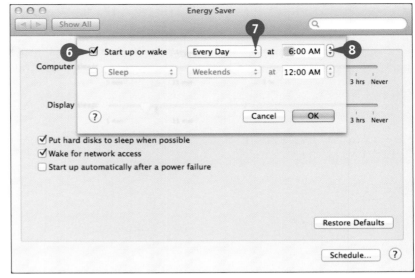

9 Click the check box on the second row (☐ changes to ☑).

10 Click the pop-up menu (⇳) and select **Sleep**, **Restart**, or **Shut Down**, as needed.

11 Click the pop-up menu (⇳) and select the frequency.

12 Click the stepper control (⇳) to set the time.

13 Click **OK**.

The Schedule dialog closes.

14 Click **Close** (⊗).

System Preferences closes.

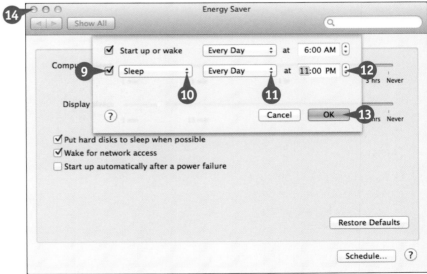

TIP

Which button do I press to wake my iMac from sleep?
You can press any key on the keyboard to wake the iMac. If you are not certain whether the iMac is asleep or preparing to run a screen saver, press **Shift**, **Ctrl**, **Option**, or **⌘**. These keys do not type a character if the iMac turns out to be awake instead of asleep. You can also move your mouse or move your finger on the trackpad to wake your iMac.

Control Checking for Software Updates

OS X's App Store app enables you to check easily for software updates available through the App Store. These include updates for OS X itself, the apps that Apple releases, and third-party apps sold through the App Store. To keep your iMac running smoothly and protect it from both online and offline threats, you should apply software updates when they become available.

You can configure the App Store feature to check automatically for updates on a schedule. You can also check for updates manually.

Control Checking for Software Updates

1 Click **Apple** (🍎).

The Apple menu opens.

2 Click **System Preferences**.

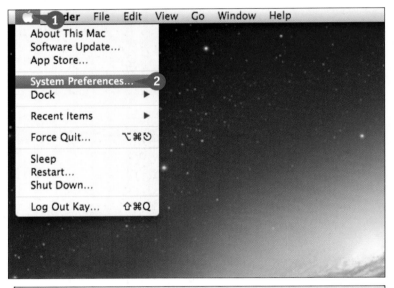

The System Preferences pane appears.

3 Click **App Store**.

The App Store pane opens.

④ Click the **Automatically check for updates** option (☐ changes to ☑).

⑤ Click the **Download newly available updates in the background** option (☐ changes to ☑).

Ⓐ You can click the **Install app updates** option (☐ changes to ☑) if you want OS X to install app updates automatically.

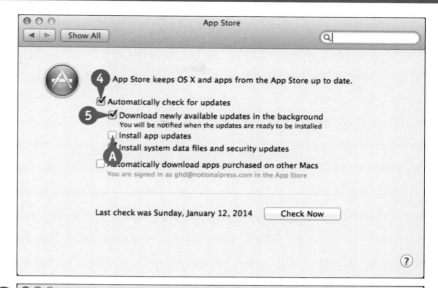

⑥ Click the **Install system data files and security updates** option (☐ changes to ☑).

⑦ Click the **Automatically download apps purchased on other Macs** option (☐ changes to ☑) if you want to automatically add apps you buy on other Macs using the same Apple ID to your iMac.

Ⓑ You can click **Check Now** to check for updates.

⑧ Click **Close** (⊗).

System Preferences closes.

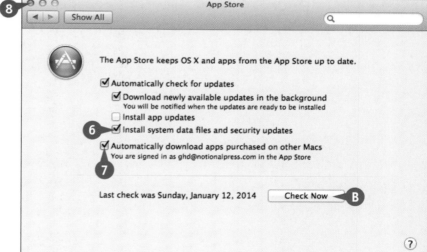

TIP

Which updates should I install?

It is normally a good idea to install all updates to keep your iMac protected against threats and to make sure you have the latest fixes and upgrades for OS X and your apps. For security, click the **Install system data files and security updates** option (☐ changes to ☑) to make App Store install these items automatically. You may prefer to install the app updates manually at a time of your choosing.

CHAPTER 13

Networking and Protecting Your iMac

OS X enables you to share files, printers, scanners, and optical drives across networks. OS X includes many security features for protecting your iMac against network and Internet threats.

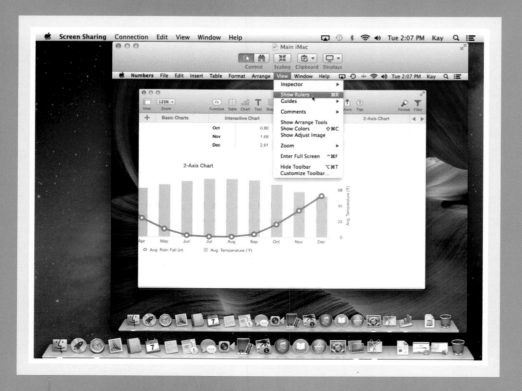

Transfer Files Using AirDrop

OS X's AirDrop feature enables you to transfer files easily via wireless between your iMac and another nearby Mac. Activating AirDrop in a Finder window shows you all nearby Macs that are currently using AirDrop. You can then drag a file to the AirDrop window and drop it on the Mac to which you want to send it. If the recipient accepts the file, AirDrop transfers it. Similarly, nearby Macs can send files to your iMac via AirDrop, and you can decide whether to accept or reject each file.

Transfer Files Using AirDrop

Send a File via AirDrop

1 Click **Finder** (🖼) on the Dock.

A Finder window opens.

2 Click **AirDrop**.

The AirDrop screen appears.

Note: To use AirDrop, both your iMac and the other Mac must be running OS X 10.7, Lion, or a later version, such as OS X 10.9, Mavericks, and must have compatible hardware; see http://support.apple.com/kb/HT4783 for details. OS X 10.6 and earlier versions do not have the AirDrop feature.

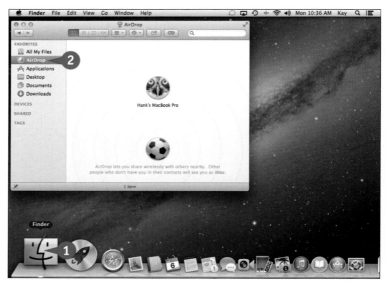

3 Press ⌘+N.

A second Finder window opens.

4 Arrange the Finder windows so you can see both.

5 Click and drag the file to the icon for the Mac you want to send it to.

Note: You can also click and drag a file from the desktop or from another tab in the same Finder window.

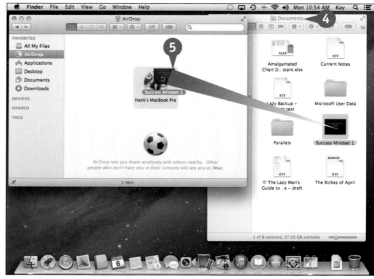

A confirmation dialog appears.

6 Click **Send**.

The Finder sends the file to the recipient.

Receive a File via AirDrop

When someone sends you a file via AirDrop, a dialog appears on-screen.

1 Click the appropriate button:

A Click **Save and Open** to save the file and open it for viewing.

B Click **Decline** to decline the transfer.

C Click **Save** to save the file so you can use it later.

If you accept the file, your iMac receives the file.

If you click **Save and Open**, your iMac opens the file in the default application for that file type, if it has a default application. You can then work with the file.

TIP

Should I use AirDrop or a shared folder on the network to transfer files?

If your iMac connects to a network with shared folders, use those folders instead of AirDrop. By storing a file in a shared folder, you and your colleagues can work on it directly without transferring copies back and forth. AirDrop is useful for sharing on networks that do not have shared folders or for sharing files with Macs to which your iMac does not normally connect. As an alternative, you can use Messages to transfer files.

Connect to a Shared Folder

OS X enables each Mac to share folders with other computers on the same network. You can connect your iMac to other Macs and work with the files in their shared folders.

The user who sets up the sharing can assign other users different levels of access to the folder. Depending on the permissions set for the folder, you may be able to view files in the folder but not alter them, or you may be able to create, change, and delete files in the folder.

Connect to a Shared Folder

1 Click **Finder** (🗿) on the Dock.

A Finder window opens.

2 If the Shared category is collapsed, position the mouse pointer over it, and then click **Show** to expand it.

3 Click the computer that is sharing the folder.

4 Click **Connect As**.

The Connect As dialog opens.

5 Click the **Registered User** option (◯ changes to ◉) if you have a user account. Otherwise, click the **Guest** option (◯ changes to ◉) and go to step **8**.

6 Type your username.

7 Type your password.

Ⓐ You can click the **Remember this password in my keychain** option (☐ changes to ☑) if you want to store your password for future use.

8 Click **Connect**.

The Connect As dialog closes.

B The shared folders appear.

Note: The shared folders you see are the folders you have permission to access. Other users may be able to access different folders.

9 Click the folder whose contents you want to see.

10 Work with files as usual. For example, open a file to work on it, or copy it to your iMac.

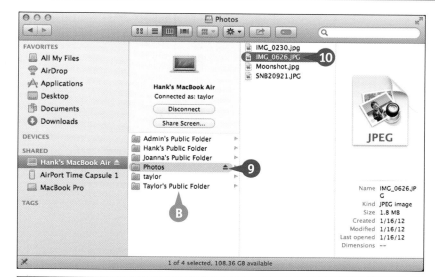

11 When you finish using the shared folder, click **Eject** (⏏) next to the computer's name in the Shared list.

Your iMac disconnects from the computer sharing the files.

C You can also click **Disconnect** to disconnect from the sharing computer.

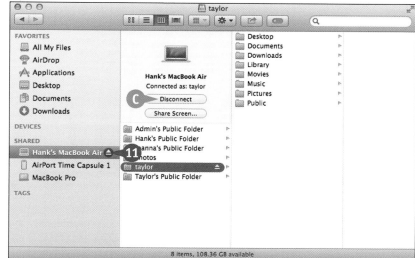

TIP

How can I connect to a shared folder that does not appear in the Shared list in the Finder window?
If the shared folder does not appear in the Shared list, find out the name or IP address of the computer sharing the folder. Click **Go** on the menu bar and click **Connect to Server**. The Connect to Server dialog opens. In the Server Address field, type or paste the computer's name or IP address; for a Windows computer, type **smb://** and then the IP address. Click **Connect**, and then provide your username and password if prompted. To reconnect to a server you have used before, click **Choose a Recent Server** (⊙▾) in the Connect to Server dialog and then click **Connect**.

Share a Folder

OS X enables you to share folders on your iMac with other users on the network. When you share a folder, you control what other users can access it. You can set different levels of permission for different users, such as allowing some users to change files while allowing other users to view files but not change them.

To share a folder on the network, you configure the File Sharing service in Sharing preferences. System Preferences sets up sharing for Macs automatically. You can configure sharing for Windows users manually.

Share a Folder

1. Press **Ctrl**+click **System Preferences** (⚙) on the Dock.

   The contextual menu opens.

2. Click **Sharing**.

   System Preferences opens and displays the Sharing pane.

3. Click the **File Sharing** option (☐ changes to ☑).

   System Preferences turns on file sharing.

4. Click **Add** (➕) under the Shared Folders box.

   A dialog for choosing a folder opens.

5. Click the folder you want to share.

6. Click **Add**.

The dialog closes, and the folder appears in the Shared Folders list.

7 Click the folder.

8 Click **Everyone**.

9 Click the **Permissions** pop-up menu (⬍) and select the appropriate permission. See the tip for details.

10 If you need to configure sharing for Windows users, click **Options**. Otherwise, go to step **16**.

The Options dialog opens.

11 Click the **Share files and folders using SMB** option (☐ changes to ☑).

12 Click the **On** option for a user (☐ changes to ☑).

The Authenticate dialog opens.

13 Type the user's password.

14 Click **OK**.

The Authenticate dialog closes.

15 Click **Done**.

The Options dialog closes.

16 Click **Close** (⊗).

System Preferences closes.

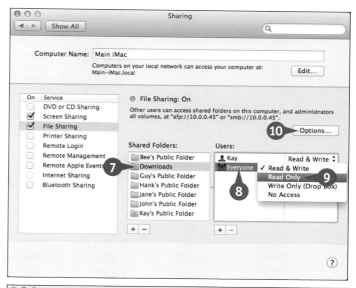

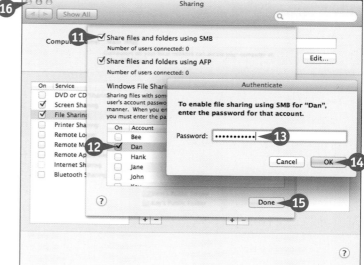

TIP

What permissions should I assign to a folder I share?
Assign **Read Only** permission if you want other people to be able only to open or copy files in the folder. If you want other people to be able to create and change files in the folder, including renaming and deleting them, click **Read & Write**. If you need to create a drop box folder that people cannot view but can add files to, click **Write Only (Drop Box)**.

Connect to a Shared Printer

OS X enables you to connect to shared printers on the network and print documents to them. By sharing printers, you can not only enable each computer to print different types of documents as needed but also reduce the costs of printing.

To use a shared printer, you first set it up on your iMac using Printers & Scanners preferences. After you set up the printer, you can access it from the Print dialog just like a printer connected directly to your iMac.

Connect to a Shared Printer

① Click **Apple** (🍎).

The Apple menu opens.

② Click **System Preferences**.

The System Preferences window opens.

③ Click **Printers & Scanners**.

The Printers & Scanners pane appears.

④ Click **Add** (⊞).

Ⓐ If the printer appears on the pop-up menu, click the printer and go to step **9**.

Note: If no printer or scanner is available on the network, the pop-up menu does not appear. Instead, the Add dialog appears. Go to step **6**.

⑤ Click **Add Printer or Scanner**.

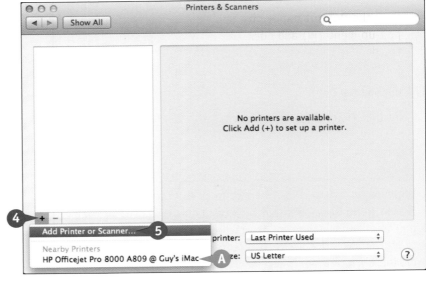

The Add dialog opens.

6 Click **Default**.

Note: Click **Windows** to see printers shared by Windows PCs on the network.

The Default pane appears.

7 Click the printer.

B You can change the name shown in the Name box.

C You can change the location shown in the Location box.

8 Click **Add**.

The Add dialog closes.

The printer appears in the Printers & Scanners pane.

9 Click the **Default printer** pop-up menu (⬍) and click the printer to use as the default. Your options are Last Printer Used or one of the printers you have added.

10 Click the **Default paper size** pop-up menu (⬍) and click the default paper size, such as US Letter.

11 Click **Close** (⬤).

System Preferences closes.

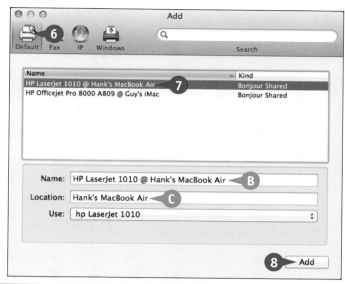

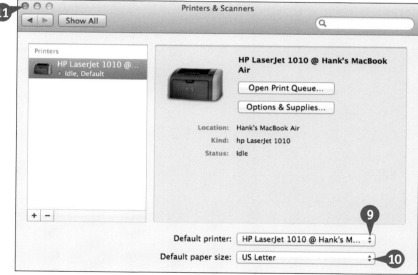

TIP

What should I do when the Use pop-up menu says "Choose a Driver or Printer Model"?
This message appears when OS X cannot identify the driver software needed for the printer. Click the **Use** pop-up menu (⬍) and then click **Select Software**. The Printer Software dialog opens. Type a distinctive part of the name in the search box to see a list of matching items, and then click the driver for the printer model. Click **OK**.

Share Your iMac's Printer

OS X's Printer Sharing feature enables you to share a printer connected to your iMac with other computers on your network. You can choose what users can print on the printer and block other users from accessing the printer.

To share the printer, you turn on the Printer Sharing feature in Sharing preferences, specify the printer, and set permissions for using it. Permitted users can access the printer from the Print dialog on their computers any time your iMac is running.

Share Your iMac's Printer

1 Click **System Preferences** (![icon]) on the Dock.

Note: If System Preferences (![icon]) does not appear on the Dock, click **Apple** (![icon]) and select **System Preferences**.

The System Preferences window opens.

2 Click **Sharing**.

The Sharing pane opens.

3 Click the **Printer Sharing** option (□ changes to ☑).

OS X turns on Printer Sharing and displays the Printer Sharing preferences.

4 Click each printer you want to share (□ changes to ☑).

A OS X makes the printer available to everyone by default.

5 To control who can use the printer, click **Add** (⊞).

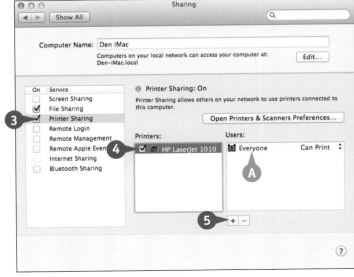

A dialog for selecting users opens.

6 Click the user you want to add.

Note: To select multiple users, click the first, and then press ⌘+click each of the others.

7 Click **Select**.

B Each user appears in the Users list.

C OS X automatically changes the Everyone item from Can Print to No Access.

8 Click **Close** (⊗).

System Preferences closes.

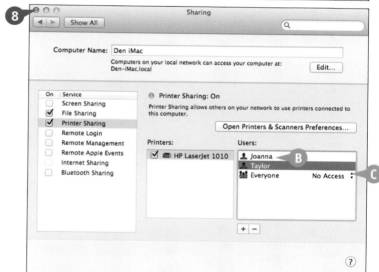

How can Windows users share my iMac's printer?
Users of PCs running Windows need to install Apple's Bonjour Print Services for Windows to access shared printers. Bonjour Print Services for Windows is available free from http://support.apple.com/kb/DL999.

How can I print from my iPad or iPhone to my iMac's printer?
If the printer is AirPrint-capable, you can print by selecting the printer on your iOS device. If not, either add Printer Pro to your iOS device or install handyPrint (www.netputing.com/handyprint/) on your iMac.

Connect Remotely via Back to My Mac

OS X's Back to My Mac feature enables you to connect one Mac remotely to another Mac across the Internet. You can use Back to My Mac either to use your iMac to control another Mac remotely or to use another Mac to control your iMac. Back to My Mac lets you view the remote Mac's screen and control the Mac.

Back to My iMac requires you to have set up iCloud on both the remote Mac and the Mac you use to connect. You turn on Back to My Mac in iCloud preferences.

Connect Remotely via Back to My Mac

Turn On Screen Sharing

1 Click **Apple** (<img>).

The Apple menu opens.

2 Click **System Preferences**.

System Preferences opens.

3 Click **iCloud**.

The iCloud pane opens.

4 Click the **Back to My Mac** option (☐ changes to ☑).

5 Click **More**.

Note: The More button does not appear if file sharing and screen sharing are already turned on. If you need to configure sharing, click **Show All** and then click **Sharing** to display the Sharing pane.

The More dialog opens.

6 Click **Open Sharing**.

The Sharing pane opens.

7 Click the **Screen Sharing** option
(☐ changes to ☑).

The Screen Sharing controls appear.

8 Click the **Only these users** option
(☐ changes to ◉).

9 Verify that the list shows the users
who will need to connect. You can
click **Add** (⊞) to add a user or
Remove (⊟) to remove a user.

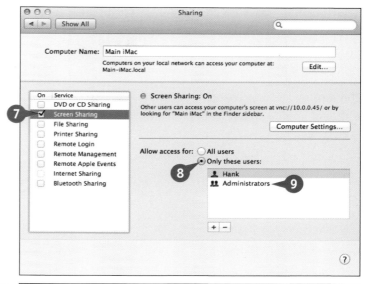

10 Click the **File Sharing** option
(☐ changes to ☑).

The File Sharing controls appear.

11 Verify that the Shared Folders list
shows the folders you want to share.

12 Verify that the Users list shows the
users who will need to connect. You
can click **Add** (⊞) to add a user or
Remove (⊟) to remove a user.

13 Click **Close** (⊗).

System Preferences closes.

Why does Back to My Mac fail to connect and instead gives me a message about NAT-PMP?
Back to My Mac establishes a two-way path through your Internet router to the iCloud servers using either
the Network Address Translation Port Mapping Protocol, NAT-PMP, or Universal Plug and Play, UPnP. If Back
to My Mac cannot connect, turn on NAT-PMP or UPnP on your router. Most routers support one, the other, or
both. Consult your router's documentation to find out how to turn on NAT-PMP or UPnP.

continued ▶

After enabling Back to My Mac on both the remote Mac and the local Mac, you can use Back to My Mac to connect remotely across the Internet.

You use the Sharing section of a Finder window to establish the connection. The remote Mac's desktop appears in a Screen Sharing window on the Mac you are using. You can control the remote Mac using the mouse and keyboard, enabling you to work much as if you were sitting at it, although screen updates appear more slowly.

Connect Remotely via Back to My Mac (continued)

Using Screen Sharing via Back to My Mac

1 Click **Finder** (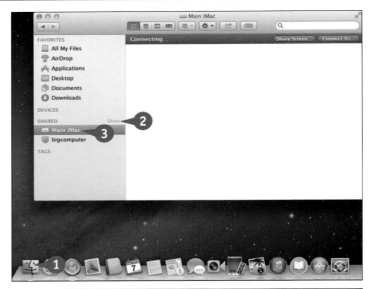) on the Dock.

A Finder window opens.

2 If the Shared category is collapsed, position the mouse pointer over it and click **Show** to expand it.

3 Click the Mac to which you want to connect.

A Finder establishes the connection.

B The remote Mac's shared folders appear.

4 Click **Share Screen**.

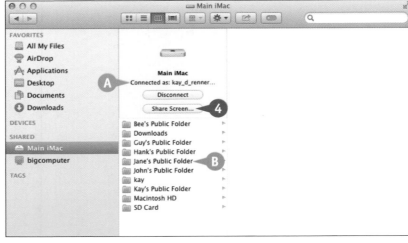

A Screen Sharing window opens, showing the remote Mac's desktop.

⑤ Work on the remote Mac using normal techniques.

⒞ Click **Scaling** (▦ changes to ▦) to scale the remote screen to the window.

⒟ To transfer data via the clipboard, click **Clipboard** (▥) and click **Get Clipboard** or **Send Clipboard**.

⒠ Click **Full Screen** (▱) to view the remote Mac full screen.

End Your Screen Sharing Session

① Click **Screen Sharing**.

② Click **Quit Screen Sharing**.

The Screen Sharing window closes.

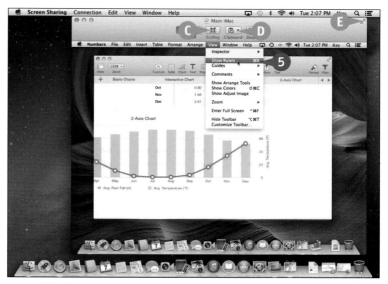

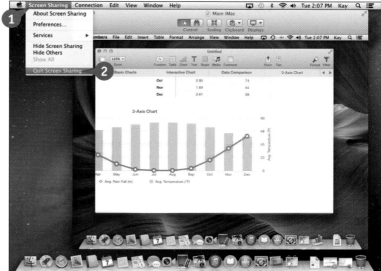

TIP

What may be preventing Back to My Mac from connecting to the iCloud servers?
If you use the OS X firewall to protect your iMac from dangerous Internet traffic, you must allow File Sharing connections and Screen Sharing connections for Back to My Mac to work. If you use the Block All Incoming Connections feature of the firewall, Back to My Mac cannot work.

Install Antivirus Software

As well as turning on the OS X firewall, you should install and run antivirus software to protect your iMac from malevolent hackers. You can buy and download antivirus software from the App Store, buy it on a disc from a physical store or by mail order, or download it from a website. Some antivirus apps are free; others are pay software.

You install the antivirus software in a similar way to other apps. However, after installing the antivirus software, you may need to restart your iMac.

Install Antivirus Software

Install Antivirus Software

1️⃣ Click **App Store** (🔘) on the Dock.

The App Store window opens.

2️⃣ Click in the search box and type **antivirus**.

The search results appear.

3️⃣ Click the app you want to see.

The app's screen appears.

4️⃣ Read the details of the app.

5️⃣ Click **Free** or the price button.

The Install App button appears.

6️⃣ Click **Install App**.

Note: If App Store prompts you to sign in, type your password and click **Sign In**.

App Store downloads and installs the app.

Note: Restart your Mac if App Store prompts you to do so.

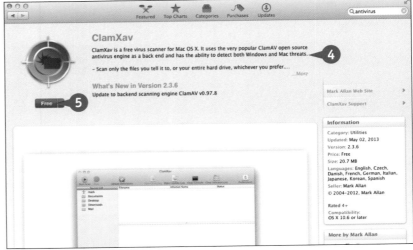

Keep Antivirus Up to Date

1 Click **Launchpad** () on the Dock.

The Launchpad screen appears.

2 Click the icon for the antivirus app you installed.

The app opens and checks for updates.

Note: Many antivirus apps check automatically for updates. You can also check manually for updates by clicking the app's menu and then selecting **Check for Updates**.

3 Click **Update Now**.

The app downloads and installs the latest updates.

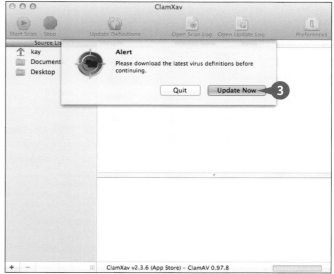

TIP

What features should I look for in antivirus software?
The main feature to look for is protection against malevolent software. This includes viruses, Trojan-horse programs that hide harm in a program that seems helpful, and rootkits, which try to build secret entry points into your computer. Protection against spyware programs, adware programs, and infected websites are useful, too. Features designed to detect phishing messages may also be helpful, but you may find that Mail's Junk Mail feature and your own evaluation give you more consistent results.

Scan for Viruses

After installing antivirus software, you should scan your iMac to detect any viruses. If the scan detects viruses or other malware, you can use the tools in the antivirus software to remove the viruses or quarantine the affected files.

Scanning your iMac for viruses can take several hours. The time depends on the number of files your iMac contains, the speed of its processor, and how much RAM it has. It is best to set aside plenty of time to run the scan.

Scan for Viruses

1 Click **Launchpad** ( ) on the Dock.

2 Click the icon for your antivirus app. This example uses ClamXav.

The app window opens.

3 Click the drive or folder you want to scan.

Ⓐ You can click **Add** (+) or **Remove** (−) to change the folders in the Source List.

Note: Scan your user folder to check all your files. Scan your iMac's drive to check all the files it contains.

4 Click **Start Scan**.

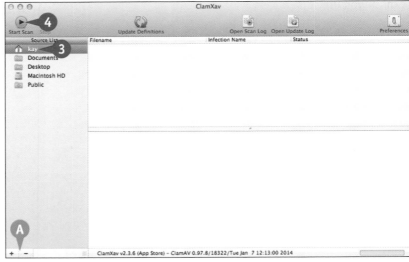

ClamXav scans the contents of the folder and its subfolders.

B The upper pane shows a list of infected files.

C The status bar shows the current file and a progress indicator.

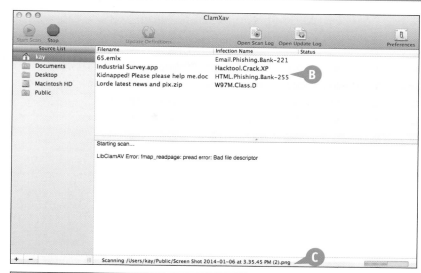

When the scan finishes, the app displays a summary of what it has found.

5 Press ⌘+click an infected file.

6 Click the appropriate command, such as **Quarantine File** or **Delete File**.

Note: Click **Exclude from Future Scans** if you are sure the file is safe and you want to prevent ClamXav from checking it again.

7 Press ⌘+Q.

The app closes.

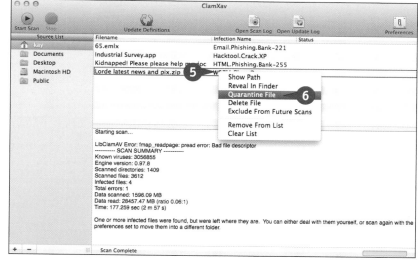

<table>
<tr><th>TIP</th></tr>
</table>

When should I ignore an infected file?
Normally, you should not ignore an infected file. Unless you are certain that a file is harmless, and that your antivirus application has falsely accused it of harboring malware, you should repair the file. Some antivirus applications also give you the option of placing a file in quarantine, putting it in a secure area so that you can review it later. Quarantine prevents the infected file from damaging your iMac but does not remove the infection.

Turn Off Automatic Login

OS X enables you to set your iMac to log in one user account automatically, bypassing the login screen. Automatic login is convenient if you are the only person who uses your iMac, but you can make your iMac more secure by turning off automatic login so each user must log in.

To turn automatic login on or off, you use the Login Options pane in Users & Groups preferences. You must have an administrator account or provide administrator credentials to change these options.

Turn Off Automatic Login

1 Press **Ctrl**+click **System Preferences** (⚙) on the Dock.

The contextual menu opens.

2 Click **Security & Privacy**.

System Preferences opens and displays the Security & Privacy pane.

3 Click **General**.

The General pane appears.

4 Click the **lock** icon (🔒).

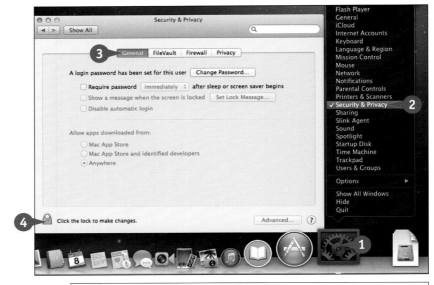

The authentication dialog opens.

5 Type your password.

6 Click **Unlock**.

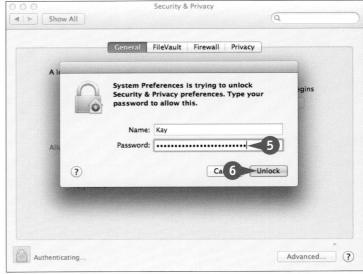

System Preferences unlocks the preferences (🔒 changes to 🔓).

7 Click the **Disable automatic login** option (☐ changes to ☑).

8 For greater security, click the **Require password *N* seconds after sleep or screen saver begins** option (☐ changes to ☑).

9 Click the pop-up menu (🔼) and click **immediately** or a short time: 5 seconds, 1 minute, or 5 minutes.

10 Click **Advanced**.

The Advanced dialog opens.

11 Click the **Log out after *N* minutes of inactivity** option (☐ changes to ☑).

12 Click the pop-up menu (🔼) and click the period of inactivity.

13 Click the **Disable remote control infrared receiver** option (☐ changes to ☑) if you want to prevent the iMac from responding to a remote control.

14 Click **OK**.

The Advanced dialog closes.

15 Click **Close** (⊗).

System Preferences closes.

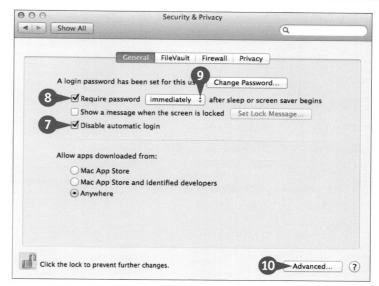

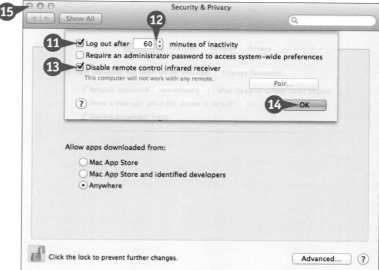

TIP

What other options can I set to tighten my iMac's security?

In Users & Groups preferences, click **Login Options**. You can then click the **Name and password** option (◯ changes to ◉) to hide the list of usernames so that anyone logging on must type a username as well as a password. Click the **Show the Sleep, Restart, and Shut Down buttons** option (☑ changes to ☐) to remove these buttons from the login screen, so that nobody can shut down the iMac without logging in unless he turns off the iMac's power. Click the **Show password hints** option (☑ changes to ☐) if you want to prevent password hints from appearing.

Tighten the Firewall's Security

OS X includes a firewall that protects your iMac from unauthorized access by other computers on your network or on the Internet. OS X enables you to configure the firewall to suit your needs. To configure the firewall, you use the Firewall pane in Security & Privacy preferences.

Even if your Internet router includes a firewall configured to prevent Internet threats from reaching your network, you should use the OS X firewall to protect against threats from other computers on your network.

Tighten the Firewall's Security

1 Press **Ctrl**+click **System Preferences** (🎛) on the Dock.

The contextual menu opens.

2 Click **Security & Privacy**.

System Preferences opens and displays the Security & Privacy pane.

3 Click **Firewall**.

The Firewall pane appears.

4 Click the **lock** icon (🔒).

The authentication dialog opens.

5 Type your password.

6 Click **Unlock**.

System Preferences unlocks the preferences (🔒 changes to 🔓).

7 If "Firewall: Off" appears, click **Turn On Firewall**.

The firewall starts, and "Firewall: On" appears.

8 Click **Firewall Options**.

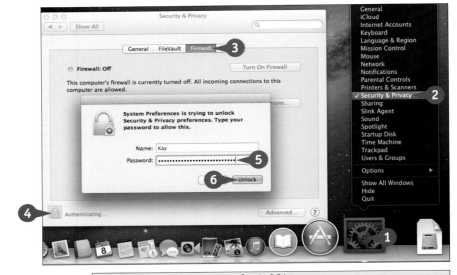

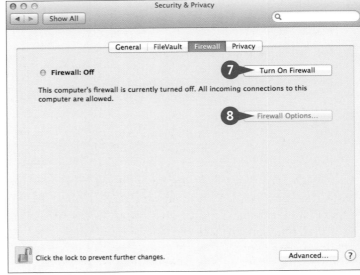

The Firewall Options dialog opens.

9 Click the **Automatically allow signed software to receive incoming connections** option (☑ changes to ☐) if you want to prevent your iMac from accepting connections automatically across the network.

10 Click the **Enable stealth mode** option (☐ changes to ☑) if you want to prevent your iMac from responding to network test applications.

11 To allow incoming connections to a particular application, click **Add** (⊞).

The Add dialog opens.

12 Click the app.

13 Click **Add**.

System Preferences adds the app to the list.

14 Click **OK**.

The Firewall Options dialog closes.

15 Click **Close** (⊗).

System Preferences closes.

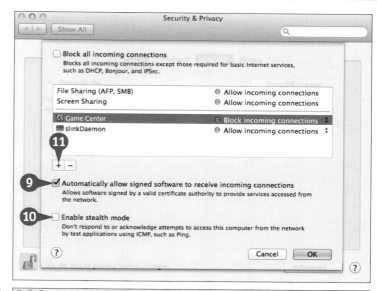

TIPS

When should I use the Block All Incoming Connections option?

Click **Block all incoming connections** when you need to tighten security as much as possible. The usual reason for blocking all connections is when connecting your iMac to a network that you cannot trust, such as a public wireless network.

How do I block incoming connections only to a specific application?

Add that application to the list in the Advanced dialog. Then click the application's **Allow incoming connections** button in the list and click **Block incoming connections.**

Recognize and Avoid Phishing Attacks

Phishing is an attack in which someone tries to make you provide valuable information such as bank account numbers, login names, passwords, or credit card numbers. After acquiring this information, the phisher either uses it directly — for example, withdrawing money from your bank account — or sells it to criminals.

Mail and Safari help protect you against phishing. Mail scans your incoming messages and marks any that may be phishing. Safari enables you to check a website's digital certificate to make sure it is valid.

Recognize and Avoid Phishing Attacks

Recognize a Phishing E-Mail Message

1 In Mail, open the message.

2 Look for signs of phishing:

Ⓐ Mail has detected suspicious signs in the message.

Ⓑ The message does not show your name as the recipient.

Ⓒ The message has a generic greeting, such as Dear Customer, or no greeting at all.

Ⓓ The message claims you need to take action, such as clearing a security lockout or reenabling your account.

Ⓔ The message contains links it encourages you to click.

3 Position the mouse pointer over a link but do not click.

Ⓕ A ScreenTip appears showing the address to which the link leads.

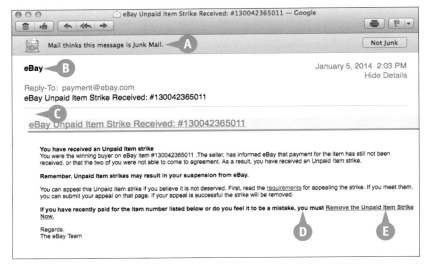

Connect Securely to a Website

1. Click **Safari** (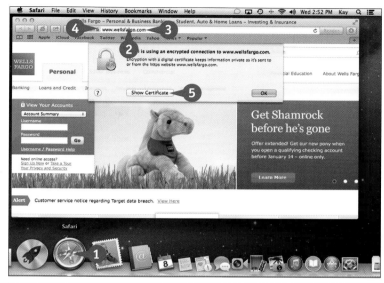) on the Dock.

2. Click the address box.

3. Type the address of the website and press [Return].

4. Click the **padlock** icon (🔒).

Note: Safari displays the padlock icon when you have connected securely to a website. The address of a secure connection starts with https:// instead of http://.

A dialog opens.

5. Click **Show Certificate**.

The dialog expands, showing the details of the digital certificate that identifies the website.

6. Verify that the certificate is valid.

7. Click **OK**.

The dialog closes.

8. If you are convinced that the website is genuine, log in to it.

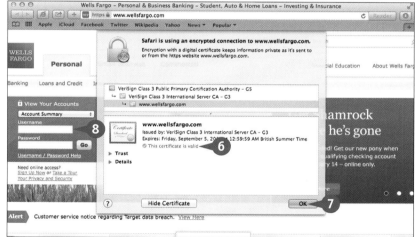

TIPS

Is it possible to make a secure connection to a dangerous website?
Yes. The padlock icon means only that the connection between your iMac and the website server is secure and cannot be read in transmission. The website may be safe or it may be dangerous; it is up to you to establish which.

Is a message definitely genuine if it includes my name?
Even if a message includes your name, be alert for other signs of phishing. Some phishers send customized phishing messages in the hope of ensnaring particular high-value victims. This technique is called *spear-phishing*. Evaluate the message's content for sense and likelihood, and remember that anything too good to be true is usually not true.

CHAPTER 14

Troubleshooting Your iMac

To keep your iMac running well, you need to perform basic maintenance, such as emptying the Trash, updating OS X and your apps with the latest fixes, and backing up your files. You may also need to troubleshoot your iMac, solving problems such as corrupt preferences files, disk permission errors, or drive failure.

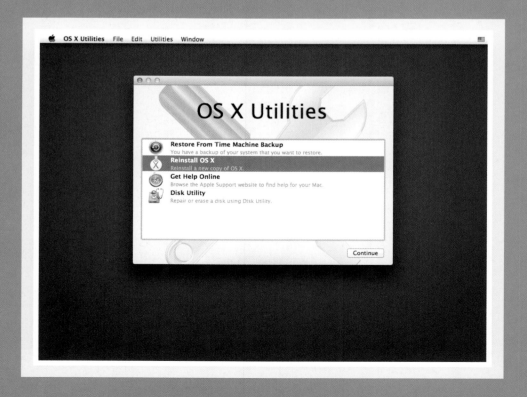

Using OS X's Help System

OS X has a built-in help system that enables you to solve problems that you encounter when using your iMac and its software. You can launch the help system from the menu bar of the Finder. You can then either browse or search to find the information you need.

Most apps that run on OS X include help files. In such apps, you can use the Help menu at the right end of the menu bar to browse or search the help files.

Using OS X's Help System

1 Click anywhere on the desktop.

The Finder becomes active.

2 Click **Help**.

The Help menu opens.

3 Click **Help Center**.

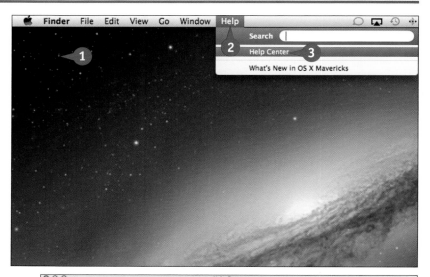

The Help Center window opens.

4 Click the search box.

5 Type a question or some keywords.

6 Press **Return**.

The Help Center window shows a list of topics related to your search terms.

⑦ Click the topic you want to view.

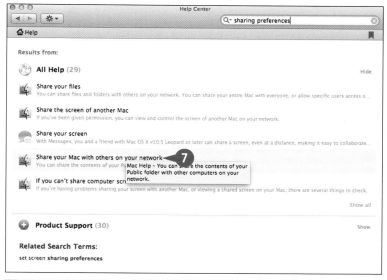

Help Center displays the topic.

Ⓐ Click **Show** to expand a topic.

Ⓑ Click a link to open another topic, an app or utility, or a web page.

Ⓒ Click **Help** (⌂) to return to the Help Center screen.

Ⓓ Click **Back** (◀) to return to the previous screen you viewed.

⑧ When you finish using Help, click **Close** (⊗).

The Help Center window closes.

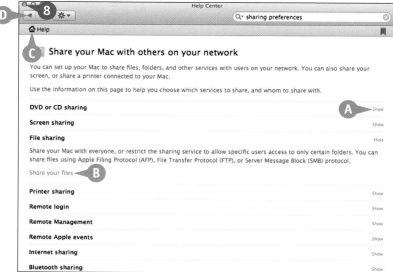

TIPS

Can I print out a help topic for reference?
To print the current topic, click **Action** (⚙▾), and then click **Print** on the pop-up menu. This menu also includes commands for making the text in the Help Center window larger or smaller and for searching for text in the current topic.

How do I get help for other applications?
Each application has its own Help menu. Activate the application, click **Help** to open the Help menu, and then click the help topic for the application or type your search terms and press Return.

Reclaim Space by Emptying the Trash

I n OS X, the Trash is a receptacle for files you delete from your iMac's drives. Any file you place in the Trash remains there until you empty the Trash, or the Trash runs out of space for files and automatically deletes the earliest files it contains. So if you find that you have deleted a file unintentionally, you can usually recover it from the Trash.

You can reclaim drive space by emptying the Trash manually. You can look through the Trash to make sure you no longer want the files it contains.

Reclaim Space by Emptying the Trash

Empty the Trash

1 Click **Trash** (🗑) on the Dock.

Note: If the Trash icon on the Dock is the empty Trash can (🗑), the Trash is already empty.

2 Look through the files and folders in the Trash to make sure it contains nothing you want to keep.

To quickly view the contents of a file, use Quick Look. Click the file, and then press `Spacebar`.

Note: You cannot open a file while it is in the Trash. If you want to open a file, you must remove it from the Trash.

3 Click **Empty**.

A dialog opens to confirm that you want to permanently erase the items in the Trash.

Note: You can turn off the confirmation of deleting files. Click **Finder** and then click **Preferences**. Click **Advanced** and then click the **Show warning before emptying the Trash** option (☑ changes to ☐).

④ Click **Empty Trash**.

OS X empties the Trash and then closes the Finder window.

Restore a File or Folder to Its Previous Location

① In the Trash folder, click the file or folder.

② Click **Action** (⚙).

③ Click **Put Back**.

Note: You can also press Ctrl+click an item and click **Put Back** on the contextual menu.

OS X restores the file or folder to its previous location.

Note: To move a file from the Trash to another folder, drag the file to that folder. For example, you can drag a file to the desktop.

TIPS

Is there a quicker way to empty the Trash?
If you are sure that the Trash contains no files or folders you need, press Ctrl+click **Trash** (🗑) on the Dock. The Dock menu opens. Click **Empty Trash**. A confirmation dialog opens. Click **Empty Trash**.

What does the Secure Empty Trash command do?
The Secure Empty Trash command overwrites files and folders to ensure that no one can recover them. Click the desktop, and then choose **Finder** and **Secure Empty Trash**. A confirmation dialog opens. Click **Secure Empty Trash**.

Keep Your iMac Current with Updates

OS X includes a feature called Software Update for keeping your iMac, its operating system, and your App Store apps up to date. You can use Software Update to check for updates and to install them. You can choose which updates to install.

Your iMac must be connected to the Internet when you check for updates and download them. You can install most updates when your iMac is either online or offline. Some updates require restarting your iMac.

Keep Your iMac Current with Updates

1 Click **Apple** (🍎).

The Apple menu opens.

2 Click **Software Update**.

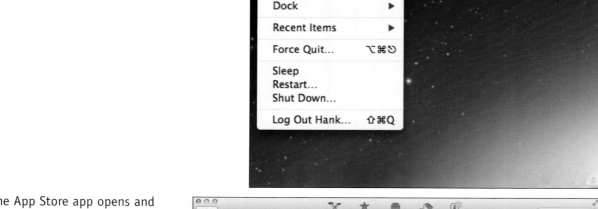

The App Store app opens and displays its Updates pane.

App Store automatically checks for updates.

If updates are available, the Updates Available list shows the details.

Note: If the message No Updates Available appears, go to step **5**.

Ⓐ You can install an individual update by clicking **Update**.

3 To install all the updates, click **Update All**.

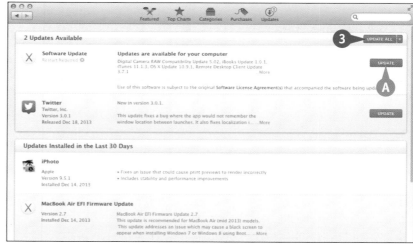

If installing the updates requires a restart, App Store displays a dialog.

④ Click **Restart**.

Ⓑ You can click **Not Now** to postpone the updates if necessary.

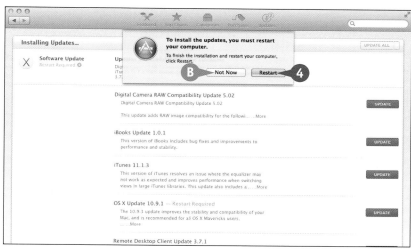

OS X installs the updates, restarting your iMac if necessary.

App Store appears and checks for updates.

Note: If App Store finds further updates, click **Update All** to install them.

⑤ Click **App Store**.

The App Store menu opens.

⑥ Click **Quit App Store**.

App Store closes.

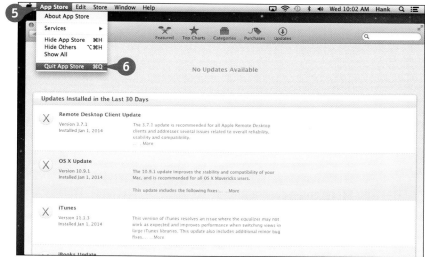

TIPS

Why does Software Update sometimes prompt me to install updates?

In OS X, Software Update comes set to check for updates automatically; when it finds updates, it prompts you to install them. You can change the frequency of these checks, choose whether to download important updates automatically, or turn off automatic checks. See Chapter 12 for instructions.

Which updates should I install?

Normally, it is best to install all available system updates unless you hear that a specific update may cause problems with your iMac. In that case, wait until Apple fixes the update. For app updates, it is wise to wait for user feedback, because some updates create incompatibilities for documents created in earlier versions.

Back Up Your Files

To enable you to keep your valuable files safe, OS X includes an automatic backup application called Time Machine. Time Machine automatically saves copies of your files to an external hard disk or an AirPort Time Capsule. You can choose what drive to use, how frequently to back up your files, and what folders to include.

To protect your data, you must back up your files. Time Machine is the most convenient choice because it takes only a few minutes to set up and thereafter runs automatically.

Back Up Your Files

1 Connect an external hard disk to your iMac.

Note: When you first connect an external hard disk to your iMac, a dialog may open prompting you to use the disk for Time Machine. Click **Use as Backup Disk** or **Cancel**, as needed.

2 Click **System Preferences** (⚙) on the Dock.

3 Click **Time Machine**.

4 Click the switch to move it to On.

The Select Disk dialog opens.

5 Click the disk or AirPort Time Capsule you want to use for backup.

Ⓐ You can click the **Encrypt backups** option (☐ changes to ☑) to encrypt your backups.

6 Click **Use Disk**.

The Select Disk dialog closes.

Ⓑ You can click the **Show Time Machine in menu bar** option (☐ changes to ☑) to give yourself easy access to Time Machine.

7 Click **Options**.

The Options dialog opens.

8 Click the **Notify after old backups are deleted** option (☐ changes to ☑) if you want notifications of deletions.

9 Click **Add** (⊞).

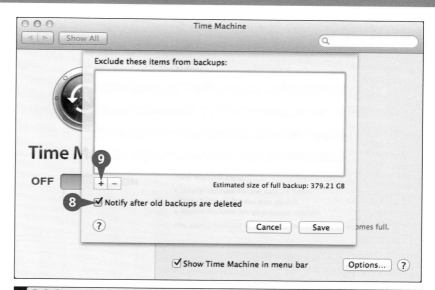

A dialog opens.

10 Select each drive or folder you want to exclude from backup.

11 Click **Exclude**.

The dialog closes, and Time Machine adds the items to the Exclude These Items from Backups dialog.

12 Click **Save** to close the Options dialog.

13 Click the **System Preferences** menu and click **Quit System Preferences** to close System Preferences.

TIPS

What kind of disk should I use for Time Machine?
You can connect an external hard disk to your iMac by using Thunderbolt or USB. Thunderbolt is faster than USB but is usually expensive. Buy a high-capacity disk — for example, four terabytes (TB) or larger — so that you have plenty of space for backups.

How often does Time Machine back up my files?
Time Machine starts to back up all your files two minutes after you set it up. After that, it creates an hourly backup of files that have changed since the last backup. Time Machine consolidates the hourly backups into daily backups, and then consolidates those into weekly backups.

Recover Files from Backup

OS X's Time Machine feature enables you to recover files easily from your backups. So when you delete a file by accident, or discover that a file has become corrupted, you can recover the file from backup by opening Time Machine. You can recover either the latest copy of the file or an earlier copy.

If you still have the current copy of the file that you recover, you can choose whether to overwrite that copy or keep it. Time Machine refers to this copy as the "original" file.

Recover Files from Backup

1 Click **Time Machine** (⊙) on the menu bar.

The Time Machine menu opens.

2 Click **Enter Time Machine**.

Note: If the Time Machine status icon does not appear on the menu bar, click **Launchpad** (⬚) on the Dock, and then click **Time Machine** (⊙) on the Launchpad screen.

Time Machine opens.

Ⓐ The front window shows your iMac's drive or drives in their current state.

Ⓑ Backups of the selected drive or folder appear in the windows behind it, newest at the front.

Ⓒ The timeline on the right shows how far back in time the available backups go.

3 Click the date or time from which you want to recover the files or folders.

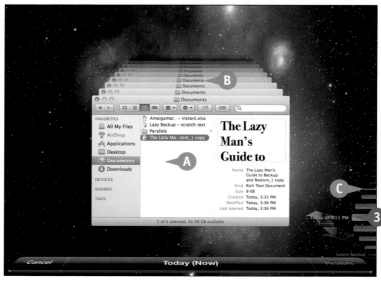

Time Machine brings the backup you chose to the front.

④ Select the item or items you want to restore.

⑤ Click **Restore**.

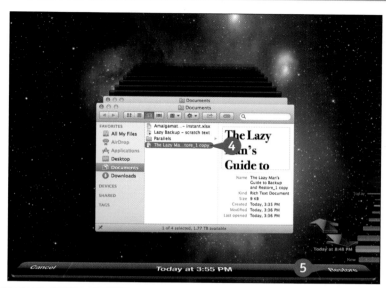

Time Machine disappears.

If restoring a file will overwrite the current version, the Copy dialog opens.

⑥ Choose how to handle the file conflict:

ⓓ Click **Replace** to replace the current file with the older file.

ⓔ Click **Keep Original** to keep the current file.

ⓕ Click **Keep Both** to keep both versions of the file. Time Machine adds "(Original)" to the name of the current version.

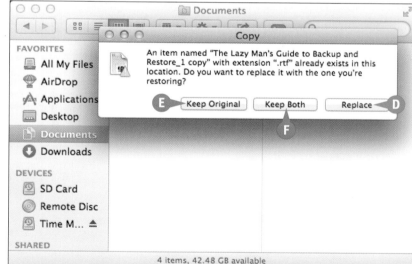

What do the arrow buttons above the Restore button do?

The two arrow buttons enable you to navigate among the available backups. Click the upward arrow to move to the previous backup, further in the past. Click the downward arrow to move to the next backup, nearer to the present.

How do I create Time Machine backups manually?

Click **Time Machine** (🕐) on the menu bar and select **Back Up Now**. The menu also enables you to enter Time Machine and open Time Machine preferences.

Recover When OS X Crashes

Normally, OS X runs stably and smoothly, but sometimes the operating system may suffer a crash. Crashes can occur for various reasons including power fluctuations, bad memory modules, an app having become corrupted, or problems with disk permissions.

Your iMac may detect that the crash has occurred and display an informational message, but in other cases the iMac's screen may simply freeze and continue displaying the same information. Normally, you can recover from a crash by turning off your iMac's power and then turning it on again.

Recover When OS X Crashes

Recover from the Screen Freezing

1 If the mouse pointer shows the "wait" cursor that looks like a spinning beach ball, wait a couple of minutes to see if OS X can recover from the problem. If the mouse pointer has disappeared, go straight to step **2**.

2 To verify that your iMac is not responding, press keys on the keyboard or move the mouse.

3 Press and hold ⌘+Ctrl and press the iMac's power button.

4 If the iMac does not respond to that key combination, press and hold the iMac's power button for about four seconds.

The iMac turns off.

5 Wait at least 8 seconds, and then press the power button once to restart the iMac.

Recover from a Detected Crash

When your iMac detects an OS X crash, it dims the screen and displays a message in the center.

1 Read the message for information.

2 Press and hold the iMac's power button for about four seconds.

The iMac turns off.

3 Wait at least eight seconds, and then press the power button once to restart the iMac.

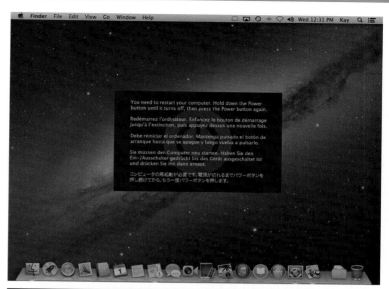

Note: Depending on how your iMac is configured, OS X may log you in automatically or display the Login dialog.

The login screen appears.

4 Click your user name, and then log in to your account as normal.

TIP

How can I avoid crashes?

- Limit the number of apps you run at the same time. When you finish using an app, close it.
- Keep at least 15 percent of your iMac's disk free. Click the desktop, click **Go** on the menu bar, and then click **Computer** to open a Finder window showing the Computer folder. Press `Ctrl`+click **Macintosh HD** and click **Get Info**. Look at the Capacity readout and the Available readout.
- If running a particular app causes your iMac to crash, uninstall and reinstall that app.
- Verify and repair disk permissions.

Troubleshoot Corrupt Preference Files

OS X and many apps enable you to set preferences to customize the way they run. Each app stores its configuration in a special file called a *preference file*. Sometimes a preference file becomes corrupted, which may prevent the app from running properly or cause it to crash.

To fix the problem, you delete the preference file. This forces the app to create a new preference file from scratch with default settings. When the app is running properly again, you can choose your custom settings again.

Troubleshoot Corrupt Preference Files

1 Quit the problem application if it is running.

Note: If you cannot quit the application by using its Quit command, force quit it. Press **Option**+click the app's Dock icon and click **Force Quit**.

2 Click an open space on the desktop.

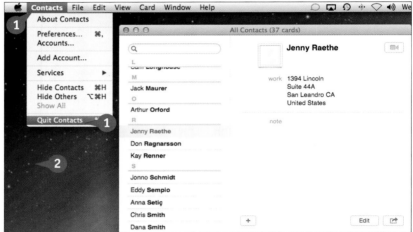

The Finder becomes active.

3 Click **Go**.

The Go menu opens.

4 Press and hold **Option**.

The Library item appears on the Go menu.

Note: OS X hides the Library item on the Go menu until you press **Option**.

5 Click **Library**.

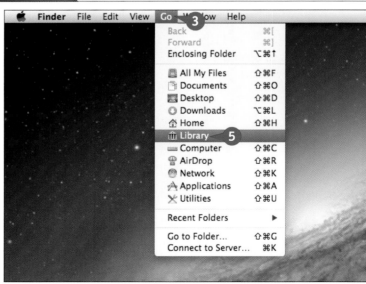

The contents of the Library folder appear.

6 Click **Preferences**.

The contents of the Preferences folder appear.

7 Click the preference file for the problem application. See the tip for help on identifying the file.

Note: If the application has two or more preference files, move them all to the Trash.

8 Click **Action** (⚙-).

The Action menu opens.

9 Click **Move to Trash**.

OS X moves the file to the Trash.

10 Start the application.

The application creates a new preference file containing default settings.

11 Set preferences in the application. In most applications, click the application's menu and click **Preferences** to open the Preferences window.

The application saves your preferences in the new preference file.

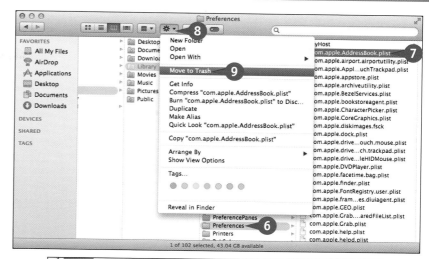

How do I find the right preference file to delete?

The names of most preference files use the format com.*company*.*application*.plist, where *company* is the manufacturer's name, *application* is the application's name, and .plist is the file extension for a property list file. For example, com.apple.mail.plist is the preference file for the Mail app, and com.microsoft.Excel.plist is the Excel preference file. If you cannot locate the preference file by browsing the Preferences folder, search online to learn the exact name.

Troubleshoot Disk Permission Errors

OS X uses a complex system of permissions to control what users, apps, and the components of the operating system itself can do. You can set some permissions by configuring user accounts or set them manually by working in the Finder. OS X sets many permissions automatically, and the OS X Installer sets permissions on apps you install using it.

Sometimes the permissions on files become corrupted, which may prevent OS X or the apps from running as normal. When this happens, you can often fix the problem by repairing the disk permissions using the Disk Utility app.

Troubleshoot Disk Permission Errors

1 Click **Launchpad** (📷) on the Dock.

The Launchpad screen appears.

2 Press **D**.

Launchpad displays only those items that include a word starting with *D*.

3 Click **Disk Utility**.

Disk Utility opens.

4 Click your iMac's hard drive.

The controls for manipulating the hard drive appear.

5 Click **First Aid**.

The First Aid pane appears.

6 Click **Repair Disk Permissions**.

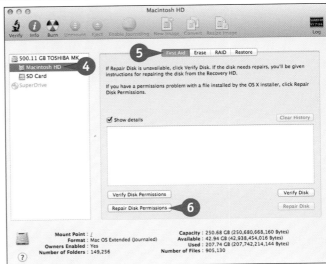

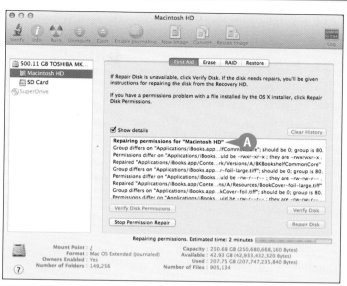

A Disk Utility repairs the disk permissions. The process may take several minutes.

Note: Disk Utility repairs permissions by resetting them to the values in a file called the *bill of materials file* for the relevant app. When you install an app using the OS X Installer, OS X creates a bill of materials file for the app. When you install an app by dragging it from a distribution file, OS X does not create a bill of materials file, so Disk Utility does not repair permissions for such apps.

7 Click **Disk Utility** on the menu bar.

The Disk Utility menu opens.

8 Click **Quit Disk Utility**.

Disk Utility closes.

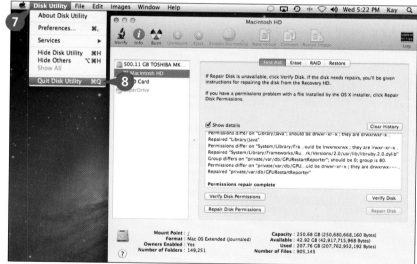

TIPS

What are the symptoms of problems with permissions?

Your iMac may run more slowly than usual. Apps may quit unexpectedly or freeze so that you have to force quit them.

What causes problems with permissions?

The two main causes of problems with permissions are installing software and power outages. A badly written installation script can set permissions nonoptimally on its own folder and incorrectly on other folders. Power outages can leave files or folders with permissions temporarily changed to enable certain operations but not changed back as they would normally be.

Repair Your iMac's Hard Drive

As well as repairing permissions, OS X's Disk Utility tool enables you to repair your iMac's hard drive. If your iMac does not start properly or if it crashes frequently, and repairing permissions does not fix the problem, you may need to repair the hard drive.

Repairing the drive may take a considerable amount of time, so you should try repairing permissions first. To repair the disk, you must start your iMac from the OS X recovery partition or another startup volume instead of starting from the hard drive.

Repair Your iMac's Hard Drive

① Start your iMac by pressing the power button.

Note: If your iMac is running, restart it by clicking **Apple** (🍎) and then pressing `Option`+clicking **Restart**.

② At the startup chime, press and hold `⌘`+`R` until the Apple logo appears.

Your iMac starts from the recovery partition.

The OS X Utilities screen appears.

③ Click **Disk Utility**.

④ Click **Continue**.

The Disk Utility window opens.

⑤ Click your iMac's hard drive.

The controls for manipulating the hard drive appear.

⑥ Click **First Aid**.

The First Aid pane appears.

⑦ Click **Repair Disk**.

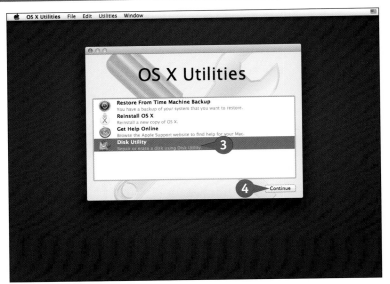

🅐 Disk Utility repairs the drive, displaying its progress.

8 Click **Disk Utility** and click **Quit Disk Utility**.

Disk Utility closes, and the Install OS X dialog opens.

9 Click **OS X Utilities**.

The OS X Utilities menu opens.

10 Click **Quit OS X Utilities**.

A confirmation dialog opens.

11 Click **Restart**.

Your iMac restarts into OS X from the hard disk.

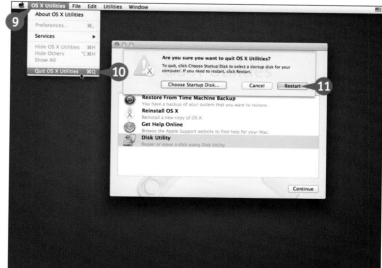

TIP

What do I do if my iMac cannot start after repairing the drive?
If your iMac cannot start after repairing the drive, try using a different startup volume. At the startup chime, press and hold ⌘+R. In OS X Utilities, click **Restore From Time Machine Backup** and then click **Continue**. Click **OS X Installer** and click **Quit OS X Installer**. In the Time Machine System Restore dialog that opens, click **Choose Startup Disk**. In the Choose Startup Disk dialog that opens, click the startup volume, and then click **Restart**. Your iMac starts from the volume you selected.

Reinstall OS X to Solve Severe Problems

If your iMac suffers severe software damage, OS X may not be able to run. When this happens, you can fix the problem by reinstalling OS X. You may also need to reinstall OS X if your iMac runs but crashes frequently and you are not able to restore stability by repairing the permissions or repairing the disk.

OS X includes a recovery partition that enables you to begin reinstalling the operating system. Once connected to the Internet, your iMac can then download the files it needs from Apple's servers and complete the reinstallation.

Reinstall OS X to Solve Severe Problems

1 Press the power button.

2 At the startup chime, press and hold ⌘+R until the Apple logo appears.

Your iMac starts from the recovery partition.

The OS X Utilities screen appears.

3 Click **Reinstall OS X**.

4 Click **Continue**.

The Install OS X screen appears.

5 Click **Continue**.

A dialog opens telling you your computer's eligibility will be verified with Apple.

6 Click **Continue**.

The Software License Agreement screen appears.

7 Click **Continue**.

A confirmation dialog opens.

8 Click **Agree**.

The screen for selecting the installation disk appears.

9 Click the disk.

10 Click **Install**.

The Sign In to Download from the App Store dialog opens.

11 Type your Apple ID.

12 Type your password.

13 Click **Sign In**.

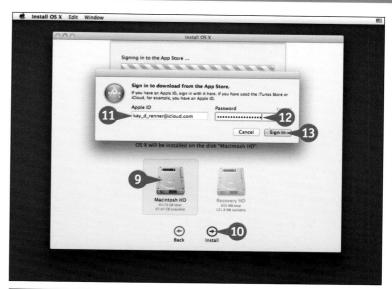

Install OS X begins downloading the components it needs to install OS X.

14 After the reinstallation finishes and your iMac restarts, log in. You can then access your files as before.

<hr>

TIP

How do I start the reinstallation if my iMac is powered on?

If your iMac is powered on and OS X is responding normally, restart your iMac by clicking **Apple** ( ), clicking **Restart**, and then clicking **Restart** in the Are You Sure You Want to Restart Your Computer Now? dialog.

If your iMac is powered on but OS X is not responding normally, press and hold the power button until the iMac shuts down. Wait for about eight seconds, and then press the power button to start your iMac.

Index

Index

There's a Visual book for every learning level...

Simplified®

The place to start if you're new to computers. Full color.

- Computers
- Creating Web Pages
- Digital Photography
- Excel
- Internet
- Laptops
- Mac OS
- Office
- PCs
- Windows
- Word

Teach Yourself VISUALLY™

Get beginning to intermediate-level training in a variety of topics. Full color.

- Access
- Adobe Muse
- Computers
- Digital Photography
- Digital Video
- Dreamweaver
- Excel
- Flash
- HTML5
- iLife
- iPad
- iPhone
- iPod
- Macs
- Mac OS
- Office
- Outlook
- Photoshop
- Photoshop Elements
- Photoshop Lightroom
- PowerPoint
- Salesforce.com
- Search Engine Optimization
- Social Media
- Web Design
- Windows
- Wireless Networking
- Word
- WordPress

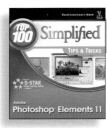

Top 100 Simplified® Tips & Tricks

Tips and techniques to take your skills beyond the basics. Full color.

- Digital Photography
- eBay
- Excel
- Google
- Office
- Photoshop
- Photoshop Elements
- PowerPoint
- Windows

...all designed for visual learners—just like you!